A rebel, a visionary, an uncompromising champion of human rights—Robert Nesta Marley rose from the slums of Kingston, Jamaica, to make reggae music and his own message of rebellion, self-determination, and the power of the individual a spiritual and political force throughout the world. The author of the highly acclaimed *Reggae Bloodlines* has created an intimate portrait of the charismatic artist through interviews with those closest to Marley and interviews with Marley himself, including the last one before his tragic death in the spring of 1981. The Wailers' recording sessions, concerts, and life at 56 Hope Road, Marley's residence, are all part of a sensitive, authoritative, and authentic look at the king of a musical movement that swept out of Jamaica and into Western and Third World countries alike.

Bob Marley

Bob Marley

Conquering Lion of Reggae

STEPHEN DAVIS

Plexus, London

Copyright © 1983, 1985, 1990, 1993 by Stephen Davis
Published by Plexus Publishing Limited
26 Dafforne Road, London SW17 8TZ
First Printing 1993

British Library Cataloguing in Publication Data

Davis, Stephen
  Bob Marley. – New ed
  I. Title
  781.64092

  ISBN 0 85965 179 7

The right of Stephen Davis to be identified as author of this work has been asserted by him
in accordance with the Copyright, Designs and Patents Act, 1988

First published in 1983 by Arthur Barker Limited; in 1985 by Doubleday & Company Inc,
USA; and in 1990 by Schenkman Books, Inc

Printed in Great Britain
Cover Design by Phil Smee

Contents

Acknowledgments

Special thanks to Judith Arons.

Thanks to Bob Marley's family and friends who shared their experiences: Cedella Booker, Rita Marley, Diane Jobson, Peter Tosh, Joe Higgs, Judy Mowatt, Tyrone Downie, Al Anderson, Don Kinsey, Neville Garrick, Lee Jaffe, Tony Garnett, Ernest Ranglin, Alton Ellis, the Wailing Souls, Jimmy Riley, Danny Sims, Lee Perry, Martha Velez, Jeff Walker, Michael Manley, Neville Gallimore, Leghorn Coghill, the Meditations, Charlie Comer, David Steinberg, Yvonne and Miss Wainwright, Clement Dodd and the people of Nine Miles, St. Ann.

Thanks to those who provided valuable information, videos, insights and interpretation: Roger Steffens, Garth White, Randy Grass, Carl Gayle, Peter Simon, Tim White, Paul Issa, Andy Bassford, Alan Greenberg, Don Williams, Peter Frank, Richard Skidmore, Joe Menell, Rob Partridge and Island Records in London, Adrian Boot, Vivien Goldman, Gordon Rohlehr, Trevor Fearon, Christopher Davis, Dermott Hussey, Luke Ehrlich, "Shirt," George Nelson, Janine Fay, Ed Dwyer, George Page, Hansel Dunn, David Burnett, Bruce Talamon, the James Isaacs Archives, the David Beiber Archives and the Reggae Beat Archives.

And thanks to those dearly beloved friends who supported the research and writing of this book: Ron Bernstein, Stephen de Sautoy, Lindy Hess, Marcia Fenwick, Shaye Areheart, Tim McGinnis, Thomas Landshoff, Howard Greenberg, Phyllis Wiseman, David and Anne Doubilet, Rob Friedlander, Howard and Hana Davis, Dan and Rebecca Mortimer, Roy Pace and Lily Aisha.

Most of all, thanks to Bob.

Author's Note

Jamaican English is a language that loses everything when translated to the printed page, and the problem is compounded in a biography of Bob Marley because of the way he spoke. Bob's words slurred and tumbled into one another in almost total defiance of conventional tense and syntax. And his speech came in different voices, depending on who he was speaking to and how strongly he wanted to make a point. In order to write a talking biography, in which Bob tells his own story as much as possible, I use phonetic writing when working with quotes Bob gave in taped interviews, in an attempt to convey some of his patois. But when employing quotes given to other writers, Bob's speech is reproduced as originally published.

S.D.

Suffering
should
be
creative
should give
birth
to something
good
and
lovely

Chinua Achebe

Joseph is a fruitful bough, even a
fruitful bough by a well; whose branches
run over the wall:
The archers have sorely grieved him,
and shot at him, and hated him:
But his bow abode in strength, and the
arms of his hands were made strong
by the hands of the mighty God of
Jacob; (from thence is the shepherd,
the stone of Israel.)

Genesis 49:22–24

1

Started Out Crying

Interviewer: *Bob, how did you start out in singing?*
Bob Marley: *Started out . . . crying. Yeah, started out crying, yunno.*

(1973)

Bob Marley spent the first half of his life in Jamaica growing under the influence of a series of strong teachers, advisers, family and friends. The first of these was his maternal grandfather, Omeriah Malcolm, a cultivator of the hills and valleys at Eight Miles and Nine Miles, Rhoden Hall, near Alva in the parish of St. Ann's.

Omeriah was often called "Custos" by his people, the large, almost tribal extended family that lived in the district, with almost every soul in the little country villages related to everyone else by blood or marriage or both. Officially, of course, the title of custos referred to the chief magistrate of the parish who presided over the courthouse at St. Ann's Bay, fifteen miles away on the north coast of the island. But in the speech of the Jamaican country people, the custos is a man who, though short of stature, still commands enormous respect.

Omeriah was a man of property and some authority in the district, a "big man" despite his height. He was also called O.M. and Manhame, and went by other nicknames as well, like many Jamaican men prominent in their communities. Omeriah Malcolm was a peasant landowner and a farmer, and his grandson Bob Marley would tell prying interviewers that he too was just a farmer after all, a cultivator of the soil like his grandfather Omeriah back in St. Ann.

In Jamaica, St. Ann is known as the "garden parish," and in many ways the parish is the spiritual center of the island nation. Located in the island's extremely fertile north-central sector, St. Ann has a special cachet for many Jamaicans as a place of abiding beauty, restlessness and rebellion. In Jamaica, St. Ann is known for the sweetness of its fruit, the abundance of its produce, the strength and head of its meticulously cultivated *sensimilia* marijuana and the special, somewhat fiery quality of its

1

people. Every Jamaican remembers St. Ann as the home ground of the island's two international heroes, Marcus Garvey and his spiritual descendant, Bob Marley.

Most of all, St. Ann is a parish of incredible tropic fecundity and splendor. On its northern border are the aquamarine inlets and beaches of the Caribbean. Inland from the north coast, the landscape turns to rolling hills and vales of every conceivable shade of green and blue, in turn shimmering with hot tropic humidity and shaded by vast sailing ocean clouds. Turkey buzzards (called "john crow" locally) swoop low over the little hamlets and villages that dot the winding rural roads, where peasants walk along in the slow, deliberate step of country people anywhere on the planet. A man's machete, carried everywhere as both agricultural implement and personal totem, might be gently brushing his leg. A woman might stop a moment to adjust the heavy basket of mango and yam on her head. In St. Ann, life takes on a measured, unhurried proportion. When waiting for something in St. Ann, people tend to say "Soon come," and sit back and hope for the best.

St. Ann is bordered on the west by the more roughly hewn parish of Trelawney, the ancestral home of the Jamaican Maroon tribes, a semiautonomous nation of the descendants of slave warriors who fought the British redcoats to a bloody draw during an eighty-year rebellion between 1660 and 1738. To the south of St. Ann is the parish of Clarendon, which has produced many of Jamaica's best singers, and St. Catherine, the gateway to the island's broad southern plain and the capital at Kingston. To the east is St. Mary, equally beautiful but lacking some of the majestic qualities of its neighbor. For some special reason, among all Jamaica's thirteen parishes, St. Ann stands alone, brimming with mystery and the dreamlike natural glories of the planet's tropical zone.

The history of the parish seems emblematic of the story of the whole island. When Christopher Columbus, sailing west from Hispaniola on his second voyage to the New World, discovered Jamaica in 1494, he anchored at Dry Harbour on St. Ann's northern coast. Columbus found the island populated by its aboriginal inhabitants, the Arawak indians, with the thickest settlement in the area of St. Ann itself. When the Spanish began to colonize Jamaica in 1509 (under license from Columbus's son Diego), they established their first town, Sevilla Nueva, at St. Ann's Bay and began their genocidal enslavement and extermination of the Arawak. Under the Spanish, St. Ann was used as a vast and rich grazing area, with gigantic herds of swine and cattle wandering over the countryside and great annual slaughters for the fat, the meat and the hides. As the Arawak began to succumb to disease and mass suicide, the Spanish began to import large numbers of African slaves from Angola, the seed of the present Jamaican population.

By the time the English took Jamaica from the Spanish, first by piracy and military force in 1655 and then by treaty in 1670, the island had a substantial black population. (Upon the arrival of the British, several large parties of former slaves of the Spanish took to the Clarendon hills to fight harassing actions against the new occupiers. These mountain guerrillas became known to the Spanish as *cimarrón*, wild and untamed. In time, and with fresh recruits from the harsh conditions of the English sugar plantations, they would be called the Maroons.)

Whoever named the Jamaican parishes, most likely some early British colonial governor or missionary, must have had some appreciation for the romantic and mystic aspect of the St. Ann landscape, heaving choppily like a green storm-tossed ocean of earth and limestone. For St. Ann herself is a mysterious figure, traditionally recognized in folk culture as the mother of the Virgin Mary and the grandmother of Jesus, but unmentioned in Scripture. Yet her cult is ancient, and in Europe St. Ann is still invoked by women in childbirth.

Under the British, Jamaica was used as a huge agricultural factory and transshipment port for the slave trade. Sugar from the West Indies was the great energizer of Europe in the eighteenth century, and vast fortunes were cut from the cane fields of St. Ann and the rest of Jamaica. To work the cane, the British stepped up the slave trade with West Africa, which resulted in one of the largest forced migrations in human history. To satisfy the European lust for sugar, millions of Africans were transported to the sweltering fields of Jamaica, Cuba, Hispaniola, Barbados and the rest of the West Indies. To defend its Jamaican prize, the British employed pirate and privateer fleets. These buccaneers ruled the Caribbean Sea under the black flag until the Crown tightened its control after the Jamaican pirate capital at Port Royal, known as the "wickedest city in the world," sank Gomorrah-like beneath the waves during an earthquake in 1692. As late as 1722, the St. Ann coast was raided by pirates, and sixteen people were burned alive in a besieged plantation house.

Black slavery lasted in Jamaica until 1834. On the plantations, Africans and their descendants were developing their own culture, with half-remembered African traditions and rhythms and newly acquired British and Caribbean influences. Wrenched from ancestral, tribal custom and tradition, the slaves coped with an unfamiliar environment by creating a culture and world parallel to that of their captors. Medical care was handled by herbalists, blessings were conveyed by myal priests and curses were invoked by obeah men. Tradition and religion were reconstructed

3

from the King James Bible and the African stories of Ananci the spider and Jesta the trickster. Although African drumming by slaves was outlawed in Jamaica early in the 1700s, a popular Jamaican music began to develop during the next century, based on the quadrilles fashionable in planter society and the chanteys brought in by seamen.

By the 1830s, agitation for abolition in Jamaica was pressed by missionaries of the three dissenting Protestant faiths—the Quakers, the Methodists and the Baptists. In 1834, a peculiar sort of Jamaican Emancipation Proclamation announced that all slaves were apprenticed to their masters. In St. Ann many slaves simply refused to work under the terms of the so-called apprentice system. By 1838, the slaves in Jamaica were freed unconditionally; with no one to work the large plantations, the fabulous Jamaican sugar economy began its long decline. By 1845, the sugar estate owners, desperate for labor, began to import East Indian indentured workers to replace the freed black slaves. It is these East Indians who are generally credited with (or blamed for) the introduction of marijuana seeds to the island.

After emancipation, Baptist missionaries began to set up "free villages" of liberated black families on five-hundred-acre tracts in the hills of Jamaica. Some of the earliest of these were in St. Ann, and it is believed that the tiny villages where Bob Marley was raised were founded in these times by former slaves and their preachers.

Many of the free villages were (and are) almost completely self-sustaining communities of small farmers growing fruit, vegetables, root crops and herbs, raising poultry and pasturing cattle and goats. To this day it is a conceit among some educated Jamaicans that the life-style of the typical Jamaican peasant is among the highest standards of living in the world. But it wasn't that idyllic in post-Emancipation St. Ann. In 1865, with civil war raging in the United States and basic imported food commodities (like salt cod) cut off by the Union naval blockade, starving St. Ann peasants drafted a plea for help to Queen Victoria and sent it via her Jamaican governor, Edward Eyre. In reply, Jamaica received a document that came to be known as the "Queen's Letter," recommending hard work for the laboring classes as the solution to their problems, and stating that only by their own effort would they achieve some improvement in their living conditions. Subsequently a small rebellion broke out in Morant Bay, in St. Thomas Parish to the east, but the leaders (George William Gordon and Paul Bogle) were caught and hanged, and the frustrations of Jamaican life were again suppressed. The people suffered in silence.

In 1887, in St. Ann's Bay, a son was born to a family of black stonemasons said to be descended from the Maroons. The boy was baptized Marcus Mosiah Garvey. In time, he would be known as Black Moses, who would try to lead his people out of bondage, back to Africa. By 1925, Marcus Garvey would become one of the most powerful black men in the world, and also one of the most feared.

At the age of fourteen, Marcus Garvey left St. Ann for Kingston, to find work. Garvey became a printer's apprentice; in 1907, at the age of twenty, he led a bitter printers' strike in Kingston, even though as a shop foreman he was technically on management's side. Fascinated with journalism, he followed the migrations of Jamaican workers to Panama and Costa Rica and edited newspapers for them in those countries. He traveled to London, where encounters with Africans led him to African history and black nationalism.

Back in Kingston by 1912, Garvey began to build a reputation as a brilliant orator and as a shrewd entrepreneur. In 1914, he founded the Universal Negro Improvement Association (UNIA), originally intended as a sort of fraternal organization. In 1916, he moved the organization to New York City and started a newspaper in Harlem called *The Negro World,* which took as its motto Garvey's nationalist rallying cry—"One Aim, One God, One Destiny. Africa for Africans at Home and Abroad." Through most of 1919–20 Garvey traveled all over America, a short, powerful man with a booming, inspirational preacher's style, spreading the UNIA doctrine of worldwide unity among Negro peoples and intense racial pride in their common African heritage. In his tough, uncompromising stance, rejecting integration and speaking directly to the lowest classes of blacks, Garvey was hailed as a savior by every black community he visited.

Gradually, Marcus Garvey formulated his ideas concerning the repatriation of New World blacks to Africa. He was convinced that black people could never secure equal rights in countries in which they were in the minority. He envisioned an autonomous black state in Africa, free from the domination of white men. As the first step in this dream he founded a steamship company, the Black Star Line, whose purpose was to "link the colored peoples of the world in commercial and industrial discourse." Purchase of Black Star Line stock was limited to blacks, and Garvey raised millions of dollars by selling single shares at five dollars apiece to his followers. It is said by Garveyites that Marcus never intended, as his critics claimed, that the Black Star Line would eventually provide transportation back to Africa for those who wanted to go. But the publicity angle of that concept was put to profitable use by the company's fund raisers and advertising agents. Despite harassment by New York authorities, the Black Star Line eventually purchased an old cotton freighter, renaming it the *S.S. Frederick Douglass.* In 1920, the boat began trading between New York and Jamaica.

The same year, Garvey held a UNIA convention in New York City. Newsreels and reporters flocked to cover Garveyite events that dazzled the city, from Harlem to old Madison Square Garden. Thousands of Garveyites paraded in Harlem in colorful uniforms. Marcus Garvey rode in an open limousine, in uniform and wearing plumes in his commodore's hat. The main sessions at Madison Square Garden were attended by African chieftains in tribal regalia.

At the podium, the small prophet from St. Ann was at his most spellbinding. Issuing a proclamation of anticolonialism and African nationalism, Garvey thundered from the rostrum, "We are the descendants of a suffering people. *We are the descendants of a people determined to suffer no longer.*" The pure African-ness of that statement, the sense that one's ancestors are always there to be appeased and avenged, was central to the hypnotic appeal Garvey had for his millions of disciples. Harlem tobacconists sold Marcus Garvey cigars with his image on the band. There was a popular race recording of a dance tune called "Black Star Line." Black churches and meeting halls rang to the UNIA anthem, "Ethiopia, Thou Land of Our Fathers."

Only in his mid-thirties, Garvey had achieved an unparalleled level of power for a black man in America. In 1922, his organization had almost six million dues-paying members. Garvey was so confident in his position that he met with the hierarchy of the Ku Klux Klan in Louisiana to discuss KKK financial support for African repatriation. But the following year, when Garvey was thirty-six, his troubles began. Management problems forced the Black Star Line into bankruptcy. Garvey was tried for mail fraud and tax evasion and sent to prison in 1925. Two years later, his sentence was commuted by President Calvin Coolidge, and the prophet was deported to Panama. Garvey made his way back to Kingston and began to preach again in churches from Falmouth to Morant Bay. He predicted full repatriation for New World black people by 1960. He revived the dormant UNIA and held several theatrical conventions in Kingston, where British colonial authorities did not take kindly to Garvey's black nationalism.

From the pulpit of a Kingston church one Sunday in 1927, Marcus Garvey uttered what would become, in Jamaica, his most revered prophecy: "Look to Africa, where a black king shall be crowned. For the day of deliverance is here."

Eventually, Marcus Garvey left for London, where he died of pneumonia in 1940 without ever setting foot in his beloved Africa. Fifteen years earlier, a UNIA attempt to establish a black colony in Liberia was rebuffed by the conservative black Liberian government. But in other parts of Africa during the 1920s, Garvey's message of African unity was catching fire. In Kenya a young rebel and organizer who called himself Jomo Kenyatta was a Garveyite of sorts. His war cry was *"Harambé"*—roughly, "Pull Together." Kwame Nkrumah's Pan-Africanism, Léopold Senghor's Négritude, Kenneth Kaunda's Humanism and Julius Nyerere's *Ujamaa* ("Familyhood") were all descended from ideas that had been African for centuries, but which had become crystallized in the lessons of Marcus Garvey of St. Ann's Bay. Forty years after Garvey's passing, the nationalist and revolutionary movements he helped spawn had forced Africa, from Angola to Zimbabwe, back into the hands of Africans.

The map of St. Ann is mostly white space in the middle, denoting the dense mountain jungle and limestone terrain in the interior of the parish. Bob Marley's country is off the one-lane paved road that cuts through the hills between the village of Alexandria and the market town of Claremont, twenty miles to the east. At Alexandria, turn east toward Alva and start searching for the tiny settlements on dirt roads where Bob Marley wandered as a barefoot country boy driving his grandfather's goats before him. If you come to the village of Albion, you've gone too far. Turn back and start looking again. Most likely, anyone along the roadside will be happy to tell you where you want to go.

Most important, anyone who travels these roads can't help but be astounded by the ironies of the place, so scenic and lush on the surface, and yet so hobbled by extremes of wealth and grinding poverty. Born into a seeming paradise, Jamaicans are among the most handsome, most generous, hardest-working people in the world. But the beauties of their birthplace aren't sufficient to support them all. Restless, many move on, seeking fortune in the island towns and, eventually, in foreign lands.

In 1940, Marcus Garvey died in England, and the world went to war for the second time in the century. Forces would be unleashed that were millennial and apocalyptic, and the world changed forever. These forces would also affect a union between a middle-aged white man and a young black woman deep in the hill country of St. Ann, Jamaica, West Indies.

Today, sitting on the patio of the suburban South Miami house that her son bought for her after her second husband died in 1977, Bob Marley's mother remembers little of World War II and the events that led her to marry her first husband, Norval Marley. Now a bright-eyed, articulate matron in her late fifties, Cedella Booker remembers the war in terms of the increased air traffic over St. Ann that delighted and mystified all the children, and the concerned discussions of her father Omeriah Malcolm and his brothers.

Cedella was born on July 23, 1926, in her father's house at Nine Miles, the sixth of the nine children of Omeriah Malcolm and his wife Alberta Wilby, from the village of Alva in the adjoining district. The family farmed O.M.'s various landholdings, but principally cultivated the rich valley bottom of a prized property of her father's they called "Smith," located down the road at Eight Miles. O.M. was a proud farmer, and his family worked hard, spending long days in the field. Much of Cedella's youth was spent walking barefoot, a basket on her head, between her father's house and his various plantings.

In the evenings, after many a hard day's work, there was often music. Omeriah played violin and accordion, and one of Cedella's uncles was a semiprofessional musician who played violin, guitar and banjo with several of the various St. Ann quadrille bands that provided dance music for country parish life—village dances, fairs and tea-meetings staged by community organizations and churches.

The quadrille styles and figures played by his relatives were probably the first music Bob Marley was exposed to as a child. Quadrille (called "katreel" in St. Ann) might be termed a Jamaican variant of bluegrass; it was developed by black country ensembles trying to reproduce the stylish European dance music of the mid-nineteenth century—the quadrille, the scotch reel, the waltz and the polka. The usual quadrille group even today usually has two guitars, a fife and a four-stringed banjo of the type Cedella's uncle played. Sometimes a fiddle and a rhumba-box are added for special occasions. Doubtless the earliest music Bob Marley ever heard was his great uncle's band jamming on classic quadrille tunes like "Titantic," "Jane and Louisa" or any of the popular quadrille round dances based on native Jamaican melodies.

One can imagine a skinny, sharp-featured boy hovering around the musicians as they played for some wedding or party, closely observing the guitarists and banjo player as they provided percussive, syncopated accompaniment for the dancers, who would accent the quadrille figures by stomping their feet in unison at certain points as a mischievous and very African fife darted around the music, providing both melody and focal point. Today the quadrille bands are dying out, vanishing from the Jamaican countryside, but during Bob Marley's childhood they were the principal form of entertainment for country people, and the quadrille musicians, despite their legendary appetites for St. Ann's puissant ganja and white rum, were accorded special status within their communities.

Cedella's mother Alberta was a small, beautiful woman from the village of Alva, a few miles to the west. Cedella remembers her singing in the fields. "She sang really well, echoing across the field so that everyone who was working could hear her, in a high tone of voice. If she could tell that people were depressed because of working so hard in the sun, she'd just sing it out. Just sing it out!"

One of the songs Alberta used to sing was called "Careless Mother":

> *Careless mother*
> *Who wandered away*
> *Only a step to the grave*

Alberta Wilby Malcolm passed away in 1936, when Cedella was ten years old. From then on, Cedella was raised by Omeriah and her older sister Enid. Cedella's childhood routine of primary school and fieldwork was interrupted only on Sunday, when the family walked down the road to the Shiloh Apostolic Church in Eight Miles. When she was fourteen, Cedella joined the choir and began to develop a fine voice, singing gospel for churches and little concerts around the district. By the time she turned sixteen, in 1942, she was beginning to get restless. The rigors of rural life in Jamaica turned young people old by the time they were thirty-five. Cedella wanted something different.

Two years later, in 1944, she found it.

In that year Captain Norval Marley, a quartermaster attached to the British West Indian Regiment, took up a new post as overseer of Crown "contingent lands" in the districts around Rhoden Hall. Norval Marley was short, dark, handsome and lonely. They met while the captain was making his rounds on horseback. Cedella remembers that it was the captain's gentle sense of humor that attracted her to him at first. Although Captain Marley was almost fifty years old and Cedella was not yet eighteen, they became lovers while Cedella was living in her grandmother's house.

Norval Marley's family were white Jamaicans from the parish of Clarendon. The Marleys were respectable, active in business and agriculture. Norval's mother, Miss Edith Marley, resided in one of Kingston's better suburban neighborhoods, near Hope Road in lower St. Andrew Parish. According to longtime residents who remember her, Edith Marley's two sons, Robert and Norval, were her complete pride and joy.

Cedella Booker doesn't know many details of Norval Marley's life.

9

She believes he was born in Clarendon before the turn of the century, and went to live with his mother in Kingston when his parents divorced. Like many white Jamaicans of the middle and upper classes, Norval might have received some of his education in England. Cedella is not sure. "Bob's father's early life, I don't know anything too much about," she says after straining to recall some point. "At the time we were together, I didn't have the experience to ask these things of him."

Cedella does remember that, in spite of the considerable difference in age, their love affair was a passionate one. "He was a very handsome, loving and sweet gentleman. He told me he loved me, and I believe that he did. He was always honest with me in that time. He told me he was the black sheep of his family, because the Marleys did not like black people, but Norval liked them very much." For a while, the romance between the pretty, unshy black teenager and the aging army captain went unnoticed but for the usual whispering and rumors that affect country life everywhere. When Cedella discovered she was pregnant, in May 1944, she was both afraid and very proud.

Cedella told Norval that she was expecting his baby, and the captain said that he would marry her and support the child. Flushed with her secret, Cedella returned to Nine Miles and blurted the news out to her most trusted sister, and began to make secret preparations for her wedding. But within twenty-four hours, sister had whispered to brothers who whispered to cousins who whispered to their mothers, Omeriah's sisters, and Omeriah got wind of what was going on with his little Ciddy and erupted with the fury of a sudden St. Ann thunderstorm.

Terrified of her father's wrath, Cedella ran away from home before O.M. could lay a hand on her. She got as far as her grandfather Daniel Wilby's house in Alva before O.M. caught up with her and took her home to Nine Miles to find out exactly what was going on. Her father told Cedella that Captain Marley was even older than the fifty years he claimed, and to think carefully about what she was doing.

Somehow Cedella got word of the crisis to Norval Marley, who rode out to Nine Miles on his horse to ask Omeriah for Cedella. "That man came right to my father's house and asked my father for me," Cedella says. "And my father told him right out that I was too young. My father said to the captain, 'She may be your girl, sah, but she's still under my protection.' I can remember this like yesterday. They were two big men arguing with each other, and I was a little girl." To add to the tension, the whole village and extended tribe was in an uproar of gossip and innuendo, of which Cedella had to bear the brunt. "But I outgrew that, yunno," Cedella says bluntly. "Because I'm strong anyhow. And if someone's sayin' something I don't like, I tell them to stop. When they teased me about the captain in those days, I just told them to stop."

After a few hours of polite but tough-minded negotiation, the two men agreed on the marriage of Cedella Malcolm to Norval Marley. The wedding was set for June, and a parson was engaged. It's doubtful a marriage license was ever taken out for an informal country marriage of convenience and necessity. And a week or so before the wedding, Norval visited Cedella at her grandmother's house to give her some unhappy news.

Norval told Cedella that an old back problem had returned to haunt him. His job in St. Ann required horseback inspection of government properties, and all the hours of walking army horses on mountain trails and back roads had aggravated a chronic hernia. On a visit to Kingston to see his mother, a doctor had told him either to seek an operation to cure the hernia or to find a job that didn't require long hours in the saddle. Norval had applied for and been ordered to a new assignment near Kingston as a foreman on bridge construction projects. But he promised to visit Cedella every week in St. Ann, and to support the baby when it arrived.

Cedella Booker heaves a long sigh, a world away from her other life in Jamaica, and conjures up her wedding night. "We got married on a Friday night, the ninth of June 1944, at my grandmother's house in St. Ann. Parson Aljoe, the minister for Stepney Church, was hired and came to the house. That was a Friday. Norval married me because I was pregnant then, and he was leaving to go away. By marrying me in our house he let me know that he would take care of us. We married Friday, and he left Saturday evening, the next night, for Kingston to take his new job."

As the seasons changed, Cedella continued to work on her family's ground. Her belly swelled, and she waddled with all the pomp and pride of a typical young Jamaican mother. She watched her diet and prayed. She lived with her father, her grandmother YaYa, and sometimes in a house in a neighboring vale called Calderwood, where her problems with her husband's family had their genesis.

It turned out that a white Jamaican woman named Mrs. Morris also lived in Calderwood. Mrs. Morris was a friend of Miss Edith, Norval Marley's mother in Kingston. Mrs. Morris heard that Cedella was going around claiming that Captain Marley had married her and was the father of her baby, and went and relayed that information to Miss Edith Marley, who had a fit.

Norval visited Cedella twice during her pregnancy, and told her disheartening stories about his family's reaction to the marriage when he had finally admitted it to his furious mother.

"Y'see," says Cedella, "here's what happened to my life with Captain Marley. I was a little black girl then, and still is today, and the prejudice in those days was so strong. Captain Marley visited me while I was pregnant, and he said his mother was very wroth with him because he had married a little black girl in the country. The next time he visit, before Bob was born, he told me that Miss Edith disinherit him in favor of his brother Robert's two sons, Peter and Alan. It turned out not only that she didn't give Norval a thing because he had married me, but also she treated him very bad too. His whole family was very against him because of me."

Cedella felt bad about the familial pressure on her husband, and didn't know what to do. When she asked Omeriah about the situation, O.M. told her not to worry or cry, and everything was going to be all right. At night, lying by herself now in Omeriah's house, waiting for the baby to come, Cedella prayed and prayed, hoping for a son.

Cedella had been baptized into the church while she was expecting her child, and she remembers no fear or apprehension of the birth. On a Tuesday night in February, she began to go into labor. Cedella's son was born at two-thirty on Wednesday morning, February 6, 1945, at his grandfather Omeriah's house at the bottom of the hill at Nine Miles. Cedella was attended by her sisters, and a local midwife was on alert in case of any problem, but the delivery was smooth and everyone in the Malcolm family was thrilled with Omeriah's first grandson, a light-complexioned child who was happy and smiling from the moment he entered the world. Taking the baby, swaddled in a receiving blanket, Omeriah reverently weighed the child on a produce scale and shouted the precious weight for all to hear: "Six-and-a-half pound!" Cedella remembers that Omeriah was "great and proud" of the baby boy, who from that moment on Omeriah considered his heir.

The Malcolms didn't name the baby, but waited for the boy's father to return from Kingston, and shortly after word was gotten to him that his wife in the country had delivered a son, Norval Marley came back to St. Ann for a week. He named the boy Nesta Robert Marley. The name Robert was chosen in honor of Norval's brother, and the name Nesta was carefully spelled out for Cedella by Captain Marley without any explanation as to why it had been chosen. To this day the name remains something of a mystery to the family. (In 1962, when Cedella emigrated to the United States, she tried to buy a passport for Bob, only seventeen at the time. The official at the Jamaican passport office—"You had to wet his palm," Cedella says—told her that Nesta Robert sounded too much like a girl's name, and the U.S. immigration authorities wouldn't like it. He suggested that the boy's passport should say Robert Nesta Marley. That's how the names were reversed.)

To the family the baby was Nesta, a radiant light-skinned child with curious black eyes who charmed everyone in the village. So the Malcolms were terrified by an incident that occurred when the baby was four months old. Cedella was patching her brother Gibson's trousers and had propped Nesta on pillows, lying on a rubber sheet. When the child dozed off, Cedella went to the grocery shop to get a bite to eat. When she returned she woke the baby and began to breast-feed him. Suddenly, Nesta seemed to convulse. Water dribbled out of his nose, and he threw up his feeding. The baby was hot to the touch, and his stomach felt as hard as a rock. Terrified, Cedella called for her sister Enid and, as the two women worried over the child, Nesta lost consciousness. His head went slack in Cedella's arms, and his eyes rolled up in his head. As her sister began to panic, Enid ran down to Smith to summon their father.

Omeriah Malcolm was an herbalist and root gatherer, and when he arrived at his house he kept a cool head as he examined the baby, still unconscious but at least breathing regularly. After due consideration, O.M. told Cedella that an evil spirit had attached itself to Nesta's body. Then he went out to his kitchen and mixed a drink from the herbs and other medicinal ingredients he kept on hand. He poured a bit down the child's throat himself. After a while, the baby threw up again, and then the fever dropped. After a day or two, the child recovered completely.

Cedella recalls another mysterious incident about that time. Baby Nesta was especially cherished by his grandmother, an ancient woman everybody called YaYa. YaYa loved the baby up, and made an amulet to protect Nesta. Cedella says that one day, while she was bathing and changing him, the amulet somehow disappeared. The whole family searched the whole house in vain. The amulet was never seen again.

"After Bob was born," Cedella says, "his father came and visited him and supported the child. He send supportance. I was so young then, just a child in the country without much sense. My husband would send the money to my father and my father would give it to me accordin' to how I'm in need of it. That's how immature I was then."

Every month or so, when he could get away, Norval Marley came up to St. Ann to visit Cedella. He gave Omeriah the money to build a tiny cabin for Cedella and the baby, and eventually set Cedella up in a little grocery shop of her own. But under pressure from Marley's family, especially his mother, the romance between the white army captain and the black country girl cooled off. As Nesta grew into a bright little boy, his father's visits became more infrequent and more single-minded. Norval Marley wanted the child.

"Now at one point," Cedella remembers, "my husband came and visited me. He told me very seriously that his nephew want Bob to adopt, to be his little boy. And I seh no. My husband told me if they take the child, you'll not know him as your son again. I said no no no no no, that could *never* be. They couldn't tek my child and I nuh see him.

"Then he went to my daddy with the argument, and my daddy called me in, and he said, 'Never you ever let him tek that child from you.' I said, 'No, Papa, I could never do that.' We done that argument. We didn't talk about it no more. My husband left, and he went right back to Kingston."

As Bob was growing up, his mother moved around the villages a bit. "After I moved from Calderwood, I live in Stepney on a little parochial road, not a road where car can run, just foot walkin' and bicycles. Bob start going to school there when he was four. It was called Stepney School. That's where we're all schooled, to the little that we know. The school was up at the top of the hill in Stepney, and I have a little grocery shop down at the bottom." When it was too hot the classes were held outdoors, and Bob, with his shiny high voice, would lead the class in reciting their numbers and letters. "I'd stay down there watching him, and my head was *this* big. I felt so proud. And then his teacher, Mrs. Isaacs, praised him so much. She always used to tell us how bright he was and how helpful he was to her."

There are people in Nine Miles and Stepney today, many of course with blood ties to Bob Marley, who remember him well from the days when he was a "pickney" in their villages. Bob is remembered with particular fondness by men and women now in their late middle age, whose descriptions give the sense that Bob grew up as a cherished little boy in these hill communities, the bubbling presence singing behind the counter of Auntie Ciddy's grocery at the bottom of the hill. The little boy was responsible for a few of his grandfather's prized goats, and he would tend Omeriah's mango walk in season and perform dozens of farm chores, spending half his life scampering barefoot between school and the fields.

In 1951, when Bob was almost six years old, Norval Marley again appeared in St. Ann. "Bob's father wrote to me and said he wanted to school him in Kingston. He called him Nesta. OK, so he come up and we talk it over with my father, all of us, and we talk it over with Bob. Him father seh, 'I think the school in Kingston could be better for the child, that he would get better teaching and everything.' So I told Bob's father that, yes, it would be all right for Bob to go to Kingston with him and get his schooling.''

Mrs. Isaacs, the teacher at the Stepney School, was against the move. Nesta was her brightest star, and she told Cedella she was afraid that the boy would not be able to compete with the children his age in the Kingston schools. But the decision had been made, and the family prepared the little boy as best as they could and sent him off to Kingston to live with his father. Bob was six years old.

Without her son, Cedella Marley was disconsolate. "I would write to him all the time, because I could not go to see him, because of Norval's family. I was not accepted. I was rejected. So I just stayed on the outskirts and kept on writing."

For several months, Norval put Cedella off by writing her that Bob was in school and doing well. After six months, Cedella wrote to Norval and told him she was coming to Kingston, that she had to see her son. Norval wrote back that Nesta was in St. Thomas Parish on a vacation with his teacher, so there was no point in coming all the way to Kingston. "All this wasn't true," Cedella says now. "But I stayed in St. Ann and waited patiently, and prayed for my little boy."

After a year passed with no word from Norval Marley, Cedella began to despair. Her letters went unanswered, and she was afraid to go to Kingston and demand her child back from her husband's family. "One day, a lady came to the shop in St. Ann where I was. Her name was Maggie James." Cedella was now a respectable village matron, and everyone in the district called her Auntie Ciddy. "And Maggie James said, 'Auntie Ciddy, I just went to Kingston and guess me who I saw?'

"I said, 'Nesta?'

"And she said, 'I saw Nesta!'

"I said, 'Where you saw him?'

"And she said, 'I was walking on Spanish Town Road and I heard somebody call "Hi! Miss Maggie!" And when I look around it was Nesta, the likkle bwai who everybody used to love so much in the country down there. And I said, "What are you doing here?" He had a bag in his hand and he said he was going to the coal yard to buy coal for Mrs. Grey.'

"And then she ask him who is Mrs. Grey? And Nesta said, 'She's the lady that I stay with.' And then he said, 'Where is me mother?'

"And she said, 'She's at home.'

"And he said, 'Ask her why she don't come look for me. Tell her I'm

at so-an-so Heywood Street and tell her she must come look for me here.'
So Maggie James run with the tiding to me that morning. She told me the
whole story, but then she said, 'One thing, Auntie Ciddy. I don't remember the number.'

"I said, 'What?'

"She said, 'Yes, Nesta gave me the address but I did not write it down.
But I know he said Heywood Street.' She told me her niece Merle was
with her that day, and that I should write to Merle to see if she remember
the address. The girl wrote back right away and said she did not remember the number but that Heywood Street was very short, and to come to
Kingston and she would help with an inquiry."

Cedella caught a ride on a farm truck as far as Claremont, and from
there she took the omnibus over the Blue Mountains to Kingston, where
the buses from the country disgorge their passengers (and their invari-
able loads of produce and chickens) along the south side of the Parade,
the great rectangular common that was the centerpiece of eighteenth-
century Kingston. Next to the bus terminal is Coronation Market, where
hundreds of "higgler" women control the market for produce and foodstuffs. Every day is market day, and when Cedella's bus let her off at the
Parade that afternoon early in 1952, she was at first bewildered by the
teeming, vivacious, *dangerous* vibration of the island's legendary capital.

Merle, Maggie James's niece, was waiting for the bus, and together the
two women began to scout Heywood Street, just off the West Parade.
The first person Cedella saw was a man sitting in a doorway of a house on
the left-hand side of the street.

"I said good evening. And he said good evening. And I said, 'Do you
know a little boy around here by the name of Marley?'

"And he said, 'Who, Robert?' And he look in the dooryard behind
him and said, 'He was just here a while ago, playing.' And then, suddenly, running from around the corner, was Robert! And when he saw
me he ran up and hugged me like this, so hard! And he looked at me and
laughed. And he said, 'Oh Mama, you're so fat!' Because I was a little
heavy at that time. I looked him up and down, and he was fat himself like
I have never seen him before, but other than that he look fine.

"And I just freeze. I just stayed there on the street and felt him and
looked at him, not even thinking about the home where he's living or
why he's there. And then afterward he said, 'Come let me introduce you
to Mrs. Grey.'

"I was a little curious, and I said, 'Who is Mrs. Grey?' And he said,
'The old lady that I'm staying with.' And I said all right, and I went
inside. He took me up the step and we went around the back and I went

16

inside and saw her sitting there, an elderly woman half in the dark. I said good afternoon. She was heavy-set and looked sick to me. She didn't look right to me. I didn't know why Bob's father had kept the child with her. And I said to her, 'I am Robert's mother.'

"She said, 'Are you?' And she told me that she was a friend of the Marley family, and that Bob's father had brought the boy to her in hopes that she would raise him as her son and heir. Bob's father believed that if Mrs. Grey adopted Bob, what she had would come down to Bob when she died. Norval did this, I believe, because he did not have anything himself to give to Bob. Mrs. Grey said that after the father brought the boy down to her, she never saw Mr. Marley again.

"And she was talking quite shaky. And all her hands were broken out in sores and her skin was peeling, and her hair was hanging in strands and falling out. She asked me why I had never come to see Robert and I told her I didn't have the slightest idea where he was. The boy just saw somebody, and I got the message, and that's why I'm here!"

Cedella told the old woman that she would take her son home, and Mrs. Grey said she would miss Bob, but she was ill and it was becoming more difficult to send him to school anyway. "Bob would fetch her coal and her groceries," Cedella says. "He was very handy to Mrs. Grey, and the two of them helped each other. You could see she was helping him from her heart. But he told us right away he wanted to go home.

"At that point, I took him home. He was seven years old."

At first, Nesta had some problems upon his return to St. Ann, although everyone was happy to see him. "All the other children wanted him to play with," Cedella says, "especially the ones older than him. He would be comin' out of school or mindin' the shop and the children would be calling, '*Nesta! Nesta!* Come and play.' Every second he and his friends would be playing football, like kicking an orange peel or whatever they had around the place."

At first he had trouble in readjusting to the regimen of Mrs. Isaacs's classroom. Then some sort of contagion hit the hill villages, and the children began to lose weight mysteriously. "Nesta became very, very thin," Cedella recalls, "and we couldn't understand why. The teacher said to me one morning, 'Mrs. Marley, I can't understand why the child is so thin. Because he was so fat when he was living in Kingston with a stranger, and now he comes back to you and gets so thin. Isn't he eating?' "

Mrs. Isaacs arranged for Cedella to buy fresh cow's milk from Mr. Jones, the head teacher at Stepney School. Put on a diet of hot milk and starchy food like roast yam, the boy gradually grew stronger. But not all the children were so lucky. Before the illness passed, one of Bob's cousins developed serious bone problems.

Nesta had also changed in another way. Before he had been taken to Kingston, he used to read palms at his mother's shop. Cedella remembers that "the district constable came to the shop one day and said, 'Auntie Ciddy, your little boy here read my hand. Listen to me. I don't know if the child realize what he was saying, but everything he told me has happened.'

"The following day, a lady called Aunt Zen came and told me, 'Did you know that your son can read hands?'

"I said, 'Read what kind of hand? A man the other day told me the same thing.'

"She said, 'No, Auntie Ciddy, it's true. Nesta read my hand and everything he told me is the same thing what happen.'

"So I said to him, 'Nes', you reading hand?' And he just smile."

After Bob came back from Kingston, he refused to read palms anymore. Aunt Zen complained to Cedella that the boy had refused to look at her hand and had told her that from then on, he was working on his singing. (Almost thirty years later, Bob's friend Diane Jobson heard the stories of Bob's childhood palmistry. One day she teasingly offered her hand for examination and said, "Bob, read my hand for me now." Bob gazed at her hand for a moment, then kissed his teeth and said, "Your hand full of crosses." Meaning he didn't read palms anymore.)

Bob used to sing for Cedella's customers in the shop, and after he was back a while, he was singing so well that local people would come to the shop and give him money to sing for them. There was a popular mento song, a Jamaican cousin of calypso, that Nesta sang all the time in the shop and which his family particularly associates with his boyhood. Bob would perform it while banging two sticks for percussion, and the people in Stepney thought it was hilarious:

> *Please mister woncha touch my tomato*
> *Touch me yam me punkin potato*
> *All you do is feel up, feel up*
> *Ain't you tired of squeeze up squeeze up*

"Touch My Tomato" is a classic Jamaican vendors' song; Cedella says it's the first song she ever heard her son sing.

In 1955, when he was ten years old, Bob Marley lost his father, whom he had never really known. Norval Marley died that year in Kingston (Cedella thinks that either cancer or malaria carried him off), leaving only a daughter, Constance Marley, by a second marriage. (Cedella and Bob never had any contact with the Marley family after Norval's death in 1955. Diane Jobson grew up with the children of Norval's brother Robert, whose names are Peter and Alan. One is a lawyer in Kingston, the other owns a concrete plant. They have a sister, Marguerite. Diane ran into Peter Marley at the airport once, after Bob had achieved his stardom. Peter Marley told her that he would very much like to meet Bob, but didn't know how he would be received. The two cousins never met.)

Nesta also lost his mother again that year, at least for a while. Deprived conditions in the country, life without electricity or running water and the long hours of stoop labor and fieldwork reminded young Jamaicans too much of the conditions of slavery. Cedella wanted out. "Oh, I just had to get out of the country. Every young girl in St. Ann want to come out of the country and, yunno, shake up demself a little bit. So I want to go to Kingston and try also." An opportunity presented itself early in 1955, when Alberta Malcolm, the wife of Cedella's older brother Jonathan, emigrated to England to study to be a nurse. Jonathan wrote to Cedella and asked her to come to the city to keep house for him. Cedella left Nesta in Omeriah's care and took the bus to town. Nesta became his grandfather's main goatherd, taking the flocks up to pasture in the morning and then bringing the frisky animals back down again at night. All day at pasture Nes' would sing to himself or play a cane fife he had gotten from a friend. Bob's cousin Sledger, a little older than he, was his constant companion.

After a while, Nesta and Sledger were sent fourteen miles down the road to live with Cedella's older sister Amy in the village of Alderton. Amy was known to be strict, and the family thought she might be able to better control the two mischievous country boys. But Amy's tyranny and child abuse was too much for them. Nesta, then about eleven years old, had to do much of the cooking, while Sledger was responsible for the animals and other chores. One of Nesta's constant duties was to walk through five miles of craggy hill terrain to fetch firewood at a hamlet called Pedro.

One Sunday morning, Amy and her husband walked off to church after Amy had ordered Nesta to prepare a big pot of rice for their Sunday dinner. The boys gathered wood, built a fire and put on the pot of rice to boil. While they were waiting for the water to heat up, they decided to run away and go back to their grandfather's house to live. So

19

the boys ate half the rice and left, taking the rest of the meal with them. When Amy returned from church to find nephews, lunch and cookpot missing, she was properly enraged; but Omeriah Malcolm granted his fugitive grandsons sanctuary from the wrath of his insulted daughter.

Meanwhile, Cedella was trying to scratch out an existence in the slums of western Kingston. "So, t'ings and time change. I left St. Ann, and it was months between, maybe years, since I last seen Nesta. I don't know. I can't quite recollect. I'd say it was two years at the most." Cedella wanted to send for her son, but she was still dependent on the charity of her relatives and wanted the boy to live with her only when she had a proper place of her own. At first she lived on Waltham Park Road, and then moved to Bedford Street with her Aunt Ivy, who had a big apartment and wanted help with the rent. "At that point," Cedella says, "I sent for Bob, because I finally had a place where he could stay with me." It was 1957.

At first, Omeriah put up a fight. He didn't want to lose his favorite grandson and valued goatherd. But O.M. knew he had to relent. So, dressed in his best clothes and loaded down with fresh fruit for his mother, Nesta was put on a bus to Kingston early one morning. It was a typically overcrowded Jamaican country omnibus, spewing clouds of sooty exhaust as it wheezed up the steep inclines of St. Ann, before joining the main cross-island road at Moneague. The bus headed south, passing over Mt. Diablo and stopping for passengers at Ewarton, Bog Walk, Linstead and the flat bridge at Raby's Corner, where the Rio Cobre carves an imposing steep-walled canyon out of sheer limestone. The bus was delayed for a time in Spanish Town because of mechanical problems, and was an hour late when it let an excited little boy out with the rest of its passengers along the bustling South Parade. His mother, whom he had not seen in two years, wasn't there to meet him, and he began to panic for a moment before he heard her excited shout: *"Nesta! Nesta!"*

Bob Marley was, in many ways, an abandoned child, and this condition was a key to his poetic sensibility. Throughout his career, from the time he began to write protest lyrics in 1965 to the time of his passing, the sufferings of the poor and the oppressed were equated with the imagery of children and childhood. "No Woman No Cry" is now sung as a lullaby by a whole generation, all over the world. Throughout his life, Bob identified his audience with children. "C'mon, children" was one of his favorite exhortations to his band and to people grooving to the Wailers' music. Family and friends invariably say that as the pressure of international fame and cultural power built up around him, Bob Marley was the most relaxed, the least shy and withdrawn, the most *himself* when kids were around. His friend Diane Jobson says that most of the time, children were in the room when Bob was composing, and it was children who Bob was singing to. In the music and lyrics that became the Wailers, one can hear the anguished, bad-dream crying of the orphan, the cast-off lost boy. "Started out crying," Bob Marley later told an interviewer who had asked him how he had got started in the music business.

His father was a memory with which Bob never really came to terms, especially to those who asked about his family. His answers over the years reflected a combination of bitterness and pride:

> *I'm born inna Babylon. My father, a guy who got together with my mother, he's a English . . . a guy who was a captain in the Army, go to war. Ya can't get no more Babylon than that! Yunnowhalmean? . . . My mother's a black woman from way inna St. Ann's, inna Jamaica, way inna country. Now this man's a man who came from inna England, go war. Fight inna waar. And then after that he go to Jamaica and find my mother way inna country . . .*
>
> (1973)

> *Born fatherless. Never know my fadda. My mother work twenty shilling a week fe keep me go to school . . . Me nuh have education. Me have inspiration! If I was educated I would be a damn fool . . .*
>
> (1975)

> *My fadda was a guy yunno, from England here, yunno? Him was like . . . like you can read it yunno, it's one o' dem slave stories: white guy get the black woman and breed her. He's a English guy . . . I t'ink. Cos me see him one time yunno. My mother? My mother African.*
>
> (1978)

Bob Marley grew up angry at his father, Norval Marley, who Bob felt had mistreated him and his mother. Cedella remembers, "One time Bob asked me, seh, 'I think my father was a bad man.' I said, 'No, your father was a good man, a very good man. But because of society, he couldn't do better.' I can see his [Norval's] position. The family was up against him. They took *everything* from him."

For a moment, Cedella forgets the warm winter evening by the pool of

21

her home in Miami, and her mind drifts back into the magma of memory, thinking about Norval Marley.

"A beautiful man," she says quietly, after a pause. "A wonderful person in his way."

2

Me Grow Stubborn

*Me grow stubborn yunno. Me grow without mother and father. Me
nuh have no parent fe have no big influence pon me. Me just grow inna
the ghetto with the youth. Stubborn, nuh obey no one; but we had
qualities, and we were good to one another.*

(1979)

When Bob Marley joined his mother in the slums of western Kingston in
1957, the hot, crowded Jamaican capital was undergoing a wrenching
period of transformation and struggle. The old wood-and-tin service-class
neighborhoods that had grown next to the original eighteenth-century
grid of Kingston (laid out in 1692 when the pirate metropolis of Port
Royal was devastated by earthquake) had decayed into slum housing,
rotting under the glare of the sun in the Tropic of Cancer. Attached to
the slums were the warrens of shantytowns and squatters' camps, densely
peopled by landless, dirt-poor intranational refugees from the harsh reali-
ties and social changes that had torn the veil of old Jamaican country life
and caused Kingston to swell with desperate and hungry people like an
angry boil on the neck of the Jamaican nation. It was under smoky and
reeking ghetto conditions of destitution, malnourished children, typhus,
polio and the violence of caged people that Bob Marley began to grow
into a man. In Trench Town the people were *crying*. The very literal
weeping and wailing of the people of the Kingston slums—"Sufferers"
they were called, and "Israelites," after the captive Old Testament tribes
with whom they identified—stoked the rebellious spirit that spawned
some of this century's most amazing cultural phenomena: the Rastafarians, the rude boys and reggae music. It was a spirit that possessed Bob
Marley as its fiery international beacon until the last day of his life, and
even after that.

Jamaica was a placid Caribbean subcolonial backwater, living on old
stories, bananas and a dying sugar industry until 1938, when a cane-

23

cutters' campaign of labor strikes on the sugar estates turned bloody and the Jamaican trade union movement was formed. Out of the two dominant unions came Jamaica's pair of political parties. The Jamaica Labour Party (JLP) was founded by a revolver-toting right-wing union boss named Alexander Bustamante, and represented in general the white British and Anglo-Jamaican colonial class, the mercantile middle-class of Chinese and Lebanese businessmen and shopkeepers and that elite segment of black Jamaica who worked for them. The People's National Party (PNP) was founded by a socialist intellectual named Norman Washington Manley, a first cousin of Alexander Bustamante. Manley's support came mainly from the great masses of peasant Jamaica, both rural and urban.

The two parties—socialist PNP and conservative JLP—have ruled Jamaica since the first general election was held in 1944, after years of agitation for Jamaican internal self-rule. It isn't an oversimplification to say that in Jamaica the JLP represents the Haves and the PNP represents the Have-nots. Throughout his life, and often despite his public statements and the fact that his district of St. Ann has long been a JLP stronghold, Bob Marley supported the general aims of the PNP—to promote equal rights and justice for the Jamaican poor.

Several factors contributed to poverty in Jamaica, and in turn fueled the migration from the rural parishes to the slums of Kingston. In Jamaica, more than fifty percent of the land is owned by fewer than one thousand individuals and companies. Due to a scarcity of available land for farming, few small landowners like Omeriah Malcolm could afford to buy or sharecrop enough land to support their families and dependents without some additional income or wage. Land shortage meant an ever-growing population crowded on smaller plots and holdings, with soil gradually declining in fertility. This situation spawned, especially after World War II, almost an entire generation of young rural Jamaicans looking for work beyond the socially stigmatized agricultural background of their parents. A 1955 study of rural Jamaica showed that sixty-five percent of the male population and thirty-two percent of the female population was unemployed or looking for work. It is precisely this cruel limbo of black Caribbean existence—jobless in Eden—that created the stampede of aspiring Jamaicans streaming into the western Kingston ghettos after the war years.

For country people like Cedella Booker, Kingston was the land of opportunity, where with luck one might find a respectable, nonmanual job and avoid a life of fieldwork and humping bananas. But it was all a myth. Kingston actually had very little work to offer. Newcomers without jobs or family traded the boredom and displacement of country life for a violent and competitive existence in some of the worst slums in the world. But the country people who failed to find freedom and a new life in Kingston rarely returned to their home parishes. Instead they squatted in one of the shantytowns that festered in western Kingston: Trench Town, built up over a ditch that drained the sewage of old Kingston; Dung Hill (or the Dungle), built on a municipal garbage dump; and Back O' Wall, which grew behind the wall of the public cemetery. The sufferers stayed in western Kingston and suffered, and the country legend of Kingston as the pot of gold at the end of the Jamaican rainbow was maintained for years.

When Bob Marley came to Kingston in the late 1950s, the miseries of the squatter camps were nothing new. The Trench Town settlements had been destroyed in a 1907 earthquake and rebuilt. Back O' Wall, the most notorious ghetto, dated from around 1935. After Trench Town was devastated by a hurricane in 1951, some public housing was built, but it was like holding back the hurricane with good intentions. Once a bucolic beach and fishing village outside of town, western Kingston became a dangerous cesspool more on the order of a New World Calcutta. As the Israelites poured in, they huddled in shanties of cardboard and newspaper, implausible yurts of fruit crates and fish barrels. People lived in oil drums and out in the open, with maybe a jagged scrap of corrugated iron propped up by a few splintered sticks to keep the fire dry and the dampness off the children. In the various camps, the sufferers lived between tin-sided alleys. Water, when it was available, was carried from standpipes, and cooking was done in the common tenement yards. People relieved themselves in pit latrines or in the alley. The air was thick with the smoke of cooking fires and the stink of urine. One-room shacks had nothing in them but a Formica dinette, a loud radio and three families jammed inside living on top of one another. At the city dump there was fierce competition between the vultures and the squatters for the contents of the garbage wagons as they unloaded the day's refuse. Overcrowding, disease, infant mortality and the violence of living in a human pressure cooker were and are the facts of life in western Kingston. By days, Trench Town looks like an old bombsite of sodden shacks, scorched earth and improbable tropic shrubbery. By night, lit only by the occasional flickering oil lamp in somebody's window, Trench Town looks like a desolate war zone of zinc, cement and scrap. And even more threatening (in the eyes of Jamaicans) were the sinister encampments of Rastafarians along the edges of the concrete gullybanks that drained the mountains that towered over Kingston.

Although its powerless inhabitants called Trench Town the "house of bondage," Bob Marley found another sort of family there. The friends he made, the people he lived with, the ghetto family among whom he grew to manhood, would be with him throughout his life. The yout's, as he called those with whom he came of age and with whom he sang raw harmony in the starving hours of his late teenage years, would be Marley's cronies, henchmen and retainers until he passed on. Some of them, like his friend Georgie who burned log wood through the night, would become song lyrics and enter into the heady realm of legend along with Bob Marley himself.

In Trench Town, Bob Marley found the family he had never had.

Compared to the dispossessed sufferers trying to survive amid the rising stench of the shantytowns, Bob Marley and his mother lived in the comparative comfort of a "government yard," one of the concrete units of public housing built in Trench Town after the 1951 disaster. At first, when Bob arrived in the city, Cedella was sharing a room on Nelson Road, but after a few months mother and child moved to Regent Street, living together in a tiny back room of a friend's house. Then, late in 1959, Cedella's older brother Solomon Malcolm decided to leave his job as a bus driver and emigrate to England. Solomon offered Cedella his prized flat in the Trench Town project at 19 Second Street, warning her that it was necessary for her and Nesta to move in with her furniture well before he moved out or jealous neighbors would steal the space. Since the rent was cheaper and the apartment bigger than where they were living, Cedella jumped at the chance. She worked as a housekeeper now, earning between twenty and thirty shillings a week, barely enough to pay for their rent and Bob's school uniform and books.

Most Jamaican boys end their formal education at fourteen, and Bob was no exception. Withdrawn and indifferent in the classroom, Bob passed through the Ebenezer, Wesley and St. Aloysius schools. There are dozens of present-day Kingstonians who remember him as a quiet, tough, observant classmate who couldn't wait for the day to end so he could be free to play football, fly his kite, play marbles, run with his friends and enjoy the other misdemeanors of ghetto youths whose heroes were cricket stars, soccer players and the emerging "rude boys," tough street anarchists born to raise hell in defiance of hard-eyed magistrates and the crippling sting of the whipping post.

Cedella remembers Bob as well-behaved in those days. He seemed to spend his whole life playing football with his vast corps of friends, staying out till all hours, kicking a ball even in the humid darkness of the Trench Town night. Cedella would be vexed and worried if he wasn't home by ten o'clock. When Bob was fifteen she lashed him with her belt when he ruined a hard-earned new pair of shoes playing soccer. That night Nesta had come home with his pants ripped and the soles of the new shoes flapping. In a rage, Cedella chased him around the apartment and beat him until he was screaming for his Uncle Gibson, who was living with them, to save him. But Bob made it up to Cedella. When she returned home exhausted the next evening after a day scrubbing floors, Gibson's live-in girl friend Pat took Cedella aside and showed her how Nesta had spent the whole afternoon cleaning the flat and fixing a broken kitchen table. "The whipping was good for him," Cedella now says succinctly, with the solomonic wisdom of the long-suffering Jamaican mother.

Several of Bob's ghetto friends remember an incident that took place on Second Street, perhaps in 1959, which left a deep impression on Bob. A welder and his girl friend, who lived a few doors down, had a terrible argument that everyone in the neighborhood could hear. The girl went away to cool off, and the man began to broadcast sad love songs on his phonograph at top volume. All day and into the evening the welder played bittersweet Jim Reeves ballads as loud as the machine could blast them out into the still, sultry air. When his girl friend returned home late that night, the welder dragged her into the street and beat her to death with a length of pipe. This murder occurred before criminal violence had become institutionalized in Trench Town, and everyone on Second Street and in the nearby areas was profoundly shocked. Especially Bob Marley.

In those days Bob Marley lived with and for his friends. Cedella recalls an incident which illustrates the strength of the almost tribal sense of loyalty the Trench Town boys felt for one another.

"I remember one time in Kingston, I used to work at a restaurant on Charles Street and Spanish Town Road, and one day a little boy came in and said to me, 'Are you Robert's mother?'

"And I said, 'Yes, what happen?' From the hurried way that he came in, I could tell something was wrong.

"And he said, 'Robert get a chop.'

"I said, 'He what?'

"He said, 'Robert get a chop in him face.'

"And I said, 'Where is he?'

"And then he told me, 'The school.' There was a school on the Spanish Town Road behind the market there, the Ebenezer School. So there was a man next door to me that have a shoe shop, and I asked him if he can watch the store for me while I ran to look for Nesta, to find out what was wrong. And when I went to the school to find him, all dem boys were in the classroom, and when they see me they look at each other and say

27

'Babylon,' as if the police.were coming, yunno, or whatever. I asked the boys if they had seen Nesta and dem say no. And then afterwards I go around the back of the school and I see him, and as he saw me he dived. He have a huge plaster on his face and he dived. And he went through another place, and hide from me, and then somehow got out of the school so I could not find him.

"Bob tried to hide what happened from me. He came home late, and I saw him outside and him was hiding, yunno. I step in front of him and I said, 'Nesta, what are you doing out there?'

"And he said, 'Nothing.'

"I said, 'What chop you?'

"Him say, 'The boys.'

"So I said, 'Why did you run from me when I tried to call you at the school?'

"He said, 'Well I thought you were going to call the police on dem, and is me good friend.' His face was badly cut, but he didn't want no police to come out there. The cut was deep, and he have the scar to this day. But he loved his friends so much that he take up for them so that he is not the one to make no quarrel or confusion or contention. He would do *anything* with his friends, and even when I might rough him and say 'Don't play with him' or 'Don't go there with him,' he'd still always— you know how boys are: he *had* to be with his friends."

Cedella Booker doesn't hesitate to admit that there was something strange about Bob in his childhood, a reserve and a shy sensitivity that sometimes set him apart from other children. She remembers him being selfish at times. If he asked for a piece of fruit and it was offered only grudgingly, he wouldn't take it. He hid his feelings from her, and would contract his features into a hard little mask that betrayed no emotion. Like most boys he pilfered change from Cedella, and unlike most boys confessed immediately when confronted with his furious mother's suspicions. "I told him, Nesta, that it is just the two of us in this world, and that whatever I had was his. I told him, 'Just *ask.*' And from that day he did."

What really vexed Cedella the most was her son's choice of friends. Most were older, and most were on the edge of juvenile delinquency and incipient rude boy–ism.

"I remember one time, I said to him, 'Bob, these people, dem bwais who are around you, seem like bad boys. A man is known by the company he keeps.' And he said to me, 'Yes, Mama, they *are* bad boys. But I nuh gwan do nothing that is wrong, yunno.'

"I said, 'I *know* you ain't gwan do nothing that is wrong, but *these people* can go do bad and because you're in their company, they might lead the police to believe you are in league with them.' And Bob said, 'Mama, they don't tell me what to do. Nobody can get me into any trouble. My friends, I tell *them* what to do.' "

There was another large family sharing the tenement yard at 19 Second Street, Trench Town, with the Marley-Malcolms. Thaddeus Livingston, or "Mr. Taddy" as he was called, was a carpenter and craftsman whose eight children filled the yard with clamor and mischief. Mr. Taddy's eldest son, Bunny (born Neville O'Riley Livingston on April 23, 1947), soon became Bob Marley's brother and singing partner. After school in the evenings, the two boys tried to harmonize amid the clashing noises of the neighborhood, beginning with familiar hymns and spirituals. The resourceful Bunny crafted a homemade instrument by stripping rubber insulation from electrical cord and using the fine copper wire for guitar strings. The sounding board was a sardine can nailed to a piece of wood, and a length of bamboo was the neck of the crude guitar. Their voices cracking and breaking as they changed from alto to tenor in pitch, Bob and Bunny in 1960 began to sing the first hesitant melodies of what would evolve into Bob Marley and the Wailers.

It was an auspicious era in Jamaica's turbulent history. The island's four-hundred-fifty-year colonial status was about to come to an end, and the emerging nation was busily inventing its own culture. Local musicians in Kingston were developing a new Jamaican sound based on the confluence of mento music, a kind of ragged Jamaican calypso descended from the quadrille music with which Bob was raised, and American rhythm and blues that was pumped without mercy into the culturally vulnerable Caribbean islands nightly by fifty-thousand-watt clear-channel stations in New Orleans and Miami. The new sound in Jamaica was called "ska," a fast shuffle close to mento and even closer to the hip-shaking back beat of R & B. Basically a hopping dance music with accents on the second and fourth beats, the word ska was originally the syllabic equivalent of this new music's afterbeat, chopped on rhythm guitar or banged out on the piano. The new Jamaican sound required a new generation of musicians as well, and gradually the best jazzmen in Kingston drifted into an instrumental group called the Skatalites, after the planetary orbiters which were flashpoints of East-West tension as the ska was developing in the late 1950s.

But like most boys in Trench Town, Bob and Bunny were mesmerized by the bold American R & B sounds they could pick up on Bunny's radio when the wind was blowing from the north. The locomotive rhythm sections and casually brilliant singers of New Orleans were particularly influential, especially Fats Domino, Louis Jordan, Larry Williams, Earl King, Huey Piano Smith and Alvin Robinson, among many others. As neophyte harmonizers, Bob and Bunny paid close attention to black vocal groups like the Drifters, whose "There Goes My Baby" in 1958 and "This Magic Moment" in 1960 were popular in Jamaica. Even more influential on the early Wailers were the Impressions, a Chicago harmony trio that grew out of the boyhood friendship of its two principal singers, Jerry Butler and Curtis Mayfield. Since the yard-style singing group, which didn't require prohibitively expensive instruments, was the principal form of musical expression for young Jamaicans, star harmony groups like the Impressions spawned dozens of competitive vocal trios in Jamaica. But in 1960, young Bob Marley wasn't thinking of a vocal group just yet. Later on, he would remember being equally influenced by Elvis Presley and especially early soul singers like Sam Cooke, Solomon Burke and Brook Benton. The country-and-western singer Jim Reeves was *very* popular in Jamaica, appreciated by Bob Marley as well.

By the time Bob was fifteen, he had just about given up on school and was concentrating mostly on singing. In 1959 the slender boy who sang "Touch My Tomato" for his mother's customers back in St. Ann gave his first public performance at a talent show at Queens Theatre. "Me saw dem have a little t'ing down at Queens deh," he recalled years later, "so one night me go in and sing a tune. Me nuh remember what it was, but me win a pound. The man dem tell me, me must start sing. And me *did.*"

Since Cedella had to pay for her son's schooling on a weekly basis, she would "get hot" with him when she saw that Nesta paid more attention to harmonizing with his friends in the evenings than to his schoolwork. One night Bob came home from singing, solemnly handed Cedella his schoolbooks and told her to find some friend who could use them, because he didn't want to go to the Ebenezer School anymore. Cedella informed her son that he couldn't make a living from singing, and would now have to learn a trade. At first she was dismayed because she knew that work for ghetto residents, even domestic work at that time, was extremely difficult to find; but then a friend gave her the name of the foreman at a welding shop east of the Parade, and Bob was eventually apprenticed as an electrical welder to a firm near South Camp Road and Emerald Street. The welding yard would be where Bob Marley's career as a professional musician really began.

At this point Bob Marley realized that as a singer he could go no further on his own without someone to teach him how to hold harmony and project his voice. Working with an acetylene torch and a hot shower of sparks by day was only the means by which he survived to sing at night, back in his neighborhood. Trench Town provided him a teacher through its informal university of boarded alleys and tenement yards.

That teacher was Joe Higgs.

Half of the famous pre-ska singing duo of Higgs and Wilson, whose first hit record—"Manny-O"—was produced by fledgling Kingston recording mogul Edward Seaga in 1960, Joe Higgs resided on Third Street, around the corner from Bob and Bunny's Second Street yard. In the cool of the evenings, Higgs's yard was the scene of constant harmonizing, group singing, community auditions, the clink of Red Stripe beer bottles and the sharp, sweet scent of ganja, Jamaica's marijuana and folk tranquilizer. Some of the best singers in the city (like Alton Ellis and Lascelles Perkins) showed up at the Third Street house, not only because Joe Higgs was a star and a hero of the ghetto like the other resident popular singers, but because he was also an acute, serious critic and an exacting singing coach. Joe Higgs possessed invaluable and nonnegotiable secrets—perfect pitch and the ability to teach people to sing close harmony—and he shared his knowledge freely, without thought of payment or anything other than training his talented ghetto neighbors to be the most disciplined harmony singers in the world. Most important, as it influenced Bob Marley, was that in an era when songs of romance and lost love ruled the Jamaican soundscape, Joe Higgs was writing songs and singing about taboo subjects like smoking ganja and the forbidding Rastafarians, an outcast and underground sect of sufferers that dominated a portion of the spiritual life of the shantytowns. Joe Higgs, with his hard-won moral authority and his compulsive attitude on correct harmony singing, was the perfect teacher for Bob Marley.

Bob and Bunny were both hopefully hanging on the fringes of Higgs's open-air music class when they met another youth, slightly older, who happened to have something no one else in the area possessed save Joe Higgs—a guitar. That boy—tall, lanky, baritone, boastful, angry—was named Peter McIntosh.

He was born Winston Hubert McIntosh in Grange Hill, Westmoreland, on October 19, 1944, the son of Alvera Coke and James McIntosh. Like Bob, he grew up in a farm parish rich in sugar, produce and herbs. Like Bunny, he had made his own first guitar out of a board, a piece of tin pan and plastic strings. When his father abandoned the family, around 1960, Alvera and her son migrated to Kingston and lived first with Alvera's sister, then with her brother and his wife on West Street in Trench Town. Peter, then about seventeen, was drawn like all the other musically inclined youths to the harmony sessions at Joe Higgs's place. "When I first came to Trench Town," Tosh says, "Joe Higgs and all the other singers were singing on Third Street. One day I happened to pass by Third Street and heard them singing together, and I go over there and join them musically. It was only me who could play a guitar, me and Joe Higgs. That is where I first find Bob and Bunny, singing with Joe."

In a 1975 interview, Bob Marley remembered what happened next. "We go out now, and me find some little yout's 'round me a sing. Then Bunny, who was like me brother in dem times, we form a group. We go look for Peter Tosh. We see Peter 'pon the street, me never even know him fe talk to. We hear him play him guitar and sing, and we figure seh yes, him sound *strong*. So we get together and form a group plus two girls and a next little yout', name Junior Braithwaite."

Peter Tosh remembers that after he, Bob and Bunny harmonized the first few times, the three boys were astonished by the vocal textures they could reproduce on favorite songs like Sam Cooke's "Chain Gang" and "Wonderful World," Ray Charles's "Hit the Road, Jack," Jerry Butler's "He Will Break Your Heart," the Impressions' "Gypsy Woman" and the Drifters' "There Goes My Baby," "This Magic Moment" and "Some Kind of Wonderful." Bunny's voice was high and piercing, an almost natural falsetto like the Impressions' Curtis Mayfield. Bob's tenor was smoky, like Sam Cooke or the Drifters' Ben E. King. And Tosh's deep baritone anchored the group with the commanding authority of a Jerry Butler.

"One day," Tosh remembers, "we went down to Ebenezer School and a likkle youth lend Bob an old guitar, and we hold onto that guitar for a good period of time until I teach Bob to play it, and show Bunny some chords. The Wailers were not a trio at the time. There were plenty of us, but it was *designed* to be a trio. We sounded so good together that people in the community always encourage us to go to the studio and record. And we Wailers' sounded good because we had good teachers, Joe Higgs and Franseeco Pep [longtime Wailers percussionist Alvin "Seeco" Patterson]. Joe Higgs used to direct us in harmony, as an elder one in the music business. And we used to appreciate that. Yes, mon!"

But Bob wanted to be more than just a member of a talented group of kids singing on Third Street. One day Bob sought out Joe Higgs alone and told him he wanted to sing and play the guitar, to learn the craft of musicianship. Higgs took Bob under his wing as a sort of private pupil in addition to his work with the informal group of Trench Town singers who called themselves the Teenagers—Bunny, Tosh, a strong young singer called Junior Braithwaite and two local girls who sang background vocals and call-response chants—Beverly Kelso and Cherry Smith. Higgs took Bob along to Higgs and Wilson shows in neighborhoods like Water House, and taught Bob to stay on key, to accompany himself with easy guitar chords and to write the chorus, verses and bridge for simple tunes.

By 1961, Bob was working at the welding yard at South Camp Road and beginning to write tunes. Once he was bold enough to scout the action at Beverley's, a record store owned by a young Chinese entrepreneur named Leslie Kong, who was beginning to record ska songs by Jamaican singers for local consumption. Bob asked someone behind the counter for an audition with Mr. Kong, and was impolitely advised to get lost. "Walk on bwai," they said to Bob Marley. "Leave the place."

It's not really hard to understand why Bob Marley was chased from Leslie Kong's door. A light-skinned, sharp-featured teenager with an askew mouth and darting eyes, Bob hardly looked the part of the ska idol or love balladeer that Kong and his fellow producers were trying to promote. And young Marley was only another face in the jostling crowd of hopeful singers who continually pestered Kong and other producers like Ken Khouri, Duke Reid and Clement Dodd for a chance to audition and record.

The reason the fledgling Jamaican recording industry was able to survive and thrive so close to the cultural imperialism of North American soul music had to do with Jamaican pride, the special requirements of the island's dancers and the formal independence Jamaica won from Great Britain in 1962 after one of the longest colonial administrations in British history. Jamaican recording of local music for local consumption had begun in the early 1950s, when a businessman named Stanley Motta had released calypso/mento songs on 78-rpm discs. But recording in Jamaica was fairly dormant during the great American R & B boom of the fifties, when Jamaican mobile sound systems, which broadcast the music Jamaicans danced to, were amply supplied with dance music (Ray Charles, James Brown, Little Richard) and love ballads (Nat King Cole, Frank Sinatra, Sammy Davis, Jr., Sam Cooke) from the States. But between 1958, when Elvis Presley was drafted into the U.S. Army and Little Richard's manic intensity faded, and the advent of the Motown Sound and the Beatles in 1962, the steady flow of reliable American music dried up. Of course there were exceptions: the Drifters, the Impressions and Sam Cooke continued to make black pop music that was immensely popular in Jamaica. But by the early 1960s the music imported from New Orleans and Chicago could no longer keep pace with the voracious demands of the mobile sound systems, which themselves had begun in the late 1940s and developed into the national dispensaries of dance music.

33

It was merchants like Leslie Kong and sound system hustlers like Duke Reid and Clement Dodd who turned their backs on the island's colonial complex of national inferiority—which held that anything from England or America was vastly superior to everything from Jamaica—and began to record Jamaican music to replace the diminished R & B from the States. Turning against the tide of history and ignoring the usually crippling neurosis of colonialism, these men and the musicians who played for them began to invent a new national culture for the new nation. The most talented men and women in Jamaica were on the scene and ready to sing for a pittance, for nothing even, just for the opportunity to stand forth, be identified as an artist and escape the brutal anonymity of Kingstonian street life. It was a new, popularly based party, cultural instead of political, and Bob Marley wanted desperately to be a part of it.

An accident in the South Camp Road welding yard propelled Bob even further toward his destiny as a musician. Working without goggles, he caught a tiny, jagged piece of steel in his left eye. Cedella remembers that when her son came back to Second Street that evening, his head was swollen and his whole body was in great pain. He was frightened for his sight and kept asking his mother to look at the eye, to see if she could see anything still in it. Bob slept all night with his head wrapped in a hot towel, paid two visits to the hospital and came away with what may have been a scratched cornea. Bob had to wear a bandage over his eye for weeks, even when he, Bunny and Peter performed at a talent contest late in 1961 as a vocal trio, calling themselves the Teenagers. Cedella thinks Bob's eye accident was the final push he needed to try to sell his talent after his initial rebuff at Beverley's. Bob told his mother that he hated his welding job and that somehow he had to get an audition with Leslie Kong. "Welding's not my line," Bob told his mother. "Singin's my line. If I was singin' and rehearsin', this wouldn't have happened."

One day at the welding yard, another worker who used to harmonize with Bob, named Desmond Dekker, caught a stray piece of iron in his eye and earned a couple of days off from work. Dekker had been writing songs in his spare time, and he used his sick days to audition for Leslie Kong at his shop and immediately recorded a song called "Honor Your Mother and Father," which became a big hit in Jamaica. Early in 1962, Desmond Dekker took Bob Marley over to Beverley's to meet Leslie Kong's newest sensation, a fourteen-year-old singer from St. James Parish named Jimmy Cliff. Born James Chambers in Somerton, near Montego Bay, Cliff had come to the city the year before and walked into Kong's shop. Cliff desperately improvised a song called "Dearest

34

Beverley," which in classic fashion earned its composer a recording session at Federal Records, whose studio facilities Kong used. Cliff had enjoyed a pair of local hits ("Hurrican Hattie" and "Daisy Got Me Crazy") when he met Bob Marley and heard him sing. Bob told Jimmy about being turned down for an audition with the boss previously; Jimmy Cliff took Bob Marley right in and introduced him to Leslie Kong.

Bob Marley sang for Leslie Kong without accompaniment, in the middle of the shop. The youthful but shrewd producer liked what he heard, a couple of ska-vitalized spirituals and a song Bob had written (with Joe Higgs's help) called "Judge Not." Within a few days, Bob had recorded "Judge Not" for Kong, as well as two other hard skas, "Terror" and "One Cup of Coffee," the last similar to, but not really a cover of, Brook Benton's "Another Cup of Coffee." A month later Bob Marley's first record, a 45-rpm single of "Judge Not" on the Beverley label, was released in Jamaica.

Sales were negligible, radio air play was nonexistent and the record was unsuccessful. But its earnest lyrics and quadrille fife were charming and different. Bob Marley had been given his break. Later, "Terror" and "One Cup of Coffee" were also released by Kong. Both songs attracted some attention, but few sales. Bob's share of the total proceeds from the three songs was twenty pounds sterling.

The year 1962 was both encouraging and extremely difficult for Bob. He had made his recording debut at the age of sixteen, and some kind of music career seemed possible to him, judging by the enthusiastic response he and his little group received from ghetto people when they sang in backyards and in talent contests. That year Bob appeared in a talent show in Montego Bay, a nervous, skinny kid outgrowing his clothes, warbling his song "Judge Not" in an unsure, squeaky voice.

But in the same year Bob's family life changed drastically when Cedella had an affair with Bunny's father, Mr. Taddy, and their daughter, Pearl Livingston, was born early in 1962, half-sister to both Bob and Bunny. Bob was almost seventeen by the time his sister was born, and life at 19 Second Street was suddenly different with a baby in the house. Also, tensions within the tenement complex were rubbed raw by a love affair between Bob and a beautiful fourteen-year-old neighbor named Esther. Cedella remembers "this little girl, living in the same yard. They were in love. Bob give me sign, and I saw her pass [Bob's cousin] Sledger a little love note for him. That morning, I stand on the balcony watching Bob go off to work and I saw Sledger pass the note to him. I see him take it out and start to read it and I called to him, 'Give me a read nuh!' And he look up and he laughs, and he just put it in his pocket."

The problem was the girl's older brother, who hated Bob because he was half-white. "Her brother say to Bob, 'We don't want no white man in our breed.' And besides, the girl was too young. Bob had a song for her:

When school days are over
I'll come back for you

but her family kill off the romance. Them style Bob as a white man. That made a difference in our yard, and I decided to go to America."

When her daughter Pearl was weaned at nine months, Cedella Marley married a steady, dependable man named Edward Booker, who was already established in the small Jamaican immigrant community in Wilmington, Delaware. Toward the end of 1962, Cedella procured a passport for herself and Bob, and his name was changed from Nesta Robert to Robert Nesta Marley, at the suggestion of the passport clerk. But money problems soon arose, and it was decided that Bob and Pearl would stay behind in Kingston until Cedella was comfortably settled in Wilmington.

Cedella and Mr. Booker left Bob and Pearl with her sister Enid at the house on Second Street. That lasted until Enid decided to return to St. Ann and took Pearl with her. So Pearl's father, Mr. Taddy, took Bob in, and Bob Marley lived with the Livingston tribe at 19 Second Street until a disagreement between Bob and Mr. Taddy's girl friend put an end to the Livingstons' domestic tranquility. At the age of eighteen, Bob Marley found himself living in the street, a Trench Town nomad and scuffler, a frequenter of the squatters' camps and Rastafarian enclaves at Darling Street and Back O' Wall, Denham Town and the rest of western Kingston. Bob Marley was homeless.

By early 1963 he had found a place to sleep in a corner of a kitchen on First Street. The other corner was inhabited by a friend, Vincent Ford, called "Tartar." The two young men were literally starving; Ford (still in Trench Town and confined by a crippling illness to a wheelchair) remembers they were so hungry that they would sing and make up songs to cover the heavy, uncomfortable grumblings of their stomachs.

The singing and obsessive harmonizing continued at the nightly Trench Town sessions. Bob had given up the idea of a solo career and plunged headlong into the third year of rehearsing with his friends. For hours they would experiment with old spirituals and songs like "Duke of Earl" by Gene Chandler, "Do You Love Me" by the Contours and "Playboy" by the Marvelettes. Joe Higgs remembers that "Bob was interested in having a group, so I started to give him some technical points in sound consciousness, timing and craft, because the voice was not really all that good. He need to know craft, technique, stuff like that. Bob was the leader of the group, but the lead *singer* of the group in those days was Junior Braithwaite. We had Bunny, Peter, Beverly and Cherry in those days. That was the Wailers.

"Bob needed to know about everything, but he was quick. It was kind of difficult to get the group to be precise in their sound, and put it over in their harmony structure. Just took a couple of years to get that perfect. But person to person, they were each capable of leading at any given time because I wanted each person to be a leader in his own right, able to lead anyone, or to be able to wail. That is where the concept come from." Most important, especially concerning the songwriting, social stance and personal styles of Bob and Peter, was Joe Higgs's strong authority within the slum communities. An established singing star, he lived in Trench Town, an outcast, politicized street poet whose fellow pop singers aspired mostly to slickness and shallow elegance.

Meanwhile Bob Marley, without his family and living huddled in a ghetto kitchen, was learning the true meaning of Jamaican sufferer culture. At times, as many as fifteen singers held harmony together in that little yard. It was a fiercely competitive shadow-world of both high hopes and hopelessness. Whatever food was available—fish tea, roast yam or breadfruit, a plate of curried goat—was shared with the children of the yard, but intra-ghetto conflict was quick to come and bitter when it arrived. In the alleys and yards of Trench Town, arguments were settled out of court and the blade took the place of litigation. Yet it was a place where friendship flourished and, being of an immaterial, spiritual nature, was somehow valued over everything else.

Bob's closest friends were Peter and Bunny, Vincent "Tartar" Ford and a ghetto youth called Georgie who sustained the groups' spirits by burning huge bonfires of log wood through the night, so that a pot of cinnamon-flavored cornmeal porridge could be quickly cooked when the brethren gathered to sing in the morning. Georgie's bonfires reached minor firestorm proportions some nights, and the First Street yard was often buzzed by police choppers with searchlights when Georgie's conflagrations sent flames licking high in the air.

Another close friend of Bob's eventually provided the opening for the group to record. His name was Alvin Patterson, but people knew him variously as Willie, or Pep; the Wailers called him Franseeco. Later, as the holder of the Wailers' percussion chair (1975–80), he was known by Wailers fans as Seeco. But back in the early sixties, he was a Rastafarian

37

hand-drummer, like Bob a migrant from St. Ann, schooled in the Afro-Jamaican burru style of drumming, an ancient, heartlike rhythm of liberation that originally welcomed released prisoners back to Jamaican slums and villages. Burru had been taken over by Rastafarians as they had generally taken over the cultural life of the ghetto. Franseeco was from this tradition and was a professional musician, having played with Lord Flea and various mento-calypso combos. If Joe Higgs was the vocal teacher of the early Wailers, then Seeco was the group's rhythm master, and a spiritual mentor as well. Best of all, he knew a man named Clement Dodd, who operated Sir Coxsone's Downbeat sound system and was beginning to make his own recordings. One day in the summer of 1963, after an intense period of rehearsal, Franseeco took the group over to Coxsone's new studio on Brentford Road for an audition. Bob Marley and the Wailers were about to begin.

3

Studio One

Then we used to sing in the back of Trench Town and rehearse plenty until the Drifters came upon the scene, and me love group singing so me just say, well, me 'ave fe go look a group.

(1975)

The year 1963 was a heady year for youth culture, and not just in Jamaica. In England, Jamaica's "mother country," the Beatles had exploded and the Rolling Stones were simmering in small clubs, fusing hard black urban U.S. blues with imagery of street-wise teenage lust and rebellion. In the States, Bob Dylan was riding the crest of protest music, applying angry new lyrics and a civil-rights consciousness to the old tunes and ballads of the folk song movement. Bob Marley, Bunny Livingston and Peter Tosh may have been enchanted by the Impressions and the Drifters, but they were hearing these other impolite sounds too, and the cosmopolitan influence definitely had an effect on them.

In a sense, the early "Wailing Wailers" were the Jamaican variant of the Rolling Stones. Like the English band, the Wailers had to claw their way from the bottom, and succeeded by taking a tough stance on tenderness and a tender stance on toughness. The Wailers' music always seemed more dangerous than the bubbly, almost carefree ska of their contemporaries. Like the Stones, the Wailers were lustful, contemptuous, insolent, *rude.*

When Joe Higgs and Seeco took the Wailers over to Clement Dodd's studio for an audition that day in the summer of 1963, Bob Marley's fate and future were sealed. In Dodd, Bob Marley would find his next mentor, someone who would teach him not just music but the music business. Joe Higgs had taught the Wailers to sing for pleasure. Clement "Sir Coxsone" Dodd would teach them to sing for a living.

Dodd invented the Jamaican music business when he returned from a six-month labor contract, cutting sugarcane on plantations in the American South in the mid-1950s. Dodd brought home several dozen recent

R & B records, hot new sounds from New Orleans and Chicago, and after a few more trips to the States had saved enough cash to set up a sound system of his own, Sir Coxsone's Downbeat, at the corner of Beeston Street and Love Lane in the heart of the Kingston slums. Since the two Jamaican radio stations—JBC (Jamaican Broadcasting Corporation) and RJR (Radio Jamaica Rediffusion)—were controlled by the island's white and brown elite, very little of what the majority of Jamaican people wanted to hear went out over the air. American R & B and Jamaican mento/ska were disseminated at local community dances, with music provided by the turntables and speakers of sound system men like Dodd and Duke Reid.

The sound systems were essentially the secular soul of Jamaica twenty-five years ago, and to some extent still are today. People too poor to buy records expressed themselves at sound system dances, and so naturally competition among the various "sounds" got extremely intense. When a dazzling new R & B number arrived from New Orleans, maybe "One Night of Sin" by Smiley Lewis or Fats Domino wailing on "Hey, La Bas!", the wise sound system man scratched off the record label to prevent the singer and song from easy identification, thus maintaining an exclusive over the rival sounds. Sound system men often retained squads of thugs to disrupt dances put on by competing sounds. In those days, if two rival systems set up within hearing distance of each other in the western Kingston ghettos, a violent night was guaranteed. Duke Reid wore revolvers and bandoliers to his dances. Most every record-spinner with the self-imposed title of Count or Prince carried a gun. Sir Coxsone Dodd was no exception.

On the corner of Beeston and Love Lane, Dodd gained a reputation for toughness early on. Platoon-level assaults from jealous rivals were usually beaten off at the gate, in part because one of Dodd's deejays, Prince Buster, was one of the best amateur boxers in Jamaica. One night in the early sixties, however, a Coxsone dance was invaded by a large goon squad, bigger than Coxsone's defense team. Dodd's diminutive engineer, Lee Perry, was beaten up after Coxsone and his men had fled, and was rescued only after Buster intervened and knocked most of Perry's attackers out.

Eventually, the sound systems of men like Dodd and Reid turned into the Jamaican recording industry. As the influx of good American R & B began to fail, the sound systems began to turn to recording local singers to ensure their mobile discos would be able to provide hot dance music to their steady customers. In a sense, the sound system men were the pioneers of a national attitude that expressed itself in a desire to somehow create a new system in which "truth and rights," the standards by which ordinary Jamaicans judge their society, would be cherished. When men like Sir Coxsone began to produce music by Jamaicans for Jamaicans, the political history of the island was about to change forever.

The beneficiaries of sound system recording were singers like Joe Higgs and his partner Delroy Wilson, Jamaican boogie artist Laurel Aitken, balladeer Owen Grey, Alton Ellis, Lascelles Perkins and Jackie Edwards, who did a killer imitation of Nat "King" Cole (Jamaicans weren't the only black musicians to assume they were royalty). The traditional road to local fame led singers through amateur shows like Vere Johns's Opportunity Hour, held in ghetto theaters like the Palace, the Ambassador or the Majestic.

The records cut by these singers (and mento-calypso bands like those of Lord Fly, Count Lasher and Lord LaRue) were for consumption by the sound systems only. Originally there was never much thought to selling them to the public. But one day someone convinced Coxsone to let him press a few hundred copies of one of Coxsone's self-produced sound system tunes. The record instantly sold out, and Coxsone went immediately into the record business full time, followed by Prince Buster, Duke Reid, Edward Seaga and a young Anglo-Jamaican named Chris Blackwell, who would go on to start a small company called Island Records a few years later.

At first, Coxsone recorded at the one-track studio of Federal Records. But after producing several early sixties hits by the Maytals (then known as the Vikings) and the vocal duo of Alton and Eddie, Coxsone had earned enough to build his own one-track studio on the northern edge of Trench Town. In early 1963, Coxsone opened the Jamaican Recording and Publishing Company Limited at 13 Brentford Road. Better known as Studio One, Coxsone's primitive studio quickly became the creative center of the Jamaican recording business as well as the laboratory where Jamaican ska, rock steady and reggae music were researched and developed.

It was to Studio One that Seeco guided the Wailers for an audition in August 1963.

At first, the audition was a disaster.

Perhaps it was because the six teenage singers—Bob, Peter, Bunny, Junior Braithwaite and the two backup singers, Beverly and Cherry—were exhausted from an anxious week of rehearsal under Joe Higgs. The group had walked over to the studio early one Sunday afternoon, accompanied by Seeco Patterson, who had recorded for Coxsone's sound system while a member of Lord Flea's mento-jazz band. Always on the lookout for new talent, Coxsone and his engineer (and cousin) Sid Bucknor held weekly Sunday auditions outdoors beneath the mango tree that shaded the studio. The two men were especially interested in discovering great voices from the country, people whose workaday lives prevented them from getting to Kingston any time other than the weekend.

The group had entered talent shows and amateur contests under various names, including the Teenagers and the Wailing Rudeboys, and Seeco had given Coxsone a huge buildup, especially concerning Bob. Coxsone had also heard one of the 45s that Leslie Kong had released of Bob's, without being terribly impressed. So when Bob counted off the time and the group, backed only by Peter Tosh's percussive guitar chords, launched into an original song called "It Hurts to Be Alone," with Junior singing lead, Coxsone didn't even look interested. The group did two more songs, impressions of Impressions-type harmonies, singing to the best of their abilities. After the last song, there was an embarrassed silence. Then Coxsone told them they had talent. He suggested that they practice some more and return in three months for another audition.

As the crestfallen young musicians were about to leave, Peter Tosh (the tallest, rudest, most assertive member of the group) blurted out that the group had one more song they wanted to sing, called "Simmer Down." Other members protested that the song was unfinished and un-rehearsed, but Coxsone told them to do the number anyway. Written by Bunny, "Simmer Down" immediately sounded like something special to Coxsone, who recognized it as a song in which young Jamaicans spoke directly to other young Jamaicans, using their own language and imagery rather than the secondhand material borrowed from American soul singers. Coxsone's commercial instinct sensed a big hit, and he told the group to come back the following Thursday to record "Simmer Down."

Elated, the group almost ran back to Trench Town to celebrate, and to continue rehearsing. At first, Bob and Bunny were somewhat skeptical about working for Coxsone, because of the producer's reputation for dishonesty and ruthlessness. But Tosh especially was confident in a bright future for the group, and pressed them to work as hard as possible.

When the group returned to the Brentford Road studio that Thursday, they discovered they were to be supported by the best professional musicians in Jamaica, the Skatalites. The Skatalites originally consisted of Don Drummond on trombone, Roland Alphonso and Tommy McCook on tenor saxes, Lester Sterling on alto sax, Johnny Moore and Leonard Dillon on trumpets, Jackie Mittoo on piano, Lloyd Brevette on bass, Lloyd Nibbs on drums and guitarist Jah Jerry. Also on hand were regular

Kingston session musicians like guitarist Ernest Ranglin, Rico Rodriguez on trombone, drummer Arkland "Drumbago" Parks and bassist Cluett Johnson. These musicians supported not only the early Wailers, but virtually all the important singers and vocal trios of the ska era. And something else, something socially important and emblematic, was also happening at Coxsone's studio when the Skatalites played in support of vocalists. The tough, volatile port city of Kingston, fractional and jealous, was symbolically united when the Skatalites and other musicians, who all came from the eastern neighborhoods of the city, played for the singers, who tended to emerge from the slums of the western part of town. In Coxsone's poorly lit, one-track recording studio, the two geographic sides of Kingston's unique ghetto culture were united to the loping rhythm of ska.

"Simmer Down" was recorded by the Wailers in two quick takes, after rehearsing in the studio all morning. The instrumental arrangement was the work of Coxsone, reedman Roland Alphonso (with whom Coxsone had a strong friendship) and pianist Jackie Mittoo. The recording was a fast, jumping ska dominated by the horns, with Bob Marley taking the angry, rasping lead vocal. The admonitory, blaring chorus was dominated by Tosh's loud bass voice and the high, monotone singing of the girls, who sounded like bold Baptist choristers from some up-country parish church. The verses were full of folk aphorisms about nanny-goat bellies, and the chorus was built on a relentless call/response pattern: *simmer down/control your temper/simmer down/the battle will get hotter/simmer down/and you won't get no supper/simmer down/and you bound to suffer/ simmer down/hear what I say/simmer down/I'm a-leaving you today . . .* Halfway through the song, Roland Alphonso steps in with a growling tenor sax solo, working the changes like a veteran bebopper before the group steps back in to finish the tune's stark chanting. Listening to the playback, jammed into Coxsone's tiny control booth, everybody involved —Wailers, Skatalites, Coxsone and his staff—knew they had a hit.

"Simmer Down" by the Wailing Wailers on the Downbeat label was released in the last weeks of 1963, just in time to catch the Christmas market. The song went to number one on the JBC chart in January 1964 and stayed at the top for the next two months. The Wailing Wailers (the group had been renamed by Coxsone without consultation) were instant stars.

"Simmer Down" defined the way a new generation of Jamaicans talked to each other, in the same way that in England the Beatles and Rolling Stones were talking to their own generation. Young Jamaicans of the Wailers' age had been recorded before (mostly notably Toots and the

43

Maytals), but their sound had drawn on gospel or spiritual music and was directed more at the general Jamaican people rather than at its rebellious youth. Speaking directly to the emerging rude boy movement, the song proudly proclaimed total empathy with these bad shantytown juvenile delinquents by playing their dance rhythms for them while at the same time telling them to "simmer down, control your temper." Perhaps sensing the forthcoming change in the scale of violence in Jamaica, the Wailers were attempting to function as peacemakers at a time when Jamaican society seemed to be coming under increasing social pressure. "Hooligan, hooligan," they sang, "make up your mind." Jamaican independence in 1962 had focused attention on national problems as never before, and the whole island, with the exception of the apolitical and still underground Rastafarians, seemed split along the opposing ideological lines of the two political parties. Also, in 1963, Jamaica's perception of the Rastafarians as a strange and violent sect was partially validated when a small group of Rastas went berserk at a place called Coral Gardens, in the hills above Montego Bay. They burned a gas station and hacked two people to death with machetes before losing a shoot-out with a posse of police, army units and landowners who thought they were witnessing the beginning of an old-fashioned Jamaican slave rebellion. The Coral Gardens Massacre, as it came to be known, shocked the whole island, especially Jamaicans who knew that the majority of Rastamen were peaceful artists, craftsmen and herb farmers who wanted merely to be left alone to smoke some of the most narcotic marijuana in the world and to worship their living God, Emperor Haile Selassie of Ethiopia, in some semblance of peace.

By the time "Simmer Down" caused a sensation in Jamaica, Bob Marley had been homeless for six months. The kitchen he shared with Tartar and others gave him no room to be alone, and for a time Bob grew adept at "cotching," moving from one roof to another every night like hundreds of other homeless unemployed people in shantytown.

But after "Simmer Down" made a lot of money for Dodd and the Wailing Wailers had begun recording regularly at Studio One, Coxsone followed his instincts and singled out Bob for special attention and care, even allowing the young songwriter to sleep in a shed in back of the studio. It wasn't much, but for Bob Marley in 1964 and 1965, the room in back of Coxsone's studio was home.

Two hits followed "Simmer Down" in quick succession, and both were completely different in tone. "It Hurts to Be Alone" (written by Junior) was a slow, plaintive ballad with a brilliant, penetrating lead vocal by Junior Braithwaite, who sounded almost exactly like Anthony Gourdine (of Little Anthony and the Imperials). Junior turned an ordinary doo-wop torch song into feelings of loss with which every young Jamaican whose parents were working abroad or who couldn't afford the rites of courtship could identify. A spare Ernest Ranglin guitar solo, again very bebop-flavored, exactly caught the wistful, yearning spirit of the song. The next Wailing Wailers hit, "Lonesome Feeling," was written by Bob and Bunny as a follow-up to Junior's song. Again describing a life of loss and loneliness, "Lonesome Feeling" was a popular success as a dance tune with the sound systems. Bunny's lead vocal and lyrics were buried under organ vamps and handclaps as the Skatalites smoldered behind a fevered trumpet break from Johnny "Dizzy" Moore.

Gradually, under Coxsone's direction, the Wailers sextet evolved into a prolific recording group. Later, Coxsone would tell an interviewer: "When they first came in, they were like most other groups just starting out—young, inexperienced and willing to learn. I coached them, and gave them a lot of ideas on harmonies. I had albums from the States by all the top soul artists. Bob liked the Impressions, the Tams and the Moonglows the most." Coxsone also described how Bob would work on his songs: "Marley used to come in and sing a song for two or three hours. Two weeks later he'd come in and work on the same song. I worked with him and the group on their songwriting, going over punch lines and harmonies."

In 1964, after the initial three hit singles, the group concentrated on recording ska versions of old spirituals and duplicating the harmony sounds of their favorite soul groups. They had a minor hit with "I'm Still Waiting," an Impressions-style ballad with Bob taking the lead vocal (imbued with classic, doo-wop rain/teardrops imagery) while the group harmonized closely behind him. Even more Impressions-like was another song by Bob called "I Need You," a simple chant, just rhythm and piano, in which Bunny clones the falsetto skills of the Impressions' Curtis Mayfield. Bob also rewrote the Drifters' classic "On Broadway" into a slow ska called "Dance with Me," and followed that with "Another Dance," a close-harmony ska with a soulful Alphonso tenor break. If the lyric was undistinguished (*You don't even know her name/you wanna dance with her over again*), the harmonies were like a finely cut jewel, multifaceted and shimmering. Perhaps the Wailers' greatest harmonic masterpiece of 1964 was a version of a big American hit from New Orleans, Aaron Neville's "Ten Commandments of Love." Behind the angelic, delicate harmonies, Bob sings the song with a convincing passion and sincerity, the sheer intensity of which shows the respect Marley had for the American R & B masters whose songs he had borrowed.

Somewhat less interesting are the old spirituals the Wailers recorded for Coxsone, mostly in 1964. "I Am Going Home" is a ska version of "Swing Low Sweet Chariot," complete with a country-church "coming for to carry me home" female lead vocal by Beverly Kelso, a primitive reggae-scratch guitar (possibly by Tosh) and wild calypsonian horn parts. "Nobody Knows" was Coxsone's ska arrangement of "Nobody Knows the Trouble I've Seen"; the recording swings in a great ska fashion and was a minor sound system hit. "Wings of a Dove," the old prisoner's lament, and "Down by the Riverside" were cut as fairly straightforward gospel songs, while the ancient black spiritual "Sinner Man" has a decidedly hard R & B instrumental hook. (Years later Tosh would rerecord the song as "Downpressor Man".)

Bob spent most of the time at the studio, learning his guitar and playing the stacks of R & B and soul records that Coxsone had shipped in from the States, music by Major Lance, Lee Dorsey and Motown acts like Marvin Gaye, Little Stevie Wonder, the Marvelettes and others. Gradually Bob became an unofficial artists and repertoire man at Studio One. Marley studied the records coming in from the States, noting which songs might be right for different singers in Coxsone's stable. One song he was obsessed with for a time was the Drifters' "Under the Boardwalk," a sentimentally effective ballad with a queer inside-out rhythm and a suspicion of Jamaican sensibility in the way it sounded. When not rehearsing at the studio, Bob liked to hang out with friends in Trench Town, mostly at Joe Higgs's place on Third Street, or else with the Rastas down at the beach. Always, there was soccer. Always, there were intense discussions of the "runnings," current events in Jamaica. And in 1964 there was a great deal to discuss. Jamaican music was changing fast, at least in its vanguard represented by musicians like the Wailers. The good-time themes and rhythms of ska were changing into something else, a new sound preoccupied by a slightly slower, steadier beat, heavily influenced by rock and roll. This new music wasn't quite rock steady, conventional wisdom's next step on the evolutionary ladder of Jamaican music from mento to reggae. This new music was identified by the dangerous social phenomenon that provided its lyrics—the Rude Boys. Within a year, the Wailing Wailers would become the kings of Rude Boy music.

When Chris Blackwell's tiny London-based company, Island Records, sold six million copies of a bouncy ska tune called "My Boy Lollipop" by Millie Small all over the world in 1964, the Jamaican government began to take note of the music coming out of Kingston's worst slums. Record producer and former anthropologist Edward Seaga had become a politician, representing some of the most dreadful ghettos in the world (Back O' Wall—now Tivoli Gardens—and the Dungle) in the Jamaican House of Representatives and serving as minister of development in the postindependence JLP government. Seaga decided to send a Kingston show band, Byron Lee and the Dragonaires, to the 1964 World's Fair in New York as representatives of Jamaican ska. Millie Small, Jimmy Cliff and Prince Buster went along to provide some "native" examples of ska singing.

At Coxsone's, everyone was saddened and outraged. The musicians complained bitterly that the Skatalites were the best ska band in the world, and that Lee and the Dragonaires were exploiting the real inventors of the music. Everyone knew that the Wailing Wailers were the most popular group in Jamaica. Everyone also knew the choice had been made on the basis of class: the conservative Jamaican government was not about to send red-eyed ganja-smoking slum dwellers like the Skatalites and dirty rude boys like the Wailers to New York, no matter how popular they were, when it could send out sanitized, image-conscious show-biz professionals instead.

Although the Wailers constantly complained about the poor treatment they received from Coxsone, Dodd remembers his relationship to the group as more of an "adoption" than anything else. Not only was Bob Marley literally taken in off the street and given shelter and a job, but Peter Tosh recalls Dodd paying the group fifteen to twenty pounds each for every song they recorded, as well as a retainer of three pounds per week, supposedly as an advance against royalties. Coxsone also bought the group its stage clothes. One ensemble worn by "Bob Marley and the Wailing Rude Boy Wailers" (as they were billed at one 1965 show at an uptown Kingston club called the Glass Bucket) consisted of collarless gold lamé "Beatle jackets" and black and white polka-dot shirts. Other times they wore tight-fitting black suits (the cuffs on Tosh's trousers rode way above his ankles), white socks and sharply pointed black shoes. The early Wailers, like every other musician in Jamaica, were completely dependent on the good will of their producer; there were no contracts, royalties, residuals or any of the other usual guarantees. In the Jamaican music industry, the *producer* was the star and took credit for the recordings, not the musicians.

Conditions at the studio were crude and very rough. Coxsone may have pioneered modern Jamaican music, but to survive in a ghetto business he had become a very hard man. He kept a revolver in the studio to intimidate the steady parade of desperate singers looking for payment for songs they had cut for him. Joe Higgs was beaten by Coxsone's henchmen when he demanded a large sum that he claimed Coxsone owed him. Other singers were slapped down by Dodd, or simply told to get lost. The atmosphere was further complicated by crowds of loiterers and young singers hoping for an audition, or a chance to sing. Everyone was so hungry that during mango season, recording sessions would crash to a halt when the musicians heard the ripe fruit bounce off the tin roof when it dropped off the big mango tree in back.

Singer Alton Ellis, one of the greats of the rock steady era, recalls how loose things were at Studio One in those days. "At the time, I had a group called Alton and the Flames, which gave me most of my hits. There were times when I was recording for Coxsone and none of the Flames were present at the studio. So anybody who would be there would be a Flame for the moment, like Ken Boothe, Delroy Wilson, *anybody*. If Bob Marley is doing something in the studio and there is no harmony, he come over and say, 'Back up this song.' We're supposed to be paid for this, but sometimes we didn't do it for the money, because in those days we were singing for recognition in the eyes of the public more than anything else."

The earliest Wailers public performances took place at the "Opportunity Hour" put on at the Palace Theatre on South Camp Road by an entrepreneurial talent scout named Vere Johns. In addition to singers, the Opportunity Hour shows featured comedians, jugglers and "legs" dancers like Persian the Cat. After the Wailers became famous through their recordings, they could usually be found singing at dances put on by sound systems like Downbeat or Sir George, or at music shows at the Success Club or Odd Fellows Hall, where fans could see all the current big acts—the Skatalites, the Wailers, the Clarendonians, the Gaylads, Alton Ellis—in a single evening.

Bob Marley was tough long before he began to work with Coxsone Dodd. In Trench Town he was known as a musician and peacemaker, and his natural charisma kept him out of most violent situations. Like many prominent and respected singers, Bob maintained close friendships with various neighborhood gunmen and Rude Boys. In fact, many singers on the Wailers' level were forced to seek alliances with local gangsters in order to have some muscle or firepower behind them when the time came to demand money from their producers.

Clement Dodd's influence was so strong that gradually Bob, too, began to be feared for a certain ruthlessness in achieving his goals. On the street Marley acquired a new name, Tuff Gong, connoting the air of ghetto authority and rude swagger with which he carried himself. And Bob Marley's toughness wasn't always so implied.

One night in 1965 the Wailers took part in a show called "Battle of the Groups," held at the Ward Theatre on the North Parade in downtown Kingston. The other groups were the Paragons, the Melodians and the Uniques, the latter a duo featuring two of the best young singers in Jamaica, Jimmy Riley and Slim Smith. The Wailers went on stage second to last, sang "It Hurts to Be Alone" and "Lonesome Feeling" and had a difficult time holding harmonies, which infuriated Bob because he had rehearsed the group especially hard for the show. When the Uniques came on stage last and Slim Smith blew everyone away with a version of "Baby, I Need Your Lovin'," the Uniques were declared the winner of the battle. Backstage, Bob glared with rage and challenged Slim Smith to a fight. But the other Wailers dragged a distraught Bob Marley off before any blows could be landed, or blades could be drawn.

The Wailers' reputation as rude boys came mostly because the group sang rude boy music on rude boy home ground. The Ward Theatre audience was acknowledged to be tough, but it was nothing compared to some of the other places the Wailing Wailers played. The Majestic and the Ambassador (before it burned down) were rude boy snake pits, and at King's Theatre, a roofless open-air cinema, the crowd responded to acts that didn't sound right with a lethal barrage of broken Dragon Stout and Red Stripe beer bottles.

By 1965, the height of the Rude Boy era in Jamaica, living conditions in western Kingston had gotten progressively worse. Late in August, downtown Kingston erupted in a race riot, pitting poor blacks against the Chinese merchants who controlled most of the small businesses downtown and in the ghettos. When the riot was finally put down, eight had been shot, a policeman had died and ninety had been arrested and accused of burning and looting dozens of Chinese shops. In the Wailers' neighborhood, the era of respect for "Brother Man," the peaceful Rastafarian ritualist and herbsman, had passed, and the ghetto had a new hero, "Rudie." Rude boys were youthful street anarchists who celebrated the criminal life and hatred of authority as the only freedom left open to them under the racist structures of the colonial system. The term "rude" applied equally to the anarchic and revolutionary youth of the slums, the young gunmen, gangsters and mercenaries who were pressed into shantytown goon squads by the two political parties, and the Rasta-inspired cultural rudies like the Wailers, who rejected traditional colonial religion and morality. The major emblem of the rudie was his ratchet, a curved German gravity knife (Okapi was a favorite brand), made for scaling fish, that could be whipped out in the time it took an upset domino game to hit the floor. The rudies redefined Kingston street life into a phantasmagoria of insolence, mugging, trolley-hopping and purse-snatching. The rudies operated in a haze of ganja smoke and hallucinogenic white rum, and when the pressure dropped on them the rudies got *really* crazy, indulging in haphazard, almost slapstick violence toward each other, but more likely toward anyone who happened to be in the alley and unarmed. They were ghetto poverty's shock troops and scapegoats, whose self-image came from the lurid American gangster films to which all true rudies flocked with the same reverence that sends religious people to church. The rudies loved the timeless moment in *Kiss of Death* when Richard Widmark pushes an old woman in a wheelchair down a flight of stairs, and *laughs*. They adored the early James Bond films (the first of which, *Doctor No,* was filmed in Jamaica). Later they would revel in the brutal orgies of death depicted in Italian "spaghetti westerns" like *Fistful of Dollars* and *Hang 'Em High.* After that the rudies became infatuated with the cartoonlike violence of Bruce Lee's martial arts films. The earliest rudies all had nicknames like Richard Widmark, Bogart, Alan Ladd and Yul Brynner. Later rudies called themselves 007, Ocean's Eleven, Clint Eastwood, Kung Fu and Death Wish.

The rude boys were never exactly beloved ghetto freedom fighters. Most rudies eventually became predatory, spreading a reign of terror over the slums and squatter camps. But both varieties of rudie—ghetto guerrilla and urban terrorist—became the subject and raison d'être of the intermediate step between ska and rock steady—the rude boy songs.

Most of the songs about the rude boys (by singers or groups other than the Wailers) were judgmental and extremely antirude. Some tunes took the form of mock court trials, in which both rude boys and the blind Jamaican judiciary are severely belittled. In "Tougher Than Tough," the rudie states his position as a bomb-thrower and ratchet-user. He's tougher than tough, he says, and he is *free.* In "Dreader Than Dread," he calls for anarchy and revolution and urges his brothers to *Stand fast together and unite/And deal with one hundred or one thousand years!*

In the Slickers' "Johnny Too Bad," Johnny is *Walking down the road with a ratchet in his waist/Robbing and stabbing and looting and shooting.* In "Shanty Town," *Now rude boys have a wail/Cause dem out of jail/Rude boys cannot fail/Cause dem must get bail/dem a loot, dem a shoot, dem a wail/in shantytown.* In "Rudy, a Message to You," the voice of the decent citizen pleads with the rudies to *Stop your running around/making trouble all over the town.* In Prince Buster's legendary "Judge Dread," the minimum sentence for being a rude boy is one hundred years. A plea of innocent is equal to contempt of court and draws another hundred years. The song shows how, for rude boys, Jamaican justice was perverted by blind accusation and absurdly harsh reprisal. But ambiguity and confusion over the rudies persisted. In "The Appeal," Prince Buster's sequel to "Judge Dread," he sentences the rudies to a thousand years in jail with the spoken words: *Count how many white people are dying, how many other nations are dying, and multiply them, and that does not amount to the number of black people that are being killed by these rude boys.* Judge Dread refuses their appeal.

The rude boy situation was an obsession for many Jamaican musicians between 1964 and 1967, like Bob Marley's old friend Desmond Dekker and his group the Aces, Derrick Morgan and especially the Clarendonians. They described a bitterly harsh urban landscape in which the rude boys were responsible for tension, violence and anguish.

From the beginning, starting in the days of "Simmer Down," Bob Marley and the Wailers took a different view. "Put It On," for instance, the best of the group's early dance hits, was a chanting ska-rock that identified the group with the rude no-limits spirit: *Feel dem spirit/Feel all right now/I'm gonna put it on/I'm gonna put it on/I'm gonna put it on/I'm not boasting/Feel like toasting/I rule my destiny/I rule my destiny/I rule my destiny/In the morning, in the night, anywhere, any time.*

"Let Him Go" (written by Bunny) warned Jamaica about its attitude toward disadvantaged youth in a fast ska-rock arrangement with a hummed, evil-sounding harmony intro. *Rudie come from jail cos rudie get bail/Rudie come from jail cos rudie get bail/you shame him you say things he didn't do/You rebuke and you scorn and you make him feel blue/Let him go/let him go/Let him go/Whhyyyoh!* Bunny sings the song with grim conviction, and the rhythm is attacked at breakneck speed without any bridge or instrumental solo, as if to emphasize that, in rudie music, the bass and drums drove the song, not the horns of the fading days of ska.

"Rude Boy," recorded late in 1965, established the Wailers as the ultimate champions of the rude boys. A mysterious litany of rude slogans and folk sayings, "Rude Boy" was again recorded as a fast dancing ska. *Walk the proud land with me my friend,* Bob invited, showing the prideful restlessness of the rudie. *I've got to keep on movin'/I've got to keep on movin'/I've got to keep on movin'/I've got to keep on movin'/I've got to keep on movin'/Rude boy rock/Rude boy strut/Ska quadrille/ska quadrille.* The bridge consists of an utterly timeless Jamaican country aphorism: *Wanty wanty cyaan getty/Getty getty nuh wanty.* It's the classic plight of deprived people, lusting for what is unavailable, disdaining what's already there. "Rude Boy" was a huge hit in Jamaica, especially at the sound systems.

"Jail House" (written by Bob) was slower, somber, even ruder. *Jail house keeps empty/Rudie gets healthy/baton stick get shorter/Rudie gets taller/ Can't fight against the youth now/cause its wrong/Can't fight against the youth now/Cause they're strong/The people going wild/Dem a rude rude people/We're gonna rule this land.* Other significant Wailers paeans to Rudeness were "Rule Dem Rudie" and, a year or so later, Peter Tosh's "I'm the Toughest" and the bad-ass, boasty "Stepping Razor" with its sinister ratchet imagery.

If the Wailers were the rudest of them all, then the brain-numbing alienation the musicians expressed was a logical psychological extension of the group's early songs of loss and lonesome feelings. In Trench Town, depression and hopelessness turned to anger, turned neighbor against neighbor, turned a generation against the whole nation. But out of the anger the Wailers expressed in their rude boy songs would emerge the uncompromising revolutionary faith that would eventually propel Bob Marley and the Wailers, almost ten years in the future, into cultural arenas all over the world.

Although Junior Braithwaite was by far the best singer in the group, his role diminished gradually during 1965. Most of the Wailing Wailers' love songs ("I Don't Need Your Love," "Your Love") were bitter and unpleasant, and weren't their biggest sellers. The group stole innumerable riffs and hooks from American pop tunes; the Contours' "Do You Love Me" became "Play Boy" in the Wailers version, which in turn stole its title from the contemporary Motown hit by the Marvelettes. Junior Walker's jerk-era "Shotgun" became "Ska Jerk," with an abrasive lead vocal by Bob. "What's New, Pussycat," a smash worldwide for Welsh sex crooner Tom Jones, was covered by the Wailers as a piano ska with a sumptuous, show-band horn section. In his lead vocal, Bob Marley takes the song seriously, and sounds much more sexy and sincere than the unctuous Jones. Bob Marley was also a fan of the Beatles and listened carefully to all their records with a craftsmanly appreciation of songwriting genius at work. The Wailers covered "And I Love Her" for Coxsone, and Bob helped supervise a Skatalites instrumental version of "I Should Have Known Better," retitled upon release in 1966 as "Independent Anniversary Ska." (The Skatalites broke up in 1965. The same musicians continued to back the Wailers as the Soul Brothers and later, after reedman Roland Alphonso quit the band, as the Soul Venders.) Although few of Bob Dylan's early records reached Jamaica, Bob Marley was very attentive when one of Dylan's mid-sixties AM radio hits would come beaming in from Miami. One of the most amazing Wailers cover versions

Bob Marley in 1975. *Adrian Boot*.

Bob, Cedella Booker and baby sister Pearl
at Nine Miles, 1963.

The Wailing Wailers (Bunny, Bob and Peter)
at the height of the rude boy era, 1965.

Bob reads his Bible on the site of his tomb
in a snapshot taken in St. Ann in 1973. *Lee Jaffe.*

The Wailers on the road in San Francisco, 1973. (From left: Carlie Barrett, Bob, Family Man, Wire,
Lee Jaffee, Peter Tosh and spouse.) *Chuck Krall.*

The Wailers broadcasting a set from the Record Plant, Sausilito, California, 1973. *Chuck Krall.*

Bob suffering from road fever in a Las Vegas motel room, 1973. *Lee Jaffe.*

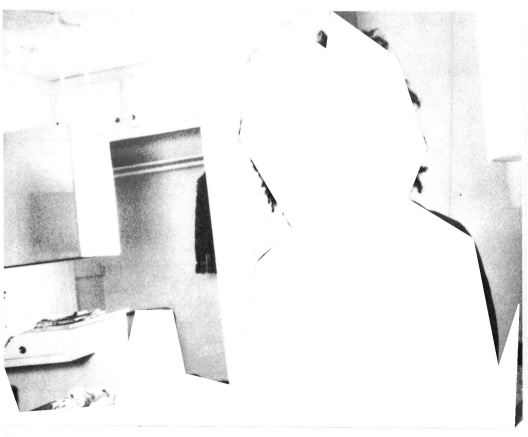

Bob peels a carrot under the tree behind his house on Hope Road, 1974. *Lee Jaffe*.

Bob rolling a giant spliff, the only photograph for which he was really happy to pose. *Kim Gottlieb*

Rita Marley. *Adrian Boot*

Live at the Lyceum, London, 1975. *Island Records.*

Tuff Gong works on a big spliff, 1976. *David Burnett.*

Table tennis was a favorite Wailers pastime at Hope Road, 1974. *Dennis Morris.*

Bob under the waterfall at Cane River, 1975. *Lee Jaffe.*

was the group's take (credited to Bunny and Coxsone) of Bob Dylan's "Like a Rolling Stone." After a spooky blues piano intro, the Soul Brothers slip into a sinister groove that's a mixture of 1965 American folk-rock and early Jamaican rock steady. Although the chorus is the same as Dylan's, the verse and the melody are different: *Nobody told you he was on the street/But that's what happens when you lie and cheat/You have no nights and you have no morning/Cause time lights come just strike without warning/How does it feel/To be on your own/With no direction home/Like a complete unknown/Like a rolling stone?*

It's a sentiment that Bob Marley knew all too well.

Cover versions and desultory love songs aside, the Wailers also produced some beautiful songs of their own in this period, music that would endure for the band's entire career and would be recorded by the three original Wailers time and time again. The first of these was "Love and Affection," cowritten by Bob and Bunny and dating back to the early days on Second Street. Like many Wailers songs about relationships, "Love and Affection" dealt with loss in a ska/doo-wop mode: *It hurts to be alone/I'm a king sitting on an empty throne.* A similar song, "One Love," is one of the Wailers earliest masterpieces. A fast ska version with Bob and Bunny trading leads, the song echoes Marcus Garvey's rallying cry and calls for unity among the youth: *One Love, One Heart/Let's get together and I'll feel all right.* The Wailers recorded a second version of the song toward the end of their tenure with Coxsone that indicated the kind of spiritual turn the Wailers began to take as their sound gradually turned away from rude themes around 1967: *One Love, One Heart/Let us pray to the Lord and I will feel all right.* A Rasta-encoded Bible-oriented song, "One Love" was further distinguished by Roland Alphonso's smoldering tenor break and an impossibly smooth vocal harmony underlay, by then a Wailers trademark.

Later in 1965, personnel changes reduced the Wailing Wailers to its elemental trio—Bob, Peter and Bunny. The changes started when Junior Braithwaite left the group during the summer in order to migrate north to Chicago with his family. Not only did Braithwaite's departure change the group's sound, the name changed also, to Bob Marley and the Wailers. Speaking of that era in a 1974 interview, Marley remembered: "Junior used to sing high. It's just nowadays that I'm beginning to realize that he sounded like one of the Jackson Five. When he left we had to look for a sound that Bunny, Peter and me could manage.

"We go on like that until we had to leggo the two girls. Them was good in recording, but fe go pon stage and mek a mistake that doesn't record over . . . But them sisters did *great.* Could sing *high.*"

But even as the Wailing Wailers were molting into a trio format, there was another "sister" on the scene, one who would play an important role in the group's future. Her name was Rita Anderson. Eventually, she became Rita Marley.

In those days, the mid-sixties, the Wailers' hangouts were still in back of Trench Town—First Street, Second Street, Third Street—where the group would rehearse, eat, meet with friends and plan for the future. To get to Coxsone's studio on Brentford Road, the Wailers and their friends used to walk up West Street, where Peter was then living, and then use a shortcut by Calvary Cemetery and Greenwich Park Road. The path the group used ran near the back of 18 Greenwich Park Road, where Rita Anderson was living with her uncle and auntie in the section called Ghost Town.

Rita Anderson used to watch them amble by, sometimes harmonizing as they went, moving with the swagger and slouch of the rude boys. Of course Rita knew who they were; the Wailers' non-rude records were played on the radio, and their rudie records were staples at sound system dances. Later she would remember: "They sounded like angels." Often, when she would see them on their way to the studio, she wanted to call out to them just to give her a chance because she could sing too. Rita had a group called the Soulettes, consisting of her, her friend Marlene (who was called "Precious") and her cousin Constantine Walker, a great harmony singer known as "Vision" or sometimes as "Dream." But the Wailers seemed too rude for Rita to approach them like that, and they bore the reputation of rough guys as well. And Rita was a pillar of the ghetto community, a Sunday school teacher and church singer with her own reputation to guard. So Rita waited until a friend, who knew the group, took her over to Coxsone's to meet them. At first they were indifferent to her, but then she reminded them that she was the little girl they used to see on their way to the studio, and they warmed up. When she told Peter she had a little group of her own, an audition was set up for the Soulettes with Coxsone, who liked what he heard and agreed to take the group on as trainees. Coxsone assigned Bob Marley to act as manager for the Soulettes, to rehearse them, groom them professionally and keep the men away from Rita, a beautiful, plump, bright-eyed girl of eighteen. At first, Rita was more attracted to Peter because, she recalls, "Bob was very strange from those times. He didn't talk much, and he didn't laugh much. He was more *observing*. Also he would lead the rehearsals, and we were very scared of him because of the discipline he would put on his rehearsals and the type of harmony that we sing. So he wasn't a favorite of ours at that time. We used to think that this man is *very* cross. Nothing but music. No girls, no anything. He was totally different."

But after several months of arduous daily rehearsals, Bob's attitude began to soften, especially when the attraction between Rita and Peter cooled off. One day Bunny told Rita that Bob had said that he was in love with her. Rita was shocked because Bob had been such a strict disciplinarian with the Soulettes that he had become more of a father figure to her than anything else. Then Bob began to write love notes to Rita, with Bunny acting as mailman, and an unlikely love affair developed between the hard but shy young ghetto artist and the Sunday school teacher. Rita asked Bob about his family, and he told her about his parents and his childhood in St. Ann. Rummaging in a dusty corner of his little room in the back of the studio, he showed Rita a huge pile of letters from his mother in Delaware, all urging him to come and live with her and find work. Rita asked Bob why he let Cedella's letters pile up like that, and he replied he was just too busy to answer them. So Rita volunteered as Bob's secretary, helping him with his papers, writing out the songs that he wrote and answering his mail. One of the first letters she wrote was to Cedella up in Wilmington, politely introducing herself and explaining why Bob had not answered any of his mother's letters.

As the two young singers became closer, Rita came to sense that Bob was under some other pressure beside the daily grind of conducting auditions and rehearsals for Coxsone. He complained to her of severe headaches and frequent nightmares, and Rita felt badly that she might have mistaken his suffering for aloofness and ganja-induced introversion. She was also concerned that the barely human living conditions behind the studio might be contributing to Bob's problems. Finally, Bob confided to Rita the source of his nightmares, after extracting from her a strict vow of secrecy. Speaking very seriously, Bob said that he had been attacked every night by a "duppy," a dead spirit, universally feared in Jamaica, whose burial was incomplete or whose grave has been violated. To Jamaicans, a duppy isn't a friendly ghost, but a deeply disturbed spirit who wanders between dimensions, unable to take its rightful place as an ancestral voice or protector of the clan; often the duppy is snared by a wicked obeah man, a black necromancer and herbal wizard whose black arts are descended from ancient Afro-Caribbean strains of magic. Once a duppy is under the control of a powerful obeah man, it can cause terrible suffering and destruction among the living.

Talking in hushed tones, Bob told a barely comprehending Rita that the duppy was pulling him out of his bed every night and ruining his sleep. Afterward, he would get a terrible headache. Bob seemed almost ashamed to be telling Rita his troubles, especially since Rita, a churchgoing ghetto Christian, believed in Jesus, not in duppies, and Bob knew it. But Rita told Bob that she wanted to help him, and agreed to stay with him one night behind the studio so she could experience the duppy for herself. Together, she told him, they would deal with the problem.

That night she stayed behind with Bob when Coxsone and the other musicians left for the night and Coxsone locked the studio behind him. It was the first night Rita Anderson had ever slept away from her home. Their bed was an old door laid out on two blocks. Rita had brought some sheets from her auntie's house so she and Bob would be able to cover themselves.

Sometime later, after Bob and Rita had gone to sleep, Rita was painfully wrenched awake. She found herself on the floor, with the breath knocked out of her, trying to scream out to Bob, who was still lying fitfully asleep. But no sound came from her mouth, and utter terror set in, something Rita explains as feeling herself "going through changes." It was a terrible, paralyzing sense of dread, something that her Christian faith had never given her room to fear before. When she was able to regain her speech, she woke Bob and told him what had happened. Then Rita vomited with a violence she had never before felt. When the tremors had subsided, Bob took her out to the standpipe and washed her off, and tried his best to calm the frightened girl.

Now Rita understood what Bob was going through. But where could he live? Before Coxsone had taken him in, Bob had been cotching on the streets or staying in Vincent Ford's kitchen. With his mother away, and sleeping space in the ghettos at an absolute premium, Bob was very much the rolling stone, without a home. One day Bob Marley would be locked into the articulate beliefs of the Rastafarians, and would proclaim himself Duppy Conqueror. But now, in 1965, struggling with a bewildering array of philosophical loyalties from rudeness to black power, from Christianity to Rasta, from country to city, from subjection to rebellion, Bob gave in to his duppy and resolved to find someplace else to live.

With no other choice, Rita took him in. The next night she asked Bob to stay with her in the room she shared with her cousin (Rita's parents were working in England) and Rita's baby daughter Sharon, whom she had conceived during a brief affair and birthed the year before. That night, Rita waited until her uncle and auntie had gone to bed; then she and Bob sneaked into the house through a back window that her cousin had left unlatched, as quietly as possible because her aunt was very strict. In spite of harsh conditions in the slum communities, parents tended to be as strict or stricter than their middle-class counterparts, and children like Rita Anderson were often raised as angels in surroundings that were hellish.

Bob wriggled out of his clothes and got in bed with Rita and her cousin, and at first everything seemed all right. But then their giggling woke up the baby, and Rita's auntie came in and turned on the light and found the three of them cowering in bed. Auntie exploded with rage and threw Rita and Bob out of her house, refusing to unlock the front door and making them leave by the same back window through which they had come. The two lovers sat out all night under the stars, and talked of things to come.

The situation was temporarily resolved when Rita pleaded with her auntie, threatening to leave the household if a place was not made for Bob. When she heard this, Auntie knew that Rita was serious, because the girl had been raised as a shining example of the good ghetto child—disciplined, hard-working, talented, respectable—and even enjoyed a kind of moral authority around the Greenwich Park Road neighborhood, where people called Rita "Goddie," short for godmother. Finally, Rita's aunt built a little shack for Bob in back of the house so the young musician would have a place to sleep.

Late in 1964, a little more than a year after she had remarried and moved to Delaware, Cedella had saved enough money to send Bob a plane ticket so he could join her in the States and start a new life. But by the time Bob received the ticket, he had already met Rita and his star was rising in the Jamaican music world. He decided to postpone any northward migration for a year, since he hoped the Wailers would be able to earn enough from their records to lift the group out of Trench Town, without having to leave the familiar climate and diet of Jamaica. Bob spent the rest of 1965 working at Coxsone's, managing the Soulettes, living with Rita on Greenwich Park Road, playing his guitar incessantly as if it had been magically grafted to his body, singing and composing snatches of song about the things they heard on the sidewalk in the cool of the evening. "We were poor and underprivileged and always wanting," Rita says now. "But we knew there was a chance and a way out."

At Christmas 1965, the Wailers went to Coxsone and demanded money for the royalties they thought were owed the group for the string of Wailing Wailers hits that year. At first Coxsone claimed that the weekly retainer he paid each Wailer meant that he didn't owe them anything. Then, after hours of haggling, recriminations and shouted threats, Coxsone paid out sixty pounds in cash, to be split among the group. Peter Tosh says that the band had been expecting a big payday at the end of the year because they had been getting "something like six dollars a week when we had positions number one, two, three, seven and nine on the local charts."

Under Coxsone Dodd, Wailermania in Jamaica left a deep impression on the national psyche but little or no money in the pockets of the Wailers. For the time, Bob's hope of achieving success on his own terms was crushed. Disgusted and embittered with Coxsone, Bob consulted with Rita and they decided that he would go to America to live with his mother and try to earn enough to start up his own record company when he got back to Kingston. The Wailers now realized that the only way for a musician to survive was to join the rat race, in which one man records, presses, labels and distributes his own records. Only by controlling the entire production could a musician hope to earn a living.

But, Bob told Rita, there was one condition. He told Rita she had to marry him before he went, so that it would be easier to send for her if he decided to stay in Delaware. At first Rita told him she didn't want to marry, for the same reasons she gave Bob the year before when he had also asked her to marry him: Rita's father was working in Sweden, her mother was in England and Bob's mother was in Delaware. Rita said her auntie would never grant her permission for the marriage without Rita's parents meeting Bob and giving their blessing. But Bob persisted and swore he would never leave for America until he had married Rita Anderson. After several more days of discussions and arguments and tears, Rita relented and told Bob that she would marry him if he could get her aunt to agree. So Bob took Auntie a bottle of wine and formally asked to marry Rita so he could sponsor her for entry to the United States after he had gotten himself settled. At first she flatly refused, but Bob argued and argued and wore Auntie down until, late in the evening and weakened by the wine, she grudgingly gave her consent.

Bob Marley and Rita Anderson were married in a religious ceremony on February 10, 1966. Bob wore his black Wailers stage suit and his biggest smile for the occasion. A short rude boy–style haircut exposed Bob's ears and made him appear even more slender than he was. Rita wore an above-the-knee wedding dress of purest white, which set off her ebony color, and a white veil clasped by a tiara of pearls above her forehead. For those who knew them it was a joyous occasion, two of the best singers and brightest hopes of ghetto culture joined in a storybook bond. Remembering that day, and the courtship that led up to it, Rita now says, "It was something out of a dream, like a fairy book. Turn to a page, and there it is."

But Rita's joy was quickly tempered by sadness, confusion and loneliness. The morning after the marriage, Bob flew off to find work in Delaware, just as his father Norval Marley had left for Kingston the day after he married Cedella back in St. Ann.

4

Soul Rebel

Name Wailers from the Bible, some place in the Bible. There's plenty of places you meet up with weeping and wailing. Children always wail yunno, cryin' out for justice and alla dat . . .

(1974)

By 1966, Cedella Booker had her own home and a little grocery shop in Wilmington, an industrial port city at the mouth of the Delaware River, and was surviving on the small scale of most hard-working first-generation immigrants to the United States. Although she had never heard the Wailing Wailers perform, their records had been brought up to her by new arrivals from Jamaica, and Cedella was extremely proud of her son. So when a friend had written to her from Jamaica and told her that Bob was married, Cedella had known it was a lie because her son would *never* marry without consulting her first, and seeking her blessing. Cedella knew of Rita from the letters she wrote on Bob's behalf; the year before Bob had written to Cedella to say that Rita had conceived a baby with him, but had lost it early in her pregnancy. Later, Bob told his mother, "I know why God take that baby, because I wouldn't have anything to support it."

When Bob arrived in Wilmington that February, Cedella drove out to the airport to pick him up, along with her niece Enid and Enid's husband. After a joyful reunion at the airport, Cedella eavesdropped on the laughter and whispering she heard in the backseat during the ride back to her house. She heard Bob whisper to Enid that he had married, but by that time Cedella wasn't really surprised. She had known something was in the air.

When they arrived at the house, Bob bounded up the steps two at a time (he always climbed stairs that way) and exulted to Cedella that, back in Jamaica, he had had a strong premonitory vision of her house, and now that he was there the house was *exactly* as he knew it from his dream. Bob was amazed at the size of the house and the opulence of Cedella's household and furniture, and was even more surprised to learn that he would have a room and a bath to himself. That night Enid's husband bought a lot of beer and there was celebration and good stories and singing. Later, when things had quieted down, Bob took Cedella aside and told her: "Mama, I get married, yunno." Cedella told Bob that she was aware of it, and felt a little hurt.

"How come you marry and never tell me?" Cedella asked. Bob replied that it wasn't his intention to marry just then, but that Coxsone had told him to marry his girl friend Rita before he left for America so that it would be easier to send for her if he wanted to. But Bob also made it clear there was more to the marriage than mere convenience. He told his mother, "You'll like her, Mama. She's a *wonderful* girl. She's my queen." Cedella says that during the seven months he lived with her in Wilmington in 1966, Bob never looked at another woman. When he wasn't working, he stayed at Cedella's and played his guitar, trying to recapture some of the spirit he felt had been washed out of him by Coxsone's manipulation. Over and over, he sang the refrain from a new song he was working on, playing two parts of a sexy rhyme against each other, lingering over the lines as if they had special meaning, as if they were a love call: *Bend down low/Let me tell you what I know . . .*

Bob worked hard in Wilmington, trying to earn and save enough to get a little record company off the ground when he went back to Jamaica. He worked as a laboratory assistant at the DuPont Chemical Company, under the alias of Donald Marley. For a few months he worked a shift on an automobile assembly line at a Chrysler plant, and later worked a night shift at a warehouse as well. He also had part-time work as a parking lot attendant and as a dishwasher in a restaurant. Later, he would remember how much he disliked his experience as a cog in the industrial world. "Everything was too hot, too noisy, too rush-rush."

At Cedella's house, mother and son were in religious conflict. In the four years they had been apart, the Christian youth Cedella had left in Trench Town had been exposed to the powerful attraction that the Rastafarian religion had for young black Jamaicans in the slums. Here was a black religion that held that Haile Selassie I of Ethiopia was the black king whom Marcus Garvey had prophesied would deliver redemption for the Negro race. Early Rasta preachers, like Leonard Howell in Kingston, had read in the *Daily Gleaner* in 1930 that an Ethiopian warlord, Ras Tafari Makonnen, great-grandson of King Selassie Shoa, had been crowned emperor of Ethiopia and had taken a new name and assumed ancient titles: Haile Selassie ("Power of the Trinity"), King of Kings, Lord of Lords, Conquering Lion of the Tribe of Judah. The emperor claimed to be the 225th ruler in a line traced from Menelik, the son of Solomon and Sheba. To Garveyite preachers in the Kingston slums, Selassie must have been the black Messiah that Marcus Garvey had forecast. They consulted their New Testaments for a sign, and found Revelation 5:2–5: "Weep not; behold, the Lion of the tribe of Judah, the root of David, hath prevailed to open the book, and to loose the seven seals thereof." When Leonard Howell began to sell one-shilling postcards of Selassie to slum dwellers, telling them the pictures were their passports back to Africa, he was arrested and committed to an asylum. But colonial Jamaica, church and state, couldn't kill the Ras Tafaris. "Cyaan stop prophecy," they insisted. And concerning Haile Selassie, there was prophecy aplenty. When Benito Mussolini's Italian Army invaded Ethiopia in 1935 and Selassie was forced into British exile after initially leading his country's resistance, the Rastamen again looked to their Bibles for a sign: "And I saw the beast, and the kings of the earth, and their armies, gathered together to make war on him that sat on the throne" (Revelation 19:19). In 1945, after Winston Churchill engineered Selassie's return to Ethiopia, the prophecy of the next verse (Revelation 19:20) was fulfilled: "And the beast was taken, and with him the false prophet that wrought miracles before him, with which he deceived them that worship his image. These both were cast alive into a lake of fire burning with brimstone." Hitler was the beast, Mussolini the false prophet. Jamaicans are a Bible-oriented people; to many, the evidence was plain and irrefutable. When Howell was finally let out of the asylum in 1940, he moved a large group of Ras Tafari followers from the slums of Kingston to an old estate in the mountains called Pinnacle, which was maintained as a Rastafarian commune and ganja plantation until the police raided and closed it down in 1954. The Pinnacle Rastas, distinguished by their long, flamboyant dreadlocks (uncut and uncombed hair, respecting several Old Testament admonitions against the razor), moved back to Kingston, mostly into Back O' Wall and Moonlight Village. The Rastas became the spiritual alternative to the negative anarchy of the rude boys. The asceticism practiced by the Rastas—shunning alcohol and salt and eating only fruits, roots, grains, vegetables and fish—was a philosophical alternative to the degradations of poverty and the general hopelessness of ghetto life. The Rastafarian sacrament of smoking marijuana as a path to righteous meditation validated an old Jamaican custom, as opposed to the repressive laws of colonial Jamaica. For the Rastas, the Jamaican government, the police, the established churches—all were extensions of the biblical wickedness of Babylon, with the black people of the New World as the metaphorical captive tribes of Israel, sold into Babylonian captivity. For the Rastas, the notion of any kind of Jamaican nationalism was a cruel joke. Home was Ethiopia in its original sense, as the Greek word for Africa. More important, Haile Selassie was a *black* redeemer, the "Almighty Ever-Living God" on earth. For Bob Marley's generation, the new black consciousness that emerged in that decade was more than just civil rights and black power. It was black religion. For them, the Messiah was on earth.

In those days, though, Cedella Booker saw it differently. She was born and raised a fundamentalist Christian, and she didn't want to know about Haile Selassie. She was a member in good standing of the United Church of the Lord Jesus Christ of the Apostolic Faith, and here was her firstborn son sitting at her kitchen table in Delaware, letting his hair grow into knots and talking to her about Ethiopia. Cedella then thought that she knew better about Rastas, about how, after Pinnacle was closed down and the Rastas had dispersed throughout the ghetto, many criminals and bad boys had taken to wearing dreadlocks to have easier access to the slums. For Cedella, Rastas were men who didn't vote and didn't work and didn't go to church and smoked ganja all day long and talked only about suffering. And here was Nesta Robert pounding on the table, raising his voice at her and quoting Scripture, reminding Cedella that "What is hidden from the wise and prudent is not hidden from children."

Cedella Booker remained unconvinced. Her worst fear was that when Bob returned to Jamaica, he would let his hair knot up and become a Rastafarian. For conservative Jamaicans like Cedella, hair length and style clearly indicated social differences; straight silken hair was the ideal, while naturally kinky hair denoted the lower orders. So the Rastafarians, who declared complete secession from society by sporting matted twenty-inch ropes of dreadlocks down their backs, were looked upon with revulsion and real dread by the mass of Jamaicans. The idea of her boy wearing dreadlocks was almost too much for Cedella to bear. Finally, when Cedella capped off a discussion by telling her son that she could never agree with what the Rastas were putting about, Bob blew up. He assumed that hard and distant look he employed to indicate displeasure ("Bob's screwface," a friend called it), and spoke with a hard coldness that Cedella had never heard her son use with her before. "Yunno, the only reason me chat with ya at all is because you're me mother, yunno. Because when me a-tell ya the truth and you fumble y'self, me just feel *hot* with ya now. But yunno what? You tell about Jesus Christ. It's hard for me as your son to come and tell ya, seh, *His Majesty Haile Selassie the First is God.*"

Bob lived in Wilmington until October, when he decided to go home.

But before he left, he had a visionary experience in his mother's house. Bob was alone on a Sunday afternoon, and had a dream in which an old man, wearing an army coat and a slouch hat, appeared and handed him a ring, a gold ring with a tiny diamond set in onyx. When Cedella came home, Bob told her of the dream. Shaken by what her son had told her, Cedella went to her room and produced the same ring that Bob had been given in his vision. It had belonged to his father, Norval Marley, and was one of the few talismans of Norval that Cedella possessed. Bob wore the ring for a time, but eventually decided that it made him uncomfortable. He returned the ring to Cedella before he left for Jamaica, where eventually the dream and its meaning would be given a very different interpretation.

When Bob told his mother he was going home, Cedella was upset at first. "You're goin' go back home and turn *Rasta,*" she spat. But there might have been other pressures on Bob as well. Years later, he hinted to a reporter that he had applied for social security in Delaware, and a local draft board then became interested in him as cannon fodder for the war in Vietnam.

In October 1966, Bob Marley returned to Kingston and moved back in with Rita Marley at 18 Greenwich Park Road. He had been gone less than a year, but in Kingston things had changed. Rastafarian consciousness had exploded when His Imperial Majesty Haile Selassie I of Ethiopia had made a state visit to Jamaica the previous April. Although Rita had written to Bob in detail of the visit, when they were reunited she spilled out the story of Selassie's hand. For weeks before the emperor arrived, Jamaica had whipped itself to a peak of anxiety and expectation. If Jah, Ras Tafari, was coming in person to bestow his blessing on Jamaica, could the last days, the days of judgment, atonement and salvation, be far behind? Devout Rastas from the Trelawney cockpits, the hills of Clarendon and the Blue Mountains of Portland began walking to Kingston weeks before Selassie's arrival, and thousands camped out on the Palisadoes, the narrow strip of land that leads to the Kingston airport. At first, Rita and her friends weren't sure if they would come out to greet Selassie; the very idea of him seemed so momentous. Could this man possibly be the Redeemer, whose coming Rita had taught in Sunday school? Would Spirit really return in Flesh? They said Selassie had nailprints on his palms. Rita made a pact with herself: if she went to see Selassie, and if she could see the nailprint of the crucifixion in his hand, then she would believe in him.

The morning of April 6, 1966, began with a drenching wall of thundershowers that soaked the thousands of Jamaicans who had turned out to welcome the emperor. Rita and her friends walked from Trench Town toward the airport as far as the cement works on Windward Road. At the airport, there was utter pandemonium when the emperor's jet broke through the cloud cover and descended to the runway. From nowhere, a flock of snow-white doves materialized and flew over the impatient throng. When the assembled Rastafarians beheld the imperial lion on the plane's fusilage, thousands rampaged through police lines and swarmed all over the plane even as the engines were being shut down. Rasta brethren fired up the giant ganja water pipes they call "chalices" in the shade cast by the imperial wings. The air was full of singing and chanting and the recitation of psalms. Hundreds prostrated themselves on the tarmac and waited for the emperor to come out. Slowly, the door was opened and the faithful beheld Selassie standing in the doorway of his jet. A shout of such raw religious frenzy went up that Selassie quickly ordered the door to the plane shut, and refused to come out for an hour. Eventually, all pretense of an elaborate state ceremony of welcome was dropped, and the event would enter Rastafarian lore as the "capture of ceremonies." The emperor was finally coaxed to leave his plane when Mortimer Planno, a Rastafarian elder who served as a kind of ex officio bishop of the Kingston brethren, climbed up the ramp and persuaded the multitude to give His Majesty some room.

Hours later Selassie's motorcade flashed past Rita and her group. The young musicians had been expecting to see a great and noble king, larger than life itself, so they were surprised when Selassie proved to be a tiny man with a mild aspect to his eyes, almost hidden in the back of his open car. Rita thought to herself, *Bwai, if I could only see his hand,* and, just as the thought ran through her head, Selassie raised his hand and waved to her. "And when I looked into his hand," she said later, "there was the nailprint, the mark, that black mark in the center of his hand. I said, 'My God! This is the man!' "

Most important, during the remainder of Selassie's visit, prominent Rastas like Mortimer Planno were included in the official delegations that accompanied Selassie. The Jamaican government, which regarded the Rastafarians as antisocial dropouts and potentially dangerous, was forced to deal with them almost on the level of a new national religion. The JLP government had been hoping that Selassie would deny the divinity proclaimed him by his Jamaican followers, but the emperor hardly said a word. Anyway, the Rastas said, the prophecy could not be gainsaid.

Selassie's visit may have temporarily altered some official Jamaican attitudes, but after the emperor went home again things went from bad to worse for the Rastas. In July, while Bob Marley was still in Delaware, the squatters' camp at Back O' Wall, home to many Kingston Rastas, was bulldozed to make way for the Tivoli Gardens housing project. Thousands lost their homes, and many Rastas were arrested and otherwise brutalized by the army and police. Once again, hundreds of Rastas were forced to disperse further through the neighborhoods of western Kingston.

Bob also found that some interesting changes had occurred in his musical family as well. Bunny's "Rude Boy" had been a big hit in his absence, and Rita's first single for Coxsone, "Pied Piper," had sold well also. The Wailing Wailers had continued to record while Bob was in the States, with Rita's cousin Vision filling in Bob's harmony behind Bunny's lead on a sunny ska-spiritual called "Who Feels It" (an early version of Bunny's "Who Feels It Knows It") and on "Dancing Shoes," a hot dance number that featured a great hard-bop tenor sax break.

Even more important were the major structural changes that had altered Jamaican music. Some time during the extremely hot, uncomfortable summer of 1966, Jamaican dancing had slowed and the sound systems subsequently demanded a new beat. Almost overnight, the quick bouncy ska step evolved into a slower beat the musicians were calling "rock steady." The prevailing rhythm now was much slower, more relaxed and sensual. But there were other factors in the evolution from ska to rock steady besides a hot summer and dancers wanting something different. The race riots of 1965, the destruction of the Back O' Wall ghetto in July 1966 and the emerging black power movement had raised the social temperature in Kingston to a feverish degree. The struggle for control of Jamaica—then ruled by JLP prime minister Hugh Shearer— was turning into armed conflict, and agents of the two political parties began pressing the previously anarchist rude boys into goon squads along lines of party loyalty. After early 1967, violence in the ghetto became systemized, turning once-open neighborhoods into militant enclaves controlled by gunmen and party bosses. The slower beat of rock steady, and the accompanying rise in lyrics of protest and social concern, was no accident of climate alone. Out of Kingston's social chaos emerged the throbbing pulse of rock steady, almost as if Jamaica's musicians were making a conscious effort to cool the nation down.

Bob Marley had his own analysis of the change, which he later described to a reporter: "The guys who were in control robbed the older musicians up, and they get frustrated and stop playing. So the musicians changed from the older musicians to the younger, hungrier ones who was coming up underneath them. People like I, we love James Brown and we dip into that American bag. We don't want to stand around

67

playing and singing that ska beat anymore. The young musicians, dem have a different beat. It was rock steady now, *eager to go!"*

The rock steady era in Jamaica conjured up a new generation of talented singers and musicians from the ghettos and hill villages, young men and women unafraid to express intimate feelings and social protest. The new wave included some holdovers from ska—Alton Ellis and the Flames, the Maytals, Stranger Cole—and newer groups like the Heptones, the Gaylads, the Melodians, Slim Smith and the Techniques, and the Paragons. Singers like Ken Boothe elevated the Jamaican love ballad to new heights; when Dobby Dobson sang "Loving Pauper," every young person in Jamaica could identify with the singer's concern for character and spiritual values over the empty glitter of materialism.

Bob Marley's identity as an observant Rastafarian began to blossom after his return to Jamaica. His hair, uncut during his last months at Cedella's house in Wilmington, began to knot up and a sparse beard sprouted. Peter Tosh also let his hair grow now, and Bunny had been a Rasta enthusiast for at least four years. The Wailers then, early in 1967, were the first of the Jamaican vocal groups to adopt the abstemious, testifying style of the Rastafarians, eating a fairly strict diet, smoking voluminous amounts of ganja, reading the Bible daily and speaking in the esoteric patois of the dread adept.

The group's religious and social consciousness eventually brought the Wailers into long-overdue conflict with Coxsone Dodd. Dodd was a Jamaican businessman of the old school, who paid musicians with bus fare and sweets on Fridays and responded with violence to any protests. While Bob was in America, Tosh and Bunny had staged an impromptu sit-down strike in Coxsone's studio after Tosh refused to play the organ for free on someone's tune and refused to leave the studio when Coxsone tried to throw him out. Tosh told Coxsone to get his gun, but Coxsone called in the police. All this put Bob in a strange position, since he was more Coxsone's employee than either Peter or Bunny. Bunny remembers that Bob occasionally got a little weird and seemed to side with Coxsone.

Eventually, the Wailers decided to leave Coxsone and form their own label, using some of the money Bob had saved while working in Delaware. They recorded one last song with him, "Bend Down Low," based on the riff that Bob had been developing in America. They had recorded over fifty tracks for Coxsone—soulful ballads, ska-rockers, rude boy anthems (the last was Peter's "I'm the Toughest," released in 1967) and rock steady shuffles. Coxsone had more than twenty hit singles in Jamaica alone, and had licensed dozens of Wailers singles to British record companies, like Chris Blackwell's Island Records. But the group had seen almost no money, and they were especially infuriated when "Bend Down Low" was a hit and the group was uncompensated. "Them rob we out of it again," Marley said later. "Man, all is robbery."

Years later, Dodd gave his own version of the parting. "Well, they started to get into this Rasta thing . . . and I wasn't ready to go with that. Then they broke the contract because they figured that they were underage [when they had signed] and I had used my own lawyer to straighten out things between us. Bob Marley was more or less like an adoption, 'cos he used to stay by me, yunno, and I used to provide whatever he needed."

After he left Coxsone's stable, Bob came next under the guidance of Mortimer Planno, the Rastafarian elder of western Kingston. Recognizing that the youth had visionary qualities far beyond his own, Planno assumed the role thrust on him by Bob, that of spiritual advisor and de facto manager of Bob Marley and the Wailers. As his faith deepened (and when Rita became pregnant with their first child), Bob moved out of Kingston, back to St. Ann and the one-room cabin that Omeriah (who had passed away in 1965) had built for Cedella twenty years before. He and Rita and their baby, a girl they named Cedella, would remain in St. Ann until 1970, commuting to Kingston when business required.

Life in St. Ann was both hard and idyllic. Rita remembers it as the best time of her marriage to Bob. Bob Marley was a farmer again, planting corn and a little ganja on the side, wearing blue denim bib overalls most of the time, his hair getting longer and knottier (though he kept it pent up in a wool cap much of the time). He and his cousins and friends spent long days wandering the St. Ann hills, walking the proud land, cementing a covenant between themselves and the land of their birth. And the deeper Bob delved into the Bible, the deeper his Rastafarian faith became. But Bob spent most of the time sitting on a boulder next to the cabin, playing his guitar incessantly, working on songs. Composing together much of the time, Bob and Rita wrote three songs that year: "Nice Time," "Stir It Up" and "Chances Are." Another song, "Belly Full," began to take shape. And an early version of "Trench Town Rock" was chorded out one winter evening in 1967 while Bob was perched on his boulder, watching the sun disappear behind the mountain at five o'clock. It wouldn't be recorded for another three years.

Not long after the group left Coxsone, the Wailers started their own label, which they called Wailin' Soul Records. (Some of the labels of the singles they issued during the few months the company existed read "Wail'n Soul'm.") Among the early Wailin' Soul releases were "This Man Is Back," announcing Bob's return to Jamaica, and "Selassie Is the Chapel," in which Bob atones for missing Selassie's visit to Jamaica the year before. Sung to the tune of the old Sonny Til and the Orioles tearjerker, "Crying in the Chapel," "Selassie Is the Chapel" was Bob Marley's first recorded song of Rastafarian faith. Another song from this era, "Bus Dem Shut," reaffirms the Wailers' commitment to the youth of Jamaica, who "burst dem shirt" with pride and hard work.

At first, Wailin' Soul Records seemed like it might be a success. Recording with young producer Clancy Eccles, the Wailers had several popular dance hall hits. "Nice Time" was slow rock steady, great for dancing, with the rock-steady big-sounding bass line that had replaced the blaring horns of ska as the instrumental focus of Jamaican pop. One of Bob's greatest songs of seduction, "Nice Time" boasted Bunny's soaring high harmony and an acute longing in the lyric: *Long time we no have no nice time/what do ya think about that?/This is my heart to rock you steady/I'll give you love anytime you're ready.* On the flip side was "Hypocrite," a favorite target of Bob's: *See de hypocrite/Dem a galong dey.* Also successful locally was "Stir It Up," an early version of the love song Bob cowrote with Rita in St. Ann.

But despite the early successes, the Wailers were too inexperienced to run their own label. Based on their past reputation as hitmakers, the Wailin' Soul records were played at dances and sound systems, but air play on the radio was nonexistent. Marvin Gaye and James Brown ruled Jamaican radio. The group didn't have any of the necessary show business connections. "We were too young for producing," Peter Tosh says. "We never understood certain important things, like how to get on the radio or sell our records. We only knew how to make them. And the other producers were holding us down as little producers, as usually big guy control small guy."

Later on, Bob would recollect the disappointment the group felt about the label. "We fight *hard,* mon. But when Christmas [1967] come and we go to collect money, the mon seh the stamper mosh and alla dat." (Apparently the Wailers were told that the "stamper," the machine that actually presses the records, had broken and so no records had been sold.) Wailin' Soul Records went quietly out of business toward the end of 1967.

The year 1968 was one of worldwide turmoil and revolution. Young black Jamaicans looked north and saw that Detroit was on fire and Har-

lem and other American black ghettos were burning up. Stokely Carmi-
chael, Malcolm X and H. Rap Brown echoed the firestorm rhetoric of
Marcus Garvey in new, more militant voices. In California, the Black
Panthers were patrolling ghettos with shotguns, saying that they were
protecting ghetto people from police violence. And there was a new map
of Africa, redrawn by the various successful anticolonial movements. In
Paris and all over Europe, university students were agitating against war
and what they felt was a dehumanizing capitalist system. The student
protest movement reached its boiling point in Jamaica in 1968, when a
popular University of the West Indies history professor from Guyana
named Walter Rodney was refused reentry to Jamaica at the Kingston
airport when he returned from a black writers' conference in Canada.
While teaching in Jamaica, Rodney had encouraged political activities
among the sufferers in western Kingston, journeying to ghetto neighborhoods like Rollington Town to reason with street people and local activists. (One of these was a young thief named Orlando Wong, who later, as
Oku Onuora, would become one of Jamaica's most famous poets.) When
word reached the U.W.I. campus that Rodney had been banned, a protest meeting was held, attended by both radical students and Rodney's
friends from the slums. The meeting turned into several days of rioting,
leaving many injured and arrested. (Walter Rodney eventually became
leader of the opposition Working People's Alliance in Guyana, where he
was assassinated in 1980 while working against the repressive regime of
Forbes Burnham.)

Perhaps reflecting this new spirit of general rebellion among the
young, especially among young black radicals, Bob Marley cut off his
locks and combed out his hair in the fashionable "Afro" style. Peter Tosh
was arrested in 1968, along with Prince Buster, after Buster had organized a street demonstration in downtown Kingston to protest the situation in Rhodesia, where a racist white government under Ian Smith had
seceded from Britain and declared an independent state, founded upon
white supremacy. Both Bob and Bunny were also arrested that year for
possession of ganja. Bob had been a passenger in a car whose driver had
been busted at a police roadblock. Bob was in jail for a month, and felt
the experience deeply, identifying himself with prisoners and captives for
the rest of his life. Bunny, however, had been caught with several pounds
of herb, and was sentenced to a year in the General Penitentiary and,
later, at Richmond Farm, a work camp for minimum security prisoners.
While Bunny served his time, the Wailers' career sputtered to a near halt.
Bob spent much of his time playing football, listening intently to the Jimi
Hendrix Experience and the new funk modes of Sly and the Family Stone

and working on songs. When Rita gave birth to their first son in 1968, Bob was ecstatic. He named the boy David Marley, but everyone called the child Ziggy

In the same year, Bob entered one of his new songs, "Don't Rock My Boat," in a national competition to decide which new song would represent Jamaica at Carifesta, the annual pan-Caribbean cultural festival. Bob's hope was that his song would win, and the group's career would revive. "Don't Rock My Boat" didn't even place among the top five songs entered, and Bob Marley was again disappointed.

The late 1960s were as confusing for the Wailers as they were for everyone else. Outwardly, the Wailers styled themselves in the black power trappings of the day—the ghetto identity, the fists in the air, rebellious music, Afro hairstyles. (Peter Tosh, then living in Kingston 11, became a skilled carver of Afro picks, the long-tined wooden combs used to tease out hair for a "natural" look. Tosh's Afro picks were in demand all over western Kingston, and were particularly admired by a twelve-year-old Kingston 11 comb carver named Tyrone Downie.)

But the real Bob Marley was moving away from rude boy confrontation, and leaning precipitously into the prevailing wind of Rastafari. Mortimer Planno guided Bob to understand Rasta as an alternative spiritual nationality for the descendants of slaves who found themselves caught between their heritage and their destiny. Planno's teachings were simple, that every black person has an African consciousness that most in the New World fail to recognize. Most important, God was again on earth, in the person of Haile Selassie. In western Kingston Rasta circles in those days, there was a millenarian sense of impending salvation and the fall of Babylon. Something, the Rastas were sure, was bound to happen.

Bob Marley responded to the spiritual thrust of the times by entrusting all his temporal affairs to his adviser, Mortimer Planno. Planno applied some of his natural charisma and leadership abilities toward advancing the Wailers' cause during 1968, but without much luck. At the same time, Bob was beginning to be influenced by a new Rastafarian sect that had been founded in Jones Town that year, the Twelve Tribes of Israel. Members of the Twelve Tribes are basically Christians who hold that the second coming of Christ has already occurred, in the person of Haile Selassie. Selassie's words are thus revered and his speeches referred to constantly. As Bob became more interested in the esoteric doctrines of Rastafari, he increased his attendance at the "groundations," Rasta prayer meetings that combined hours of drumming and religious chanting with herbal meditation.

One of the guiding forces of the Twelve Tribes was astrology, and each new member is assigned a tribe according to the month of his birth. Many members discard their "slave names" and adopt the name of their natal tribe—Dan, Levi, Gad, etc. Vernon Carrington, the Rasta philosopher who founded the movement, is known as Gad the Prophet.

Bob Marley would later explain: "Gad revealed back to I and I [the Rasta form for "we"] the secret of the lost Twelve Tribes. I was born in February, so I'm from the tribe of *Joseph.* Now someone born in April could say they were from Aries, and that's what they will be, because the word is power and you live it. But if you say that you are *Reuben,* then you realize you find your roots because you become Jacob's children, which is Israel. Jacob said, 'Thou art Reuban, thou art my firstborn, the beginning of my strength, the excellence of my dignity.' "

It was at a Rasta groundation in 1968 that Bob Marley met Johnny Nash, a young black American singer who would get the Wailers back into business and eventually out into the world at large.

Johnny Nash was already a star when he met Bob Marley.

Born in Houston in 1940, Nash grew up in church choirs and developed a clear, ringing tenor voice and a passionate delivery, especially on ballads. In 1955, when Johnny Nash was fifteen, he was "discovered" by American broadcasting personality Arthur Godfrey while caddying for Godfrey on a Houston golf course. Nash became a member of Godrey's radio family, and his voice became familiar to millions of Americans via Godfrey's weekly network broadcasts. When the Godfrey show made the transition from radio to television, Johnny Nash became one of the first black Americans to be regularly featured on network television in the United States, breaking through racial barriers that had blocked black advancement in American entertainment for decades. By the early sixties, Nash had starred in two Hollywood films, *Take a Giant Step* and *Key Witness,* and was considered a hot property. He had recorded five albums of white-oriented pop music for ABC-Paramount, which had sold well. But Johnny Nash, handsome, successful, dynamic, felt something was wrong. There was a new spirit for blacks in the land, but Johnny's audience was completely white. He was already beginning to change his style by the time he met a young black New York promoter named Danny Sims.

Born in Mississippi in 1936, Danny Sims was a former college football player who came to New York because he wanted to get involved with the entertainment business. In the late fifties he opened a restaurant in Manhattan called Sapphire's, the first black supper club in New York that was "downtown," that is, not in Harlem. Sapphire's quickly became a hangout for black performers on Broadway—Sammy Davis, Jr., Harry Delafonte, Ossie Davis—and young music stars like Johnny Nash, all attracted by some of the best soul food in New York. Danny had been dating Johnny's sister, and Johnny and Danny became friends. When Johnny was about to leave for a concert tour of the Caribbean, he asked Danny to manage the tour for him. Sims's promotions for Johnny Nash were so successful that Nash outdrew even Sammy Davis, Jr., in Puerto Rico and Trinidad, and Danny Sims was out of the restaurant business for good. In 1960, Sims brought Brook Benton, the New Orleans soul singer who was a great favorite of Bob Marley's, to Jamaica for a series of successful concerts. Less than a year later, Sims's New York company, International Attractions, was the biggest promoter of American acts in the Caribbean, dispatching talent like Aretha Franklin, Otis Redding and Curtis Mayfield on tours of the Caribbean circuit.

In 1964, Johnny Nash and Danny Sims started a record company called JODA Records (JODA stood for Johnny and Danny). In the next two years JODA would have a dozen hit singles (one of their acts was the Cowsills), but, unable to sell albums, the main source of cash volume in the record business, the company filed for bankruptcy in 1966.

But Danny Sims had other plans, plans that were years ahead of their time. From promoting American singers in Jamaica, Sims knew of the incredible, untapped vitality of the music scene in Kingston. So at the end of 1966, Danny Sims liquidated his New York companies and went offshore. Realizing that he could record American "product" cheaply in Kingston, Sims moved his family, Johnny Nash's family and that of producer Arthur Jenkins to the lush mountain suburbs of Kingston. Sims reestablished his music publishing company in the Cayman Islands, an offshore tax haven and banking center between Jamaica and Cuba, and renamed his company Cayman Music. He bought a big villa in Russell Heights, one of suburban Kingston's better districts, and settled down to make music and wait out "the revolution" that he felt was hurting black record business in the United States.

At first, Nash and Sims had little interest in Jamaican music, which sounded primitive to these sophisticated New York music pros. The Jamaican ska and rock steady forms had until then been deemed too weird for the American market. But local musicians began teaching the rhythms to Johnny Nash, who was questing for a new way to present himself to the black soul audience. Nash began writing songs with a subtle Jamaican flavor, some of which ended up on the first album Nash recorded at Federal Studio in Kingston, *Hold Me Tight,* which clearly showed its Jamaican influence even though the music was mostly played by top New York studio musicians that Danny Sims had flown in for the recording sessions. More important, the album sold well around the world on the wings of its two best songs, "Hold Me Tight" and a version of Sam Cooke's "Cupid," almost pure rock steady.

Nash was also intrigued by the Rastafarian spiritual revival he was hearing about from the Jamaicans he was jamming with, so when Neville Willoughby, one of the top radio disc jockeys in Jamaica, offered to escort him to a Rastafarian groundation, Nash readily accepted. Willoughby took Johnny Nash to one of the Twelve Tribes' Jones Town "street meetings," where the Rasta faithful gathered on Sunday afternoons for "Satta Amassagana" (literally, "give thanks and praise" in Ethiopia's Amharic language). After the chanting and prayer session, Nash was introduced to two of the island's most popular younger singers, Bob and Rita Marley.

Danny Sims remembers Johnny Nash coming back to his house in Russell Heights that night, excited by the scene he had witnessed. Nash talked about a beautiful black woman he had met named Rita, and her husband Bob, who had all these wonderful songs. Nash was so enthused that he had invited the young couple up to Russell Heights the next afternoon, so Danny Sims would have a chance to hear the Marleys sing for himself.

When Neville Willoughby brought Bob and Rita up to his house the following day, Danny Sims says, "Bob Marley must have sung twenty straight goddamn hit records." With Rita deftly harmonizing as Bob strummed chords on his acoustic guitar, Bob sang "Nice Time," "Chances Are," "Don't Rock My Boat," "Lively Up Yourself" and many others into the hot tropic afternoon, his porkpie hat tilted at a rakish angle. Sims was impressed, and both he and Nash immediately wanted to work with the Wailers, especially after they met Peter Tosh and heard the records of the third Wailer, Bunny Livingston, stuck in the penitentiary. Bob and Peter began spending time at Sims's place (the neighbors immediately started to complain of the presence of Rastafarians in their exclusive area), and the Wailers' long professional relationship with Danny Sims began. But it was some time before they actually began to work with Sims, especially with Bunny in jail. So Bob and Rita went back to St. Ann for several months to work on songs. Later, Bob tersely recalled his life in 1967: "The politics get hot and the city get hot, so I was in the country planting corn. Johnny Nash and his manager came down to me, to write songs for them. They felt like I was finished with music. They didn't know that I was only resting."

Sims says that he met with Bob and told him that he would like to represent the Wailers internationally, as songwriters. Marley referred Sims to Mortimer Planno, who was still managing the Wailers. Sims and Planno conferred, and a deal was struck. Bob, Peter and Bunny were all hired as songwriters by Cayman Music at a weekly retainer of fifty dollars each. Mortimer Planno, according to Sims, asked for and was given a piece of the action.

When Bunny was released from prison near the end of 1968, the Wailers began cutting demonstration recordings of the songs they had written for Danny Sims's company. Over the next four years the Wailers recorded over eighty tracks for Sims, first at West Indian Recording (now Dynamic Studios) and later at Harry J's studio in uptown Kingston. Bob Marley refused to record at Sims's first choice of studios, Federal Records, because of some long-simmering feud with the owner, Ken Khouri. At Dynamic Studios, Bunny says, "We used to do some *wicked* late night work. Sometimes we done the next morning. Me can recall musicians like Hux Brown on guitar and Jackie Jackson on bass. We did a version of 'Nice Time' with Hugh Masakela playing trumpet . . . me nuh get no pay all now." By early 1969, Sims had formed a new record company called JAD Records, which stood for *J*ohnny, *A*rthur and *D*anny. Arthur Jenkins, the new partner, was an arranger and producer responsible for some of the music on the sessions the Wailers did for Sims. (Years later, after Bob Marley's star had risen considerably higher, there would be a heated dispute as to whether the Wailers' sessions for Sims that began in 1968 were ever meant to be released by JAD Records, or were in fact merely demo sessions for Wailers songs written under contract to Cayman Music.) Some of the songs, although not released for years, provide a fascinating glimpse at Bob Marley and the Wailers' more commercial side in the late 1960s.

According to Danny Sims, "There was no 'Jah' in the music Bob was making back then. It was all 'Jesus' this and 'Lord' that. The revolutionary music didn't come until the Manley government in 1972." More likely, the three Wailers songwriters assumed that Sims, being in part self-exiled from black power struggles in the States, was only interested in rock steady dance music. "Mellow Mood" was a scorching Bob Marley seduction song, laced with amorous boasting *(Gonna play your favorite song/darlin'/gonna rock you all night long)* and Jamaican folk imagery. If the thrust of the song was typically priapic Marley, the meticulous harmonies were ethereal and angelic, showing a more soulful side of love. A new rock steady version updated the Wailers ska oldie "Put It On," while "How Many Times" and "There She Goes" recall the group's history as a Jamaican street corner doo-wop ensemble. By the late sixties, with ultramodern James Brown ascendant as Soul Brother Number One, the Wailers had really lost interest in this old-fashioned material but still performed it dutifully, as if they thought the Jamaican fans demanded it.

Somewhat more successful are two of Peter Tosh's songs, "Hammer" (which injected a slightly rude note into the otherwise politically sanitary sessions) and "You Can't Do That to Me," an early version of Tosh's later "Stop That Train," which became a staple of the Wailers' early tours. A sorrowful love ballad by Bob and Rita, "Chances Are," was undistinguished especially when compared to "Hold On to This Feeling," a knockout Bob-and-Rita duet styled after Marvin Gaye and Tammy Terrell and never released. "Touch Me" stole the melody of the American pop hit "Dream Lover," and "Treat You Right" was a song by Bunny in very early reggae time.

Perhaps the best of the early sessions for Sims was the first version of "Soul Rebel," a post-rude boasting song that indicated a more "soulful," humane direction for the Wailers. But none of this music matched the power of the Wailers' most recent local hits, like "Bend Down Low," a love song that spoke directly of the romantic dilemmas of the poorest young Jamaicans: *You keep on knockin' but you can't come in/Don't you understand you been living in sin?*

The sessions for JAD, with the exception of the great "Mellow Mood," just didn't articulate the Trench Town experience, which is what young Jamaicans expected from the Wailers by now.

In early 1969, the hottest producer of Jamaican music was Leslie Kong, the proprietor of Beverley's Records. Kong's 1968 production of a song called "Israelites" by Desmond Dekker, Bob's old friend from the South Camp Road welding yard, was the first Jamaican record to be a worldwide hit since Millie Small's "My Boy Lollipop" back in 1964. Another Kong record from 1968, the Pioneers' "Long Shot Kick the Bucket" (the tale of a dead racehorse), was a big hit among England's West Indian population. Jamaican music was just beginning to change its basic rhythms again, this time shifting down a gear from rock steady into the even slower, rasta-influenced and ganja-pollinated mode called *reggae.* In 1968, Leslie Kong had produced a dance tune by the Maytals called "Do the Reggay," which validated the new beat and inadvertently named it as well. The word "reggae" had several mysterious connotations. Toots Hibbert of the Maytals, who wrote the song, later said the word meant "regular," referring to its steady, ticking rhythm. Joe Higgs identified the word with "streggae," a ghetto patois term denoting uncouth rudeness. Others say reggae means ragged, rough, of the streets. Some observers equate the slowed beat to the massive early 1970s rise of "herb culture" in Jamaica. In any case, Kong's artistic stable included some of the island's best singers—Ken Boothe, Delroy Wilson, the Melodians—and a crack early-reggae studio band, Beverley's All-Stars, which included bassists Lloyd Parkes and Jackie Jackson, drummer Paul Douglas, Gladstone Anderson and Winston Wright on keyboards and guitarists Rad Bryan, Lynn Tait and Hux Brown.

This was the band that backed the three Wailers when they recorded an album's worth of tracks for Leslie Kong early in 1969. Nominally, the group was still signed to Cayman Music, but Nash and Sims had cut back JAD Records operations and agreed to let the Wailers record for local Kingston producers after Bob had complained that the group needed to make a living. The only stipulation was that the recordings be released in the Caribbean only, leaving the potentially more lucrative English and American markets for the JAD partnership.

The ten songs the Wailers recorded for Leslie Kong in 1969 are the most modern-sounding of the Wailers early period, and all have that special Beverley's trademark swing, emblematic of the new energy and enthusiasm that went into the earliest reggae recordings. The jazzy saxes and trumpets that dominated ska and rock steady disappear, and instrumental breaks are now played by the more populist electric guitar. Most of the songs are dance tunes, but the Wailers' irrepressible social concern manages to surface now and then. The nonsense dance lyric of "Soul Shakedown Party" was countered by Tosh's "Stop That Train," which told of the mental anguish of a Rasta prophet without honor in his own country: *All my life I've been a lonely man/Teaching people who don't understand/Even though I try my best/I still can't find no happiness/Stop that train, I'm leaving/Won't be too long, whether I'm right or wrong . . .*

"Caution" is a brooding Bob Marley composition whose mystery is to be found in obscure lyric imagery dealing with psychic traffic warnings for black people. The track is punctuated by the modulated electric guitar stuttering that was standard in Leslie Kong's records, over which Bob exults *Hit me from the top, you crazy mother-funky!* in true James Brown style.

Peter Tosh sang an authoritative lead vocal on a version of the civil rights–era spiritual "Go Tell It on the Mountain," as well as on his own song, "Soon Come," which bewails the Jamaican national attitude of better late than never. Although these were "message songs," the crisp and bright arrangements made perfect sense to dancers. And Tosh was starting to be recognized as a writer with the same kind of tough and direct voice as the more visible Bob Marley. Another Tosh song, "Can't You See" (previously recorded for Coxsone as an uncharacteristic, almost Stones-ish rocker), was modernized and softened by Kong, inflected with the more African touch of new sound coming from his studio.

Two of the Wailers' tracks for Kong were in a more serious vein. "Soul Captives" was basically a harmony showpiece with the hook line, "Soul captives are free." More substantial was the beautiful "Cheer Up," which set the tone of black unity that would preoccupy an older Bob Marley.

The Kong sessions were rounded off by a pair of classic Wailers sex chants. "Back Out" was one of the first Wailers songs to feature Bob singing in a style that ached with desire, that communicated a palpable lust, sparked by perfectly timed James Brown grunts—"Back out, *unh,* and shut your mouth." Bob was in such control now as a singer that he could produce instant biochemical reactions in attentive dancers, rocking the groove of a song with scat phrases and repetitive soul slang. This kind of singing, coupled with the appalling chop of hard reggae rhythm guitar, was nothing less than a setup for secular Jamaican spirit possession, trance music of the highest order. Equally seducing was another Marley love song, "Do It Twice."

Although Leslie Kong released eight or nine Wailers singles both in Jamaica and in England, the response was lukewarm and the records failed commercially. A year later, Kong notified the group that he intended to put out an album of tracks the Wailers had cut for him, to be called *The Best of the Wailers.* Bunny flew into a rage and told Kong that the title was a lie, since the best of the Wailers was obviously yet to come, and threatened that if the album was released, Kong would die. Although Bunny was rumored to have more than a passing acquaintance with the black arts of obeah, Kong paid him no mind and the Wailers album was issued in Jamaica. A year later Leslie Kong, at age thirty-eight the most important producer in Jamaica and one of the prime developers of reggae music, suffered a sudden and massive heart attack in his studio and dropped dead. He had only recently finished recording the seminal Jimmy Cliff songs for the sound track to a new film called *The Harder They Come.*

The Wailers' main hangout in 1969 was called the Soul Shack, a little record shop (presided over mostly by Rita) in an alley behind producer Joe Gibbs's studio near Half Way Tree Boulevard in Kingston. But neither the Wailers recordings nor the shop brought in the kind of money that Bob needed to realize the dream he had for the group: a custom record label, one where the musicians would actually control their music. Toward this goal, Bob left Jamaica again in the spring of that year, and went back to the United States to live with his mother and find work in Delaware.

He worked for Chrysler that year, spending his days on a truck assembly line, and working a variety of other part-time jobs as well, including a stint on the night shift at a warehouse. At Cedella's house, Bob incessantly played his guitar and worked on songs, most notably "Comma Comma" and "It's Alright," a lively affirmation that hard-working people can get it if they really want: *The sun shall not smite me by day/Nor the moon by night/But everything that I do/shall be hopeful and right.* Later, Bob would look back with wry amusement at the wage slavery he endured in Delaware, and seven years later he reworked the song for an album, retitling it "Night Shift."

Meanwhile, back in Kingston, Peter Tosh continued to record for Leslie Kong, trying also to earn money to start the new label. Under the name "Peter Touch" he released several unmemorable songs, including "Selassie Serenade," "The Return of Al Capone" and "Sun Valley."

When Bob's plane landed at the Kingston airport in the autumn of 1969, he wasn't much wealthier than when he had left earlier in the year. The money he had managed to save went to support Rita and the three children, and the rental of a small house on First Street in Trench Town where the Wailers could get together and rehearse. But Bob had returned creatively refreshed, with new songs and ideas. Almost immediately the Wailers started a new collaboration, one that would galvanize Jamaican music within the coming year. The Wailers' new producer and cowriter was an old friend from their days with Coxsone, a tiny wizard of a sound engineer who went by the usual schizophrenic roll call of nicknames—"Upsetter," "Little," "Scratch."

His real name was Lee Perry.

Born in Kingston in 1939, Lee Perry went to work for Coxsone Dodd in 1959, holding auditions and rehearsals at Dodd's Downbeat Record Shop on Orange Street before Coxsone built his own studio. Prior to that he worked on Coxsone's sound system in the days of the sound system wars with sonic rivals Duke Reid and Prince Buster. One of his first productions for Coxsone was the epochal "Six and Seven Books" by Toots and the Maytals, a wild fusion of jumping 1961 ska and the fervor of a Wednesday night prayer meeting. Perry continued working for Dodd until about the time the Wailers left the Studio One label in late 1967. Like many of the great artists of reggae, Perry felt that Dodd had failed to adequately compensate him for his work, but he also acknowledged that his apprenticeship with Sir Coxsone had given him an invaluable education.

In the late sixties Lee Perry was the baddest maverick in Jamaican music, and he combined an extremely rude attitude with brilliant new rhythms and eccentric African-sounding percussion. Styling himself "The Upsetter" (and dearly wanting to upset Coxsone's dominant position on the scene), the elfin Perry expressed his rage with singles like "Run for Cover" and "Return of Django," whose slow, sinister beat left a definite, chilling menace in the hearts of his listeners. Perry's music exploded with new ideas: one single, "People Funny Boy," is credited by some scholars as the record that literally gave birth to the slow, sexy reggae beat that *ticked*. Perry claimed that the inspiration for his hard new sound came after he attended late night services at a Trench Town Pocomania church, the Afro-Jamaican revivalist sect whose breathy religious shuffle encourages spirit possession among the faithful.

"At the same time," Perry says, "me want to upset Downbeat [Coxsone], upset him technically. And all the others too. 'Cos they were all doing something same all the way, alla dem just go *ska-aska-ska-aska*. And when the people hear what I-man do to them, they hear a different beat, a slower beat, a waxy beat, like you stepping in glue. And dem hear a different bass, a rebel bass, coming at you like sticking a gun.

"Me knew Wailers from Downbeat days, of course, and when dem come a-see Downbeat, dem a-come and see me, and Jackie Mittoo, and we help them with music and recordin'. But then when Bob drop into my hands [in 1969], him really take on the power of music now. Bob rebirth . . . it was a different level for him completely. As Bob a-come out of my section, was when him roots manners start, because my rhythm fresh, a harder type of thing, and nothing else could carry Wailers more than dem kind of beat and that kind of feeling. I the right man to go with their kind of soul. Is there me show dem see what to sing and how to do it."

Working with Bob, Bunny and Peter in the back room of his Upsetter Records shop at the corner of Beeston Street and Luke Lane, Perry completely recast the basic Wailers sound. Bob's lead vocals were transformed into something more urgent and raw, devoid of pretense and smooth edges. Out went the old-fashioned Wailers doo-wop harmonies, to be replaced by terse but melodious backup parts. Perry dropped horn sections from the Wailers' music, as well as every trace of Leslie Kong–style frothy reggae bounce. Now the dark and primitive bass was the lead instrument, offset by the metronomic chop of electric guitar. Palpitating with this dread new bass warfare, the Wailers' music became *evil* once again, tough as nails, as in the days of "Rude Boy" and "Rule This Land."

Much of the credit for the Wailers' powerful creative surge goes to Perry's elite young studio band, the Upsetters, the nucleus of which, the two Barrett brothers, would eventually merge with the Wailers to create the best reggae band in the world. The key to the Upsetters was Aston Francis Barrett, born in Kingston in 1946, called "Family Man" or just "Fams" for his prowess at fathering large numbers of children. The lock that Family Man's key fit was the drumming of his younger brother Carlie, born Carlton Lloyd Barrett in 1950. Together, the Barrett brothers developed a stupefying rhythm harmony sound, a driving, percussive harmonic counterpart to the Wailers' strong vocal harmonies. In 1975, Family Man recalled how he became the Wailers' "melodic superintendent":

"I build my own bass. I don't go to school you know, no one teach I. I build one out of board and put on four guitar string." Working with his brother Carlie's automatic sense of time, Family Man developed fast as a musician. "I really take it serious in '68. Two week hard practice and the third week a band, the fourth I go studio." (The Barretts' first session was for "Watch This Sound," which Jimmy Riley recorded with Slim Smith in a group called the Uniques. "Watch This Sound," the Barrett brothers' first recorded "riddim," was a big hit in 1968 for Winston Lo's Tramp label.)

"The first little group," Family Man continues, "we call it the Hippy Boys, that was a road band. Studio-wise, we were the Upsetters. My brother Carlie was in it, and Alva Lewis guitar, and Glen Adams keyboard. That was the four who toured [in Britain] in '69. Within them times we do studio work, yunno. Well, we was the only group capable enough to back Wailers. 'My Cup' and 'Conqueror' and all dem things . . . Bob is the leader of the Wailers, and I am the leader of the musical part of the group. The Wailers was the best vocal group and I group was the best little backing band at the time, so we say, why don't we just come together and smash the world."

And they did.

The Wailers/Lee Perry/Upsetters sessions were held at Studio 17, Perry's record shop, during the last months of 1969 and on through 1970. Many partisans of the Wailers still feel that these recordings are the best the band ever made. The new songs reaffirmed the band's status of rude shamans and soul rebels, spokesmen for a generation of Jamaicans determined to suffer no longer.

The sessions had actually started earlier, after Bob's return. Hanging out at Upsetter Records, Bob, Peter and Bunny talked music with Lee Perry, drank fish tea, built countless spliffs, ate roasted fish and cornbread. Scratch (after "Chicken Scratch," a popular dance tune he had cut) wanted the Wailers to record exclusively for his Upsetter label, but Bob still badly wanted a label of his own. Two of the earliest Perry/ Wailers collaborations, "Duppy Conqueror" and "Who's Mr. Brown," were released as singles in Jamaica on the fledgling Tuff Gong label, backed with their respective "dubs," the rhythm tracks of the recordings with the vocals "dubbed" out so local deejays could boast and toast to the rhythms at sound system dances. The label was named after Bob Marley's street handle in Trench Town. Mindful of what had happened to the group's earlier label venture, when Jamaican radio refused to play the discs because they didn't have proper labels, Bob asked a friend named Guy Coombs, who designed handbills for local advertisers, to design a label for the new record company. Coombs recalls that he drew up the early Tuff Gong label and had it printed at his own expense, because Bob was broke. The label was simple: "Tuff Gong—a Wailin' Soul production." Half the label was left blank so that song titles could be written in by hand. Today, Coombs remembers Bob Marley as "someone who showed heavy discipline at all times. He was never talkative, and even when you talked to him most times, he never cared to talk back. He always preferred more to sing than to talk, and always had his guitar." When the label's second single, "Who's Mr. Brown," was issued, Coombs designed and printed some handbills similar to the dance announcements that were passed out all over the city. One side of the card was a picture of the group, Bob on the left, Peter in the middle, Bunny on the right, wearing T-shirts and very short haircuts. The caption read: "Here Comes Bob Marley and the Wailing Wailers." The reverse hopefully touted "Who's Mr. Brown," proclaiming it "a sure HIT."

Unfortunately, Tuff Gong Records quickly sank back into the same exploitative ooze of the Kingston music business that had consumed Wailin' Soul: no radio airplay, no distribution, no money. Bob Marley later dismissed the early rise and fall of Tuff Gong with "The Wailers came forward again, but we couldn't hold a groove."

So they began to record with Lee Perry for Upsetter Records, a relationship between Bob and Scratch that lasted through 1978. Perhaps the reason the collaboration was so *right* was that the scrappy, jabbering Scratch was such a good foil for the reticent, moody Marley. While Bob strummed chords and brooded, Perry would croak out catchphrases and brainy doggerel, trying to find the right lyrics to match the sputtering, bumpity Afro-style percussion tracks that the Barretts were experimenting with. Perry seemed slightly demented to outsiders, with his alternate astral identities fueled by copious amounts of white rum and ganja; but he was also a witty and imaginative lyricist who contributed immeasurably to the great records the Wailers made with him. As to who actually wrote the songs (Bob or Scratch—Peter's and Bunny's songs are unmistakably their own), confusion still reigns. The early Upsetter/Wailers releases credited most of the songs to Lee Perry. When the same songs were later released on albums in Britain, some of them were credited to Bob Marley or sometimes to "R. Marley." Most likely, they were written by both men and the band, improvising in the studio. Trying to clear the matter up, a reporter asked Perry in 1977 about the songs he wrote with Bob. Who wrote what? "That part now, me no wanna discuss," Scratch said. "Because we have work to perform and me and him live too close like a brother. These are minor problem, something between me and him, and I don't think anyone should get involved in that. Is a me and him problem, so let we solve it."

"Duppy Conqueror," "Small Axe," "Stand Alone," "Don't Rock My Boat"—these and other early Wailers masterpieces seem even more singular when isolated from their times. In 1969, Jimmy Cliff's "Wonderful World Beautiful People" was a hit record all over the world, as Desmond Dekker's "Israelites" had been to a lesser extent in 1968. The dominant sound in the Caribbean was definitely James Brown, Soul Brother Number One, with his epileptic squawks and insane, pleading declarations of love. In America, though, James Brown was riding the escalator over the hill, and Sly Stone and Jimi Hendrix were ascendant, not pleading for mercy anymore.

"Duppy Conqueror" was written jointly by Bob and Lee Perry, and describes the quiet exultation of the released prisoner, feelings Bob knew well from his own prison term as a ganja smoker: *Yes me friend/Dem set me free again/Yes me friend/Me deh pan street again/The bars could not hold me/ Force could not control me/They try to keep me down/But Jah put I around.* Bob goes on to sing that he must take a pilgrimage to Mount Zion, and that nothing is going to stop him. *If you are a bull-bucker/well let me tell you/I'm a duppy conqueror.*

In 1969 and the following year, when "Duppy Conqueror" was popular, the term "duppy conqueror" generally implied a hoodlum, someone so bad that even duppies are afraid. But in speaking in the voice of a prisoner, the Wailers were making a subtle political point in the song. If duppies are the wandering souls of the dishonored or disinterred dead, so can the iniquitous Jamaican judicial system be seen as a duppy, as a malevolent spirit from the rotting corpse of Jamaican history. Here now the duppy conqueror is no mere criminal, but a shamanic, resurrected victim who lives in Jah's grace and cannot be suppressed by injustice.

A similar point was made by another Perry/Marley song, "Small Axe," which on its surface seemed to be a Third World proclamation and warning to the colonial powers, with imagery lifted directly from the Old Testament: *Why boasteth thyself, oh evil men?/Playing smart without being clever/I say you're working iniquity to achieve vanity/But the goodness of Jah-Jah I-ndureth for I-ver/If you are a big big tree/We are a small axe/Sharpened to cut you down/Ready to cut you down.* But the song actually referred to more immediate issues for the group. When the Wailers had originally merged with Lee Perry, his record company, Upsetter, was facing unified competition from the "big three" studios in Kingston—Federal, Studio One and Dynamic. One day Bob and Peter and Scratch were playing with lyrics at the Upsetter shop and Scratch was complaining about the "big t'ree." Brash and boasty as usual, Tosh spoke up: "If dem is the big t'ree, we name the small axe!" And one of the canniest double entendres in reggae music was born. "Small Axe" was irresistible because it threatened with both the voodoo mystery of obeah and the authority of the Bible: *These are the words of my master/Telling me that no weak heart shall prosper/And whosoever diggeth a pit/Shall fall in it.* And Scratch's wicked, clicking polyrhythms gave the music even more of a hoodoo edge, like a Jamaican myal priest exorcising demons.

The earliest sessions at Studio 17 produced several new songs and a handful of remakes of earlier pages from the Wailers' songbook. "Mr. Brown" was another version of "Who's Mr. Brown," originally the sequel to "Duppy Conqueror." Laced with ominous rattles and ghoulish cackling, "Mr. Brown" was an aural horror show: *Mr. Brown is a clown who rides through town in a coffin,* a duppy who "upsets the town" from Mandeville to Sligoville. "My Cup" was a more old-fashioned Wailers song about suffering. The cup was the singer's eyes, brimming with tears, the main lubricant of Wailer imagery: *Yes I've got to cry, cry, cry.*

"It's Alright" was the song that Bob had written in Delaware, produced by Perry in a sort of experimental stop time. But "Corner Stone" hit a really rocking groove, and took its theme from the Psalms (always a wellspring of Bob Marley's lyrics): *The stone that the builder refuse/will always be the head corner stone/Cos the things people refuse/Are the things they should use.* The lines are borrowed from Psalm 118:22–23. But in "Corner Stone," Bob's spiritual intent is peripheral; what he really wants is some love: *You are the builder baby/And I am a builder's stone.* Ten years later, the same potent builder/stone imagery would surface again in "Ride Natty Ride."

Among the older Wailers' songs re-created by Lee Perry were Peter's "No Sympathy," "Rebel's Hop," a remake of "Rude Boy" with new verses and more actively rebellious now than rude, and "Soul Rebel," which had been recorded for Danny Sims. Among the newer songs were "Try Me," a seductive challenge in the form of a harmony chant; "Reaction," a lesson in social physics warning that for *Every little action/There's a reaction;* and "Souls Almighty," a goofy slice of proto-reggae in which Bob intones: *funky funky chicken/mash potato/do the alligator/let's do it together* . . .

If the first set of sessions the Wailers recorded for Lee Perry was less than world shaking, a second series of recordings cut in early 1970 was much more important. "Small Axe" emerged from these dates, as well as "Lively Up Yourself," "Kaya," "400 Years" and several other Wailers staples. "Kaya" was particularly significant for the era of the early 1970s, when "herb culture" began to predominate among Jamaican artists and musicians; in response, the basic beat slowed down into classical reggae time so both players and dancers wouldn't have to exert themselves. "Kaya" is a Rasta term for ganja, and the feeling of being high on herb, *feelin' Irie-I,* is ingeniously combined with chanting visions of rain and falling skies. The effect is pure, colorful musical impressionism. "Lively Up Yourself" was an anthem of unity and dancing with knockout harmonies, Bob exhorting his people that reggae is another bag, and a blistering horn solo, probably from Tommy McCook. "400 Years" contained the polemics that Jamaicans had come to expect from Peter Tosh: *400 years 400 years 400 years/and it's the same philosophy/400 years 400 years 400 years/and my people/they still can't see/why do they fight against the youths of today/without the youth, they all go astray.*

Some of Bob Marley's most passionate and transcendent love songs came out of these sessions as well. "Don't Rock My Boat" might be the ultimate example of the synthesis of Bob's subdued but lusty soul singing and the Barretts' patented trance groove. Family Man's utterly *pelvic* bass line cushioned the sensual pillow talk of the lyric, with Bob telling his lover how happy he is, *happy inside all the time.* "Stand Alone" is sadder in tone, a gentle song about the pain of reconciling lovers: *Here you are/crying again/and your loveliness/won't cover your shame.* The song is a lacework of hidden meanings and indecipherable lines, and displays a strong hint of the paternalistic attitude that Bob maintained toward the women who passed through his life.

In addition to new versions of "Put It On" (delivered in the heartbeat tempo of Rasta burru drumming, which redressed the original rude boy spiritual in Rastafarian robes) and "Keep on Moving," a harmonic tour de force adapted from a Curtis Mayfield song, the Wailers also cut several new tunes. "Fussing and Fighting" was hard reggae-rock, a plea for peace among warring ghetto factions. "Sun Is Shining" is a very weird dance poem, acid-reggae, with a melodica accompaniment that adds a surreal touch to lyrics that seem psychedelic in their looseness and high spirits. "Brain Washing" is a very poignant Bunny Livingston condemnation of the Mother Goose nursery rhymes, which Rastafarians considered contaminated by Babylonian mythology and witchcraft: *Is just old brainwashing/coming through for poor man's child.* One of the cleverest of Perry's recordings is called "All in One," which reprises in medley form the Wailers' greatest hits to 1969—"Bend Down Low," "Nice Time," "One Love," "Simmer Down," "It Hurts to Be Alone," "Lonesome Feeling," "Love and Affection," "Put It On" and "Duppy Conqueror," all seamlessly translated into one three-minute track.

In "African Herbsman," the Wailers as observant Rastafarians are evident as Bob paraphrases the lyric of a Richie Havens song. Calling himself a "retired slaveman," Bob calls on his brother the African herbsman to retrieve him from the clutches of Babylon: *African herbsman/Seize your time/And take this illusion/from the edge of my mind.* The song spoke for all black people in the West, separated from their home culture by slavery and the legacy of the whip.

The best of the Upsetter/Wailers sessions were released in Jamaica and England during 1970 and 1971 on the Upsetter label. "My Cup," "Duppy Conqueror" and "Small Axe" all were minor hits. But it wasn't until the release of the stupendous "Trench Town Rock" during the summer of 1971 that the Wailers again exploded in Jamaica.

5

Reggae on Broadway

We're sick and tired of your bullshit game
Die and go to heaven inna Jesus name
We know and we understand
Almighty God is a living man
You can fool some people sometimes
But you can't fool all the people all the time
And now we've seen the light
We gonna stand up for our rights

"Get Up, Stand Up"

As the new decade began in 1970, the Wailers were sitting in limbo. The best work of their Lee Perry sessions was yet to be released; their old harmony style was passé, and the group was broke.

Early in 1970, Danny Sims and Johnny Nash liquidated their record business in Jamaica, and Nash accepted an offer to act in and score a movie being shot in Sweden, where Nash's Jamaican-produced records, "Hold Me Tight" and "Cupid," had been big hits. Nash and Sims invited Bob Marley along to help with the sound track, and Bob decided to go. On his way to Sweden he took Rita and the children to Wilmington to live with Cedella. For the next year Rita worked in a Delaware hospital as a nurse. Just before he left for England, on his mother's advice, Bob had his hair cut.

While Bob was in Europe, the rest of the Wailers stayed in Kingston. Under the direction of Lee Perry, they recorded behind various lead singers: "Peter Touch," Ras Dawkins and Lee Perry himself in a molten extravaganza called "Son of Thunder," which Perry released as the flip side of "My Cup." The Wailers/Upsetters rhythm section, the Barrett brothers, also found work in a short-lived group called the Youth Professionals, assembled by a local club owner as the house band for his sleazy night spot. The Youth Professionals included a very young but extremely talented keyboard player named Tyrone Downie.

Born in eastern Kingston in 1956, after his mother had gone into labor at a sound system dance, Tyrone was raised in the Victoria neighborhood, not far from Vineyard Town and the Catholic cathedral on North Street. It was an area that produced some of Jamaica's best piano players and footballers, like the most famous soccer player in the history of modern Jamaica, Alan "Skill" Cole. Tyrone was raised by his mother, Gwendoline Edwards, a strict Christian, and sent to prestigious Kingston College, an Anglican school. Somebody gave Tyrone a harmonica, and he quickly became addicted to music. He enlisted in the cadet band and used to sneak into the school's chapel after hours and play the organ. When he got caught, he was caned. By the time he was thirteen, Tyrone was playing piano in church and had started to build a reputation in an area already full of hot players. One day a local club owner came to the gate and gave a classmate two shillings to bring Tyrone to see him. When Tyrone came out, the man told him that Tyrone's friend Horace Swaby (later to be renamed Augustus Pablo) had been spreading the word that Tyrone was one of the most talented musicians around. Tyrone was invited to play in the band of a new downtown nightclub. Since Tyrone was only fourteen, he took the club owner home to meet his mother to ask her permission. When Gwendoline Edwards was assured that her son would only play on the weekends and that his schooling would not be interrupted, she gave her consent.

The businessman then took the young teenager over to his club to show Tyrone his new instrument—a new Farfisa 5 electric organ. The Farfisa is the cheapest, cheesiest-sounding keyboard available, and in time Tyrone would grow to be one of the most sophisticated synthesizer players in modern music. But back in 1970, the Farfisa 5 seemed "like a spaceship." He began to experiment immediately, and within a few days mastered everything the instrument could play.

But Tyrone was intimidated when he first met his fellow Youth Professionals. Family Man and Carlie Barrett, the pulse of the Upsetters, were the *hardest* rhythm section in Kingston. But Family Man made Tyrone feel at ease, and shared his knowledge. When the Youth Professionals began to build a local reputation, the club owner wanted the band to work weeknights as well. Tyrone was making money, and told his mother he wanted to leave school. "She was disappointed," he remembers with a wry touch in his deep voice. "She thought I had a brain."

Now Tyrone began to hang out with Family Man and his family, at Pembroke Hall on the northwest outskirts of Kingston where the bassist lived. Family Man told Tyrone about the Wailers and the big plans the group would hatch when Bob came back from Sweden. Family even hinted that Tyrone might one day become part of those plans. Tyrone was flattered beyond belief, and gained a great deal of confidence from Family Man, of whom Tyrone says: "He's a very serious person. If he doesn't know you, he doesn't want to deal with you."

In Sweden, during the winter and spring of 1970, Bob Marley was cold. To avoid the frigid Scandinavian climate, Bob stuck close to his Stockholm hotel room and worked on songs for Nash's soundtrack, collaborating with Nash's Texas-born keyboard player, John "Rabbit" Bundrick. Bob also spent time with two African hand-drummers who played on the sound track sessions, Remi "Rebop" Kwaku Baah and Coffee, talking about Africa and smoking hashish.

Before leaving Sweden, Bob Marley accompanied Johnny Nash and his backup band, Rabbit and the Jungles, on a short tour of Swedish cities, where Nash's Jamaican-style records had been popular. With the tour over and the sound track finished (neither film nor record would ever be released), Johnny Nash and his entourage decamped for London, where Danny Sims was trying to secure a record deal for Nash with the British branch of CBS Records. When the deal was signed, Bob was joined in London by the rest of the Wailers—Peter, Bunny and the Barrett brothers. The Wailers originally thought they were coming to support Nash on a tour of England, but instead they found themselves living in a seedy hotel in Bayswater with no way to cook their own food, rehearsing by day in the basement of a company called Rondor Music, in Surrey. The band was extremely unhappy with the squalid living and working conditions, and Peter and Bunny complained constantly. Bob was angry too, but was less inclined to complain loudly since Danny Sims was trying to get Bob a recording deal with CBS as well.

Early in 1971, the Wailers went into the CBS studio at Soho Square to cut some of the backing tracks for Johnny Nash's forthcoming album. Among the songs they worked on were Nash's "I Can See Clearly Now" and four numbers by Bob Marley: "Stir It Up," "Guava Jelly," "Comma Comma" and "You Poured Sugar on Me." Since the music was meant for international soul fans and not the Jamaican reggae audience, the tracks were polite and somewhat subdued as arranged by Rabbit Bundrick. But at the same sessions the band recorded a tune of Bob's that Sims hoped to sell to CBS as a single. The song, "Reggae on Broadway," was a rock-hard rhythm chant, unlike anything Bob had cut before, charged with a Sly Stone back beat and James Brown grunts. But despite the dancing, upbeat vibe, there was something sad and frantic about the song, as if it recalled the lonely feelings of exile and burning ambition described by the Drifters' "On Broadway," which had been a hit ten years earlier. Reggae was almost on Broadway, but the Wailers were penniless and homesick in London.

In the spring of '71, the Wailers returned to Jamaica to visit and record, while Sims and Nash remained in London to oversee the production of Nash's album. The group began working at Dynamic Sounds and at a comfortable new studio built by producer Harry Johnson on Roosevelt Road in uptown Kingston. They were scheduled to return to England in the fall to support Nash on a British tour.

For the next four months, the Wailers embarked on an incredibly prolific recording spurt, cutting dozens of new songs that signaled many artistic changes in the band. They were energized by some important new musicians and a new manager. Alan "Skill" Cole was Jamaica's finest young soccer star, a tall and friendly natural leader who became a close friend of Bob Marley's, sharing Marley's Rasta enthusiasm and love of herb. It was a perfect match for a friendship; Jamaica's greatest footballer and music fan with Jamaica's greatest musician and football fanatic. When the Wailers had returned to Jamaica, Bob asked Skill Cole to help the band by producing some local recordings and taking care of business in Kingston, drawing on Skill's prestige as an athlete of national stature.

When the Wailers began to record again in Jamaica, the old keyboard player from Lee Perry's Upsetter sessions, Glen Adams, had emigrated to New York, and the Wailers began to think of a replacement to join the band for recording and touring. The keyboardist on the band's great 1971 sessions was the fifteen-year-old former Youth Professional, Tyrone Downie, then a resident of Cockburn Pen, Kingston 11.

Tyrone recalls the era: "So from the Youth Professional gig, I'm a musician now, right? So being a musician, you get curious. You listen to records, you love records, artists and musicians. You want to know who plays on the records, and the only way to know is go downtown and look, because they're all there. So I'd go and hang out at different record shops to find out what was really happening.

"Bob's shop wasn't called Tuff Gong then; it had another name, Soul Shack. A real small shack in an alley back of Joe Gibbs's studio, next door to a little food shop. They sold records, Afro picks carved by Peter, anything to do with soul 'cos then it was still the soul era, black and proud and all that. One day I saw the shop, and Rita was at the counter, and I said to myself, 'Wah! This is where Bob Marley and dem is.' Rita called me into the shop and gave me a mango; she was so nice that I was surprised, I'm just a likkle school guy and alla dat. But I was afraid to go into the shop because I knew there wasn't anybody my age or any real young person working at recordin' then.

"Bob confirmed that for me when he arrived. He looked at me and said, 'Wha you doin' here? Gwan back to school. Gwan home.' But he said it nice, as if me mother would be worried about me. So I said, 'Waaah,' yunno, and left. But the vibe at the shop was so great for musicians that I kept going back and hanging around."

One day the Wailers gathered at the Soul Shack to rehearse a new song, "Lick Samba," which the band was going to record. By then, Tyrone had played a couple of sessions for star producer Bunny Lee (most notably singer Carl Dawkins's "Walk a Little Prouder"), and was hanging around the Wailers, waiting for a chance now that Glen Adams was gone. Family Man beckoned a jumpy Tyrone into the studio, and told Bob that the boy was a former Youth Professional. From then on, Tyrone says, Bob was cool. Adding to Tyrone's appeal was that he was happy to play for free. "I was young then," Tyrone says, "I don't care about money, and was always ready to play with the Wailers. I was like their groupie!"

The first tune Tyrone played on was one of the first the Wailers cut that year, "Lick Samba," produced by Bob with Lee Perry engineering. Not long after that, the Wailers recorded a song that Bob had begun to develop as early as 1967, during his retreat to the hills of St. Ann. When it was released in the early summer of 1971, "Trench Town Rock" tore up Jamaica, defining ghetto residents as the righteous and outsiders as . . . *outsiders.* For young Jamaicans, the lilting melody, pulsating riddim and prideful language redrew the invisible boundaries between "dem" and "us." "Trench Town Rock" was number one in Jamaica for the next five months, and it turned Bob Marley into a national hero.

In a Jamaica where slum culture and music represented the only freedom of expression offered to poor people, "Trench Town Rock" literally exploded, contributing to the attitudes that would soon bring enormous changes to Jamaica. In confirming the positive side of the Trench Town experience, the Wailers emerged as spokesmen of the ghetto and the Jamaican poor. It was an honor the Wailers would never lose. *One good thing about music: when it hits you feel no pain.*

The song was also a big breakthrough for the band, because they were suddenly in demand for recordings and stage shows. Even more important, Bunny Livingston later would say, " 'Trench Town Rock' is the tune that made us *really* start to search." After the new social forces of "Trench Town Rock" had been released, the Wailers could never again return to easy songs of love and romance. As Peter Tosh said of the song, "We were now gone into a twelfth dimension." And a contemporary (1971) literary magazine in Trinidad observed the Wailers from afar as "three musicians struggling to unearth the inner feelings of the Kingstonian man in the street, through the media of rock steady, reggae and their own unique, as yet unnamed beat. It might be food for thought for non-Jamaicans to take a lesson or two from West Indians who refuse to bow to imported acid rock and the omnipresent Motown sound and fight off the commercialism and artistic prostitution which this obeisance can easily breed in a people not yet free from the colonial yoke."

With the band's new notoriety came enough cash for Bob and Rita to abandon their Soul Shack record shop and establish Tuff Gong Records, first on the Parade and later on Beeston Street. With Lee Perry busy releasing some of the records he had cut with the Wailers—"Small Axe," "Kaya," "All in One," "More Axe" and Peter's "Down Presser"—Bob decided to crank up his Tuff Gong Productions to meet the demand for new Wailers music. Recording at various studios, the Wailers began to produce an enormous amount of new material. After the "Lick Samba" session, the Wailers recorded "Midnight Ravers," "Craven Choke Puppy" (a sharp riffing vocal in true reggae rhythm), "Satisfy My Soul" (a hypnotic meditation on power and the powerless), "Redder than Red" ("red" meaning high on herb), "Mr. Chatterbox" for producer Bunny Lee, Peter Tosh's "Stop That Train" and "Burial" (also called "Funeral") and a pair of Rasta gospel songs by Bunny, "This Train" and "Dreamland," the last a passionate tune about a utopian Africa.

Among other Wailers sessions recorded in the summer of 1971 were a new version of "Guava Jelly," produced by Skill Cole, a new song called "Screwface," scolding complainers and naysayers in general, and the first versions of "Natural Mystic" and "Concrete Jungle." Also cut were several songs intended for a Bob Marley album if the already recorded "Reggae on Broadway" was a hit in England. These included a follow-up, "Dance Do the Reggae"; new versions of two older ballads, "Chances Are" and "Mellow Mood"; two interesting pieces ("Stay with Me" and "Gonna Get You") by other songwriters under contract to Danny Sims; and a devastating new song written by Bob, "Hurting Inside," which laid bare the memories of a man who had once been lost and abandoned: *When I was just a little child/Happiness was there awhile/ And from me it slipped one day/Happiness come back I say/Cause if you don't come/I'm gonna go lookin'/For happiness/Cause I'm hurting inside/Yes I'm hurting inside.*

Bob Marley's was a hectic life in those times. Days were full of recording and strenuous exercise under Skill Cole's training-like discipline. Nights were devoted to communal I-tal meals, composing and rehearsing. Because the work was so hard and the rewards so few when compared to the fabled riches of the rock stars who passed through Jamaica, there were bound to be tensions within the group, involving the usual group issues: leadership, direction, songs and money. The Wailers had been together for ten years since the early rehearsals in Joe Higgs's yard. Though they sensed an impending breakthrough, the frustrations of low cash flow and lack of recognition took their toll within the group. Long periods passed when Bob and Bunny wouldn't speak to each other, and the dispute would be settled through the mediation of friends. Peter Tosh especially was frustrated when Bob's songs often took priority during precious studio time.

During the summer of 1971, Bob Marley's political life began to heat up. An alliance was formed then between the Wailers and the People's National Party that would continue, informally but always understood, for years. It would almost get Bob Marley killed.

The Jamaican political scene had been relatively placid for some years. The Jamaica Labour Party had rather sleepily governed Jamaica in the decade since the island's independence in 1962. Though little had happened since the riots and turmoil of the late 1960s, the climate in Jamaica was repressive and unabashedly neocolonial. Jamaica was being run by lazy bureaucrats for the benefit of the middle class and the old planting and mercantile families. An easy tropical life for a relatively few people was supported by an enormous pool of cheap black labor, a system whose grinding injustice the Wailers knew intimately, as in Bunny's song "Who Feels It, *Knows* It."

With a general election announced for the following year, the opposition People's National Party began a hard-fought campaign to capture Jamaica for socialism. Leading the fight was the party's candidate for prime minister, Michael Manley, a charismatic union leader who was the son of the party's founder and the island's prime minister during the last years of British rule.

Michael Manley was not only an able leader and a master orator, he carried with him a palpable moral authority as well, especially for spiritual young Rastas like Bob Marley. It was Michael Manley who, on a visit to Ethiopia, had invited Emperor Haile Selassie to make his state visit to Jamaica in 1966. When he arrived, Selassie presented Michael Manley with his imperial staff as a present. For the Rastas it was a sign. The emperor had chosen. The staff was dubbed the "Rod of Correction," and

95

when Manley brandished it in the air during his months of campaigning in the Jamaican hill villages, people would whoop with awe. "Joshua stick," they would call. They saw in him a modern Joshua, following in the footsteps of his Mosaic father, Norman Washington Manley, who had led the nation to independence.

Ten years later, Michael Manley would recall how he was first influenced by the Wailers. "I first knew Bob Marley in 1971, in the days of 'Trench Town Rock.' At this stage his music was still visceral protest carried on the wings of a relatively uncomplicated commentary on the ghetto. Throughout that year, he performed as part of a group of artists who traveled all over Jamaica with me while the party which I led prepared for the general elections of 1972. Until that time, my own political perceptions had reflected a mutually reinforcing marriage. On the one hand, there was the political theory which I had absorbed from my father as a youth and had developed into explicit socialist doctrine as a student in university. On the other hand, were some twenty years as an organizer and negotiator with the Jamaican trade union movement. To this was now added a vital and new ingredient. I could never pretend that the lyrics of the protest music which were the driving motivation of reggae taught me things that I did not know. From an intellectual point of view, they were confirmatory of all that I believed as a socialist, and have struggled against as a trade unionist. But I had not myself been born in the ghetto and was not personally part of that experience. Reggae music influenced me profoundly by deepening the element of emotional comprehension."

For several weeks Bob and Rita joined the "PNP Musical Bandwagon," playing from the back of a flatbed truck. Bob played guitar and sang, and when Rita was along she harmonized. Although most Rastafarian purists were shunning the elections and politics in general as the devil's work, Bob Marley had been impressed by Michael Manley's leadership, his ability to sympathize with and speak to the common Jamaican and his Ethiopianism. Some people said that when Manley and socialism took over in Jamaica, herb would be legalized and the repression of Rasta as an alternate spiritual nationality would cease. When Bob Marley finally jumped off the PNP Musical Bandwagon as the group was about to return to England, he was optimistic that things in Jamaica were about to change.

In the fall of 1971, Danny Sims summoned Bob Marley and the Wailers back to London. Johnny Nash's album *I Can See Clearly Now,* with four songs by Bob, had been released and was beginning to climb the

British charts. It looked like a smash hit. Sims wanted to sign Bob Marley to British CBS and rush-release "Reggae on Broadway" to coincide with Nash's soft-core popularization of the Jamaican sound. So the Wailers prepared to winter in London, with Bunny complaining about the cold, Peter complaining about Danny Sims and Bob looking hopefully to the future.

As the five Wailers left Jamaica for London, they realized that Jamaican culture was about to catch fire. The American pop singer Paul Simon was in Kingston recording a song called "Mother and Child Reunion" at Dynamic Studios, supervised by producer Leslie Kong and using the best session players in Jamaica. Not far away, in the streets of Bob's Ghost Town neighborhood, a movie was being shot by a young Jamaican named Perry Henzell. The working title of the film was "The Harder They Come," and it starred Bob Marley's old friend from the days at Beverley's, Jimmy Cliff.

Back in London, with his first single about to be released by CBS, Bob Marley was determined to see his career take off no matter what the sacrifice. The Wailers were again installed in the seedy, inexpensive hotel in Bayswater, on the northern edge of Hyde Park, where they had stayed earlier in the year. They rehearsed and worked on songs during the day, and spent the evenings pub-crawling with Johnny Nash and Danny Sims, checking the action at black clubs in South London like the A Train and Mr. Bee's in Peckham. Gradually they made contact with young fans in London's large West Indian community and, like thousands of Jamaican immigrants before them, began to feel more at home in the damp, sooty British capital. With Johnny Nash's "I Can See Clearly Now" firmly at the top of the British charts, Bunny became increasingly impatient and angry at having to sit back and wait while a black Yankee like Nash appropriated the Jamaican idiom and made money with it. In part to placate Bunny, Danny Sims hired a black Londoner from Trinidad, Brent Clarke, to be the Wailers' manager in London. The first thing Clarke did was to move them out of their hotel and into a small semidetached house in Neasden, with separate bedrooms and a kitchen where the group could prepare food that was more familiar to them than the greasy fish and chips and Indian cooking on which the Rasta Italists had been barely subsisting. Immediately the band's morale improved, and they began attracting other young black musicians and the subculture of girls, herbsmen and hangers-on that supported the scene. Bob and Peter adapted quickly to London life, acquiring local girl friends and enjoying their stature as brave soul rebels among the restive black youth of Notting Hill and Brixton. But Bunny was unhappy in England and remained withdrawn and meditative, reading the Bible and pining for Jean Watt, the beautiful woman who was waiting for him back in Jamaica.

By the end of 1971, Nash's *I Can See Clearly Now* album was number one all over the world. Nash and Sims had retooled the basic tracks recorded earlier in the year for the four songs Bob Marley had written for the album. "Stir It Up" now sounded overproduced to Bob, cluttered with horns, flutes and mushy string arrangements. "Guava Jelly" was a little less antiseptic, with Rabbit Bundrick's organ vamps and an aggressive, suggestive lyric. Another Marley song, "You Poured Sugar on Me," used the same chords as "Guava Jelly" and Bundrick's swelling organ to build an inoffensive ballad, while "Comma Comma" came off as easy-listening reggae—refined, polite, definitely not dangerous. Thanks in part to Bob Marley, Johnny Nash's sagging career had been given a huge boost.

But Bob Marley's own single, "Reggae on Broadway," although simultaneously released by CBS, bombed. Nobody in Nash's now-large audience knew what real reggae was; nobody knew how to dance to the new beat. CBS was devoting its promotional energies to Johnny Nash, and "Reggae on Broadway" (the B side was "Oh Lord I Got To Get There") was ignored. In all, it sold about three thousand copies. In an attempt to expand Nash's audience and find one for Marley, Sims convinced CBS to finance a three-week tour in November and December. For eighteen days Johnny Nash and Bob Marley toured seventy-two English high schools, playing four schools per day, just Nash, Marley and their acoustic guitars. The shows consisted of fifteen minutes of Bob's music, then fifteen minutes of Johnny Nash, followed by thirty minutes of questions. Although Bob was not wearing Rasta dreadlocks at that point, he spent much of his time telling the students about Haile Selassie and the repatriation of blacks to Africa.

When the exhausting road trip had finished, according to Danny Sims, Bob Marley was as popular in England as Johnny Nash. But "Reggae on Broadway" still failed to take off, and the Wailers were stranded in Neasden with no money when Sims and Nash ran off to New York to try to rescue Nash's album, which had stalled in America without their attention. With Danny Sims gone, the Wailers were without "visible means of support," and their passports were being held by the British Home Office over a dispute about the group's lack of work permits. The Wailers had no cash, no work and no return tickets to Jamaica. The thick English winter was upon them, Bunny was miserable, the group desperate.

In December 1971, Bob Marley played what he thought was the Wailers' last card. He walked into the Basing Street studios of Island Records and asked to see the boss, Chris Blackwell.

At that point, Chris Blackwell was probably the only person in the record business in a position to help Bob Marley and the Wailers. Not only was the young Anglo-Jamaican boss of Island Records the proprietor of the hottest independent record company in the world, but Blackwell had been following the Wailers' progress for years, from a distance, and harbored a shrewd, instinctive knowledge of the group's strengths and weaknesses. Eventually he would emerge as interpreter and translator of Bob Marley's prophetic music to the world at large.

Chris Blackwell was born in London in 1937. His Irish father was related to the Blackwell family that had founded the Crosse and Blackwell company. His mother was a Lindo, one of Jamaica's most esteemed Jewish families, descended from Sephardic refugees who had arrived in Jamaica in the 1600s in the flight from the cruelties of the Spanish Inquisition. Once in Jamaica, the Jewish merchant families emerged as middlemen between the buccaneers plying their trade on the Spanish Main and the British Crown, which purchased most of the pirated loot. In the late 1700s, the Lindo family had become wealthy selling rum and sugar, and were cattle ranchers on a vast scale.

Six months after his birth, Chris Blackwell was taken to Jamaica to be raised in the Lindo's enormous mansion on Waterloo Road, Kingston's most prestigious suburb. The house was called Terra Nova, a tropical fantasy of open verandas and formal reception rooms, stately gardens and a large azure swimming pool. The window of Chris's room on the second floor had a spectacular view of the mountains overlooking the plain of Kingston. Here Chris Blackwell grew up without siblings, almost alone, a sickly asthmatic child with few friends and a rich, secretive imagination.

When he was ten, Blackwell was sent back to England for his education. Four years later he was at Harrow, one of Britain's more prestigious public schools. He left in 1955, when he was seventeen, and returned to Jamaica, finished with his formal education. But the rich young playboy soon found himself back in London, sent by his family to study accountancy at the firm of Price Waterhouse so he could eventually return to Jamaica and enter the Lindos's many businesses. Blackwell's impatient mind lasted only a few months as an accountant, and instead he studied the arcane secrets of professional gambling. Blackwell played bridge, poker and blackjack in London clubs, played the ponies at Newbury and Ascot and bet on greyhound races at White City and Wembley. Later on, he would say that his skill at gambling when quite young was a better

education than the four years at Oxford for which he had been programmed. It was at the racetrack that Blackwell discovered the value of
money, at the betting tables of London clubs where he learned to bluff,
negotiate and win—skills required of any person to survive and dominate
in the shady world of the recording business.

By 1958, when Bob Marley had joined his mother Cedella in the
squalor of Trench Town, Chris Blackwell returned to Jamaica and took
his place in Jamaican society. He worked as aide-de-camp to Sir Hugh
Foot, the British governor-general of Jamaica, and sold real estate. Later
he taught waterskiing at a resort near Montego Bay, on Jamaica's north
coast. When he stopped enjoying whatever he was doing, he quit.

A few years previously Blackwell made his first contact with the people
usually shunned and feared by his lofty social strata—the Rastafarians. It
happened when he and some friends were following the desolate coast of
Hellshire, west of Kingston, in Blackwell's motorboat. The boat hit a
submerged reef and swamped. After Blackwell and his friends had swum
for shore, Blackwell left to find help. He followed the shore for hours
until he was ready to expire from exhaustion and thirst. Finally, in the
distance he saw a hut. When he drew closer, a dreadlocked Rastaman
looked out at him, and Chris Blackwell almost died from fright. "All you
ever heard was that Rastas were killers," he says. "All you heard was that
they were anti-white." But the Rasta gave Blackwell a drink of water and
a place to lie down for a few moments to regain his strength. Blackwell
collapsed instead into a deep sleep, and awoke hours later to find himself
being watched by six Rastas and a small dreadlocked boy. The Rastas fed
Blackwell and talked to him, preaching about Haile Selassie and reading
from the Bible the relevant passages relating to the divinity of the Ethiopian emperor. Then they took Blackwell back to Kingston. Only eight or
nine hours elapsed between the shipwreck and the eventual rescue of
Blackwell's friends, but Chris Blackwell had stepped into another world
altogether. From then on, he would view the Rastafarians with sympathy.

By 1959, Chris Blackwell had begun recording music in Jamaica. Early
that year he had hung around New York jazz clubs and immersed himself
in Miles Davis and John Coltrane. Back in Jamaica he heard a jazz combo
at the Half Moon Hotel, where he had been water-ski instructor, led by a
pianist from Bermuda named Lance Heywood. Blackwell quickly incorporated a small record company whose name, Island Records, was chosen
because of the success of Alec Waugh's 1957 novel, *Island in the Sun,* and
the subsequent movie. He recorded the group at the studios of radio
station RJR in Kingston, because there were no other recording studios

in town, and some weeks later released Island Records's first album, *Lance Heywood at the Half Moon.*

In 1960, a turn in the Lindo family fortunes necessitated the sale of Terra Nova, Blackwell's childhood home. The young producer was devastated that he was unable to save the house, and decided then to apply himself to his business so that his family would never endure such a humiliation again. Terra Nova was transformed into a hotel, lost to them forever.

In 1961, Island Records had its first hit: "Little Sheila" by Laurel Aitken went to number one in Jamaica. Blackwell's next single also went number one, and he plowed his profits of fifteen hundred dollars back into the business and opened an office in Kingston, with his Chinese girl friend answering the phones. Later that year Ian Fleming, who wrote many of his James Bond stories near Orcabessa in the parish of St. Mary, recommended Blackwell to be producer Harry Saltzman's factotum in Jamaica during the filming of *Dr. No.* Eventually Saltzman offered Blackwell a permanent job, but a fortune-teller advised Blackwell to stick with music.

Very little Jamaican popular music that wasn't mento or calypso had been recorded by the time Blackwell started out. His only early competition was from folklorist-turned-producer Edward Seaga and Clement Dodd. But then, in 1962, the Jamaican recording business burst into flower and dozens of young artists—Jimmy Cliff, the Maytals, the Wailers among others—began their careers. Almost overnight, competition between Coxsone, Duke Reid, Leslie Kong and King Edwards became fierce and cutthroat. Chris Blackwell, too much the gentleman to compete directly, opted out. Since he was selling more records to the growing West Indian immigrant community in England than he was in Jamaica, Blackwell chose London, and made deals with the other Kingston producers to be their representative and in some cases their licensee in Britain. In the summer of 1962, Island Records was established in an office in Knightsbridge, and the new company's first single—"Twist Baby" by Jamaican singer Owen Grey—sold out its first pressing of five hundred copies, all distributed to tiny black record shops in Brixton, Lewisham and sometimes Birmingham by the tireless Blackwell working out of the trunk of his Mini-Cooper. Best of all, he had no competition. Blackwell genuinely loved the Jamaican music he was selling, and the small enterprise earned enough so that he could almost ignore the early sixties London pop scene that was careening around him.

Chris Blackwell's big break came in 1964. Island had issued a single called "We'll Meet" by a Jamaican duo, Roy and Millie. The song had done good business. Blackwell searched out the singer, Millie Small, in Jamaica and flew her to London and gave her a song called "My Boy Lollipop" to record. Blackwell had discovered the song back in 1959 as a 78-rpm R & B record in a New York shop. He licensed Millie Small's bouncy ska version to the Phillips music conglomerate, and within a year the single had sold six million copies around the world. Blackwell now had his first star, and some real money. He appointed himself Millie Small's manager, and went on the road.

On a Millie Small tour of Midlands clubs in 1964, Chris Blackwell discovered one of her opening acts in Birmingham. The Spencer Davis Group had a fifteen-year-old lead singer with the voice of a whiskeyed-up blues belter from Memphis—Steve Winwood. Blackwell fell for the band, signed them to Island, licensed them again to Phillips and had his first English hit with "Keep on Runnin' " in 1965. Two years later the group had two worldwide hits with "Gimme Some Lovin' " and "I'm a Man." When the group broke up in 1968, Winwood formed a new band, Traffic. Putting all his marketing acumen behind the new group, Blackwell took his label out of the business of black music. Island became a rock company, eventually working with such English folk and rock musicians as John Martyn, Fairport Convention, Cat Stevens, Free, King Crimson, Jethro Tull and Emerson, Lake and Palmer.

By the time Bob Marley walked into Chris Blackwell's office in 1971, Blackwell was a millionaire from his white rock business and had all but ignored Jamaican music for five years. Jimmy Cliff was the only Jamaican signed to Island, but since 1967 he had been releasing records only on the Trojan label, which Blackwell had formed in partnership back in 1967. But if he had been focusing on rock music, Blackwell hadn't lost his feeling for great music from Jamaica. When he met with Bob Marley, Chris Blackwell knew exactly who he was talking to. Blackwell had been interested in Johnny Nash's progress, and told associates he had been interested in the Wailers for years but hadn't made an approach to the group because of their reputation as latent rude boys who wouldn't sign a contract.

When Nash and Sims left for the States, Brent Clarke, the young promo man from Trinidad, had gone to Island Records to look for work. Later he played Blackwell some of the demos the Wailers had cut for Sims, and Blackwell was said to have been impressed. When they finally met each other, Bob Marley reminded Chris Blackwell that ten years before Island had released Bob's first single, "One Cup of Coffee," in England as Leslie Kong's licensee. As it turned out, Bob Marley didn't really have to sell the Wailers to Chris Blackwell. Within days of their meeting, Blackwell had agreed to advance the band eight thousand pounds so the Wailers could return to Jamaica and record their first album for Island Records. Blackwell didn't seem to mind that the Wailers had contracts with Danny Sims. It was his style to worry about those kinds of problems only when they came up.

The Wailers' morale shot up when Blackwell agreed to back the band. The Wailers' entire career had been mismanaged and exploited, and now a white rock producer was taking a chance on them, assigning an unheard-of sum (although a mere pittance by rock standards) for the group to cut the rhythm and vocal tracks for their own album.

When the Wailers returned to Jamaica, they collected their Island advance from bandleader Byron Lee, whose Kingston bank had been the conduit through which Blackwell's money had been wired, and set about rebuilding their lives. Bunny, immensely relieved to be back home, left Trench Town and moved to the Rasta enclave at Bull Bay, about ten miles east of the city along the coastal road. This community was noted for its fresh fish and vegetables, and for the talented people in sports, music and the arts who were living there. Bob took some of his share and brought Rita and the children home from Delaware, where Rita had been working as a nurse. A new Tuff Gong record shack was set up at Beeston Street and Chancery Lane, and the Wailers began to rehearse. Bob and Rita had already decided to move out to Bull Bay after the album was recorded.

The recording sessions for the album that would be called *Catch a Fire* took place early in 1972. Up to then, reggae had been a music that existed primarily on 45-rpm singles. Reggae songs were one-shot concepts, interrelated only through common rhythm and attitudes among the musicians. But the European and American audiences that Blackwell wanted the Wailers to penetrate were accustomed to getting their music from albums on which ten or more tunes clicked together in a more sustained atmosphere. Chris Blackwell in effect had told Bob Marley to go back to Jamaica and make the first reggae *album,* which Blackwell would then transform into a record that could appeal to the rock fans who were his principal customers.

The sessions were held at three studios—Dynamic Sound, Harry J's and Randy's on the North Parade. The tracks mingled several familiar Wailers numbers that had previously been released in Jamaica with new songs designed to flesh out the densely packed themes of alienation and rebellion the Wailers were projecting—"Catch a Fire," "Kinky Reggae," "No More Trouble" and "Baby We've Got A Date." Various Kingston studio musicians rounded off the basic Wailers quintet. Bobbie Shakespeare played bass on "Concrete Jungle," while Tyrone Downie played the organ on the same song and on "Stir It Up." Veteran keyboardist Winston Wright also played organ, and Seeco supplied additional hand percussion on aketé drums. Several backing vocal tracks were also sung by Rita Marley and two friends, Marcia Griffiths and Judy Mowatt, who had been recruited when Peter and Bunny weren't around for a session.

As soon as the rhythm and vocal tracks were complete, Bob Marley was on a plane back to London, to overdub and mix the album with London session players. Guitarist Wayne Perkins, who had made his reputation at Muscle Shoals Studios, Alabama, supplied the sinuous rock guitar lines on "Concrete Jungle" and "Stir It Up." Rabbit Bundrick overlaid clavinet, electric piano and Moog synthesizer parts on most of the tracks. A percussionist named Chris Karen played tabla on "Concrete Jungle." Blackwell also artificially accelerated the Wailers' basic rhythms a beat, perhaps figuring that the slowish pulse of reggae would turn off the rock crowd. Blackwell and Marley spent months fine tuning the album, postponing the actual release date until the very end of the year. Johnny Nash, Danny Sims and CBS had to be dealt with first. Fortunately for the group, entangled with Danny Sims by five years of contracts and agreements, Blackwell knew that in the Wailers he had a winner, a good investment.

The Sims/Nash team was back in London by then, preparing for a short tour to promote *I Can See Clearly Now,* which had finally hit in America, selling almost two million copies. Bob Marley met with Sims and agreed to open the shows, backed by Nash's touring band (the Sons of the Jungle), singing "Reggae on Broadway." Bob appeared on tour wearing tight pants and an Afro hairstyle and sang like James Brown. At this point Sims thought the Wailers were still in his pocket; he was trying to convince CBS to release another Marley single and began negotiating for a Wailers tour of England. The rest of the band was flown to London and installed in a studio, where they rehearsed in preparation for a tour that was often delayed and postponed. When rumors spread through Anglo-Jamaican London that the Wailers were rehearsing, a couple of hundred young West Indians would show up to jam the space, dancing when the band locked into its signature mesmerizing groove. Finally, backstage at Johnny Nash's London concert, the three Wailers confronted Sims with their desire to go with Island. Sims stalled the young musicians, explaining that he had already given CBS five tracks toward the Wailers' album and persuaded the company to release a sequel to "Reggae on Broadway." Sims and Nash again decamped almost immediately for New York, where Nash's American label was panicky. Nash's version of Marley's "Stir It Up" had been released and was failing to perform as well as "I Can See Clearly Now," which had been number one for five weeks. At the same time, CBS sent their lawyer over to Island to remind Blackwell that the Wailers were signed to CBS through Danny Sims. The document the CBS lawyer produced was a photocopy of a typed contract half a page long. Blackwell was reluctant to face a lawsuit from Cayman Music. So he suggested that Marley fly to New York to ask Danny Sims how much he wanted to release the band to Island.

Danny Sims had failed Bob Marley but, in fairness, it was not for lack of trying. Sims explains the situation very simply: "What happened was that Johnny broke in the U.S., and Bob didn't." CBS was trying to back off from releasing another Bob Marley record in England, and so when Bob appeared backstage at Nash's New York show and told Sims he wanted his contract back, Sims listened to what Marley had to say. Sims told Marley that the Wailers owed CBS for their advances and expenses, but offered to release the group if they signed a new songwriters contract with Cayman Music. Sims also wanted Island to pay five thousand pounds for the Wailers' contract and grant Sims a two-percent override on the Wailers' first six albums. Early the next morning, Marley phoned Sims's demands to Chris Blackwell, and Blackwell agreed to the terms. Island had the Wailers. Danny Sims had the Wailers' all-important publishing.

While he was in New York, Bob linked up with Traffic, his fellow Island artists, who were on the New York stop of their last American tour. Traveling with Traffic was Dickie Jobson, an old friend of Blackwell's from Jamaica who worked alongside Blackwell for Island. Jobson invited Marley to a party for the band after the New York show. The scene at the band's suite at the Windsor Hotel on West 58th Street that night was right out of "Midnight Ravers." Groupies were in hot competition with drug dealers for the musicians' attention. Traffic's Jim Capaldi was jamming with some friends, record bizz types were shouting at each other and Bob Marley sat quietly in a corner, taking it all in.

Eventually a young New York artist and harmonica player named Lee Jaffe struck up a conversation with Bob. Jaffe was a friend of Capaldi's from London, where they had met while working on a film with a beautiful Jamaican actress named Esther Anderson, who was also at the party. Bob Marley shared a joint with Lee Jaffe and eventually took out his guitar; Jaffe produced his harmonica and started to play the blues. Bob was a sucker for blues music, and began to jam. A friendship was begun that night that was to last the rest of Bob's life. For the next three years, Lee Jaffe went almost everywhere with Bob, road managing the earliest

Wailers "tours" in America and eventually becoming the only white musician to play with Bob Marley and the Wailers.

Lee Jaffe spent the next few days helping Bob and Dickie Jobson buy new equipment for the Wailers. When it was time for Bob to return to Kingston, he invited Jaffe to come down and check out the scene. Dickie offered a place to stay, and Esther Anderson was going too, so Lee decided to see for himself what these Wailers were all about. He stepped into the tropic glare of the Kingston airport a few days later, and soon found Bob Marley at the Wailers' new rehearsal studio, an outbuilding at the back of a large mansion that Chris Blackwell had just bought at 56 Hope Road. The big pink manse, now rechristened "Island House," was in the same suburban Kingston neighborhood as Jamaica House, the prime minister's official residence, and it was ironically only yards from where Norval Marley and his family had lived. Now Blackwell was turning the pink house into Island Records' Jamaican headquarters and had given Bob Marley the run of the place. Since Bob was used to living in his studio from the Coxsone days, he eventually took over Hope Road with his entourage of reggae musicians and Trench Town constituents. The neighbors were unhappy, and the police often came around to sniff for ganja. But by then Bob Marley knew how to talk to cops, and there was no trouble.

Soon after Jaffe arrived in Jamaica, Chris Blackwell chartered an old DC-3 and the Island circle set out for Carnival in Trinidad. Lee Jaffe went along, joining Bob, Chris, Dickie Jobson, Jim Capaldi and Esther Anderson. All the seats had been taken out of the plane, and the party was spread out on cushions all over the deck. The plane island-hopped all the way to Trinidad; when Blackwell noticed a nice beach somewhere below, he'd tell the pilot to land so everybody could swim.

Back in Jamaica, Lee Jaffe settled into accompanying Bob Marley on his daily routine. Rita Marley had birthed Bob's second son, Stephen Marley, and left their Ghost Town home for a little house at Bull Bay in early 1972. Bob was alternately living with her and sleeping at 56 Hope Road, where he was carrying on a torrid affair with Esther Anderson. Bob and Esther had started out as friends (she had been linked romantically with Marlon Brando and Blackwell), but a strong attraction soon drew them together and developed into something heavier. Bob also spent occasional nights with "the mothers of his babies," as the Jamaican euphemism goes. By 1970 one of Bob's Trench Town girl friends, Pat Williams, had borne him a son, named Robbie, and another, Janet, was then pregnant with another of Bob's sons, to be named Rohan Marley at birth. During his second stay in London, Bob had impregnated a black

English girl, also named Janet, who would have a daughter called Karen Marley. Bob told friends that he could always tell one of his children by its mouth.

If Bob had spent the night at Hope Road, his days would begin just before sunrise. As dawn broke over Long Mountain, someone would pack and light a chalice full of herb, and pass it among the waking brethren. Skill Cole was back from a season playing for Santos Brazil, one of the top soccer teams in the world, and he had Bob and friends in training for weeks at a time, subsisting on little but fresh juices, hard running and football. As Rastas, they saw their bodies as temples that should be kept strong and unprofaned by processed and forbidden foods like meat, salt and shellfish. The group would then pile into Bob's Ford Capri or Lee's rented car and drive to Bull Bay for an hour of running on the beach, Bob and Skill in front. Some days they ran up a long hillside to a spectacular waterfall at Cane River. Bob quickly shed his steaming clothes down to his striped briefs and plunged into the icy water. The young lions would leisurely shampoo their locks in the clean spring, spending long luxuriant moments rinsing their heads in the falling water. Bob usually looked in on Rita (who was rebuilding her house by herself, hauling beams and pouring concrete) and the children before leaving for downtown Kingston and the Tuff Gong record shop on Beeston Street, where Bob could hang out, check up on sales and the downtown reggae scene. When the Wailers had signed with Island, they had retained the rights to all their records in the Caribbean, so as not to depend too heavily on problematic foreign royalties for daily survival. The Tuff Gong record shop stocked dozens of obscure singles by the Wailers, Bob Marley, Peter Tosh, Bunny Livingston, Rita Marley, Family Man and all their permutations. The shop was the main Wailers hangout and office, and the source of a fairly constant trickle of petty cash. A food shop next door sold box lunches of sprats and rice, and Bob would usually eat and drink a couple of jellies before collaring Skill and driving over to Trench Town in search of fresh herb to smoke.

Uptown, at Island House, Bob Marley was still an unwanted outsider. But driving slowly through Trench Town to avoid the flocks of ghetto children darting around the car, Bob Marley progressed like a hero returning home. Everyone on the street knew him and called out to him, and while he was bartering for herb in some yard, men and boys would line up to shake his hand or ask for a few shillings. The next stop was usually the ball field at Boy's Town, where Bob and Skill played soccer almost every day, as Bob had done as a boy. Skill Cole was like a god in Jamaica then, around the time he played for Santos, and when he teamed with the fast passing of Bob, their pickup football squads were usually unbeatable. By the time the game had finished it was usually four o'clock, and time for daily rehearsal back at Hope Road. Island had a phone and a secretary working there, and after the day's crucial Wailers business had been transacted, it was hit-me-with-music for the rest of the evening. The Wailers would rehearse until midnight and beyond, and the harsh red coal of the ganja chalice would glow brightly until Bob slept. Four or five hours later, at dawn, someone would fire up the chalice again, and a new day would go through its cycle.

When the Wailers weren't rehearsing, or when Bob wanted or needed a few days away from the smoky atmosphere of Kingston, they drove up to St. Ann to hang out at Nine Miles. Omeriah's place was now "Auntie's house," and Bob liked to go there and relax, cook I-tal food and take long hikes through the deep mountain bush to the herb fields. Bob would walk through the waving stands of marijuana, whose bright green leaves seemed to glow in contrast to the lush dark chlorophyll of the St. Ann hillsides. The days at Nine Miles restored Bob Marley's sense of place, his roots, his grandfather, his *home*. For hours he sat on hilltops, reading the Bible aloud to Skill or Lee or whoever was about. His favorite book then was the Psalms, and as he read the verses his features would assume the same mask of concentration and astral travel that they assumed when Bob took the stage and sang. Nine Miles was Bob's anchor. In Jamaica, the worst that can be said about a person was that he didn't come from anyplace.

On the day appointed to return to Kingston, the group would drive off before sunrise, as the morning mists covered the dirt roads of the parish like a blanket, and the sound of the motor startled sleeping cattle egrets into flight.

It was no accident that the Wailers' first album, *Catch a Fire,* which effectively launched the era of reggae music, should have coincided with the election of Michael Manley in 1972 as the new prime minister of Jamaica. For just as *Catch a Fire* changed Jamaican music and helped launch it into the cultural arenas of the world, the election of a socialist government transformed Jamaica from a sleepy banana republic to a struggling, morally preoccupied nation at war with its own history.

At 56 Hope Road, at Bull Bay, in Trench Town, the election was the hottest topic of the year. It seemed the whole island was ready for a change to the visionary politics of sharing that Michael Manley espoused. "When I look at my people," Manley cried, "my heart *bleed.*" The island's best singers weighed in behind the PNP: Delroy Wilson's "Better

Must Come" was the campaign's theme song; Clancy Eccles's "Rod of Correction," Max Romeo's "Let the Power Fall on I," Junior Byles's "Beat Down Babylon" and Ken Lazarus's "Hail the Man" all proclaimed the rise of a Jamaica yearning for equal rights and justice. But for all the militancy of the reggae musicians, JLP prime minister Hugh Shearer's government countered with strict censorship. All pro-PNP songs were banned from radio stations JBC and RJR. The Wailers were included because of their rebellious associations and because Bob had played on the PNP Musical Bandwagon the year before. The ban was so effective that Tuff Gong didn't bother to release any records in Jamaica in 1972. When the general elections were held that autumn, Michael Manley had won the largest majority in Jamaican parliamentary history, marred only slightly by Jamaica's traditional election-eve violence. It was the beginning of a new order in old Jamaica.

Catch a Fire was released by Island Records in England in December 1972, and in America the following month, January 1973. Dark, ominous, threatening, the album was a rebel's indictment of slavery and colonialism, a celebration of reggae trance and sexuality. Chris Blackwell had taken the bottom-heavy Jamaican rhythm tracks and given the music a new "top" with layers of rock guitar and synthesizer. The album's package was an expensive die-cut cardboard Zippo lighter that seemed to burst into flame when opened, emblematic of the bitter protest contained in Bob Marley and Peter Tosh's lyrics.

Catch a Fire didn't catch on at first; the album was released in America through Capitol Records, which thought reggae was sheer savagery and allowed only minimal promotion. Since *The Harder They Come* was not yet in general release, reggae and Jamaican culture were alien commodities to the rock audience. Nevertheless, the first reviews were excellent in England, more familiar with West Indian music, and good in America, where *Rolling Stone* critic Rob Houghton opined that the record had "a mature, fully realized sound with a beautiful lyric sensibility that turns well-known stylistics into a fresh, vibrant music." Despite the lack of crucial promotion, *Catch a Fire* sold a modest fourteen thousand copies that first year.

Most important, *Catch a Fire* changed reggae's direction. Years later, the Anglo-Jamaican dub poet Linton Kwesi Johnson wrote that the album's effect was such that "a whole new style of Jamaican music has come into being. It has a different character, a different sound . . . what I can only describe as 'International Reggae.' It incorporates elements from popular music, internationally: rock and soul, blues and funk. These elements facilitated a breakthrough on the international market . . . Instead of concentrating exclusively on a bottom-heavy sound with the emphasis on drum and bass, you had on this record more of a 'toppy' mix, a lighter sound. The emphasis is more on the guitar and other fillers. On no other Jamaican reggae recording . . . was such a clear-cut attempt made to incorporate the modern electronic sounds of metropolitan music." Perhaps *Catch a Fire* was the first Anglo-Jamaican reggae record. Its stereo engineering made the other Jamaican records—all monaural—sound tinny and crude.

At first, *Catch a Fire* had more of an impact upon the watchful and restive music media than on the public. Many writers and music fans were repelled by the excess of the glitter-rock musicians; people wanted to dance again, and Bob gave them a new beat and lyrics that wouldn't rot their minds. The great heroes of the rock era were dead or retired; as they faded from fashion, Bob Marley—the Rasta rebel street poet—became more attractive. Reggae was something wholesome and true, something that one could believe in again. *Catch a fire, you're gonna get burned!*

With the release of their first album in 1973, the Wailers became a professional rock band, with all the responsibilities and expectations of any other pro band on the Euro-American circuit. In return for financial backing and huge amounts of artistic control, Island Records expected "The Wailers" (as they were billed on *Catch a Fire)* to tour frequently to support album sales, and record new albums within a specified time to meet the demand for their music. As soon as *Catch a Fire* came out, Chris Blackwell told Bob Marley that he wanted another album from the Wailers as soon as possible and that Island would finance a tour of the United Kingdom in the spring and American clubs that summer and autumn. Bob and the band rehearsed songs for the new album, and auditioned for a keyboard player to take on the road. Once a keyboard player was hired, the Wailers became a six-piece group.

His name was Earl Lindo, born in Kingston in 1953. Everyone called him "Wire" (pronounced "Wya"); all the musicians called him a genius. He was the keyboard player for a Jamaican show band called Now Generation, and he was *hot,* with a brooding, organic melodic sensibility that easily matched the Wailers. He was replacing the juvenile Tyrone Downie, the Wailers' unpaid keyboard player and fan, who had become disillusioned with the Wailers and fled for the security of a North Coast hotel band up in Ocho Rios, JoJo Bennett and the Fugitives. At first Wire didn't mean to join the Wailers. He took a leave from Now Generation to travel as a hired keyboard man for the Wailers until their next album was recorded and for the duration of their tours. It wasn't as if he were really *joining* the band.

Rehearsals took place in the Wailers' quarters behind Island House. By then Perry Henzell's *The Harder They Come* had opened. A brilliant evocation of a famous Jamaican gunman of the late 1940s, the film starred Jimmy Cliff as the bandit Rhygin', who in real life was shot down by police outside Kingston harbor in 1948. The film's sound track, released by Chris Blackwell's specialty label, Mango, anthologized classic rocksteady hits by Desmond Dekker, the Maytals, the Melodians and Jimmy Cliff. The soundtrack was even more important than *Catch a Fire* in advancing Jamaican music around the world. Based on its success, Blackwell signed Toots and the Maytals, for whom there was an international demand based on "Sweet and Dandy" from the sound track, and was also starting to work with the Heptones, Lee Perry, an old ska group called Justin Hinds and the Dominoes and a new group of uptown Rasta boys who were calling themselves Third World.

The working title of the Wailers' second album was *Reincarnated Souls,* from one of the new tunes Bunny had written. The pattern of trusted old songs besides new, more immediate broadsides was continued from the *Catch a Fire* sessions. Recording at Harry J's comfortable uptown studio (financed in part by Chris Blackwell so Island's Jamaican artists would have decent recording facilities), the Wailers quickly cut new versions of old hits: "Put It On," "Small Axe" and "Duppy Conqueror." The band also cut three new songs by Bunny ("Reincarnated Souls," "Hallelujah Time" and "Pass It On"), one by Peter Tosh ("One Foundation") and a soulful, dramatic burra meditation called "Rasta Man Chant," with which the group was planning to open upcoming shows in England. These peaceful, almost hymnlike songs contrasted sharply with the angry and vengeful new material that Bob Marley was bringing the Wailers, perhaps foreshadowing the philosophical differences that would later dissolve the spiritual glue that held the group together. Songs like "I Shot the Sheriff," "Burnin' and Lootin' " and "Get Up, Stand Up" (cowritten with Peter Tosh) prefigured a hard and fearless new sound for reggae, very much in tune with the militant socialist "Camelot" mentality that prevailed in Jamaica during the early years of Michael Manley's government.

It was at Countryman's place on the beach that "I Shot the Sheriff" was born. Bob and his entourage had taken to hanging out at Countryman's after Dickie Jobson had discovered the young Rasta fisherman/herbsman while searching for locations to shoot commercials. Not only was Countryman the most righteous dread around, but he was said to produce lightning bolts on command and grew the sweetest ganja—"goatshit" it was called—to be found near Kingston. One of Countryman's favorite pastimes in those days was to swim out to sea as far as he could, just for the sheer gamble of seeing whether he could make it back to shore alive. It was Countryman's wild life-force that appealed to Bob Marley, who liked to come out with his guitar, light the chalice with his friends and work on songs. On the day that "I Shot the Sheriff" was born, Bob, Skill Cole and Lee Jaffe were singing the song and laughing with delight when two enormous fat girls waddled up the beach. As Bob sang out "I Shot the Sheriff" and Skill and Lee roared back, "but I didn't shoot no deputy," the two fat girls started to dance and gyrate. Bob knew he had a *big* hit.

Recording at Harry J's was an easygoing affair for the Wailers, who didn't have to worry about studio time anymore. Bob sat around for hours, almost naked in the tropic afternoon, rolling spliffs the size and shape of an ice cream cone. Between songs the play would get physical, Bob and Skill wrestling and slap-fighting around the yard. There was a constant parade of hangers-on, including an older disc jockey who provoked the infamous Marley glare when he asked Bob if he could watch him record.

"Cho," spat Bob, a Jamaican negative. "Me nuh wan' ya fe stand 'round an' *watch* I."

The man stammered that he didn't want to stare at Bob, but Marley got there first.

"It look like ya wan' find out where I head rest. Ya gwan round all kinda corner tryin' fe smart me to find out where I head rest. Just come and ask me where I head rest. If ya wan' know where I head rest, I head rest with *Jah.*"

The following month, the Wailers packed their instruments, sweaters and overcoats and took off for London and their first tour. On the way, Bob went to Delaware to see his mother. Although Bob had worn his hair in modified dreadlocks twice before, he had worn an Afro style for the past three years. So when he got to Delaware, Cedella was surprised to see Bob's hair pent up in a red, green and gold tam, the colors of the flag of Ethiopia. At the kitchen table, Bob smiled and said, "Momma, look at this." He pulled off his tam and a new crown of sprouting locks popped out, kinky as kinky can be.

"You growing it again?" Cedella asked, still dubious.

"Yes, Momma."

"Nes', you locksing up forever now?"

"Yes, Momma."
Bob Marley never cut his hair again.

When the Wailers arrived in London in April 1973 to begin a three-month tour of the British hinterland, they found a surprise waiting for them. London record shops were carrying a Wailers album, *African Herbsman* on the Trojan label, that the group knew nothing about. The best of the Wailers records cut for Lee Perry, including "Trench Town Rock," had apparently been sold by Scratch to Lee Goptal, the Anglo-Indian accountant who had founded Trojan in partnership with Chris Blackwell. Goptal and Blackwell had parted ways the year before, with Goptal retaining Trojan. The Wailers now found their music a pawn in a businessman's game. Island may have had the Wailers, but Goptal and Lee Perry wanted a piece of the action too. And they got it, partly because *African Herbsman* was a brilliant album of essential early Wailers. When *African Herbsman* became available in America, its hypnotic allure captivated many listeners who had passed over *Catch a Fire* the first time around. For some Wailers fans, the power of *African Herbsman* has never been equaled.

The new six-piece Wailers began a grueling ninety-day tour of British cinemas and black dance halls at a London club called The Greyhound on Fulham Road. Playing two shows a night, the band was ragged in the early dates, perhaps because Wire and the new arrangements were just beginning to jell. Then the Wailers hit provincial England in a tiny van without even a road manager, carrying and setting up their instruments themselves. Wire Lindo tuned the bass and the other two guitars before the shows. The group spent a week playing black clubs in Birmingham, in England's industrial Midlands, and eventually got as far as Belfast, where they played before a shocked and subdued pub audience that had never even heard any kind of West Indian music before. Afterward, Peter Tosh remembers, people came backstage to say how much they liked the band.

By the time the Wailers returned to London, the musicians had tightened into a crack reggae-rock band but were on the verge of disintegrating from the rigor of touring on a low budget and lack of familiar nourishment. Bunny in particular was suffering from depression brought on by lack of food. A strict Rasta I-talist who forbade himself any processed food, Bunny would fast for days on the road, and would often go without sleep as well. Relations between the three original Wailers were strained, with both Peter and Bunny complaining of the dominant role that Bob Marley had assumed, fully backed by his friend Chris Blackwell.

In London, the Wailers were hot. Island Records booked them into a super-cool club called the Speakeasy as a media showcase for the band, and the Wailers delivered blistering, stop-out performances that turned the chic club into a steamy dance in Trench Town. On May 20, they played the BBC television program "Old Grey Whistle Test," doing "Concrete Jungle" and "Stop That Train." Bob stood in the middle of the stage set, wearing leather pants and a sweater, his hair just turning to locks, strapped into a Telecaster. Bunny was on the right, in striped pants and his trademark knitted Rasta vest, alternately playing akete drums and timbales with brushes. Peter stood on the left, a tam pulled tight over his head, eyes hidden by shades, concentrating on his nervous, rhythmic guitar tick. Bob provided the visual focus, "rocking back and forth like a hobbyhorse" according to the *New Musical Express*'s reviewer.

During the following week, the Wailers gave an extraordinary live concert at the BBC's Paris Theatre, which was broadcast as part of the "Top Gear" pop music series. Performing on the British radio network for the first time, the Wailers were on their best behavior, and the performance emerged as a perfect jewel, almost "chamber reggae" in the band's precision and attention to detail. After a well-meaning but fumbling compere, Peter Drummond, introduced the group to raucous whistles and applause from the Wailers' loyal West Indian claque, Bob said thank you and the group clicked into the show-opener, "Rastafarian Chant." The band was nervous and Bunny's opening drumbeat was tentative, but then the Barrett brothers synched in and the angelic Wailers harmony rang out: *Said I hear the words of the Rasta man seh/Babylon your throne gone down gone down/Babylon your throne gone down.* After three minutes and fifteen seconds of harmony, the Wailers were cut off and the compere began his between-song patter. "That was a chant, which is sort of a roots song for the Wailers, to do with a cult which is Rasta Faria [sic] which a lot of West Indians are turning to, which was extremely popular in the 1920s. Rasta meaning 'head,' Faria meaning 'creator.' This next number is on their current album, *Catch a Fire,* composed by Bob Marley. It's called 'Slave Driver.' " Carlie Barrett tapped out the opening beats, and a subdued version followed, driven by Tosh's cruelly chopping guitar and Wire's vivid, passionate organ breaks. When the number was through, the compere gently urged the crowd to dance, and the party was under way. A great rendition of "Stop That Train" was next, with Tosh delivering his strongest singing of the tour over the breathless harmonies of Bunny and Bob. The Wailers' vaunted harmonies were again on display in the dramatic a cappella choral intro to "No More Trouble," which segued into a hard-rocking groove as soon as the rhythm section

114

kicked in. Tosh followed this with an improvised lyric on "400" Years": *Won't you come with me/You're black and you're proud/So you got to be free,* as the band supplied impeccable dub on the song's coda. *Look how long . . . 400 years!* Now the intensity of the set was starting to really build. "Midnight Ravers" was a bass/dub showpiece, six minutes of apocalyptic imagery, the "music of stampede" invading the staid precincts of the BBC. "Stir It Up" seemed even more of a simmering sex litany when colored with Tosh's obscene wah-wah guitar solo on top of the instrumental passage. "Concrete Jungle" followed fast, Carlie rushing the beat a little after a sharp snare intro. Wire made a mistake halfway through the song, starting his solo halfway through the second chorus. Bob shot Wire an evil look and killed the song early, going right into the Wailers' new clarion call from their forthcoming album, "Get Up Stand Up." The version was pure 1973 Wailers, brimming with tension, never giving up the fight. The compere announced the last number, and the audience protested vehemently. "Kinky Reggae," the story of looking for herb in Piccadilly Circus, finished an entrancing set. Backstage after the show, Bob Marley got hot with Wire, who had blown a passage in "Concrete Jungle." Always the perfectionist, Bob Marley didn't like mistakes.

Three months after they arrived in England, the Wailers headed home. Everybody was exhausted and in bad shape. Peter and Bunny had lost weight, Wire and Carlie were acting strange and Family Man kept whatever was bothering him to himself, as usual. Only Bob seemed to thrive, and why not? He had a new English girl friend and increasing control over the Wailers and his future. As soon as their plane touched the ground of Jamaica, Bunny left the band. He would never tour with the Wailers again.

Back in Jamaica, Bob returned briefly to his familiar life, living intermittently with Rita and the children, hanging out with Skill and the boys at Tuff Gong on Beeston Street and Island House, visiting the mothers of his children, playing football, rehearsing for a brief North American tour. Immediately there was a crisis when Bunny announced that he wouldn't go to America, that his future as a Wailer would include only recording and performances in Jamaica. Bunny hated airplanes and had vowed never to fly again. Bob and Peter conferred on the situation and decided to ask their harmony teacher, Joe Higgs, to go on tour to sing Bunny's ethereal high harmony parts. Higgs said yes immediately, and joined the rehearsals behind Island House.

At this point the Wailers were operating without a manager. The group was dependent on Chris Blackwell for the things a manager usually provides—recording supervision, artistic direction and finding the band work so the musicians' children could eat. Blackwell knew that the Wailers had to make a few key showcase performances in the States in order to support *Catch a Fire,* so Lee Jaffe was flown to New York and installed in a suite at the Windsor Hotel. Lee took a copy of *Catch a Fire* over to Max's Kansas City on Park Avenue South, and persuaded New York's premier pop showcase to book the Wailers for the second week of July 1973, as opening act for a new young troubadour from New Jersey named Bruce Springsteen. Then he called Paul's Mall, a jazz club in Boston, and booked the Wailers for the first week of July at one thousand dollars a week for the band. Gradually other dates began to fill in, and the Wailers had a little tour. Island Records picked up the tour's expense as part of the promotion campaign the company was preparing to launch.

The Wailers went out again as a six-piece, Joe Higgs subbing for Bunny. Higgs recalls his involvement:

"The tour was pending, but something went down between Bob, Bunny, Peter and Island Records that I don't know. Bunny refused to tour, and realizing that it was really something in the air hanging for Bob, he ask me to fill in for Bunny. So I went along in 1973, the first North American tour the Wailers went.

"It was the first Jamaican band to go on tour to expose our Jamaican music. Our first major acceptance came from Boston. We toured from east to west, north to south in the States. We went to California, Chicago, New York, all those places. We went to Lexington, Kentucky. We went to Tampa, Florida. We went to Cambridge in Massachusetts, and Pittsfield—a whole itinerary that a lot of people have never been to in the reggae circuit.

"At first the audience showed mixed emotions . . . it was something they weren't ready to accept immediately. It was like reminding them of something. And we noticed it was a ninety-five percent white audience most of the way. Even though we were playing for capacity, we were concerned with the composition of the audience we had seen on tour.

"The tour was hard work. We had to clear our own luggage, and pack our own instruments, because we had to be very economical. It was an economical tour to promote *Catch a Fire.* And Bob Marley was very inspirational to me, because I remembered how we used to sing in Trench Town, when he would show what he could do by singing for seven or eight hours a day, yunno, stopping to eat, stopping to smoke and returning to sing again. And on tour he did two hour concerts, like two shows per night, yunno, with just an hour rest between shows . . . I was satisfied to see that he was so strong on tour, capable of doing two shows a night for three nights straight."

Bob in Battersea Park, 1975. *Adrian Boot*

George Harrison visits Bob at the Roxy, Los Angeles, 1975. *Island Records*

Bob Marley and the I-Threes (Judy Mowatt, Rita Marley and Marcia Griffiths), 1976. *Kim Gottlieb.*

David "Ziggy" Marley fronts for his father, 1976. *David Melhado/Island Records.*

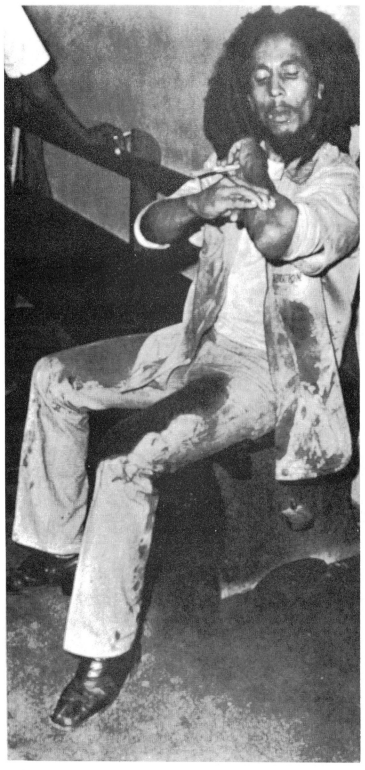

Bob checks his wounds after the shooting at Hope Road, December 3, 1976.

Clive Williams, Jamaica Daily News.

A pensive Bob at Hope Road with his ring, 1978. *Adrian Boot.*

Peter Tosh joins Bob for "Get Up, Stand Up," the encore of a Wailers concert at Burbank, California, 1978.

Bob at a press conference in Paris, 1978. *Phonogram*

Bob consults his Bible while on tour, 1979. *Island Records*

Bob at Hope Road. *Frank Spooner Pictures*

Cindy Breakspeare with her son Damian.
Frank Spooner Pictures

The soccer-addicted Bob
enjoying his daily habit.
Frank Spooner Pictures

At Paul's Mall in Boston, the Wailers drew packed houses every night. The ultrahip all-white audience yelled standard Rasta salutations like "Ites" and "I-rie" up to the bandstand. The opening act, the rock band Orleans, were rabid Wailers fans and staked out their own seats as soon as their set was over. For those early American club audiences, the Wailers shows were like astral transport to Uranus. As they gradually learned to identify with Jamaican youth culture—trance music, ganja, rebellion— they were sucked in by the relentless spiritual tug of the Wailers' reggae chop.

A week later at Max's Kansas City, opening for Bruce Springsteen, the Wailers threw down another blistering performance before a nonchalant audience of Springsteen fans. Playing three sets a night on the weekend, they opened with the new version of "Put It On," whose old fabric was stretched to its limit by the whacking, almost drummed rhythm guitar licks. The sound system was terrible, and although Carlie was hot and prominent, Family Man was inaudible, drowned out by Wire's cheesy-sounding organ. Even with the jabbering crowd and distorted blats of electronic feedback, the band hit a fast, rocking reggae groove by the time it led into "Slave Driver." Bob's singing was threatening and direct, without the cunning vocal embellishments of later years. Gradually, the relentless Wailers rhythm section shut up the nervous audience, and by the end of the set Bob stood immobile in the spotlight, one hand pressed to his head as he sang, and even the waitresses had stopped hassling the customers and were staring, openmouthed. The shows were all like that for the duration of that first Wailers tour, which finished at the Matrix Club in San Francisco early in August.

Back in Boston, writer James Isaacs visited the band in their motel room, and captured the ambience of the Wailers on tour, vintage 1973: "In the minuscule lobby a small, somewhat frayed desk clerk directs us to the second floor. The door opens before we can knock. It is Lee, a long-haired young white New Yorker who is the road manager. He ushers us into another land.

"The air inside the suite, sticky and as thick as stew, is an olfactory collage of heavy *ganja* smoke, fish being boiled in the kitchenette, last night's incense, watermelon and bathwater. The Wailers are staying here, Lee says, because there is the kitchenette and they eat *Jamaican* food.

"It is 3:30 in the afternoon on the Wailers' second day in Boston. And Aston 'Family Man' Barrett, the bassist, is lying soundlessly on the floor, his head resting against a guitar case. It is difficult to tell whether he is napping, *incommunicado* or just stoned, for his ever-present shades shield his eyes from the visitors with their tape recorders and notepads. His brother 'Charlie,' the drummer with whom he stirs up the lascivious reggae meter, is in front of the kitchenette stove preparing a kind of fish stew. He wears a pin with Haile Selassie's picture on it. Like the others in the band, he is a Rasta.

"Wire, the newest and youngest Wailer, sits at a table, on which there is a watermelon and a cabbage, while Peter MacIntosh plays the chicken-scratch shuffle through a cigar-box amp. In the middle of the room Bob Marley, 28, sits contemplatively. He wears only a striped bikini and the ends of his tangled, fleecy hair are still wet from the tub."

"Does Marley consider his songs to be political?"

"It is not really political, yunno. Is reality and fantasy. Is right and wrong. Material vanity mek people suffer most. The good suffer for the bad. Is respect we tryin' to teach.

"These are the last days," Marley continues. "Signs are there. President exposed!"

"Children havin' children," Peter intercedes.

"You can get it from reality, mon," says Marley. "Reality, what is *real*. Dat what we're teachin'."

"Rastafari not a culture, it's reality of life," Bob explains. "Our god is a living man, yunno? The Bible tell you, black King of Kings, Lord of Lords. I can't pass that, yunnowhaImean? If I see that in the Bible, I know it's true!"

Many hard-core Jamaican fans of the Wailers, who felt that *Catch a Fire*'s murky gloss represented a sellout to a Babylonian music cartel, were relieved when the Wailers' second album was released in October 1973. The album was retitled *Burnin'* when Bunny's "Reincarnated Souls" track was scrapped from the LP and issued as the B-side of the "Concrete Jungle" single that Island released in England to coincide with the spring tour. *Burnin'* had much more of a rootsy Jamaican sound—organic, I-tal, more acoustic and "wooden." Reflecting the differences among its musicians, the album presented a mixed message: Bob's neo-rude protest anthems verses Bunny's paeans to the grandeur of Rastafarian theology. It was two sides of the same coin. The title song, "Burnin' and Lootin'," was inspired by the new political wars that were beginning to develop in the slum neighborhoods of Kingston as PNP socialism tightened its control. Wire's dark organ and Tosh's guitar describe a people under curfew, confronting "uniforms of brutality." The song shows the cleansing side of street violence. *Burnin' and a-lootin' tonight/Burnin' all pollution tonight/Burnin' all illusions tonight*. In the end, for the people of the ghetto, there is only despair and illusions going up in flame. The album finished with the burra/akete vocal harmony of "Rasta Man Chant." The soaring three-part male harmonies on that track marked the end of the days of the old Wailing Wailers. What would emerge was the new African singing style of Bob Marley, previewed in subtle spots on *Burnin'*.

A few weeks before the Wailers' fall tour was to start, Bob was sitting under the big tree behind Hope Road, peeling a mango with a kitchen knife, when the first shipment of *Burnin'* T-shirts arrived. The pale yellow shirts were part of Island's promotional paraphernalia for the new album, and they were spectacular. One of Esther Anderson's photos of Bob from the album sleeve, a locks-back profile with a six-inch ganja cigar jutting defiantly from Marley's beak, was silk-screened in brown in front. Bare-chested, Bob Marley reached in the carton and pulled out a shirt, one marked small. He put the shirt on, and Bob on the shirt puffed away, while Bob in I-rality went back to peeling his mango, his pointed beard and Caucasian nose and the sharp planes of his face standing out against the rounded contours of the faces around him. Everyone was thrilled with the shirts, and Bob shook out his locks and smiled too.

In October the Wailers continued their drive for fame and fortune, joining a seventeen-city Sly and the Family Stone tour as opening act. Joe Higgs again replaced Bunny Livingston, who refused to tour. Sly Stone was the hottest thing in black music then, and the Wailers were pleased to be working with him despite Sly's eccentricity and habit of missing shows.

Four shows into the tour, the Wailers were fired. They had been both blowing the vaunted Family Stone off their own stage and drawing boos from Sly's fans. Broke and stranded in Las Vegas, where they had been dropped from the tour, without money or a manager, the band's spirits were abysmal. Bob was upset, and sat for hours in his hotel room, his luggage strewn about the room, his collarless brown suede jacket zipped tight to stay the cold of the desert night, his eyes a million miles away.

Somehow the band got to San Francisco, where the Wailers' jam-packed shows at the Matrix had won a lot of fans, in order to fulfill a commitment for a live in-studio broadcast over the pioneering rock station KSAN-FM. In San Francisco the Wailers' herb supply was replenished and their spirits lifted. On the morning of the broadcast, Bob pulled on his sleeveless blue sweater and went to the motel coffee shop for breakfast. Over coffee he scanned the headlines of the San Francisco *Examiner*: "Stunning collapse of Nixon tape strategy; Cox and Ruckelshaus are fired; Atty. General Richardson out." The head of another story

119

read: "Angry, bipartisan impeachment talk." The rest of the front page: "Israelis say they've pushed to within 45 miles of Cairo." Ignoring these stories, Bob turned immediately to the astrology page to check the forecast for Aquarius, then checked the entertainment section to see if there was a mention of the Wailers. Then he threw the paper into the garbage and went out into the bright light to join the rest of the band.

That afternoon, the Wailers broadcast their new show from the Record Plant, a top recording studio for the San Francisco music scene, located in Sausalito. Playing to about five people in the studio, the Wailers delivered another set of perfect chamber-reggae. After a warm intro by KSAN deejay Tom Donahue, who pointed out that San Francisco had been gripped by Wailermania, the set opened with Peter, Bob and Joe Higgs seated in front of their mikes, laying out the heartbeat Rasta pulse on hand drums. Joe played an alto drum called funde, Bob played the repeater and Peter supplied the deep boom of a huge, red green and gold bass drum. During the fade-out of "Rasta Man Chant," Bob scatted the melody of a current hit, Manfred Mann's "Pretty Flamingos."

The song over, Bob quietly gave the Rasta benediction: "Ites." Then the band swung into a resurrected Wailers oldie, "Bend down Low." The love song was now a fast reggae-rocker and a staple of the Wailers' new repertoire. "Catch a Fire" was next, with Wire's organ dominant while the rest of the band functioned as rhythm section. The set changed pace with Peter Tosh's new showpiece, "You Can't Blame the Youth." A litany of the villains of revisionist black history (Columbus, Marco Polo, Henry Morgan), the song made the point: *When every Christmas come/You buy the youth a fancy toy gun/So you can't blame the youth of today/You can't fool the youth.* Tosh continued with a passionate version of "Stop That Train," before the band swung back into Marley's groove with "Burnin' and Lootin'." There was a lull after the tune stopped, and Bob asked what to play. Joe Higgs said, "Do the reggae song," and Carlie tapped out the drum opening to "Kinky Reggae," full of whiplash guitars and Wire's out-of-control organ lines.

The final three numbers of the broadcast were breathtaking. "Get Up, Stand Up" was taken slow, a very roots-reggae tempo that let people hear the song's new lyrics from Peter and Bob: *We're sick and tired of your bullshit game/Die and go to heaven in Jesus name/We know and we understand/Almighty God is a living man.* On the "preacher man" verse, Bob launched into a jazz/scat vocal over the Barrett brothers' dub system, and the effect was transcendent, pure Marley tongue-talking in the spirit of Jah. Then the first encore was "Rude Boy," a rocking reggae version of the old trench warfare song from the lost days of Rude. *Walk the proud land,* they wailed, in the city by the bay. *I've got to keep on movin'/I've got to keep on movin'/I've got to keep on movin'/ska quadrille . . .* As the band hurriedly tuned for the finale, Bob hushed them with "Lively up yahself, sah! Cool foot, cool foot, cool foot." The show ended with an extended jam on "Lively Up Yourself," the song the Wailers had once cut for the Upsetter; now Bob was thinking of using it to open the Wailers' next album. Its first public performance was at KSAN that afternoon in October, 1973. *Lively up yourself and don't be no drag/Lively up yourself, cause reggae is another bag.*

The North American tour was over. The Wailers had become famous and promoted their records, but they hadn't made any money. Disgruntled, Joe Higgs caught the first plane back to Jamaica after the KSAN gig, and the Wailers played their last show as a five-piece. It was a televised benefit for the Ethiopian Famine Relief Fund, a charity dear to the hearts of Bob and Peter, and the Wailers flew a thousand miles, to Edmonton in Canada, to take part. Someone videotaped the show.

"And now we have the number-one reggae group in the world, ladies and gentlemen, Bob Marley and the Wailers, one time!! (Party whistles and scattered applause.) Bob: "Ites. *Ites!!!* Iree, yunno. I and I play, uh, will play some music. I and I'll do 'Slave Driver,' yunno." No applause. A great fast version followed and again got no applause. On the scratchy videotape, Bob seems boyish, stoned and slaphappy. "Dat was 'Slave Driver,' yunno. It seems as if you don't get the message . . . eh? So now you can't blame the youth, as Peter would say, so stop that train cause we're leavin'." Wire's keyboard delivered an incredible yawp of feedback and the band went into the tune, sounding as if they were playing three different songs at once, science fiction organ vamps drowning out the Marley-Tosh duet. Then Bob's roogalated patter flowed again: "So we're gonna get up, stand up for your rights, because tonight's the night. Hi, how ya doin? How 'bout a smoke?" (Turns to the band.) "Get up, stand up fe ya right. Uunnh! *Fiya!!!*" Carlie blasted out a salvo and Tosh lit into his crazed whacketa-whacketa-whack guitar riff, and Bob performed an amazing, propulsive scat version of the Wailers' then-current theme, complete with a dubby drum and vocal recitation on the first verse and chorus. When the song crashed to a halt, there was a flicker of resentful applause. "Ites, yunno," Bob said. "Iree." And walked off. The emcee tried to be nice—"C'mon, put your hands together, make the boys feel good, thank you very much"—but it didn't help.

At the end of October 1973, the Wailers returned to Jamaica for two weeks of rest, and then immediately flew to England (minus Joe Higgs) to begin a quick tour of England to promote *Burnin'* and the single "Get Up Stand Up" b/w "Slave Driver." It was the beginning of a bitter winter, and the Wailers shivered and suffered through the first part of the tour, Bob and Peter fronting the band as a duo. The first gig was at Nottingham on November 19, followed by one-night stands at Bradford, Birmingham, Stafford, Blackpool, Liverpool (where they were supported by Chilly Willy and the Red Hot Peppers), Doncaster Outlook, Leeds Polytechnic and Manchester. The show at Leeds Polytechnic College was typical of the tour. The demoralized Wailers shuffled onstage in their street clothes and overcoats after Wire had tuned the guitars. The group exchanged a few grunts and played for forty-five minutes. At the end of the set they ran offstage, and then ran on again and played a short encore before calling it quits. The hall was only half full, more than on most of the shows on that desultory tour. Afterward, backstage, Bob bewildered local journalists, including the *Melody Maker* correspondent, by refusing to talk about reggae and delivering instead a long sermon concerning the divinity of Haile Selassie.

On November 30, in Northampton, a freezing snow began to fall, the first snow the Wailers had seen in years. Bob and Peter argued bitterly and came to blows, and Wire announced he was leaving the band to join the American folk singer Taj Mahal; the tour broke up. The short set at Northampton was the band's last show. The next night's date at Leicester was canceled, as were the ten remaining shows of the English tour, including the all-important London showcase. The British music press was told that Peter Tosh had become ill and could no longer work. Earl "Wire" Lindo left for San Francisco to work for Taj Mahal, and Peter and the Barrett brothers flew to Jamaica, followed by Bob after he had conferred with Chris Blackwell for a few days in London. At that point, only Bob Marley and Chris Blackwell knew that the old Wailers were finished forever. Bob Marley was taking over the band.

Another era had ended for the Wailers. Perhaps its epitaph is supplied best by Joe Higgs, speaking many years later.

"The heavier albums were the earlier ones, *Catch a Fire* and *Burnin'*, dealing with experiences totally. Confrontation, truth and rights, totally.

No compromise: those first albums were really what was going down. You can only imagine those albums now, because that experience was not to be experienced anymore, only to be thought of. You could only imagine afterward what it was like to be sad. Those days . . . was what it is."

6

Knotty Dread

Cos I feel like bombing a church
Now that you know the preacher is lying
So who's gonna stay at home
When the freedom fighters are fightin'?
                                "Talkin' Blues"

Late in 1973, Bob Marley sat for an interview with Neville Willoughby, the disc jockey who had introduced Bob to Johnny Nash six years earlier. Bob had just returned in low spirits from the aborted English tour, but he had been on the cover of *Melody Maker* in London the week before, *Burnin'* was released and doing well and his star was on the rise. On the radio he sounded young, angry and vibrant, and answered most of the specific questions with testimony on the divinity of Haile Selassie, sentiments not usually expressed on the air in Jamaica.

Asked how he had started out, Bob replied: "Started out crying. Yeah, started out crying, yunno. And then music becomes a part . . . because me grateful to *Jah*. From the beginning Jah created the start, yunnowhaImean?"

"Bob, you always seem to be aware of the suffering. You keep coming right back to it all the time. Would you say you are a bitter person, or angry?"

"Well, I man sight up earth today, Neville, and when I-man sight up earth I notice that people are living under false pretense, majority of them, yunno. And I know, seh, I and I don't 'ave fe suffer to be aware of suffering. So is not anger and alla dat, but is just truth, and truth haffa bust out of man like a river."

"But Bob, quite frankly, I don't think you would fairly say right now you're a sufferer, in the sense of money."

"Well . . . *hey!* Dig dis: I-man's a farmer, yunno, and I-man don't live with money. Dem coulda never given I a penny I a-seh. I-man haffa live. But again, I-man can play music, and if money fe come out of music, *mek*

125

money come out of music. My heart really open wide. I bleed blood, forget money. For the t'ing is, Selassie I is the king of kings 'pon earth. Now, which rich guy 'pon earth rich like king of kings? So my father is richest man 'pon earth, so I is rich man now."

"How long have you been a Rastaman?"

"From creation."

"Explain to the people of Jamaica exactly what it means to be a Rasta."

"I would say to the people, 'Be still, and know that His Imperial Majesty Haile Selassie I of Ethiopia is the Almighty.' Now, the Bible seh so, Babylon newspaper seh so, and I and I the children seh so. Yunno? So I don't see how much more reveal our people want. Wha' dem want? A white god? Well, god come black. True true."

"As a Rasta, what do you think of crime and violence?"

"Is laws cause crime and violence. Rasta don't believe in violence. Rasta don't believe. Rasta *know.*"

"Do you feel amazed with people who can't understand what you're saying?"

"I'm sorry for the people who don't understand, 'cause they be in great tribulation when they don't 'ave to. I personally now, my heart can be as hard as a stone, and yet soft as water. Yunnowhalmean? Then again, still sorry for the people who don't know His Imperial Majesty. Is like my mother used to tell me, yunno: 'People head a-go chop off, and dem waan dead and cyaan dead, inna de judgment.' *These days* are the judgment days. Only the fittest of the fittest shall survive. Like Marcus Garvey seh. And you know, so it go."

When Willoughby took note that the group was now billed as Bob Marley and the Wailers, and asked if Bob was still committed to the group, Bob answered carefully. "Well, yes. The group is the Wailers. For some reason, dem [Island Records] seh Bob Marley and the Wailers. I never tell no one fe say that, from no time at all. But maybe fe some reason dem do it. Well, I man is a Wailer. And so it rest."

"What is the situation with Johnny Nash?"

"Well, dem gimme some money, and what happen is I sign a little agreement with dem and . . . *cho!* Is like, I no wanna seh anything bad about dem, and still me nuh have nothin' much good fe seh."

Asked about "carpetbaggers" like Nash and Paul Simon who come to Jamaica to make "big money," Marley replied:

"Well, dem so something, these people out there, a-try kill we off, but couldn't do because dem people too wicked. Dem t'ing mek me vex, yunnowhalmean? Look how much good artist inna Jamaica and look what it tek for a guy like me a-go get some good recordin' done, and do a

126

t'ing with it. That why we a-try and get our own studio, because we want to mek music without going through things involving social classes. Dem try fe divide we in classes. Well, me no agree with. Is wickedness. Ya cyaan divide the people."

"Do you have any hope in the country right now?"

"Hope in the country? Well, Jamaica is a nice great place now. Me really love Jamaica, yunno, because me walk plenty stone land in Jamaica, plenty hills, but I think it really need a direction—not a big old signing up this and signing up that—but a direction of *our own country.*"

By 1974 the old Wailers had unofficially disbanded. The group, if it existed, had no manager and performed no concerts abroad that year. The Wailers hadn't even performed in Jamaica in two years. Some thought was given to the Wailers touring as a trio: Bob, Family and Carlie, with Rita and her friends Marcia Griffiths and Judy Mowatt doing backup vocals. But the idea was scrapped when Bob remembered how his other tours had failed without an experienced manager. Bob Marley spent most of 1974 perfecting the recordings for the album that would eventually become *Natty Dread.*

The songs came quickly. "Road Block." "So Jah Seh." "Talkin' Blues." "Knotty Dread." They were inspired by the political warfare that threatened Jamaica in early 1974. Michael Manley was tightening up socialism's control over Jamaica, and the middle class found itself squeezed the tightest. Jamaica was a place where every white woman and gas station manager had a couple of maids, a place where giant North American aluminum cartels carried off the raw bauxite earth for a few pennies a ton. Michael Manley was trying to change that, and the opposition fought back. By the early spring of 1974, some of the ghetto neighborhoods were under the gun. The violence got so bad that Manley declared a state of national emergency. There were tanks and troops in the streets of Kingston and a 6 P.M. curfew in Montego Bay. All violent movies were banned (including *The Harder They Come)* and the notorious Gun Court was established in Kingston, a wire-enclosed concentration camp for captured gunmen, situated in the heart of the city and painted blood red for maximum effect. The Jamaican Parliament mandated life sentences for anyone convicted of possessing an illegal handgun, or even a few bullets. The battle for Jamaica had begun, waged between the gunmen and goon squads of Jamaica's two political parties. It would be fought mostly in the slums of western Kingston, but its skirmishes would eventually engulf most of the nation.

The first time Bob got caught up in it, he was riding back to Kingston

127

at three in the morning, snuggled up with Esther Anderson and a spliff in the back of Lee Jaffe's rented Toyota, with cousin Sledger at the wheel. They had been in Negril, where Bob and Esther were building a house. At the time Esther's allure was still intoxicating Bob. Half white and half Indian, the Jamaican actress was both beautiful and intelligent. She was also in some demand professionally; her most recent role had been in *Warm December* with Sidney Poitier. Bob was proud that she was his girl, and he and Esther were true friends. Her snapshots of him had been used on the sleeve of *Burnin'*. The house they were putting up was near a Negril-area fishing hamlet presided over by a patriarch named Mr. Pringle, who had twenty-three children. Everybody in the area was named Pringle. As the Toyota rounded a curve near Mandeville and everyone was laughing about Mr. Pringle, Sledger screeched to a halt. A police roadblock was just ahead, checking Kingston-bound cars for guns and ganja. In a flash Bob's spliff and everything else combustible had been jettisoned from the windows and everyone was frantically fanning the air and trembling with apprehension. To get through the roadblock, the car was strip-searched and Esther was pawed by an M16-toting cop in Jamaica Defence Force fatigues. Bob and Sledger were reviled for their dreadlocks. Three o'clock roadblock. Flushed with humiliation and fury, the little group drove on to Kingston.

From then on, Bob spent much of his time at Harry J's, working on songs. Early versions of "No Woman, No Cry" were recorded and discarded. The group was just Bob, Family and Carlie, with a sixteen-year-old organist named Bernard "Touter" Harvey supplying organ in place of Wire. Lee Jaffe played harmonica on "Road Block" and "Talkin' Blues." (When dubbing in the harmonica part, Family Man would stand behind Lee and tap his shoulder when it was time to play. One tap meant play; two meant stop.) No guitar parts were recorded; Bob and Family Man would find a guitar player in London later in the year to overdub the lead guitar lines. The trademark Wailers harmonies were supplied by Rita, Marcia and Judy. Bob was starting to refer to the women as full-time members of the Wailers. He was calling them the I-Threes.

In May, singer Marvin Gaye, the king of the Motown Sound, brought a forty-piece orchestra to Jamaica to perform at the Carib Theatre. Because the show was in part a benefit for a new sports facility in Trench Town, the Wailers were asked to open for Gaye. The concert sold out quickly. Gaye was extremely popular from the days of "What's Goin' On," and also had a big contemporary hit, "Let's Get It On." For weeks rumors ran through Kingston that the Wailers wouldn't play. Although the group hadn't performed in Jamaica for years, their appearance was habitually advertised for dances at which the group invariably never showed. But on the night of the concert, the three original Wailers and the Barrett brothers gathered backstage at the theater. A knife fight erupted at the stage door as Bunny was pushing his way into the building. Because Touter was deemed too young to appear in public with the Wailers, Tyrone Downie played the electric organ that night. It was his first public appearance with the Wailers.

When the group took the stage, pandemonium broke loose. Bunny was at the left, barefoot, fully locksed, playing his timbales. In the middle Tosh wore fatigues with a sergeant's stripes and bell-bottomed jeans, a tam clamped down over his head. Bob was on the right, in a satin jacket, leather pants and high-heeled shoes, locks flying as he pranced about the stage with his guitar. The crowd quickly was stunned by the awesome new Wailers show, a reggae-rock style the group had never before exposed in Jamaica. When Bob gave the first performance of "Road Block" that night, the response was terrific. *Why can't we roam this open country/ Oh why can't we be what we want to be/We want to be free/Three o'clock roadblock—curfew/And I've got to throw away/My little herb stalk.* Lee Jaffe was standing backstage with his harmonica in his pocket; he had played on the "Road Block" single that Tuff Gong was about to release, but he wasn't expecting to play that night. Just when it came time to play the harp solo, Skill Cole pushed Jaffe out on the stage, saying, "It's your turn." Bob Marley walked up to the mike and said, "This is Lee. Don't turn him up too loud." The crowd adored "Road Block"; the song was so *current* and the rhythm so hard that everyone identified with it.

Backstage after the show, Bob was approached by Marvin Gaye's road manager, Don Taylor. Although Taylor was a Jamaican who had started out doing errands for sailors along Kingston's waterfront, he had gone to America and had become involved with the music business, working as a valet and road manager for singers like Chuck Jackson and Martha Reeves and soul groups like the Stylistics. Rapping out a fast-talking black Yankee jive, Taylor told Bob Marley he wanted to be his manager, and bragged about his connections in the music world. Taylor told Bob that with his knowledge and contacts he'd *guarantee* to make Bob a big star. It was exactly what Bob Marley wanted to hear. With a slick black manager like Don Taylor making things easy for him, Bob could concentrate on the music and on beaming the message of Rastafari out into the world. Bob said he would think about Taylor's offer.

The Marvin Gaye Show marked the end of the old Wailers—it was their last concert as a trio—and the beginning of the new band. "Road

Block" was released by Bob's Tuff Gong label shortly after the show, and became number one at dances and in the shops. The new sound—Bob's trilling, ethnic singing, the sharp kick of the rhythms, the I-Threes wailing in back—was an instant hit with Jamaicans but was anathema on Jamaican radio, too blunt and rebellious to be programmed by the JBC's conservative managers. Bob was furious: he had the most popular song in Jamaica, but the radio stations wouldn't play it. The problem was the nature of Jamaican radio itself, which was staffed mostly by foreigners and played almost no Jamaican music. The transistor revolution in the late 1950s made inexpensive radios available to the general public, but both Jamaican stations, JBC and RJR, continued to ignore local music.

Bob and Skill Cole got so angry they decided to take action. They rounded up Frowzer and Take-Life, two young killers who Bob used to say he was trying to reform, and went down to the JBC studio on Odeon Avenue to try to get "Road Block" some air play. Skill took the baseball bat he occasionally carried as a club, and Take-Life began to clean his nails with his ratchet knife as Bob tried to reason with the terrified disc jockeys who were unfortunate enough to be around that day. Basically, Bob threatened the deejays' lives if "Road Block" wasn't played. So it was. "Road Block" was number one in Jamaica all summer. "This is the best sound to have come out of the present Jamaican experience," said the Jamaica *Daily News,* "and those who have ears feel every word and every intonation."

In June Bob, Family Man, Skill and Lee flew to New York, where Bob and Family were supposed to work on the new Taj Mahal album, *Mo' Roots.* Wire was working with Taj, a young black folk musician who was turning away from the blues and getting into the newer Caribbean rhythms. Wire Lindo had done the arrangements for Taj's new songs, which included Bob's "Slave Driver" and the Slickers' "Johnny Too Bad." The Taj Mahal/Wailers combination might have been wonderful, because Bob and Family Man were prepared to play music; but Taj Mahal had already recorded his album by the time they arrived, and could only invite them to help him mix. Family Man overdubbed a piano part on "Slave Driver," but the sessions were frustrating and no music was played. Everyone sensed a missed chance.

Back in Kingston, work progressed on new songs. "Bend Down Low" and "Lively Up Yourself" were resurrected. Militant new songs like "So Jah Seh" and "Revolution" were in production. "Them Belly Full" was being written in the studio, a collaboration between Bob, Carlie Barrett and a longtime Marley street crony, Leghorn Coghill. A new song, "Am-A-Do (Do It to Your Bad Self)," was recorded as a demo and then shelved. Keyboards continued to be a problem, with Wire in California and Tyrone playing full time with the Caribs, the house band at the Kingston Sheraton. Touter was filling in temporarily and was acknowledged to be very talented, but he was too young and too inexperienced to endure the rigors of permanent Wailerhood. Touter played on many of the sessions and when he wasn't around, Family Man played clavinet on "Road Block" and organ, piano and clavinet on "Bend Down Low."

Wrapping up the album they were calling *Knotty Dread*, the Wailers were profiled on the cover of *Xaymaca*, the Sunday magazine of the Jamaica *Daily News*. The magazine's photographer and layout man was Neville Garrick, a Kingston-born U.C.L.A.-trained designer who would become the Wailers' full-time art director. Although the article was published on August 11, 1974, it gave no hint that the original Wailers had broken up or were in trouble. Bob talked about touring: "I love Jamaica and I love the people but I have to move up and down the earth. My mother tell me God is the father for the fatherless. So where he sends me I must go. No man can tell me what to do. I have seven children [the latest, Justin Marley, had recently been born to an Englishwoman Bob had met on the Wailers' last tour] and I could make a million tunes here and can't put my children in a room. I can't afford to make my children grow up like me. I love the brethren, and I love the children, but I can't afford to stay here and go to prison. That's the direction of the youth now. If Jah never worked it that I have to go outside and look certain things, maybe I would be in prison now."

Later, Bob spoke of his dream: "Too many people going on like only England and America are in the world. But there is a better life in Africa. I *feel* for Africa, I want to go there and write some music. Instead of going to New York, why can't we go to Ghana? Go to Nigeria—meet some black people, learn a new language. You see, people are only seeking material vanity. Black people are so stubborn. They stay here because white people give them a big hotel and a floor to vacuum."

Early in August, Bob and Family Man took the tapes for the new album to London for remixing under Chris Blackwell's direction. As they left, Tuff Gong Records released the second single to emerge from the sessions, "Knotty Dread," a fast litany of esoteric Rasta patois and a pilgrim's progress of the Trench Town cityscape: *Then I walk up to first street/And then I walk up to second street to see/And then I trod on through third street/And then I talk to some dread on fourth street/Knotty Dreadlock inna Fifth Street/And then I skip one fence to sixth street/I've got to reach seventh street/Knotty dreadlock congo bongo I . . .*

In London, the Wailers found their guitar player.

Al Anderson was a young black rock guitarist from America, born in Montclair, New Jersey, in 1953. His first band, the Centurians, covered "Expressway to Your Heart." His second, Red Bread, copied Jimi Hendrix and Jeff Beck. Al Anderson was the bass player. After recovering from a car crash, he took his savings and went to London, where he found a job playing bass with the avant-garde guitarist John Martyn. Martyn was an Island artist; he introduced Al to Chris Blackwell as a bass player and suggested the Island boss give Al some studio work. One night Al was hanging out at the home of another Island musician, Paul Kossoff, who played guitar for the rock group Free. Kossoff played Anderson the Wailers' *Catch a Fire* to illustrate a point about reggae bass playing. It was the first time Al Anderson had heard reggae.

The next morning, Chris Blackwell called Al Anderson and asked him to come to Island's Basing Street studio to play guitar on a Bob Marley session. Al Anderson was ready. He had by then given up the bass and was playing lead guitar for Shakatu, an Afro-rock band led by the Nigerian master drummer Remi Kabaka, playing the same circuit as their more famous African competitor, Osibisa.

When Al showed up at Basing Street, he found Bob and Chris Blackwell presiding over an overdub session. Al played some of his Afro-funk licks; Bob said he didn't like it. Al asked what he wanted, and Bob just said, "Play the blues, mon."

"It was really fun," Al remembers, "because when I first walked into the studio I was just a guy from the States with my hair all plaited up from the Afro-rock band, and I turn around and I see Bob and he's got a real knot-cap on his head. I got spaced out and said, Hey, look at *this* cat. I had never even *seen* a Rastafarian before.

"And at the time I was doing a lot of alcohol, drinking, and was very unhealthy, and Bob was like . . . not a pimple on his face, not a wrinkle. He was into herb and I-tal foods and was totally healthy. I noticed right away that the guy was totally physically fit and conscious of everything that was moving. But I was just a session guitar player to him, and he was into finishing off his LP and going home. It was almost October and winter was coming and he wasn't into hanging around a day longer than he had to."

Al Anderson's first session involved guitar overdubs on "Lively Up Yourself" and "No Woman, No Cry." Al played his best and was satisfied that his licks would be used; but after the playback Bob said to Blackwell, "That's not what I wanted. It's not what I hear." Anderson tried another take, and Bob still wasn't happy. Finally Bob turned to Al.

"He just said, 'One, five, four—*blues,* mon.' I said, 'OK, now I know where you're coming from.' "

When the sessions were complete, Al Anderson resumed his plans to visit Nigeria with Shakatu. But again he got a call from Chris Blackwell, saying there was interest in asking Al to join the Wailers. Al was flattered, but felt confined by the reggae format and preferred to stay with Shakatu, where he had freedom to play in the wide-open style he liked. One night he got together with Bob in Bob's flat in Chelsea, off King's Road, and the two musicians talked and jammed all night, riffing in the James Brown groove that Bob liked to play when relaxing. Bob asked Al if he wrote any songs, and then played Al a new song he was working on and about to record: *Stiff Necked Fools/You think you are cool/Tryin' to deny me/ Of my simplicity/You 'ave gone from reality/And are provin' your love for vanity.* Off in a corner, Family Man was fast asleep, with his ear next to a blaring radio.

"I just sat and talked with him that evening," Al says, "and we jammed, and I saw the guy had unlimited potential as a songwriter. He was so conscious and aware of what was going on in the world. I said, Hey man, I've never *met* a cat like this. I was drinking heavily, really drunk, and he was into helping me. He said, Man, you have to get fit. Come to Jamaica, it's a different world from what you're used to."

Al told Bob he would join the Wailers, and Bob and Family returned to Jamaica confident that they had a guitarist who could play the blues-rock music they wanted to spice their reggae for an international audience. Al assumed he would go to Jamaica and start work immediately. The new Wailers album was scheduled for release in November 1974, and Al assumed the Wailers would tour shortly after that.

Instead, Al was met at the Kingston airport by Bob, who took him to Rita's old house in Trench Town. Sledger and Leghorn were selling sticks of herb outside the front door, and an exhausted Al crashed on the sofa. Al told Bob he was prepared to play right away, and Bob replied that there had been some problems with Chris Blackwell, and that the new album would be delayed a few weeks. Al wanted the Wailers to at least play some live gigs around Jamaica, but Bob insisted the timing wasn't right. It would be another six months before Al attended his first full Wailers rehearsal.

In the meantime, he got a chance to live and learn, "yard-style." "When I got to Jamaica, I stopped drinking and got into physical shape. I got into I-tal foods and became a vegetarian. All this was Bob's influence. And the Bible was always around. He was totally into it. It was his life. He *lived* it. It was a real thing for him.

"I was in a funny position with the Wailers. I was the 'white' cat in the band, the Yank, the American guy fuckin' up the music by playing loud rock and roll. Family Man was a big help, because he was the only one who sat down with me and said, Hey man, it's not *chicka,* it's *cha . . . cha. . . .* Family Man was everything to me. It was Fams who taught me to play reggae."

Even though the Wailers were relatively inactive through 1974, Bob Marley's spirit was kept in the public eye by an incredible stroke of fortune. Other musicians had already been picking up Marley's songs for their records; Taj Mahal thought "Slave Driver" was appropriate to cover, and Barbra Streisand recorded "Guava Jelly" and put it on her *Butterfly* album. But when Eric Clapton's comeback recording of "I Shot the Sheriff" went number one around the world in the late summer of 1974, Bob Marley's destiny was fixed. Clapton, formerly of Cream, was one of the major axe heroes of sixties rock. For years he had lived in retirement as a heroin addict before deciding to clean up and make a comeback in 1974. That Clapton should choose "I Shot the Sheriff" as the music for his rebirth was not fortuitous. Lee Jaffe had played the song for Carl Radle, Clapton's bass player, with the idea of Clapton doing the song. The version that Clapton produced didn't have much to do with the feel of Jamaican reggae, but it was a heartfelt version with a suspicion of reggae in the flailing rhythm guitars. The most Jamaican thing about it was the sentiment of oppression and rebellion.

Eric Clapton's rock god status now bestowed on Bob Marley complete legitimacy in rock circles. One interviewer later asked Bob about the song, and he said: "I wanted to say 'I Shot the Police' but the government would have made a fuss. So I said 'I Shot the Sheriff,' instead. But it's still the same idea—justice!" To interviewer Karl Dallas, who asked about the message of the song, Bob said: "That message is a kind . . . of diplomatic statement. 'I Shot the Sheriff' is like, 'I shot wickedness,' because all around in my own town they're trying to track me down. It's not really just a sheriff; it's just elements of *wickedness,* yunno."

What about the deputy? How does he come in?

"Well, the sheriff shoot the deputy. If he didn't shoot the deputy, the sheriff still have mercy. He just had to kill the deputy because the deputy's a good guy and there's still a hassle. But the elements of that song is, people been judging you until you can't stand it no more, you explode, yunno, you just explode. So it carry the message. Coxsone asked me about that, because when Coxsone finish [hearing] the song, he don't know the meaning of it. He liked the type of music, and he like the melody, and he like [the title] 'I Shot the Sheriff,' yunno, but I don't know if him get it, because I think he thought he was hearing Elton John sing 'Don't Shoot Me, I'm Only the Piano Player.' Bob Dylan sang, 'Take this badge off of me, I don't want to shoot them anymore.' And one man's aim shot the sheriff, yunno? That song now fit no one else but Eric Clapton, yunno? Right beside Elton John and Bob Dylan. One man seh, 'Don't Shoot me, I'm Only the Piano Player.' Next man—Bob Dylan—him seh, 'Take this badge offa me.' Clapton seh him shot the sheriff. So you find, it's like dem guys, yunnowhaImean? *Categorized.*"

Bob Marley usually smoked a big spliff before his interviews. Then he would enjoy sluicing down through what Michael Thomas once described as "the psychic rapids of upper Niger consciousness."

In Jamaica, Clapton's version was also a hit, played on both stations as no Wailers song ever had been. Again Bob and Skill were furious. Clapton's "I Shot the Sheriff" was being played every hour on the JBC, while the Wailers' new single, "Knotty Dread," was never to be heard. Again, Bob and Skill went over to the station to protest. One of the disc jockeys complained to the police that he had been threatened. Rumors went out that Bob Marley had been banned from entering the station for two years as a result.

Late in 1974, something happened to sour relations between Bob and Chris Blackwell, and musician and producer fell out temporarily. But the battle did get hotter. At one point Dickie Jobson, who was managing the Jamaican operation for Blackwell, gave word to Bob to vacate the premises of 56 Hope Road immediately. The Wailers feverishly packed up their equipment and left. Family Man and Lee Jaffe picked up an entire piano and loaded it into a truck. The Wailers' gear was hauled out to Rita's house in Bull Bay until the fight blew over. But some damage had been done. The new album was postponed for several months, and Bob even considered another recording deal when Motown, the Los Angeles–based black music conglomerate, made him an offer. However, he decided that Chris Blackwell was the only producer he could trust with his music. When their differences were patched up, Marley made it clear to Blackwell that part of their next deal together would have to include the transfer of Island House to Bob's company, Tuff Gong. He didn't want to be evicted from Hope Road ever again.

By January 1975, the Wailers were shedding one skin and growing another. The big songs of the day in Jamaica were "Marcus Garvey," a militant song about the black prophet by a roots trio from St. Ann called Burning Spear (after the nom de guerre of Kenyan president Jomo Kenyatta), and "House of Dreadlocks" by Big Youth, Kingston's hottest sound system disc jockey and street oracle. The whole nation was rocking

135

to Spear's provocative reminder that *Marcus Garvey words come to pass/ Can't get no food to eat/Can't get no money to spend.*

The Wailers "officially" broke up that month. Peter Tosh and Bunny Livingston had been at the recent album sessions, but more as spectators than as participants. The bitterness increased when it became clear that the group was again Bob Marley and the Wailers, that Bob had taken over the group. Much of Peter and Bunny's anger was directed at Chris Blackwell, who they felt had convinced Bob to dump them. Bunny and Blackwell had argued over the question of touring, and Tosh is said to have confronted Blackwell with a rusty machete when he asked Blackwell for some money and was told that the Wailers owed Island Records forty-two thousand dollars for their touring expenses. Tosh was also angry that his artistic role in the group had been suppressed. "If you check the albums," he said later, "and you check how many songs Peter and Bunny do on those albums, you can count dem on one hand! Raas claat, you can count dem on *haaf* a hand! One album with nine or ten songs, and eight songs are Bob. Tell the whole story right there."

Bunny's case was slightly different, perhaps because of the brotherly nature of his relationship with Bob. By then it was clear to Bunny that he and Bob were trains on different tracks. While Bob had made a career out of songs of angry protest, Bunny's music preached quietism and activist religion. While Bob was belting out "Trench Town Rock," Bunny was singing "Dreamland," a soothing Rasta ballad. Bunny's music— "This Train," "Sunday Morning," "Pass It On," "Hallelujah Time"— was soft, the opposite of Bob's jagged songs. The Wailers were no longer big enough for both of them, and Bunny's attitude toward the Wailers' schism tended to be more philosophical than Peter's: "I don't really see it as a 'split,'" Bunny said at the time. "Although we are not working together physically, we're all sending the same message—*Rastafari!* So we're together still and will always be together in that sense . . . Every man has a testimony and a message, and there's so much inside one that it has to be brought out, or else it can hurt. Ideas that could have been good, dem become stagnant because you cyaan put out more than a couple of albums a year and so . . . it just happened. It wasn't planned, but it worked out that it was all for the good, because now all our material is being exposed. Bob has his album, Peter has his album and I have mine."

So the three Wailers went their own ways. Bob, supported by Chris Blackwell, kept the Wailers and pursued his destiny. Peter followed his, lashing out with a furious spew of Jamaican singles on his Intel-Diplo label—"Mark of the Beast," "Burial," "Can't Blame the Youth" and later the ganja anthem "Legalize It." Bunny worked on his own songs and released his pastoral masterpiece *Blackheart Man* the following year, on Island Records.

Bob Marley and the Wailers previewed their new lineup early that year at the Jackson Five's concert in Kingston. Bob was out front by himself with his Les Paul, playing rhythm guitar and prancing his signature dance, his knees almost touching his chin as if he were juggling an invisible soccer ball. Then he would stand stock still before the mike, one finger resting on his temple as his other hand stretched into the smoky air in a gesture of preaching and prophetic intent. The audience was enthralled by the spectacle of the three I-Threes in red, green and gold headdresses and gowns, chucking in unison and singing in harmony at stage right. Rita was in the middle, leading the harmony with her midrange soprano. To her right was Marcia Griffiths, a regal, large-boned woman who had been Jamaica's premier female singer for ten years. Marcia had been "discovered" in 1964 by the ska-era Blues Busters, and had become a national figure when she sang Carla Thomas's "No Time to Lose" on Jamaican television. Influenced by Aretha Franklin and Dionne Warwick, Marcia opened shows for American soul stars in Jamaica, and enjoyed a string of hit singles produced by Coxsone Dodd. With her singer-husband Bob Andy, she had recorded an album for Harry J called *Young, Gifted and Black* that was a big hit in Europe; she had spent almost three seasons touring in Germany by the time she joined the I-Threes.

To Rita's left was Judy Mowatt, the I-Three's choreographer. Judy was born in Gordon Town, outside Kingston, and started her career as a dancer, working in a troupe that traveled all over the islands. Her friends called her Julie Ann. By her late teens she was singing in a female trio called the Gaylettes, and later became friendly with both Rita and Marcia. When Marcia had a singing job at the House of Chin and needed backing harmony on a Diana Ross song called "Remember Me," she asked Rita and Judy to join her. Bob Marley heard the show, and decided that the ladies had the sound he wanted behind him. Later, Judy recalled how the group came to be named: "So while we were in the studio for the *Natty Dread* album, Brother Bunny and Brother Peter were in with Bob, not working with him, but in the studio. Well, we lookin' a name to call ourselves, and we said 'We Three'? Brother Bunny said, 'No, call yourselves Heat Air and Water.' But that was a much too harsh name, so we said no. We settled for the name 'I-Three.' The I in the Three is H.I.M. Haile Selassie I, who is that 'far eye' who is watching your deeds.

137

When you least think nobody is watchin', that 'far eye' is watchin'. So the name is really *mystical.*"

The Wailers' third album for Island Records was released in early February 1975. The change in the group was a shock to hard-core Wailers fans. The name of the album was a shock to Bob Marley. It had been originally titled *Knotty Dread,* after the single that Tuff Gong had released in Jamaica a few months before. The word "knotty" implied for Bob a wild jungle Rastaman, a natural, thoughtful man like his friend Countryman. Knotty was *dread,* a cultural agent provocateur, spreading psychic terror through Jamaican society, even capturing its young. But Island Records called the record *Natty Dread,* which seemed to change the meaning of the title. To Bob, as he told a friend, the word "natty" described some Rasta in a nice new cream serge suit with well-groomed locks, not the ropy street locksman that Bob knew. But Bob was also a stoic about these things. "That's the music business," he would say.

The cover of the album told the whole story. Now it was "Bob Marley and the Wailers" again, superimposed over an airbrushed painting of Bob's face and locks. The music inside was stunning, the Wailers' most sophisticated to date. The *Natty Dread* music was no less combustible than *Burnin'* or *Catch a Fire,* but seemed even more dangerous for its stark reggae minimalist quality, a smoldering flame that lingered after the fires of the previous albums had cooled. "Lively Up Yourself" introduced Al Anderson's quiet blues guitar to Wailers fans, and reintroduced the horn section to the group's sound. The alto solo (by Ray Allen of Johnny Nash's band) was typical of what Bob wanted from a reedman, a punchy, barely contained Hank Crawford style that seemed to burst out of the speakers. There was also the trilling Yoruba lookout call that started the album, Bob hailing the Wailers' new day like an African rooster at dawn. "No Woman, No Cry" followed, a sentimental collage of Trench Town memories in a cheering, optimistic format based on the self-reliance that had gotten Bob and Rita out of the ghetto. Bob would later credit part of the song to Vincent Ford, his old friend "Tartar" from the hungry kitchen on First Street.

The Wailers then delved directly into trance music with "Them Belly Full (But We Hungry)." Competition for food was a constant battle in Jamaica and Bob reminded that *a hungry mob is an angry mob.* Yet reggae music could also be a balm for a people weathered by injustice and poverty: *Forget your troubles, and dance/Forget your sorrows, and dance/Forget your sickness, and dance/Forget your weakness, and dance . . .* As backup singers, the I-Threes sounded so *right* that one could almost forget that Peter and Bunny were gone. The Tuff Gong single "Road Block" had been remixed in London and retitled "Rebel Music (3 O'clock Road Block)." New harmonica parts had been overdubbed by session player Gary Farr, over a fine Barrett brothers riddim, extending the trancelike effect of "Belly Full." "So Jah Seh" opened side two, a mélange of scriptural quotation and ghetto defiance. It is Marley the provider and father of seven speaking. (And as the album was released, an eighth child was on the way as well, to another of Bob's girl friends.) "Natty Dread" was "Knotty Dread," followed by the great, updated "Bend Down Low."

The final two songs established Bob forever as an artist-militant; the line in "Talkin' Blues" about bombing a church caused a sensation in Jamaica. And "Revolution" doubled the blow. *It takes a revolution/To make a solution . . . So if a fire make it bu'n/And if a blood make it run.* In the past, open calls to rebellion had been punished in Jamaica by jail and the whip. But the new Jamaica of *Natty Dread* was undergoing a socialist revolution, a visionary movement in which even Knotty Dread seemed to have a place. Some even said he was the conscience of the nation. Perhaps because of this, *Natty Dread* was a spectacular success, especially with the rock press in England and North America. People sensed in Marley's declarations a moral authority; the Wailers' reggae wasn't just empty, impotent pop music. Most of their Euro-American fans weren't sure just what it was the Wailers stood for—the concept of Haile Selassie (deposed and discredited the previous year) as the black messiah and Almighty God on earth was too much for some—but they liked the music, the show, the charisma and the sense of history and purpose.

In Kingston that spring, the Wailers began to coalesce into the ensemble that would tour during the summer. Arranging and coordinating everything was the Wailers' new manager, Don Taylor.

Bob had consulted with his Jamaican lawyer, Diane Jobson, about Taylor, who had been asking Bob to take him on. "Him seh him wan' manage me," Bob told Diane. "But me earnin' a lotta money nuh; how can him manage me with him likkle bruk pocket?" Bob was concerned that Taylor hadn't the resources to be a professional manager, and just wanted to make money from him. Bob asked Diane to come to Taylor's flat to meet him, so they went to Taylor's place on Wellington Avenue and Don laid on a jive-rapping spiel: "Bob, I just wanna be your manager, man, nothing else. C'mon on, man, we're *brothers.*" Right there Don Taylor sold himself to Bob. He told Bob he didn't even want a contract, and Bob, who had been burned by every piece of paper he had ever signed, said yes. Later, he asked Diane what she thought of Don

Taylor, and Diane said that she didn't know much about the music business, but that if talking alone could do it, Taylor might be all right.

Once Don Taylor had been taken on, he organized a North American tour for June and July, followed by a brief showcase tour of England. Bob set about solidifying the Wailers touring party, building around the Barrett brothers, Al Anderson on guitar and the I-Threes. Alvin "Seeco" Patterson, the Wailers old Rasta rhythm master, was added as a percussionist, more as a "vibe" than as a musician. The only slot then left to fill was the keyboards, a prime instrument in the Wailers format. Wire Lindo was still with Taj Mahal, and Touter, who had shone on several of the *Natty Dread* tracks, was still too young to make an extended Wailers road tour. That left Tyrone Downie.

Tyrone was then playing organ with the Caribs, the cocktail hour poolside group at the Sheraton Kingston. Earlier Bob had come to hear the band with a current girl friend, the Jamaican beauty queen Cindy Breakspeare. Tyrone was singing cover versions of Billy Preston hits like "Nothing from Nothing," and Bob loved Tyrone's playing and especially his voice. Bob asked Tyrone to play on the Marvin Gaye show, and Tyrone was very thrilled. "That show came off really well," he remembers, "and it was my first live gig with the Wailers. At the time I didn't take it very seriously, but if I had realized what I was doing, that I was becoming one of the band, I would have treasured every inch, every moment, every second!" Both Al Anderson and Lee Jaffe were pressing Bob to hire Tyrone for the tour. Touter was great, they said, but he was a "pretty-boy" type of musician, whereas Tyrone was a "roots boy," someone who would make the players play reggae. Touter played his keyboards like a piano. Tyrone played his like a drum. The rest of the Wailers gave Tyrone a new name—"Jumpy."

By that time, Island House had been completely taken over by Bob Marley. It isn't clear whether Blackwell ever formally sold the house and grounds to Bob, but by early 1975, Island Records was gone and Tuff Gong Records had moved in. Rasta construction crews immediately started work on the place, transforming the outbuildings into rehearsal space. Long-range plans included a recording studio for the ground floor of the house. Don Taylor ordered the building gutted and stripped of its old-fashioned window sashes, replaced by modern louvers which effectively ruined the house's period architecture. Even as the house became a construction site, Bob and his entourage moved in. It was like a Rasta encampment in the middle of uptown Kingston. Bob and Skill Cole were always around, playing football, rehearsing, writing songs. In residence were all sorts of musicians and hangers-on, doing physical training and artisanry, sharing meals, sleeping on the house's bare floors at night. Bob had his own little room upstairs where he could sleep or meditate, but when he wasn't involved with a new girl friend, he might be at Rita's for the night, or with one of his other lovers. Bob's attitude toward the concept of "home" was best summed up in a remark he made to Diane Jobson: "Birds have their nest, but son of Jah has not a place to lay his head." Upstairs, adjacent to Bob's room, was a porch dominated by a table tennis set. One of Bob's paramours in those days was Anita Bellnavis, then the Caribbean women's table tennis champion, who bore Bob's eighth child, a daughter she named Kimane Marley. By the spring of 1975, though, Bob had a new girl friend, Cindy Breakspeare, a statuesque woman of twenty who managed a gymnasium and was generally considered to be the most beautiful woman in Jamaica. Before Cindy and Bob even became lovers, Cindy had a flat at Hope Road. Now Jamaica was scandalized. Here was the flower of Jamaica's light-skinned womanhood openly consorting with a revolutionary Rasta who was rumored to smoke a pound of ganja every week. The press dubbed the couple "Beauty and the Beast."

Around this time Bob stirred up another controversy when he invited the Twelve Tribes of Israel to hold groundations and prayer meetings on the grounds of Hope Road. Known within the organization as "Joseph" (because his Aquarian birth sign corresponded to the tribe of Joseph), Bob was responsible for inducing many of reggae's hardest musicians to come to the Hope Road meetings and to join the Twelve Tribes. Freddie MacGregor, one of Jamaica's leading singers, remembers the 1975 Twelve Tribes meetings at Hope Road as the rock upon which his reborn Rasta faith was founded. But not all the behavior at 56 Hope Road was so sanctified. The scene attracted many of Bob's old crowd from Trench Town and Ghost Town, young gangsters and gunmen who recognized Bob as their spiritual leader. Few of them were Rastas; most were just former rude boys who had graduated into career criminals and killers. Bob liked to tell people he was trying to reform them, and whenever one of his friends would be arrested for armed robbery or murder, Bob would send Diane Jobson down to bail them out. "Like a bird in the tree," he sang, "the prisoners must be free." The scene around Bob was always very physical; there was lots of wrestling and horseplay. Once, Bob attacked Lee Jaffe, who wrestled Bob to the dirt and began to pin him. Suddenly Bob's pal Take-Life crept up behind Lee with a length of lead pipe, prepared to transform the back of Lee's skull to guava jelly. Just as Take-Life was about to take Jaffe's life, he was grabbed by Al Anderson, who talked him out of braining the Wailers' harmonica player.

141

Bob also paid close attention to his radio show in those days. By then, Jamaican radio had loosened up to the point that various reggae producers were allowed to sponsor fifteen-minute segments featuring their own music. Bob's Tuff Gong show was a notable exception. While it generally played music by the Wailers, Peter, Bunny, Family Man or one of the I-Threes, the show also featured any other new song that Bob particularly liked. It was also the first of these shows to send its own producer (Skill Cole) and use its own jingles. Eventually the show was taken over by the engineer Errol T., who initiated a "Culture Corner" consisting of Scripture reading, quotes from Marcus Garvey and some extremely bizarre sound effects. Bob was especially concerned that children listen to the show. "Reggae music on radio mustn't deal as a program for people to enjoy as a musical t'ing," he said. "It must be an *educational* program. That means I want to look forward to hear something 'bout all mankind's struggle for life. It can't be like, 'OK, this is Bob Marley—this is John Holt—this is Dennis Brown.' You must have *content* in this package."

On Sunday morning, Bob played soccer at Rae Town in eastern Kingston. If he was in Jamaica, he rarely missed that game. One fellow player remembers Bob from those games as "like a tiger turned loose. We were on opposing sides and whenever he tackled for the ball, you could feel his intensity. As we played and grew weary at the height of the noonday sun, unlike the rest of us he still seemed ready to play when everyone was screaming with extreme fatigue. Afterward we retired for a groundation session at the bottom of Paradise Street. As we sat reasoning together, Bob sang softly, 'Sun is shining, weather is sweet' . . ."

In April 1975, Bob and Don Taylor flew to New York to negotiate a production deal. Earlier, a company called Sire Records had sent Bob a demo tape by Martha Velez, a talented rock singer based in Woodstock, New York, asking if Bob might be interested in producing her new album. One of Velez's tunes, "Living Outside the Law," caught Bob's interest, and he sent word to Sire that he was interested. Velez and the Sire executives met with Bob and Don on a rainy day in early April. Despite the mild spring weather, Bob was swaddled in leather from head to foot, dressed for bitter cold. Bob didn't say a word, letting Don Taylor do all the talking, but he quickly made eye contact with Martha, as if to say he thought they could work together.

Three weeks later, in May, Martha Velez arrived in Kingston and was met at the airport by Don Taylor. Taken to Hope Road, she entered a darkened room full of reclining Rastafarians casually passing a burning chalice among themselves. At first Martha began to panic, and asked herself what on earth she was doing there. But then Bob emerged from the pride of dread lions and took her off to another room to begin work. First he played her some of his songs on acoustic guitar: "Bend Down Low," "Stand Alone," "No Woman, No Cry." Bob told Martha that he wanted the record to sound "international," so the two musicians began writing a song together that eventually would be called "Disco Night." Then Bob got bored and went out to play football for a while.

The loose working conditions at Hope Road were sometimes frustrating for Martha Velez. After three weeks in Jamaica, with Bob and Lee Perry producing, Velez had cut only two tracks at Harry J's Studio. She returned to New York to confer with the record company, and then came back to Kingston to finish recording. This time, Bob got down to business. "Sister Martha" went out to Negril to rehearse with the Wailers at a resort called the Sea Grape. When they returned to Kingston, the rest of the tracks for her album were recorded at Harry J's with Family Man and Tyrone Downie doing the arrangements and the I-Threes doing backing vocals. Martha remembers Bob being particularly harsh with Rita then, abusing her for any mistakes the I-Threes might have committed. This was because the haughty Marcia Griffiths would have walked out if Bob had been rude to her, and Judy Mowatt had become romantically involved with Skill Cole and Bob didn't feel he had the right to yell at Skill's woman. So Rita Marley bore the brunt of Bob's wrath whenever something happened with the singers.

Soon the backing tracks for the Velez record were almost complete. With the Barrett brothers and the I-Threes, the tapes sounded a lot like a well-mannered Wailers album. Al Anderson overdubbed his understated blues guitar, sometimes replaced by Earl "Chinna" Smith, Kingston's hottest young reggae session guitarist. Lee "Scratch" Perry did most of the actual production work on the record, and supplied some of his patented African percussive tricks. When the album was released the following year as *Escape from Babylon,* it included "Bend Down Low," "Get Up, Stand Up," "Disco Night" (cowritten by Bob), "There You Are" (a retitled version of "Stand Alone") and "Happiness" (a retitled version of "Hurting Inside") in addition to three other songs by Velez.

In June, the Wailers flew to Miami to begin their 1975 North American tour. Eight musicians made the trip (Marcia Griffiths stayed behind because she was in the last stages of a pregnancy; Rita and Judy performed as the I-Twos), accompanied by new Wailers art man Neville Garrick, who would handle the lights. The group holed up at the Attaché Motel in Hollywood, Florida, rehearsing at a nearby hall while Neville

Garrick built the red, green and gold Lion of Judah backdrops at the hotel. It was the usual Wailers routine for Bob: up before dawn, running and football on the beach, followed by a day of obsessive, perfectionist rehearsals for the band. To relieve the dietary problems the band had suffered on past tours, the Wailers brought along their own cook, Mikey Dan, a patriarchal Rasta who specialized in Bob's favorite foods—fish, stew beans, peas and rice, cornmeal or oatmeal porridge, vegetables and Irish moss, a Jamaican health drink prepared with seaweed, linseed and milk. The tour was also joined by Don Taylor and two employees, equipment manager Dave Harper and Tony Garnett, a Jamaican-born disc jockey and Wailers fan from Los Angeles who served the tour as court jester, master of ceremonies and road manager. Don Taylor ran Tony Garnett hard, sending him all over town to pick up equipment and make traveling arrangements for the band. One day Bob noticed that Tony G. was looking rather lost. Bob looked at Tony and said: "Tell me sumpin'. You ever been in dis bizzness before?" Tony answered, "No, but me can learn." Bob thought for a minute, then said: "All right. Cool runnings. Say what? What you 'ave fe say before the show? Ya got anything planned?" It was the first inkling Tony G. had that he was supposed to compere the tour.

The 1975 Wailers tour began the media's long love-hate affair with Bob Marley. Everywhere the Wailers went, they were hot copy. Bob was a great story, a new kind of rock star, an obviously principled man who wore his hair like a Gorgonian snake nest and used every interview as a platform to proclaim the divinity of the deposed Ethiopian emperor and the forthcoming redemption of the black race. In America, *Rolling Stone* proclaimed Marley "the dreadlocked, dark sorcerer/poet"; the New York *Times* hailed him as "the Black Prince of reggae"; New York's *Village Voice* dubbed Bob "the Mick Jagger of reggae." But Bob remained suspicious of journalists, while almost never refusing an interview, no matter how small or obscure the publication. He read all his press clippings avidly, and he was often angry at the misconceptions engendered by careless reporters who didn't take their responsibilities seriously enough. He would often answer annoying or disrespectful questions with sarcastic queries of his own, and after the first five minutes of many an interview, journalists would find themselves being tested by Bob on their own beliefs and values. When talking about Rasta, Bob would often consult and quote from the weathered Bible he carried with him from motel to motel. His personal Bible was a Jamaican printing of the King James version, with a photocopied portrait of the Lion of Judah in full regalia pasted on the cover, as well as other pictures of Selassie glued on the inside cover and flyleaf. Also written in ball-point pen on the flyleaf were various Marley notations: "Ethiopia is a mystery in the hands of God"; "For great is the mystery of Godliness/God is manifested in the flesh—JAH."

The tour started with a showcase concert at the Diplomat Hotel in Hollywood, Florida, and then the band flew off to Canada to begin the trek across North America. Although the group's popularity was growing, the Wailers were not yet ready to play theaters and auditoriums. Instead they played nightclubs, mostly four-hundred-seaters, and some large outdoor concerts. Again, some of their audience were white kids, but this tour brought out the hidden underground of Jamaican immigrants to the States, who crowded in beside the white youth and turned some of the gigs into pure Trench Town rock. From Canada the tour progressed to Philadelphia, then to Boston, where the Wailers played a sold-out Paul's Mall, a downtown basement jazz club. The song lineup stayed the same throughout: "Trench Town Rock" opened the set, followed by "Burnin' and Lootin'," "Them Belly Full," "Road Block," "Lively Up Yourself," "Natty Dread," "No Woman, No Cry," "I Shot the Sheriff" (which was a big crowd-pleaser because of Eric Clapton's hit of the previous year) and "Kinky Reggae." The invariably demanded encore was a long rave-up on "Get Up, Stand Up" with Bob going through twenty-five choruses before leaving his audience on their feet, emotionally spent.

Between shows, Bob sat in the cramped dressing rooms, holding court for American fans meekly offering stashes of Columbian marijuana and Jamaicans bantering with the band in rapid-fire patois. Beautiful groupies materialized in the sweet-smelling smoke of the backstage area, and occasionally Bob would take one back to the motel with him. On June 18, the Wailers played before fifteen thousand rabid fans, many of them Jamaicans, at the Schaefer Music Festival in New York's Central Park, a transcendent show that caused a near riot when the band left the stage. Spontaneous demand caused another show to be booked at the Manhattan Center, an instant sellout.

The new edition Wailers were as tight as sunburned skin, thoroughly professional, taking pains to be precise. Bob rode drummer Carlie Barrett very hard that tour, often berating him backstage when Carlie had rushed the beat or made an error. After New York, the tour headed for Cleveland, Detroit and Chicago, where the group played a club called the Quiet Night and Tony G. almost broke his back trying to get Tyrone's Hammond B3 organ down the steep flight of stairs leading to the club. In Chicago, Bob had a reunion with Junior Braithwaite, the original Wailers lead singer, who had left Jamaica ten years earlier. Later, between shows, a huge gang of Jamaican rudies refused to clear the club after the first set, terrifying the club manager, who swore never to book the Wailers again. There were also problems between Don Taylor, who was respectful only to Bob, and the other musicians, who felt that Taylor was cheap and quick to belittle them. With Tony G. rather amateurishly handling travel plans and with just one roadie to drive the truck, unpack and set up the equipment, the tour was *very* disorganized; the musicians really hated Taylor for that. And sometimes, when Lee Jaffe would come out of the wings to play his harmonica part on "Road Block," Taylor would come on stage and stand in front of him so Jaffe's whiteness wouldn't be so conspicuous. Taylor also would stand in front of the boyish Tyrone Downie during Tyrone's solos, and would sometimes upstage Al Anderson as well. It drove the musicians crazy, and they complained bitterly to Bob.

Everywhere, there were interviews. In Boston, Bob told the reporter from London's *New Musical Express* that Haile Selassie, "Him ever young, the youngest man on earth. Him control time." Asked about Selassie's overthrow the year before, Bob quoted Revelation: " 'There shall be wars, and rumors of wars, even in Zion.' " In other words, he didn't believe it. "These are the last days, without a doubt," he said quietly. "1975 is the last quarter before the year 2000, and righteousness, the positive way of thinking, must win, good over evil. We're confident of victory." Many reporters asked Bob about the line "I feel like bombing a church" from "Talkin' Blues"; it was one of Bob's favorite subjects at the time. "Politics and the church are the same thing. Dem keep the people in ignorance, and Jah nuh gwaan come and seh, 'I am God and you should praise me.' These guys who preach are false . . . the greatest t'ing dem can seh is about death, cos dem sen you die and go to heaven after all this sufferation. To go through all sufferation for that! No, the greatest thing is life, man. *Life!*"

By the middle of July, the tour reached California. The shows at San Francisco's Boarding House had been sold out for two weeks; outside the club, scalpers were getting fifty dollars a ticket. When the lights dimmed and the band bore down—*One good thing about music/When it hits you feel no pain*—the place went wild. Bob would stand frozen, singing with immense concentration, his outstretched forefinger sometimes pointing to his temple or the bridge of his nose. Then, as the beat began to surge and his energy burst its dam, he would explode across the stage, arms piercing the foggy air, face shining with perspiration and the joy of release.

On other songs Bob concentrated on driving the band with his early-model Gibson Les Paul, lashing out hard reggae rhythm guitar, pace-maker to the Barretts' thunder-heavy locomotion. Audiences and press reviews were ecstatic: the shows were described as "tight, perfect and burning with passion and dark power." "In live performance . . . the Wailers surpass rational response." Impresario Bill Graham was so impressed that he quickly promoted a last-minute Wailers show at the large Oakland Paramount Theater. The hall came within a hundred tickets of selling out.

The last stop of the American tour was Los Angeles in the second week of July. The Wailers had important showcases at the Roxy, a fashionable club on Sunset Strip, and were scheduled to videotape songs for their first appearance on network television in the United States. The Wailers checked into a kitchenette motel on Hollywood Boulevard, and Bob changed into a new green Adidas warm-up suit and prepared to play soccer and meet the press. Road conditions improved also, since Tony G. was from Los Angeles. The motel quickly filled with Wailers fans and groupies, most of them bringing marijuana, mangoes, papayas, cherries, long skeins of dried figs, myriad health food. The band was relieved at the replenished herb supply, which had been precarious in the Midwest despite the efforts of the hip little Jamaican communities in all the towns to keep the musicians refreshed. Tony G. remembers that whenever the Wailers ran out of herb and a pound had to be procured, the ganja money always came out of Bob's pocket. In one of his Hollywood press chats, Bob told reporter Richard Cromelin that he had been smoking daily for nine years, with a few periods of abstinence. But Bob also pointed out that, for him, smoking ganja was neither frivolous nor hedonistic: "When you smoke herb, herb reveal yourself to you. All the wickedness you do, the herb reveal it to yourself, your conscience, show up yourself clear, because herb mek you *meditate*. Is only a natural t'ing and it grow like a tree."

Asked whether he considered himself a revolutionary, Bob proved himself more of a Rasta realist: "You see, the revolution is a mechanical t'ing, you know. It's *them* planned it . . . If you plan revolution you can get hurt. Revolution *happen*. You know, it just happen and you see it happen around you . . . The only control you can have is if Jah really love you and Him take you from the revolution . . . The revolution'll go on, *harder*. Pure fightin', you understan'. It not like the Cuban Revolution type of revolution. Is the whole universe involved in this revolution."

Asked about the Rastafarian concept of his people's exile in Babylon,

Bob launched on a voluble dread meditation on the devil, one of his favorite subjects in those days: "Anywhere devilism is, is Babylon. Babylon fill the air with bad vibes. The Devil ain't got no power over me. The Devil come and me shake hands with the Devil! Devil have his part to play. Devil's a good friend too . . . Because when you don' know him, that's the time he can mash you down. Him can-a trick you if you don' know him well, trick you and hide behind you . . . The Devil's a dangerous guy, mon. Is-a Jah goin' to protect me. He said, 'Fear not, have no fear.' " Then he was asked if he personally feared anything. "Me? Naah." Then he reconsidered. "Well, me don't swim too tough, so me don't go in the water too deep." Around his neck Bob wore a large golden *Chai,* the Hebrew symbol for life.

Don Taylor was chauffeuring the Wailers around L.A. in a rented Cadillac convertible, a huge Babylonian bus. Early in July, Taylor drove Bob to the CBS television studio at Studio City to tape two songs for *The Manhattan Transfer Show,* a four-program summer series whose young producers were Wailers fans. At first, Taylor demanded a closed set for the taping, in order to develop the proper atmosphere. Uptight CBS officials, who had thought they were getting some slick soul brother and who had blanched when dreadlocked Bob Marley walked in, said no. The Wailers taped two songs, "Kinky Reggae" and "Get Up, Stand Up." The taping was recorded in one take, the Wailers playing a manicured reggae that clicked with the precision of an I-tal Las Vegas showband. When the show was broadcast a few weeks later, only "Kinky Reggae" was seen, but it was another small triumph. A long bass/drums skank at the end was very potent; the Wailers had achieved the first coast-to-coast reggae TV appearance in America.

The shows at L.A.'s Roxy Theater were the best of the U.S. gigs. The 1975 Wailers tour ran concurrent with an American tour by the Rolling Stones, whose guitarist Keith Richard favored a Bob Marley T-shirt for his own gigs. The Stones had asked the Wailers to open their shows on the West Coast that month, but the Wailers' booking agent, Stu Weintraub, and Don Taylor made the difficult decision to refuse. Everyone felt that the Wailers were headliners and stars, and that stars didn't open shows for anybody. It was a point of pride. Nevertheless, the Stones skipped a party in their honor to attend the first of the Roxy shows. Also in the audience were two of the Beatles (George and Ringo), the Band, the Grateful Dead, Billy Preston, Herbie Hancock, Joni Mitchell, Cat Stevens, Buddy Miles, Bob Dylan's wife and a lot of movie stars. The Wailers burned that night with an especially bright flame.

By July 16, the Wailers were in London, installed in a flat in the King's Road, Chelsea, preparing for a four-date British tour to promote *Natty Dread*. Two shows were scheduled for the Lyceum, an ornate red and gold vaudeville palace in London's Strand, with subsequent shows at the Odeon in Birmingham and the Hard Rock in Manchester. Bob Marley was now a national figure among British youth, especially young West Indians and their white friends. Bob saw himself on the cover of *New Musical Express* when he arrived at Heathrow Airport. The frantic air of expectancy that anticipated the Wailers' shows in London was caught by journalist Carl Gayle in his pivotal cover story on Bob Marley for *Black Music* magazine:

"Natty Dread is in town, the soul rebel from Kingston and Ethiopia, who, with his pride of culture and his uncompromising stance in music as in life, is breaking down the colour barrier. Is breaking down the barrier that has long prevented the acknowledgement of the power of Jamaican music. Is breaking down the barrier that puts you physically and spiritually in touch with your inner frenzy. His music has potential. It gets under your skin and into your soul and turns you loose.

"They will come to hear the music but not so much as they will come to see his face, the man and the image. To stand and watch him on stage as he puts himself, body and soul, through the various stages of emotion of which his music speaks. To watch him rebel and cry out and to be hypnotised by it all.

"They're a little awestruck by the fire they've seen in his pictures and have heard in his voice, by his aggression and his beauty. And they would be more than a little ill at ease in his presence. But they've already been hypnotised, they cannot resist. So that when he tells them to lively up themselves, there will be no alternative, he's got them under his spell . . . And there's gonna be burnin' and lootin', weepin' and wailin' tonight. An atmosphere of carnal expectancy and of revolution tonight. Tonight, tonight!"

Despite all the adulation, Bob was annoyed on his arrival that *Natty Dread* had slipped off the British charts, and he was unsure about the Lyceum shows, even though they had long been sold out. In rehearsal he worked the band extremely hard and was sharp with Tyrone and Al when they missed a cue or botched an intro. On the night of the first Lyceum show, Chris Blackwell stood at the back of the theater and watched the young Third World band, which was signed to Island, open the show. When the Wailers came on, the theater erupted in a loud blast of emotion. Bob stood for a moment, swaying and silhouetted before the Ethiopian backdrop, flanked by portraits of Haile Selassie and Marcus Garvey, until Carlie tapped out the intro to "Trench Town Rock" and Bob plunged into the show. *Hit me with music, Brutalize me with music.* When the Wailers hit the fifth song of the set, "No Woman, No Cry," and every person in the Lyceum sang along in perfect unison, Blackwell thought to himself, "That's the hit; I've gotta record that live."

On the following night, Island set up recording facilities at the Lyceum. Special microphones hung from the ceiling to capture the audience singing along. Backstage, black activists persuaded Tony Garnett to introduce the show by reading their poster protesting the imminent hanging of a young black man in one of Her Majesty's prisons. With Bob's approval, Tony G. read the poster as the band waited onstage, and then said, "But this, I wan' tell ya, is the *Trench Town experience.* All the way from Trench Town, Jamaica, *Bob Marley and the Wailers!*" Chris Blackwell's tapes were rolling as the Wailers laid on a dazzling Rasta stage musical. Every song seemed an epiphanic poem of folk wisdom, and the band crackled like sheet lightning. Dozens of fans rushed the stage and stood with their arms outstretched, trying to touch the wild-haired prophet who hopped and darted above them like some captured African imp. Introducing the band during the dub passage of "Kinky Reggae," Bob finally identified himself: ". . . and I . . . I am Natty Dread!" The crowd screamed as Bob formally assumed the mantle of the visionary Rasta rebel, someone to believe, someone to follow, someone to feel.

The following Saturday, the Wailers traveled to Birmingham for that night's gig. At the sound check, Bob was again very rough on Tyrone, who seemed visibly unhappy. That night the Wailers went on at nine-fifteen and played for two hours, performing "Talkin' Blues" for the first and only time on the tour. Again the show was a success, but the sense of strength and unity the Wailers projected on stage masked some of the dissent and unhappiness felt by some members of the band, especially toward Bob. Tyrone and Al were being paid a flat fee for the tour, and didn't really consider themselves part of the group. Carl Gayle discovered this when he accompanied the two youngest Wailers to the next day's gig at Manchester by train. In his usual hurried cadence, Tyrone voiced some of his complaints: "The treatment that you get, you know. The way it seems is that the Wailers is really Family Man, Carlie and Bob, all the interest is in them. All I want to know is that I play music and really enjoy myself. And like if it wasn't for this cat now [referring to Al] I would be strung out.

"I wouldn't come on the tour, y'know, 'cause Family Man check me fe come and I said I wouldn't because if I don't get pay in Jamaica I don't think I would get pay abroad.

"Bob say you mustn't deal with money, man, you must play music and build something. That is the usual argument you get in Jamaica right now when a man want you work fe him.

"Wailers going mek it, you know, 'cause at least they are accepted by the world. All they have to do is keep doing the same type of material. 'Cause is strictly commercial, the way I see it right now. The thing with Bob is that I like the guy. His music saying something ya can sing. Who wouldn't want play with a guy like that? But the things you have to go through, man, mental strains, you know. Bob get everybody tense because . . . I don't know, him won't relax himself. The thing is he's worried about if the show going come off alright. If the music going sound heavy when show time come. But him really no have to worry because the group heavy already. The sound is already there. But him just tense and nervous and just rub it off on everybody else."

Later, after the tour had ended and some of the pressure was off Bob, Carl Gayle asked him about the tensions within the group.

Bob said: "Me no get tense, me just tighten up because the music me play, me want it to be something someone can really concentrate 'pon. Not something where you just come play anything you want play, you know. Is a music where sometimes if you fool around too much it no sound good. You have to be directly inside o' it with all o' we a-work right. So me just a tighten up, is not really tense. If you laugh, laugh too much, everything just go in a little vain way. Somebody 'ave to tighten it up, 'ave to be like strict sometimes. And after the show over we cool again.

"Like Al and Tyrone might take a little time fe understand. Like the face what me have something me really mean war. When is music time me serious. Just so me stay, we no in a joke business." Asked why Peter and Bunny had been left behind, Bob's answer was frank and strangely prophetic:

"Is like them don't want understand me can't jus' play music fe Jamaica alone. Can't learn that way. Me get the most of my learning when me travel and talk to other people. That was a kind of worry me have, why me never so loose before. They [Peter and Bunny] can be a part of the group but me 'ave fe leave Jamaica certain time because of politics in the air. The influence from politicians we have is strong. Them love come to you and try get you, and me is a man no like turn down no one. So me leave Jamaica."

About the same time in London Bob gave a revealing interview to

R. A. Allen of the Caribbean *Times,* which displayed some interesting and sometimes contradictory attitudes. After telling Allen that he was born in "nineteen forty . . . eight" and denying that he was married ("Me never believe in marriage that much . . . marriage is a trap to control men; woman is a coward. Man strong"), Bob became offended when asked his views on homosexuality. "Sodomy?" he snorted. "Me nuh wan' deal wid." Asked if he admired any woman, Bob said he liked "dat woman in America . . . Angela Davis, a woman like that who defends something; me can appreciate that."

On his identity: "Bob Marley isn't my name. I don't even know my name yet."

On race prejudice: "Well, me don't dip on nobody's side; me don't dip on the black man's side or the white man's side. Me dip on *God's* side, who cause me to come from black and white, who give me this talent."

On his way home to Jamaica after his conquest of England, Bob Marley stopped off in Delaware to see his mother. He used the interlude to work on new songs for the album he would soon begin to record in Jamaica, tunes like "Cry to Me" and "Rat Race." For several months Bob had been working with the text of a speech that Haile Selassie had delivered to a United Nations assembly at Stanford University in California in 1968, trying to craft Selassie's trenchant warning of war and permanent struggle within the context of the Wailers' music.

By mid-August, Bob was back at Hope Road, cutting the rhythm tracks for the Wailers' next album at Harry J's familiar studio and at the studio run by veteran Jamaican producer Joe Gibbs. It was in the middle of these sessions that, on August 27, 1975, Haile Selassie died in a small apartment of his former palace in Addis Ababa at the age of eighty-three. Immediately there was a furor in Jamaica, where the question of the emperor's divinity had been hotly debated for forty years. The doubters laughed, and the faithful Rasta again pointed to Revelation: "There shall be wars and *rumors* of wars, even in Zion." Around Hope Road there was some confusion and some of the Rasta brethren wavered in their belief. Bob Marley stood firm. Late one evening in September Bob and Lee Perry commandeered Harry J's, filling the dimly lit studio with ferocious concentration and cumulonimbi of ganja smoke. As the studio clock showed 10:30 P.M., Bob stepped up to the boom mike suspended above his head and matched a poem of deep religious affirmation to the heartstopping rhythm track the Barretts had earlier laid down: *Jah Lives! Children, yeah!/Jah Jah Lives, children yeah!/The truth is an offense, but not a sin/ Is he who laughs last, is he who win/Is a foolish dog, bark at a flying bird/One sheeple must learn, children, to respect the shepherd/Jah Live . . . Fools saying in their heart/Rasta your god is dead/But I and I know, children, dread shall be dread, a-dread/Jah Lives.* By the time Bob finished his verses, his brown cotton shirt and blue jeans were soaked to the skin. The next morning, Al Anderson was brought in to overdub a guitar part, Lee Perry dubbed in percussion and the I-Threes recorded a stupendous harmonic chorale to back the track. A few weeks later, "Jah Live" was released (by Tuff Gong in Jamaica, by Island in England), credited to "Hugh Peart." Yet few people doubted that most of the song was Bob's, his response to the reported passing of His Imperial Majesty.

Early in September, Bob gave a rare Jamaican radio interview to the JBC's Dermott Hussey for broadcast on Hussey's weekly cultural program. It was a candid talk for Marley; he described some Jamaican musicians as cheap hustlers and spoke heatedly on the disbanding of the old Wailers as an inevitable event brought about by the invisible laws of change. Bob told Hussey that he received his inspiration from three main sources—Haile Selassie, the love of his mother and all the people who were against him. Bob explained that he turned struggle and confrontation into a positive vibration by writing songs, like "Road Block" or "I Shot the Sheriff," about people who vexed him. When the interview had been broadcast, Bob asked Hussey to destroy the tape.

As the sessions for the new album continued through October, Bob commuted between Hope Road and the studio on nearby Roosevelt Road. At home he kept his children close to him, mingling his three by Rita with Pat Williams's son Robbie Marley and his other children by other women. His guitar was constantly at hand, a tiny photo of Selassie and a map of Africa taped to the soundboard. After the Jamaica *Daily News* published a series about destitute and starving ghetto children foraging for food at the Kingston dump, Bob wrote a song called "Children of the Ghetto": *Children playing in the streets/On broken bottles and rubbish heap/Another little baby got nothin' to eat/Cause in the ghetto, bitter is sweet.* One day, Bob said, he would gather all his children into a group and have them record that song, so they would know from where their father had come.

But Bob's children didn't have to worry about scavenging for food. Their father was becoming a wealthy man and an international star, at once basking in the positive glow of his new fame and wary of any effects his new wealth and raw cultural power were having on his fellow Jamaicans. Bob had come of age in a Jamaica of mistrust and violent competition. He knew that most successful Jamaicans didn't stay on the island of their birth and heritage. Circumstances forced them into a more comfortable exile.

In November, Island released the album Chris Blackwell had recorded at the Lyceum, *Bob Marley and the Wailers Live!* Now the whole music world heard how stupendous those gigs had been, and the album did as much as *Natty Dread* to boost Bob as reggae's prime shaman. *Live!* had it all—the convulsive reggae anthems, the fiery scat and interpretive singing, the huge crowd singing along in unison and screaming for the truth and redemption that only the Wailers could deliver. There was the climactic jam on "Get Up, Stand Up" and Bob's bellowed incantation, "Rastafari—*Almighty God.*"

Late that November, the three original Wailers joined forces for one final concert at Jamaica's national stadium. The occasion was a benefit concert by black superstar Stevie Wonder on behalf of the Jamaican Institute for the Blind. The Wailers went on at two in the morning with "Rastaman Chant," and the packed stadium roared in appreciation. Peter Tosh got riot cops from Harman Barracks moving out of the stadium with "Mark of the Beast," and Bunny played his new song, the timely "Arab Oil Weapon." Then Bob and the new edition of the Wailers did their current show, joined in the end by Stevie Wonder, dressed in his stage costume of dozens of tinkling silver bells. As the moon began its descent to the west, the black Yankee soul star and the Jamaican soul rebel jammed on "Superstition" and "I Shot the Sheriff." The show was over at 4 A.M., and Bob Marley was ecstatic. For an encore the three original Wailers came out and did "Rude Boy." It was the last time they would ever perform together.

7

Smile Jamaica

Bob Marley isn't my name. I don't even know my name yet.
(1976)

By 1976, Bob Marley was a star. He had made it. In record parlance, that was the year the Wailers "broke"; they were in demand for concerts, advance orders for their new album flowed in and *Rolling Stone* magazine voted them "Band of the Year." It was the year after *Natty Dread,* and thousands of young Jamaicans had stopped combing their hair and started to think the Rastas might be right after all. Their leader was Bob Marley. His dark prophecies of vengeance and revolution seemed all the more immediate by January 1976, when the Manley government hosted the annual meeting of the International Monetary Fund, and the western ghettos of the city went up in burnin' and lootin' in full view of the IMF delegates in the high-rise hotels in New Kingston. Convinced the rioting was a JLP plot to embarrass and destabilize his socialist regime, Manley declared a curfew and dispatched troops to put down the disturbances. Marauding gangs of criminals and political thugs now took to the streets after dark, and even the tough Kingston police tried to stay off the streets at night. By 7 P.M., Kingston was shut down and locked in, the whole city in fear. *War inna Babylon,* Max Romeo sang, *War Inna Babylon—it sipple [slippery] out deh.* Another big reggae hit of the day was "Jah Kingdom Go to Waste"; both songs were banned by the worried Jamaican government in an effort to keep inflammatory songs off the radio. Jamaica was in trouble, but it really wasn't anything new. Bob Marley had been saying it for years.

Over at 56 Hope Road, Bob Marley was just waking up. It was ten o'clock on a morning in early March, and Bob had been up late the night before, working on the album at Harry J's. In a few hours the press officer from Island Records, Jeff Walker, would be bringing another carload of American reporters for a press conference.

Wearing only a T-shirt and cutoff jeans, Bob shook out his locks and wandered downstairs, settling on a large rock under the huge poinciana tree in back of the house. Absently, he signaled for his morning spliff and a nearby herbsman handed Bob a large one, neatly rolled into a seven-inch cone. Within minutes a woman had brought out herb tea and fresh fruit, and the motley crew of Rasta craftsmen had begun the day's labor on the house, whose interior was being repainted in red, green and gold. Portraits of Haile Selassie were tacked to most of the walls. A telegram arrived, and Bob tipped the deliveryman with a spliff. After a while, Bob walked over and sat on the hood of his latest purchase, a sleek silver-blue BMW Bavaria that he had paid fifteen thousand dollars for. Originally he hadn't wanted anything so grand, worried that it might not look right for a Ghost Town Rasta to be driving a big BMW. But Skill Cole had argued that the Bavaria would be good for the weekly treks to the herb fields up in St. Ann, whose dirt roads had destroyed most of the other cars Bob had used to drive to his ancestral lands. Sitting regally on his car, Bob held court for the day's constant stream of destitute old friends and hangers-on from the ghetto, each of whom got five or ten dollars depending on his needs. Some of them had bigger scams they wanted Bob to finance, dope deals and swindles on the Babylonian economy. Always interested in a good scam, Bob Marley listened to them all. Not many got what they wanted, but some did. All this took place to the constant roar of Honda CB200 motorcycles racing in and out of the property and the relentless throb of the Tuff Gong sound system, which broadcast the city's rudest reggae to its wealthiest district over loudspeakers at all hours of the day or night. Over the door to the kitchen was a sign: PLEASE TAKE OFF YOUR SHOE OR WIPE FOOT.

In March of that year, I was among a swarm of foreign reporters and correspondents who descended on Kingston with assignments to write about Bob Marley and the social changes sweeping Jamaica. Bob took the interviews individually, a laborious process since his interviews tended toward lengthy bouts with Rastafarian philosophy and faith. So the reporters from *Time, Rolling Stone, Melody Maker,* the *New York Times Magazine,* German and Dutch television and various American music and skin magazines were left to drink rum around the pool of the Sheraton. The more enterprising of them rented cars and ventured onto the fringes of Trench Town, with the doors locked and the windows rolled tightly up for security, even in the blare of the tropic winter sun. Trench Town wasn't happy to be gawked at—"No wan' you come col' I up"—and the reporters' Datsuns were invariably pelted with rotten fruit, Red Stripe bottles and stones.

Bob regarded interviews as an important part of his Rasta ministry, and he generally approached them in earnest, intending to cooperate and educate in order to spread the message of Rasta in his music. His seriousness was often rewarded with dozens of repetitious and foolish questions regarding his hair, his religion, the amount of dope he smoked and whether he really wanted to go back to Africa. Bob usually responded by quoting from the Bible, his own lyrics, St. Ann homilies and the Trench Town street sayings of the time. In 1976, with the *Rastaman Vibration* sessions under his belt, he quoted most heavily from a fiery Haile Selassie speech which he and Carlie Barrett had set to music for the next album.

It was my turn for an interview with Bob on a late Monday afternoon. That day he had already talked to *Time* and *Melody Maker,* and had spent an hour with photographer Dave Burnett from *Time,* who had made Bob run around with his guitar under his arm, trying for a special-effects shot that would be spread across several frames of the film. Bob ran back and forth for the photographer, much to the general hilarity of those present, until he was tired out. When another intruding white photographer asked Bob to move into better light, Bob replied that if the man wanted him in a different place, he'd have to come back another day. When the second photographer then asked Bob to take off his hat, Bob took a draw of his spliff and looked into space. Sitting on his car, dressed in denims and leather boots, Bob flicked the ash from his spliff as he patiently answered questions, distracted occasionally by the shouts of his children and the squall of motorbikes revving up and passing out of his yard. As late afternoon became evening under the big shade tree, the toads and crickets came to life in the branches, a chorus of bug song and scree. Bob Marley, his features a mask except when he laughed, would take a cheek-hollowing draw of his ganja cigar and wait for the next question.

What message, I asked, did he think he was giving the hordes of press people crowding into his life these days.

"Well, me have a message and we wan' fe get it across. The message is to live. My message across the world is *Rastafari.* 'Righteousness shall cover the earth like water covers the sea.' Right now, no one teachin' the *real* way of life. Right now the devil have plenty influence, but as far as me is concerned, all the devil influence lead to is death. While Jah lead to life."

Was he surprised to be asked so much about Africa?

"Yeah, man. Rastaman must go home to Africa. It sound funny to some people sometime; sometime it can sound like a mad t'ing, but our desire is fe go home to Africa. We like Jamaica, yunno, but Jamaica is spoiled as far as Rastaman is concerned. The history of Jamaica is spoiled, just like if you have an egg that break, ya cyaan put it back together again. Jamaican cyaan be fixed for I and I, for Rastaman. When we check out the system here, we see death. And Rastaman seh, Life. Here people have to fight for everything. Ambition and false pride. Dem people a coward."

What about criticisms that he was selling out his culture?

"Check this," Bob said, quoting Haile Selassie, " 'Until the philosophy which holds one race superior and another inferior is finally and permanently discredited and abandoned, there is *war.*' Jah say dese t'ings. Me check them out to the people. If God hadn't given me a song to sing, then I wouldn't have a song to sing. Ya cyaan sell culture . . . I'm dealing with universal togetherness."

There was talk of another election soon in Jamaica. Was Bob worried that the politicians might try to use him? Especially the Manley government?

"Only one government me love—the government of Rastafari. Politicians don't care for people; only Jah care for people. Seh, every man for himself, and God for us all. Politician cyaan fall rain, dem cyaan mek corn, yunnerstand? The only unity we wan' get is Rasta."

After relighting his dormant spliff, Bob launched on a fragmentary meditation on the kinds of music he liked.

"Rock music, soul music . . . every song is a sign. But you 'ave fe be careful about the type of song and vibration that you give to the people, for 'Woe be unto they who lead my people astray.'

"People rob me and try to trick me. You cyaan call it trick, you call it *teef.* But now I have experience, now I and I see and I don't get tricked. Used to make recording and not get royalties . . . still happen some time. Alla dem English companies *rob,* man. Dem wha' deal with West Indian music, pure *teef*-dem.

"Me love I-Threes, me love Burning Spear, me love Big Youth. All Jamaican music . . . Me love dub, if ya can tek it. I nuh really get involved with it so much. Live more 'pon the creative side. For Wailers, dub means *right and tight,* the perfect groove. When we seh to our musicians, we gonna dub this one, we mek sure we play it right and tight."

There was talk that Michael Manley would legalize marijuana in Jamaica. Did Bob believe it?

"Herb is the healin' of the nation. Manley can say whatever, but police still get their order from somebody. I mean . . . there are people who live in evil and think it is right. 'Cause for instance now, a Rastaman siddung and smoke some herb, with good meditation, and a policeman come see him, stick him up, search him, beat him, and put him in prison. Now, *who is this guy doing these t'ings for?* Herb just grow, like yam and cabbage. Policemen do it for evil. Dem don wan' know God and live, dem wan' ha' fe dead, yunno!"

What about the question of an artist's inspiration?

"Well, it is good to think good of yourself, and good of others. Inspiration come straight from out of Jah, man. Yeah, man. *Yeah, man.* Ya just 'a fe live right. The ship rock, but we still steady."

In the violent political climate of the moment in Jamaica, did Bob fear for his safety?

"No sah! No mon! Me nuh afraid fe dem. If I can avoid dem I avoid dem. If I'm goin' down the street and I see a roadblock and there's a street for me to turn off before the roadblock, ya bettah go an' turn off. It's good not fe get search.

"Now if somebody wan kill I, if somebody wan try and hurt I, than I and I mek him hurt I, and if the only thing I can do is defend I-self, then I'm the one. *I'm the one and let no one on it.*

"Rasta *physical,* yunnowhaImean? We nuh come like no sheep in dem slaughter, like one time. YunnowhaImean? Dem just don't have power fe do certain things to I and I. Dem just don't have it!

"Gun court? A wickedness, man. It's the system. The *sys*-tem. The *system!* The system kill people, so we must kill the system."

The conversation wore on as it got darker and Bob's spliff got shorter. Asked about the future, he became animated and articulate, attracted to prophecy.

"I and I reason, ya watch what a-gwan happen. It nuh tek long. I cyaan explain it because if me 'ave the power fe explain it I explain it and people will try and stop me. Me *know* it gonna happen. Reggae gwan get a real fight if it nuh happen already. This is *Third World* music . . . Ya don't have understanding in one day; ya have it little by little and it just grow."

By then it was past twilight in Bob Marley's yard, and over the horizon a sliver of waxing moon shone like a streetlamp. As we conversed, dark figures gathered in the shadows around the car under the big tree, listening intently as Marley spoke. A beautiful young black woman pressed in, concentrating on Bob's discourse with the foreigner. The still air was filled with crickets and smoke; in the big house lights were on, and the aroma of the evening meal being prepared wafted out into the courtyard. After an hour more of chat, Bob leaned back on the hood of the BMW and closed his eyes. His role was then taken over by a proselytizing young brother from the Twelve Tribes of Israel organization, who had been sitting at Bob's feet and feeding him lines and catch-phrases during our interview. The brother proceeded to challenge me on my negligible knowledge of Scripture, arrogantly demanding to know how long it takes to read the Bible a chapter a day. When I said I didn't know, the brother snorted that it takes three-and-a-half years. Bob sat up again: "Read the Bible, man. Most populous book in the world." I said that for some people it was a big decision to come back to the Bible, and the Twelve Tribes brother pointed out with irritation that all it took was your ears. Bob woke up and agreed: "Read the Bible, man. Most populous book in the world. Certain t'ings ya 'ave fe know what to do, ya read the Bible." After I said my thanks and farewell, I was followed out of the yard by the Twelve Tribes brother, who was offering some herb for sale. As I turned to talk with him I saw Bob Marley, still stretched out on his car under the tree, still surrounded by his disciples affectionately watching over his slumber.

In the dozens of other interviews Bob gave that month, he kept hammering at the same themes: the evils of the system, the black redemption offered by Rastafari, the sweetness of herb, Haile Selassie's "Until the philosophy" speech, bad writers who misinterpret him (although he also claimed that he wasn't eloquent enough to explain his true feelings) and his constant battle with the devil. He was also revising his own history, telling some reporters he was born in the late 1940s and saying that his jail term back in the sixties was for driving without a license. There was no point in alerting immigration authorities with replays of his old dope bust. Most writers looking for the *real* Bob Marley drew a complete blank, because the real Bob was down at the beach playing football with Skill Cole and the House of Dread team, or rehearsing the band. Perhaps the best contemporary portrait of Bob Marley's scene came from Chris Blackwell, interviewed in *Melody Maker:* "[Bob is] supersensitive, amazingly bright, takes in a lot of things right to the back of his head. He's a natural leader and he has some very heavy people around him, heavy in the sense of being intelligent, bright and talented . . . And it says a lot for him that they acknowledge him as their leader, because they're all very strong people in their own right . . . Basically, the attitude of Bob and the Wailers has always been that they would, on their terms, like to expand their music. They had their own shop even when I first knew them, and when they wanted some money they'd go and make a few records and sell them themselves. So they've always been a very independent crowd of people, the Wailers."

Many of the questions Bob was asked had to do with his lyrics, and he provided some interesting interpretations. To a reporter from *Oui* magazine who asked about "Burnin' and Lootin'," Bob said: "That song about burnin' and lootin' *illusions* . . . the illusions of the capitalists and dem people with the big bank accounts." And when *New Musical Express* asked if "Them Belly Full" was a tract on starvation and wealth, Bob said no, not exactly. "Your belly's full, but we're hungry for the *love* of our brethren. Food might be in your belly," he said, "but there's more to living than just filling it. Where's the love of your brother?"

Often asked by white reporters if his music was antiwhite, Bob again, patiently, said no. "My music defends righteousness. If you're black and you're wrong, you're wrong. If you're white and you're wrong, you're wrong. It's *universal*. Against white people? I couldn't say that. My music fight against the system . . . and I will keep on doing it until I am satisfied the people have the message that Rastafari is the Almighty, and all we black people have redemption, just like anyone else. Not for money will I do anything, man, but because I have something to do. There should be no war between black and white. But until white people listen to black with open ears, there must be, well, suspicion."

Bob was asked how he would know when his work is over.

"Because I will feel myself satisfied, and I will feel like I am tired. And God will tell me. And the people will see and tell me. It is *redemption* now, yunno. No one can stop it."

Eventually the foreign reporters went home and filed their stories, and Bob Marley mythology began in earnest. By April, *Time* magazine gushed: "Marley is Jamaica's superstar. He rivals the government as a political force. The mythical hero of his last album, *Natty Dread*, has already become a national symbol. Marley is a cynosure both in Jamaican society and in the Trench Town ghetto where he grew up. He seldom appears in either milieu, but when he does, it is with a retinue that includes a shaman, a cook, one "herbsman" laden with marijuana, and several athletes." A few people sensed that the social pressure on Bob Marley, and indeed on the whole nation of Jamaica, was reaching a breaking point. "At the moment the scene has a crazy-ish feel to it," Chris Blackwell told *Melody Maker,* "which is very dangerous."

Meanwhile, during the sessions for *Rastaman Vibration* and rehearsals for the planned summer tour of America and Europe, the Wailers changed musicians again. Al Anderson, whose guitar solos on "No Woman, No Cry" and "Jah Live" had endeared him to many fans, left the Wailers to play with Peter Tosh, who was preparing his *Legalize It* album at the time. Al told Bob that Don Taylor's abrasive management had driven him out of the band, and advised Bob to get a new manager. Bob objected, saying that Don was black and "We give all black people a chance." Another detection to Peter Tosh was Lee Jaffe, who had also become disillusioned by the end of the '75 U.S. tour and hadn't accompanied the group to England. Instead, he'd returned to Jamaica, where he was busted for herb in a roadblock. After a few days in jail, Bob Marley arranged to make Jaffe's bail while Bob was still in England. Jaffe would go on to coproduce *Legalize It* with the rest of the Wailers, minus Bob, as backing musicians.

Al Anderson was replaced by a nineteen-year-old Kingston guitarist, Earl "Chinna" Smith, a busy session musician who Al calls "the high priest of reggae guitar." Chinna had his own band, the Soul Syndicate, but played rhythm guitar for the Wailers during 1976. For a while, Tyrone Downie thought he was out of the Wailers too, because of the candid comments he had made about Bob in England to Carl Gayle, which had been published by *Black Music,* much to Bob's annoyance. For a month or so after the tour, Tyrone kept a low profile, half afraid to stop in at Hope Road to face the music. When he finally showed up, Bob and his entourage were in a room with the shutters closed; it was dark, with a dim candle burning, and the pungent smell of fish tea and the passing chalice tickled Tyrone's nose. "They said the tour was on, they were happy to see me, was I coming with them? It was a big relief that I was still in the band."

Even with Chinna Smith on rhythm guitar, the Wailers were still incomplete as an international touring band. Chris Blackwell, Bob and Family Man all agreed that the Wailers had to have a rock-style "lead" guitarist to appeal to an international audience. Chinna was roots, but the band also needed some flash. It would take two guitarists to replace Al Anderson in the Wailers. And, as with Al, the Wailers turned to a black American. His name was Don Kinsey.

Chris Blackwell found him, just as he had found Al. Don Kinsey was playing in a black-rock power trio called White Lightning; his brother Woody was on drums, Buster Cherry Jones was on bass and the band had an album out on Island Records. Don was twenty-three years old and had been a professional blues guitarist since he was eleven. Born in Gary, Indiana, the son of a full-time blues musician, Don started playing guitar with his father's band at eleven. By the time he was through with high school he went on the road with bluesman Albert King's band, forming the rock band White Lightning when his older brother got out of the army. Don Kinsey was just what the Wailers were looking for, a blues guitarist who liked to rock. The question always was, could he play reggae?

In March 1976, Don Kinsey's father in Indiana got a phone call from Don Taylor in Miami. Would Kinsey be interested in coming to Miami, where the Wailers were mixing their new album? Don had met Bob the previous summer, after the Wailers show at the Manhattan Center in New York, but had no idea that he was being considered to replace Al Anderson. Don flew to Miami, where he found Bob and Family Man mixing and overdubbing the *Rastaman Vibration* track at Criteria Studios. Don Kinsey sat down with his guitar in the studio and noodled a bit as he listened to the track. Bob recorded Don's practice riff, and used it on the album. Don Kinsey had become a Wailer. "It was my heavy blues roots," he says. "I was able to jell with them because reggae is a deep, deep feeling and has a lot in common with blues. I felt like I fit right in." He ended up overdubbing lead guitar throughout the album, except for "Crazy Baldhead," which Al had cut before he withdrew. Kinsey then went back to Indiana. He got another call from Don Taylor a few weeks later, asking if Don would be interested in joining the band for the summer tour. Don flew to Kingston for a week, and settled into the seductive Hope Road routine of ganja at daybreak, porridge and fish tea, running on the beach, fresh fruit all the time. Bob checked him out spiritually. "He had his Bible, and he said, 'You ever read this?' He said, 'Where you think you're from? Where's your homeland? What's your real nationality? What's your real language?' He was always testing me in those days." Kinsey survived by concentrating at band rehearsals, gradually integrating the sound of his Gibson SG blues guitar into the Wailers' groove, even pushing the beat a little more into the spectrum of rock. More assertive than the tasteful and very economical Al Anderson, Don Kinsey really changed the way the Wailers sounded while he was in the band.

Rastaman Vibration, the Wailers' fifth album for Island, was released in May 1976. Its rough jacket of simulated burlap depicted Bob Marley in fatigues and bore the inscription: "This album jacket is great for cleaning herb." The back of the jacket bore the first scriptural quotation on a Wailers record; it was the "Joseph is a fruitful bough" verse from Genesis 49. For the first time Bob Marley was publicly identifying himself as Joseph, his tribal name as a member of the Twelves Tribes of Israel. *Rastaman Vibration* was also the first Wailers album to be widely considered disappointing by Wailers fans. After the dread rhetoric of *Natty Dread* and the fiery rock music of *Live,* the new album seemed unmilitant, formulaic and a little contrived. The criticisms were for reggae's hardcore only: Bob Marley's new fans boosted the album into the charts in England and the United States. It was Bob Marley's biggest success in his lifetime.

Bob took credit for only three of the album's songs, the rest being divided between other Wailers and Bob's friends. While almost all the songs are undoubtedly Bob's, he was still signed to Danny Sims as a songwriter and he wanted to avoid paying Cayman Music the major portion of his composer's royalty. The album's opening tracks, "Rastaman Vibration" and "Roots, Rock, Reggae," are both credited to Vincent Ford, Bob's old friend "Tartar." The ballad "Johnny Was," a sad tale of violent death in Trench Town, was credited to R. Marley, Bob's wife Rita. A new version of "Cry to Me," an ancient Wailers standard, was credited to Bob, while the stern, admonitory "Want More," which spoke to the Jamaican people in folkish terms, was credited to Family Man. "Crazy Baldhead" on side two, the rootsiest number on a generally avant-reggae album, was credited to Bob and Tartar, while "Who the Cap Fit" (recorded years before as "Man to Man") was assigned to the Barrett brothers. Bob took sole credit for "Night Shift," which in a previous Wailers incarnation had been called "It's Alright," Bob's memory of his exile in the factories and warehouses of Delaware.

Rastaman Vibration's centerpiece was "War," Haile Selassie's speech on African resistance movements set to an ultramodern Carlton Barrett time signature. The hypnotic, chanting nature of Selassie's speech on the bondage Africa suffers is interpolated by Bob and the I-Threes, calling for war: *And until the ignoble and unhappy regime that now holds our brothers in Angola, in Mozambique and South Africa in sub-human bondage has been toppled and utterly destroyed/Everywhere is war.* With "War," Bob Marley and the Wailers became more than just a Jamaican reggae band. "War" forever identified them as members of a new international movement supporting African resistance that would culminate years later in the liberation of Zimbabwe and the continuing struggle against the racist government in South Africa. *Until that day, the African continent will not know peace. We Africans will fight, if neccessary, and we know we shall win as we are confident in the victory of good over evil/Everywhere is war.* "War" was credited to Skill Cole and Carlie Barrett.

The album's last (and best) track was "Rat Race," a bitter commentary on the upcoming Jamaican national elections, in which Bob reminds everyone that "Rasta don't work for no CIA." Released as a single by Tuff Gong, "Rat Race" was a huge smash in Jamaica, outselling even Bunny's big hit of the day, "Battering Down Sentence." Island released the more popsy "Roots, Rock, Reggae" as the single in England and America instead.

The Wailers went back on the road in June, ready for three months of touring in America and Europe. With two guitarists and Marcia Griffiths back in the I-Threes, the Wailers were a ten-piece; in spite of Bob's perfectionist rehearsals, it took the band a few dates to get the feel of each other. Don Kinsey recalls the initial difficulty of playing "with seven other musicians, each playing a different rhythm, and you have to sustain yours. You have to simplify your style, set back, mellow it out, play nice and sweet." Kinsey taped most of the rehearsals, sound checks and early gigs on a small cassette recorder, so he could practice in his spare time. "I spent a lot of nights in my hotel," he says, "studying that music." Also part of the touring party was Alan Cole, working as a road manager and general man-at-arms, Tony "Gillie" Gilbert, who was cooking, Neville Garrick, soundman Dennis Thompson and Tony G., Don Taylor's live-lied-up road manager. (The siren used on "Crazy Baldhead" was originally bought by Tony G. on the previous tour to blast at attractive women espied by the Wailers from their bus.)

Once again the tour began in Miami, and Don Kinsey says that for him it was an epiphany. "When we finally hit the stage, it was the ultimate experience. It really opened my head up to see that many people aware and in tune to what he sang. It was really encouraging. It made me want to play my best, every night."

The first major show of the tour was at the Tower Theater in Philadelphia, and it was unlike any show that Bob Marley was ever to perform. After Tony G.'s corny soul-show intro ("Coming rootically all the way from Trench Town, Jamaica, the proverbial, the prophetic Bob Marley!"), Bob launched into an apostolic Christo-Rasta worship service, with Tyrone's organ sounding like Ebenezer Baptist Church and the I-Threes choiring like a Wednesday night prayer meeting. "Rastaman Chant" got a new lyric: *The Conquering Lion shall break every chain/Give us the vict'ry again and again.* After a subdued "Burnin' and Lootin'" Bob was positively mellow from the stage: "Well yeah! How ya all doin'? Jah bless you all, yunno . . . 'cause Jah Live!" Some Wailers fans were puzzled; this wasn't the firebrand Marley they had expected. They didn't know that Cedella Booker was in the audience, having been driven up from Delaware to see her son perform in public for the first time. Cedella sat through the show, alternately transfixed and excited that all the people seemed to be rejoicing with Bob. "He looked like a different person up there," she says. "You could see God Himself in Bob that night." The Philadelphia show was extra long, as Bob played for his mother and the band retested concert veterans like "I Shot the Sheriff" and tried the new songs from *Rastaman Vibration*. The show climaxed with a stunning "Rat Race," a long jam on "Want More" in which Bob began to talk in tongues, a trance inducing "Rastaman Vibration" and the ritual "Get Up, Stand Up," with nine-year-old Ziggy Marley coming on stage to dance with his father on the last song.

The tour went on to Boston, then to New York, where the Wailers sold out the Beacon Theater on Broadway. "War in Rema!" Bob shouted during the New York performance. "War in Concrete Jungle, war in Tivoli. Dis is war!" The next day Bob sat for a semideranged interview with *High Times*, posing for the drug magazine's cover beaming happily over a kilo of Thai marijuana. Island press officer Jeff Walker later said that it was the only photo session he ever arranged in which Bob was an enthusiastic participant. After smoking a big spliff of the Thai herb, Bob launched into a complex lesson of Rasta rhetoric that the editors later chose to print verbatim. As with many of the interviews on that tour, Skill Cole sat quietly in a corner, interjecting when something interested him.

In Chicago a week later, Bob complained about the many writers who misinterpreted what he said, and the interviewer ventured that some writers might be confused by an artist who talked rebellion but drove a BMW and lived in a big house. Bob got annoyed at this: "Ya see, my father is in Zion," he said, trying to keep his composure. "And my father create everyt'ing 'pon the face of the earth. I mean, what is a house for I to live in? When I was living in Ghost Town, no writers came down there, yunnerstand? When I was living in Ghost Town, leaning against all that zinc, with the burial ground right in front of me, there was nobody there. So we move uptown and the writers come; me got to go somewhere where all the writers can come." Bob and Skill dissolved into sardonic laughter at the thought.

A few weeks later, the Wailers hit Los Angeles, and the tour checked into the Cavalier Motel in Westwood, where Bob was besieged by fans and reporters. A few miles away on Sunset Strip, a giant billboard advertising *Rastaman Vibration* presided over the smoggy boulevard. The album had reached number eleven on the American charts, the Wailers' highest commercial penetration ever, and gave every indication of going top ten. All the Wailers' southern California gigs—the Roxy Theater, Santa Monica, Long Beach, San Diego—were sold out. The show at the Roxy was stunning, in part because Bob Dylan was in the audience and Dylan was an old-time favorite of Bob's. ("Him really say it clear," Marley had said of Dylan earlier in the year.) The crowd at the Roxy was wild for the Wailers and sang along with every tune, and the relatively intimate showcase allowed the band to sparkle. The first three songs ("Trench Town Rock," "Burnin' and Lootin' " and "Them Belly Full") were taken slowly, as the Wailers built steam. "Rebel Music" followed, a little faster, and then Family Man's new bass line for "I Shot the Sheriff" got the building rocking hard. "Want More" was played as a dub show-case for the Barrett brothers, and segued into "No Woman, No Cry" and "Lively Up Yourself." "Roots, Rock, Reggae" was done as a tribal recita-tion with the I-Threes, followed by a spooky "Rat Race" and "Rastaman Vibration." The finale was a long show-within-a-show beginning with "Get Up, Stand Up," which blended into "No More Trouble," then the long Selassie tirade of "War," which dissolved into a vocal jam with the I-Threes, ending in a new climax of "Get Up, Stand Up," in which Bob called out the vocalism *"Woi-Yo"* and the I-Threes and eventually the whole audience answered back *"Woi-Yo-Yo-Yo."* Many Wailers connois-seurs believe it was the best performance the band ever gave.

Back at the Cavalier Motel, everything was cool. During the day Bob and Skill played football and gave interviews. By night they occasionally ran around with the pretty girls who seemed to be knocking on Bob's door at all hours. (Rita Marley tended not to live with Bob when the Wailers went on the road, preferring to frugally share a room with Judy and Marcia.) There was always cocaine being offered, but in those days Bob usually stayed away from coke and mandated that the rest of the Wailers stick to herb as well.

Some interesting clues to Bob Marley's sense of self were given in interviews. To Carl Gayle of *Black Music,* Bob said, "Me is a natural man like any other man, and me feel like any other man. Me nuh really feel like a entertainer or a star or any o' dem t'ing deh. Me really know what me a-deal wid. Me know wha' me want, me know whey me come from, and me know whey me go." To a reporter from *Chic* magazine, who asked if Bob thought much about himself and his pleasures, Bob replied: "No man, I don't think o' me that much. Me know me do t'ings, me like to do plenty t'ings. The important t'ing is that the *truth* will spread out, and the change wha' some people figure can happen, a-gwan happen. Yeah, man! I just so confident, is a *shame.*"

Asked by Carl Gayle about the violence in Jamaica, Marley replied with a candor he might not have used were he speaking in Jamaica: "Political violence, I mean *planned political warfare,* trouble political peo-ple. Check for instance we now. Through [because] we could sing a tune and ten thousand people buy it, then politician would like have you in him back pocket. So you cyaan mek dat happen yunno. Is a dangerous game."

Many reporters asked Bob about the difference between his dance music and his religious philosophy. "Well, you see is the whole educa tional thing. If you talkin' to some people you 'ave fe talk to dem 'bout what *dem* a-talk about before you talk to dem about what *you* talk about." To another reporter: "These songs, people understand them or they cyaan understand them, but ya 'ave fe sing them just the same. Ya *really* 'ave fe sing them. What the people want is the *beauties,* man."

When one reporter questioned Bob on the death of Haile Selassie in Addis Ababa the previous year, Skill Cole spoke up: "Do you have personal knowledge of this?"

The reporter stammered that he had seen pictures in the papers, and Skill scoffed. "Pictures? I don't see no pictures! It's propaganda, man!" Then Bob spoke: "Selassie-I, you can check him so. 'Cause if him eighty-three today, tomorrow you see him and he twenty-eight. And next mornin' him a baby, and today him a bird. Yeah man! Jah Live! Ya cyaan kill God!"

The Wailers moved to Europe after the southern California shows. In Düsseldorf, Germany, they played for four thousand blue-eyed blond Teutonic youths in an outdoor concert. Backstage in the dressing room, Bob was handling a precious spliff when the Düsseldorf police walked in and announced a search. For twenty minutes, police questioned Bob about drugs while he palmed the spliff. Then they asked Bob to accompany them to the Wailers' hotel so he could be present during a search of his room. As they were walking out to the car, Bob surreptitiously handed the spliff to Tony G., who was walking next to him. Tony disposed of the roach, but it was the closest call the band was to have with the law that tour. In Amsterdam, Tony G. remembers, "We left the stage with everyone in the auditorium singing *woi-yo-yo-yo-yo,* and they was still singing as we got onto the bus, and they was still singing as we drove out of the stadium, and we could still hear them singing *woi-yo-yo-yo* when we were five blocks away. That really put a smile on Bob's face."

In Paris, the Wailers again played to adoring capacity crowds, French kids and West Africans drunk on reggae music and the wiry little sorcerer who windmilled his dreadlocks and seemed to command his own shining cult of swaying priestesses and hard reggae warriors. Don Kinsey's screaming, acidic guitar showpieces were given more space in Europe, prior to the Wailers shows in England. Also in Paris, Bob gave interviews, listening patiently as a translator reworked the French reporters' questions in terms Bob could deal with. One French girl asked Bob how old he was and he answered, "Today." Another asked about his home and Bob said, "My home is what I think about. My home is not a material award out there somewhere, yunno. My home is in my head. In the other type of language, realistically I mean, I never stay away from Jamaica yet. I am always there."

A lot had changed for Bob Marley in the year since he and the Wailers had last been in London. He was now more than just reggae's first star: he was its spokesman. And even more than that, as *New Musical Express* called it at the time. "The white kids have lost their heroes; Jagger has become a wealthy socialite, Dylan a mellowed, home-loving man, even Lennon has little to say anymore. So along comes this guy with amazing screw top hair, and he's singing about 'Burnin' and Lootin' ' and 'brain-wash education' and loving your brothers and smoking dope. Their dream lives on. And for the black kids, a leader, far more than just a star to many of them. Rastafari lives in him; he carries the spirit of their religion and their God."

The Wailers' initial shows in London, at the Hammersmith Palais, were marred by sound problems, but as the tour progressed through England they hit their stride, a Rasta revival meeting careening through the British landscape. At Cardiff, Wales, there was a near-riot when fans without tickets couldn't get in.

Back in London, the tour over, Bob and Skill Cole planned a trip to Ethiopia. Tony G. ran around arranging for shots and visas (the trip was postponed because of Ethiopia's war with Somalia), the last chore he was to perform for Bob as an employee of the jealous Don Taylor, who at several instances during the tour had tried to get Tony in trouble with an easily perturbed Bob. "Once we went to a town," Tony G. remembers, "and Bob likes to have a spacious room, OK? But we didn't always have much money then for him to have a suite. So Don Taylor said to get Bob a single room, and I followed orders. I found it peculiar, because I was always getting Bob a double or a suite if it had a kitchen. So I gave him his key and took up his stuff, and later on he came down and I hear him say, very hard, 'Where Tony Garnett?' I could tell from his tone of voice that sumpin' not right. I say', 'Wha' happen?', and him seh, 'It's *Trench Town* me come from, yunno. One room!! Me nuh wan' see dem t'ing a nuh more. How come you give me this likkle room? Whey *you* room? Lemme see ya room now.' I show him my room, a big room, and him say, 'Look 'pon ya room and look 'pon that likkle room you give me. I want something *decent* and t'ing.' " Later, Bob voiced suspicions about

Don Taylor's dealings to Garnett, and asked him if he thought he could do Don Taylor's work. Garnett said no, that he just didn't have the contacts and sophistication that Taylor had.

The Jamaica that Bob Marley returned to in September, with the summer's travels behind him, was in some ways different from the one he had left four months before. Michael Manley had declared another state of emergency on the previous June 19, and was now ruling by decree in an effort to crack down on the political violence that was turning Kingston into a ghost town. A long tradition of election-year violence had gotten out of control in Jamaica, aggravated by a strange flood of thousands of pistols and shotguns into Jamaican society. The sources of all the guns were mysterious. Some said that the big ganja dealers in the rural parishes were now demanding guns in payment for their herb because the Manley government had made it illegal to have U.S. currency. Huge shipments of small arms were said to be landing on darkened country lanes in light planes out of Miami and Louisiana. The guns were then easily converted into cash in Jamaican cities and towns. Others said that the guns were smuggled into Jamaica by the JLP (under leader of the opposition and former Kingston record producer Edward Seaga) in order to prevent what some Jamaicans interpreted as a Communist takeover of the island. Michael Manley's increasingly militant socialist program, his material support for the revolution in Angola and his friendship with Fidel Castro of Cuba frightened the old Jamaican plantocracy, as well as the small middle class that had been nurtured in the last twenty years. They looked at Michael Manley—one of them, after all—and saw red. When the IMF forced Jamaica to adopt strict import and currency restrictions, the country had to tighten its belt, as the dreadful saying goes. Foodstuffs occasionally dwindled; there were shortages of rice, cooking oil, flour. Competition was fierce in Jamaica just to eat, and people wondered what had happened to Michael Manley's vaunted management abilities. At the same time, a brain drain of educated and skilled Jamaicans sapped the nation of some of its best people. Manley and his supporters began to speak darkly of "destabilization," the planned disruption of Jamaica's economy by the CIA, which in 1973 had helped the Chilean military savage that nation's experiment with elected socialist change. In Kingston's virulent street graffiti, Edward Seaga got a new name—CIAga. The big songs of the day were all militant: "We Should Be in Angola" by Pablo Moses, "MPLA" by the Revolutionaires, "Right Time" by the Mighty Diamonds, "Ballistic Affair" by LeRoy Smart. The morning *Gleaner* blared out daily headlines on the night's murders and mayhem, and it seemed to Jamaicans as if Kingston was becoming a Belfast or a Beirut, another tribal city bent on its own annihilation.

It was in this sultry, dangerous port city that the events surrounding the "Smile Jamaica" concert were played out, the attempted assassination of Bob Marley and the Wailers.

The year before, Stevie Wonder had played in Kingston with the Wailers and had offered half his fee to a school for blind Jamaicans. For months since then, Bob had talked of making a similar gesture. He wanted the Wailers to do a free concert in Kingston's National Heroes Park as a way of thanking Jamaica for its support. Jamaica House, the prime minister's headquarters, was contacted and PNP minister Arnold Bertram acted as liaison for the government. Other artists—Peter Tosh, Bunny Wailer (as he was now calling himself) and Burning Spear—were asked to play. A date was set: December 5, 1976.

The idea of the concert was to work for peace among the warring factions of Jamaica. The theme was "Smile Jamaica," and the Wailers recorded two versions of a song under that title. The first was a fast scatting Afro-ska, cut at Lee Perry's new studio, the "Black Ark," a green concrete bunker behind Perry's house in suburban Washington Gardens. The second version, slower and ironically somber, was recorded at Harry J's: *Feeling up/Feeling down/This feeling wouldn't leave me alone/Then I came 'pon one who said/Hey Dread, smile Natty Dread/Smile, you're in Jamaica now.* At the time, it made a powerful statement, Bob Marley affirming his Jamaican nationality for all to see.

Not long after the concert had been scheduled, the government announced the date of the national election for two weeks after the concert, on December 20. For Manley and the PNP, it was a brilliant stroke of political theater. On the eve of the election that would decide the destiny of Jamaica between two polarized factions for the next five years, at the height of the battle between socialism and capitalism in the Caribbean, Bob Marley and the Wailers, who had supported Michael Manley in 1972, would again appear to endorse Manley and his vision before an immense number of Jamaicans.

At Hope Road, there was consternation. Bob was incensed that his charity concert had been co-opted by the government. And where the Rasta community had generally supported Manley four years earlier, most Rastas now were embittered that Manley hadn't legalized ganja or facilitated the repatriation of Jamaicans to Ethiopia. Yet the concert also had an attractive side for the Wailers: their topical singles, "War," "Rat Race" and "Who the Cap Fit," had all been banned from the radio, but

171

"Smile Jamaica" was a staple of the airwaves, a light and positive plea to Jamaicans to "settle down, roots people." (Another song Bob cut with Lee Perry, "Rainbow Country," was given to Jack Ruby's sound system and played at dances around Jamaica.) Preparations for the concert went ahead, despite some anonymous warnings and threats against Bob, which were assumed to come from JLP sources but weren't taken very seriously.

In October, Cindy Breakspeare won the Miss World beauty competition at Albert Hall in London. British tabloids splashed the beauty queen's ongoing romance with the Jamaican reggae king all over their front pages. The "Beauty and the Beast" fuss scandalized and shamed conservative Jamaicans, annoyed that Breakspeare would carry on with Marley, who was known to be married and the father of at least eight children by various common-law wives. In New York, Don Taylor tried to put the affair in perspective for *People* magazine in their article about Cindy: "Bob loves his kids and takes care of his family, but he's a bit of a gypsy. In the Caribbean we deal with love in a much more relaxed way."

Around that time, Bob also made a trip to his mother's house in Delaware, where his stepfather Edward Booker lay dying. Mr. Booker, on his deathbed, asked Bob to look after Cedella, Pearl and the two boys, and Bob gave his promise. When Edward Booker passed away, Bob told his mother to put her affairs in Delaware in order, because he wanted to move her to the house he was buying in the suburbs of Miami. Bob went back to Kingston a few weeks later, to prepare for the "Smile Jamaica" show. It was a tense period in Jamaica. The island was "Under Heavy Manners," the PNP campaign slogan, denoting children being disciplined. With the nation up for grabs, there was the feeling that *anything* could happen.

Bob Marley and the Wailers hadn't been expecting trouble that Friday night, December 3, even though unidentified voices on the telephone had warned that Bob should cancel the concert. Rita was also telling Bob that the concert was a mistake, and Marcia Griffiths flatly refused to perform because of the danger.

There had been other omens as well, among the more clairvoyant of the Wailers. Two weeks before, Judy Mowatt had a vision of a man stoning a rooster; the stones caught three chickens and their entrails protruded from their bodies. On the morning of December 3, she awoke to find three of her chickens dead. And the previous night, Bob had stayed with Rita in Bull Bay and had a dream, as he later told interviewers Basil Wilson and Herman Hall, where "I feel the whole thing going on . . . I was in a barrage of gunshot and no gunshot catch me. The vision just say to me, 'Don't run.' And me just wake up. And in the morning when I reach Hope Road, I tell them, bwai, you want to see what happen last night, I dream seh I was into pure gunshot, so be careful."

The rehearsal began at sunset in the studio behind the main house at Hope Road. The Wailers were jamming with the horn section from the band Zap Pow, who would accompany them later on stage. The I-Threes were there, as were five of Bob's children and innumerable hangers-on. It was a warm evening; the sooty haze of the day had been blown out to sea, and stars were visible in the clear night air. The Wailers had been polishing "Jah Live," which hadn't been played much in concert. At about eight forty-five, Bob decided to take a break. He told the musicians to work on the song's bridge and went into the little kitchen of the main house to get something to eat. Another reason for the break was the arrival of Up-Sweet, the Wailers' favorite Kali-man, a ganja dealer who was known for the best herb in Jamaica.

Just then Judy Mowatt of the I-Threes, who was pregnant, began to feel ill, and asked Bob to find someone to take her home to Bull Bay. Bob was in the kitchen eating slices of grapefruit, and directed Neville Garrick to take Judy in Bob's BMW. Neville tried to get out of the chore, asking Diane Jobson to take Judy, mostly because he wanted to smoke some of Up-Sweet's famous product; but Bob's orders were law and Neville and an assistant engineer named Sticko drove the BMW through the gates with Judy in the backseat. As they left, just before 9 P.M., Don Taylor drove into the compound and parked his car. From the back of the house he could hear the group rehearsing the bridge to "Jah Live." Taylor had come to see Chris Blackwell on business but Blackwell was late, so Taylor walked into the kitchen and found Bob and guitarist Don Kinsey eating grapefruit. Taylor asked for some grapefruit and started walking across the little room to get a piece. At that moment, they heard the first shots, and the shattering of glass all around them.

Taylor's car had, after a minute, been followed onto Marley's grounds by two white Datsun compacts. One car blocked the front gate as another screeched up to the front of the house. Six gunmen jumped out: two stood guard in front while four others ran to each side of the yard and started firing at the house and anything that moved. The first sounds anyone heard were pops, like firecrackers, and then the air was rent by exploding windows and splintered wood and plaster as the bullets flew around. Trying to get the children out a side door, Rita Marley was shot by one of the gunmen in the front yard. She felt a bullet enter her head

173

and blacked out. At the same time, the other gunman guarding the front pushed into the door nearest Hope Road with a revolver in his hand. Tyrone Downie's girl friend was standing right behind him, out of his line of sight, and described him as a sixteen-year-old kid, obviously terrified. He closed his eyes and pressed his head against the wall, blindly pointing his pistol into the corner where Family Man and other musicians were trying to squeeze into a bathroom. The kid pulled the trigger, and several bullets lodged in the organ and the ceiling. Then he ran out.

Back in the kitchen, Bob Marley was puzzled at the sound of the firecrackers. Then he saw a masked man stick his head in the kitchen door and raise the barrel of a submachine gun. Don Kinsey was standing next to him, and remembers: "One guy came through the little back door there, and man, this guy pulled this gun inside the door and just emptied that joker toward the corner where we were. And man, Bob and Don Taylor were right *there*. I said, God! What is going *on!?* When I seen this gun come up in the door, it was like slow motion, like I could just see the bullets coming and going right beside me."

Don Kinsey jumped behind some equipment and Bob jammed himself into a corner, trying to stay out of the way. Don Kinsey recalls that it was a little strange that the gunman didn't kill Bob. "He looked right up at us in the corner," Kinsey says, "and he knew he [Bob] was in there. So I think he wasn't really aiming, but just firing." The man got off eight shots. The first two were wild, ricocheting around the room. The next five ripped into Don Taylor's side and upper legs as he was reaching for the grapefruit Bob was still holding. The last slug caught Bob Marley, grazing the breastbone over his heart and the biceps of his left arm. Then the gunman ran out and back, toward the cars in front of the house.

After that, there were at least five minutes of dumb silence. Everyone who wasn't wounded had his head down, unsure whether or not the murderers had left. Then panic and screaming started around the house as the reality of the ambush sunk in. Don Taylor got up and started walking around, blood gushing from five bulletholes in his side and waist. After a few minutes he collapsed from shock and blood loss. By the time the first police car arrived on the scene, ten minutes later, Bob and Rita were already on the way to the hospital, followed by Taylor and a badly wounded friend of the band named Lewis Simpson. Incredibly, despite the ferocity of the raid and the large amount of firings, no one had been killed. The rest of the Wailers melted away from Hope Road as soon as Bob and Rita had been loaded into a car. Twenty minutes after the shooting, 56 Hope Road was deserted except for the police.

Driving Judy home to Bull Bay, Neville Garrick heard about the shooting on a JBC radio bulletin at nine-thirty. After dropping Judy off, Garrick burned rubber to get back, but the BMW blew a tire on the coastal road and Neville and Sticko jumped out to fix it. Suddenly a police car pulled up: "Bob Marley cyaar dat," the police said, and drew their guns. When Neville told them who he was, the BMW got a police escort back to Hope Road. Neville ran into the kitchen and saw the grapefruit Bob had been eating, lying in a huge pool of clotting blood. Although the police wanted him to stay at Hope Road and take charge, Neville drove immediately to the hospital. His fears were allayed somewhat when he saw Bob sitting up on a bench in the emergency area, a bandage being wrapped around the sternum that had been chipped by the passing bullet. Bob's fatigue pants and *Rastaman Vibration* promotional shirt were soaked in blood. Rita was lying in a ward with her head bandaged. The bullet fragment had lodged between her scalp and her skull without seriously wounding her; she could talk and was giving a statement to the police. Out in the hall, Neville saw Don Taylor being wheeled past, looking blue, drained of blood, and dead, on his way to the surgery that would save his life. Soon after, Michael Manley came to the hospital, followed by PNP finance minister David Coore, the father of Bob's friend Cat Coore from the Third World band. Manley placed Bob under the protection of the Jamaican security service, and a few hours later, when his wounds had been cleaned and stitched and after Rita was asleep, Bob was spirited out of the hospital and whisked to a secret location to try to recover and regroup. The "Smile Jamaica" concert was still on, and Michael Manley wanted Bob to go through with it. But no one knew for sure if, Bob having survived, the assassins might try to finish the job.

Four hours after the shooting, Bob and his closest associates gathered at Strawberry Hill, an old mansion in the mountains three thousand feet above Kingston. Blackwell had made the place available to Marley as a hideout, and the grounds of the house were surrounded by heavily armed police units; local mountain Rastas were said to be in the trees with sharpened machetes, standing watch over a scarred, frightened and extremely bewildered Bob. He sedated himself with a series of spliffs and stared out into the dark, listening to the deafening night sounds of the jungle's insects and birds.

The following day, Saturday the fourth, Bob slept and rested. When he awoke, he was again faced with the decision about the concert. At that point, he had no intention of going through with it. His wife was in the hospital, his children were safe and he was alive but totally out of it. The

Wailers were in hiding, scattered around Kingston, with little hope of gathering them in time.

The Wailers held a meeting that night from eight o'clock until two in the morning, trying to reach a decision, trying to reason out who had shot at them. Most assumed it was "poli-tricks," a case of rabid JLP jealousy over the Wailers' tacit endorsement of Manley and the PNP. Others weren't so sure, noting that one of Skill Cole's notorious scams, usually financed by Bob, might have backfired into an act of gangland vengeance. For a while, Bob thought the shooting might have had to do with the success of the Wailers, or his romance with Miss World, which had infuriated some in Jamaica. In any case, Bob was almost incoherently upset, and when the meeting broke up he still hadn't made the decision to appear the following night.

Early on Sunday morning, the outlook from Strawberry Hill brightened. First came the news that Don Taylor would survive, and would be flown to Miami to have a bullet removed from his spinal cord. Then a film crew from New York, hired by Chris Blackwell to chronicle the concert, gave Bob its set of powerful walkie-talkies, so the Wailers could communicate with each other from various locations about the city. But Bob was full of anxiety because the gunmen hadn't been caught. One of their cars had been found burned and abandoned in Trench Town, but the identities of the assassins, and whether they would attack again, remained a mystery.

Confusion reigned supreme as the day progressed. Bob sat at Strawberry Hill and waited, as Island Records press aide Jeff Walker talked via walkie-talkie to Chris Blackwell and the film crew back at the Sheraton, and with Cat Coore of Third World, who had gone to the concert site with the other walkie-talkie. When neither Peter Tosh, Bunny Wailer nor Burning Spear showed up to play, it was decided that Third World would go on stage to test the climate for Bob to come down from the mountains. Meanwhile, police were searching for the other Wailers, trying to assemble the band back at Hope Road. Don Kinsey was found at a friend's house, where he had been hiding since the shooting stopped, and was given an escort to the Sheraton, where the film crew was preparing its gear. Kinsey talked to Bob over the walkie-talkie, and Bob asked if he would play. Don said he would. Meanwhile, Tyrone Downie and Carlie Barrett had come to Hope Road, and only Family Man was missing from the nucleus of the band. Next Bob talked to Cat Coore at the site, where an estimated fifty thousand Jamaicans had gathered by four o'clock so as not to miss the historic concert that, against all expectation, still hadn't been canceled. When Third World took the stage Bob could hear the crowd's enthusiastic response over the radio, as well as a warm tribute accorded Bob and the Wailers by master of ceremonies Elaine Wint. After their set, Third World spoke with Bob again, telling him the vibes were right for him to come down and play. Next Bob spoke with Carlie Barrett at Hope Road, wondering how the Wailers could play without Family Man. At this Cat Coore piped in that he would play his bass. "Get over to the concert," Bob then told his drummer. "I t'ink we a-gwan come down."

Five minutes later, Bob had a change of heart when Rita begged him not to do the show. Judy Mowatt remembers: "Rita had come out of the hospital that same evening, and she was up at Strawberry Hill still wearing her bandages and her dressing gown. Lots of people were asking Bob if he was gonna do the concert and he didn't give them any reply at all. But a few people were *insisting* that he do the concert. And Rita was there crying and saying that he shouldn't do the concert because of what had happened to him. A lot of people, myself too, was fearing that the concert might be worse than what had happened at Hope Road." When Bob looked like he was wavering, an argument erupted between him and the powerful, radical PNP housing minister Anthony Spaulding, who had been given the task of persuading Bob Marley to play that evening. (Spaulding may have called in an old favor, having given Bob a house in Bull Bay when the PNP took over in 1972.) Eventually, Spaulding's rhetoric and cajoling persuaded Bob; and the group piled into a motorcade idling outside the house. Next to Marley in the back seat of a red Volvo was the Jamaican commissioner of police. As the line of cars began a mad dash down the winding mountain roads, the commissioner opened his attaché case and casually assembled and loaded a small machine gun, just in case. When Jeff Walker contacted Heroes Park and informed the stage crew that Bob was on his way and that the Wailers would play, he could hear the jubilation on the other end of the walkie-talkie. Halfway down the mountain, the motorcade blundered into a rival JLP election rally that was just breaking up. But instead of being hostile when the crowd saw who was in the car, they began to chant *Bob-Mar-ley, Bob-Mar-ley!* At that point, Bob realized that his safety might be assured.

Down at National Heroes Park there was pandemonium. The crowd had swollen to eighty thousand, the entrances to the park were clogged and the tiny stage was surrounded by the waving, rapidly moving crowd, illuminated only by a single spotlight and the lights of Chris Blackwell's film crew. Michael Manley was up on stage, talking to the people as he waited for Marley. When Bob's car squeezed through, Bob bounded out and was rushed up to the stage where he was embraced by Manley, who then retreated to the top of a nearby van where he watched the concert in full view of any of the snipers who were generally presumed to be lurking in the crowd. "The great, the great, the great, the great Bob Marley," the MC shouted. "C'mon, people, the guy come out of his *bed* fe sing fe you!"

Rita Marley and Judy Mowatt had been in a car behind Bob's, and by the time the two women struggled through the crowd to the side of the stage, Bob was already into the first number, a churning version of "War." When he had first reached the stage, Marley had checked what musicians there were—Carlie, Tyrone, Cat Coore from Third World, the Zap Pow horns and five drummers from the akete group Ras Michael and the Sons of Negus. It was good enough. Bob turned to the cheering throng and shook out his dreadlock mane with a wild yodel of exultation. Then he asked for quiet, and said: "When I decided to do this concert two-and-a-half months ago, *there was no politics!* I just wanted to play for the love of the people." Then he muttered that the Wailers would do just one song, and lit into "War." Halfway through the song, Don Kinsey showed up and took over on guitar. Dressed in a simple brown tunic over his bandaged torso and wearing jeans and ankle boots, working without his heavy electric guitar, Bob performed a manic "War" for the first time in Jamaica, driving the pickup Wailers to a hard, military groove. Instead of leaving the stage after "War," Bob went into "Trench Town Rock," followed by "Rastaman Vibration," a murderous rendition of "Want More" and an amazing version of "So Jah Seh," perhaps the only time the Wailers ever performed that song in concert. Many in the delirious crowd were especially moved by the spectacle of Rita Marley singing onstage in her nightgown and hospital robe, an Ethiopian scarf covering the bandages wound round her head.

As the "Smile Jamaica" concert came to its climax, Bob finished his ninety-minute set with a dramatic gesture. He pulled up his loose shirt and rolled up his sleeve to expose his wounds to the people. Then he let his clothes drop and crouched into the stance of a Wild West gunfighter and pointed two fingers at the crowd like a pair of Colt .45s. Head thrown back, locks flashing in pride, Bob's bravado gesture seemed to breathe defiance and victory. The show was over. Within minutes, the nervous crowd had scattered. It was said that never had a crowd disassembled so fast in Jamaica.

Bob Marley was still terrified. He spent the night again at a heavily guarded Strawberry Hill, and at seven the following morning flew out of Jamaica on a private jet chartered by Chris Blackwell, accompanied only by Neville Garrick, bound for safety at Blackwell's new headquarters on the island of Nassau in the Bahamas. It would be more than a year before Bob Marley would set foot in Jamaica again.

An hour after the plane left Kingston, Bob and Neville Garrick landed at the Nassau airport, and Bob had to pass through a very edgy customs examination. By then, the assassination attempt was headline news all over the world, and anxious Bahamian officials asked the exhausted Marley if he was seeking political asylum. Bob said no, that he was on vacation. When customs finally let them through, a car took them to Blackwell's house at Compass Point, where Bob retired to try and get some sleep. He had been almost continuously awake since Friday morning, four days earlier. But two hours later Bahamian police and officials were at the door to escort Bob and Neville to another interview with higher immigration officials. They were eventually given the most conditional of temporary visas, so that the authorities could deport them quickly in case of trouble. Rita Marley and the children arrived a day later, followed by the rest of the Wailers in another week. Everyone's visa had to be renewed every week. Eventually Don Kinsey had enough, and flew home to Indiana with regrets and no hard feelings.

Who shot Bob Marley? Rumors ripped through every level of Kingston. Some people theorized that the attempted assassination might not have been political. One widely circulated rumor claimed the shooting was the result of a racetrack fix at Kingston's Caymanas Park, engineered by Skill Cole, who then skipped out of the country with a large amount of currency. Variants of this rumor included ganja deals, cocaine burns and a revenge hit by Jamaican gangster elements. Perhaps significantly, Skill Cole disappeared from Jamaica for several years. Later, several Wailers heard that the assassins hadn't themselves survived the weekend, having been murdered by the elements that hired them.

According to Michael Manley, speaking years later, his intelligence service "drew a blank" when the shooting was investigated. Detectives naturally tried to trace the getaway car back to Tivoli Gardens, the deep slum constituency of opposition leader Edward Seaga, but to no end. It was, Manley said, "an extremely skilled and professional job." Some said that the professionalism included the fact that no one had died, as if the shooting were a warning rather than an assassination. Others said the primary target might not have been Bob, but Don Taylor, who was known to gamble. The bullets the gunmen had used were all homemade.

The shooting did attain one objective: Bob Marley had been physically removed from the political landscape, no longer a threat to either side in the worsening battle for Jamaica. And a week later, on December 15,

179

voters gave Michael Manley and the PNP 47 seats out of 60 in the Jamaican Parliament, a convincing mandate for socialism in Jamaica. Two hundred had died in the worst election violence in Jamaican history.

Later, when asked who had shot him, Bob Marley would say he didn't know. "A man came to me and want to clear up my mind, and say, 'Bob, is politics.' He said to me he was in one place and see where I was going to get hurt, but he just could not do anything. That mean, the man tell me, is his side it come from. But that cool. Some people want to talk about is through Miss World, and through the group and dem likkle t'ings. Is *foolishness*, all dat. Seen?" Much later, interviewed by the New York *Times* at his mother's house in Delaware, Bob was more philosophical about the reason he was shot. "Maybe jealousy," he said. "Jealousy's a disease inside plenty people brain. It stir 'em up and twist 'em 'round toward wickedness. That the trut'. And when you know the trut', ya cyaan get annoyed."

The Wailers stayed in the Bahamas for the next month, through January 1977. Just before Christmas, Bob was reunited with Cindy Breakspeare on nearby Paradise Island. Cindy had been in London during the shooting, attending to her chores as Miss World, and the reunion was a joyous and tender occasion for Bob, especially when Cindy told him she wanted to have his child. The couple spent long days swimming in the azure sea; at night they went to shows by pop groups at the big hotels. They were good friends who had fallen happily in love with each other again, and work began on Bob's ninth child. When their son was born, Cindy named the boy Damian Marley.

Stevie Wonder jamming with the Wailers on "Exodus" at the Philadelphia convention of the Black Music Association, 1979.

Bob receives a traditional Maori tribal welcome when the Wailers play Aukland, New Zealand. Note the carved stick in his left hand. *Island Records.*

Bob receives a Maori greeting during the Wailers' tour of New Zealand, 1979. *Island Records*

Bob during the Wailers' last tour, 1980. *Frank Spooner Pictures.*

Bob Marley, Kingston, 1980. *Adrian Boot.*

Zimbabwe, 1980.

Bob Marley and the Wailers pose in a London elevator after returning from Zimbabwe, 1980. (Standing: Tyrone Downie, Junior Marvin, Earl "Wire" Lindo, Seeco. Below: Carlie Barrett, Bob, Al Anderson, Family Man.)

Adrian Boot.

Cedella and Bob read the Bible at the Sunshine House clinic at Bad Wiessee, Bavaria, 1981. *Monte Fresco, Associated Newspapers Group Ltd.*

After his passing in May 1981, Bob apotheosized into a Jamaican stamp.

Edward Seaga, the Jamaican prime minister, walks up the hill to Bob Marley's tomb. *Frank Spooner Pictures.*

Bob Marley's grave (left) next to the little house where he lived with Rita between 1967 and 1970. *Adrian Boot*

8

Babylon by Bus

. . . Yeah, seventy-seven, yunno? Two sevens meet, and that mean a
dangerous time, dangerous in a sense of being a dangerous *good*
time . . .

(1977)

> *The Wailers will be there*
> *The Damned, the Jam, the Clash*
> *Maytals will be there, Dr. Feelgood too*
> *No boring old farts/No boring old farts/No boring old farts*
> *Will be there*
> *Well it's a punky reggae party*
> *And it's tonight!*
>
> "Punky Reggae Party"

Early in January 1977, Bob Marley and the Wailers moved to London to
begin recording a new album. As a balm for his wounds, physical and
mental, Bob threw himself into his work. The band settled into a comfortable flat at 42 Oakley Street, Chelsea, and hermetically sealed itself
off from the world, an I-tal Rasta enclave protected by receptionists in the
lobby and the apartment block's security system. The flat was carpeted in
plush brown, the furniture was Habitat; Family Man had a mini-mixer
between the speakers of his portable sound system so he could pump up
the bass how he liked it, the color television was always on—a Babylonian hearth ("Exodus!" the band would yell at a jailbreak on some television show)—and Gillie was in the kitchen cooking and lovingly serving
huge meals of ackee and salt cod, vegetables, dumplings and Irish moss,
the spermy concoction that Jamaicans revere as a health food and which
Gillie called "life protoplasm." As soon as a batch was ready Gillie would
call out "Where's the Skip?" so that Bob, a rabid moss fan, would get the
first taste. Once, at the London flat, a female journalist asked Bob what

181

Irish moss would do for her health. As sincerely as possible, Bob told her that it would wet her poom-poom.

A river of new songs and updated Wailers standards was running through Bob's mind and he was anxious to cut, as soon as possible, the first Wailers music recorded out of Jamaica since the days of "Reggae on Broadway" six years earlier. But a new guitar player was needed to replace Don Kinsey, and Bob had begun to think about trying to lure Al Anderson back from Peter Tosh's band when Chris Blackwell mentioned Junior Marvin. Junior was a young black blues guitarist who had been born in Jamaica and then raised with relatives both in England and America. His real name was Julian; as a musician he had been known first as Junior Kerr, then as Junior Hanson. He had toured and apprenticed with the Texas bluesman T. Bone Walker, and had also worked with Billy Preston, Ike and Tina Turner and Bob Marley's friend Stevie Wonder. Junior was an experienced blues-rock player who had released two albums on Atlantic Records in the United States with his own band, Hanson, and Bob liked him immediately because he thought he could hear a streak of Jimi Hendrix in Junior's style. One day Junior was recording a track for Steve Winwood at Island Studios when Blackwell asked him out of the blue if he'd like to join the Wailers. When assured that the Island boss wasn't joking, Junior said yes. He then spent a week with Bob and Tyrone Downie, jamming and learning the new songs Bob was working on. After a few days Family Man plugged his bass into a mini-amp and joined in. Junior was a Wailer. Someone popped a cassette into a recorder and the proto-sessions for *Exodus* had begun. "Waiting in Vain" was then a slow, acoustic ballad, Bob and Tyrone duetting on the vocal harmonies the I-Threes would later re-create. "So Much Things to Say" only half-existed, as Bob was still teaching himself the verses. "Exodus" was emerging as a hard trance-rocker, goosed by Junior's beat-rushing style, while "Jamming" was still an acoustic chant, Bob searching for the song's eventual bounce. Bob was readying enough songs for the next two Wailers albums, and during the rehearsals and jam sessions in the winter of '77 the Wailers prepared more than thirty songs for recording. They were also closely monitoring the music coming out of Jamaica, taking note of the new groups that were emerging to fill the gap left by their exile, harmony trios like the Meditations, Israel Vibration, the I-tals and Culture. The big song of the day was Culture's "Two Sevens Clash," an apocalyptic prophecy that 1977 would be a time of extreme judgment for Jamaica and the world at large. Jamaicans, especially the millenarian Rastas, felt something special in the air.

In London there was a different kind of feeling. Young white rock fans were turning into punks, tearing their clothes, mortifying themselves with safety pins and razors, dyeing their spiky hair in wild colors and adopting a fetish regalia of black leather and bondage uniforms. It was wild. They *loved* reggae, just as the skinheads had gone to black clubs to dance the rock steady a decade earlier. And just as Jamaican society reviled the Rasta for his hairy cords and his no-future philosophy, the English dreaded the punk for his relentlessly blasting music, for his psychotic and mutilated appearance and for the outrages of the baddest of the punk bands, the Sex Pistols, who in the year of Queen Elizabeth's royal jubilee said "fuck" on the telly and sang "God save the queen/And her fascist regime/She made you a moron/And England's screaming!" Bob Marley enjoyed those lines.

In the middle of the sessions, Lee Perry showed up and moved into a flat above Island's Basing Street studios. The Wailers were heavily into the *Exodus* music, but work stopped for a while so Bob and Lee could catch up and talk about working together again. Perry had been producing some brilliant reggae in Kingston, working with the Heptones and Junior Murvin, a veteran singer who had cut a song Perry had written, "Police and Thieves." The song had been a huge hit in Jamaica, where it described daily life in Kingston: "Police and thieves in the street/Fighting the nation with their guns and ammunition." But now, at Basing Street, Bob and Lee Perry first heard a new version of "Police and Thieves" by a punk band who called themselves the Clash, after Culture's song "Two Sevens Clash." The Clash's version of Perry's song was horrible, a garage band on leapers, but for Lee Perry it held a certain fascination and for the punk/new wave movement it paved the way for punk's close alliance with reggae, the outcast youth of two races banding together for solace and support. The *Exodus* sessions had stopped for the day by the time Bob Marley agreed to go into the studio with Perry and record a song Perry had written about the alliance, "Punky Reggae Party." The only musicians around were members of Third World and Aswad, one of the young Rasta reggae bands that had grown up in England in the wake of Jamaican stars like Bob. They were quickly recruited to lay down a backing track as Bob put his soul into verses that described the common ground between rebellious black and white youth: *Rejected by society/Treated with impunity/Affected by my dignity/A search for reality—New Wave!* Later some of the Wailers dubbed new parts behind a long, flamboyant scat vocal by Bob, and later in Jamaica Lee Perry added backing vocals by the Meditations, who croaked "oink oink" behind Bob, reflecting Perry's distaste for the punks' general gestalt of spit and filth. "Listen, punk love reggae," Bob said later, "and some a dem seh things that Babylon no like. I thought dem was badness first, but now me give dem nine hundred percent right. Dem resist the society and seh, 'Me a punk cos I don't want you to shove me where I don't like it.' . . . Because him nuh feel like we inferior—white man feel inferior to the black man, that's why him try kill the black man. And the punk seh, 'No! We wanna join wit the Rastaman and get something outta life.' "

Bob Marley and the Wailers cut twenty new songs at the Island studios during the winter of 1977. The ten most innovative and expressive of these appeared on the *Exodus* album, released the following spring. The remaining ten came out the next year, on the *Kaya* album. (With Lee Perry, Bob also cut an epistolary version of "Keep On Moving" for his children in Jamaica.) These London sessions marked another change of direction for the Wailers. Bob's lyrics were a mixture of spiritual militance and inward-directed recrimination (his family—his children— had narrowly escaped murder), tempered by the most deeply felt and passionate love songs he would ever write, a reflection of his affair with Cindy Breakspeare. And the music itself was also changing. "Exodus" incorporated the new four-to-the-bar "militant" style of drumming (also called "rockers," devised primarily by Kingston session drummer Sly Dunbar) that had taken Jamaican reggae by storm. And the addition of Junior Marvin on guitar also seemed to notch the Wailers' basic locomotion into a higher gear. That, plus the addition of a three-piece horn section (Vin Gordon, Glen DaCosta and David Madden), gave the Wailers an even more martial and explosive sound.

Exodus was unlike any other Wailers album. "Natural Mystic" had an invocational feeling, intuitive of an impending spell. The next three songs were programmatic, all dealing with the attempted assassination. "So Much Things to Say" invoked Marcus Garvey and Paul Bogle (the executed leader of the Jamaican peasant revolt at Morant Bay in 1865), before stating a Rasta mission: *I and I nuh come to fight flesh and blood/but spiritual wickedness in high and low places.* The song decried the rumor and "labbering" that had plagued Bob since the "Smile Jamaica" concert. "Guiltiness" was an extraordinary incantation predicted by "Natural Mystic," a long-distance curse at Marley's enemies: *Woe to the downpresser/ They'll eat the bread of sorrow/Woe to the downpresser/They'll eat the bread of sad tomorrow.* "Heathen" continued this assault and boosted family spirits as well: *Rise up you fallen fighters/Rise and take your stance again/He who fights and run away/Lives to fight another day.* A restive, disturbed mood was conjured by stinging solos from Junior and Tyrone, reggae-rock fireworks. "Exodus" both described the Wailers' own hegira and called for a mental, if not physical, migration of New World blacks to Africa, forsaking the industrial materialism of the West by arming themselves with the faith of Rastafari and black prophecy.

The album's second side was much more reflective, a suite of dance and love songs. "Jamming" was mere innovation, the Wailers going slightly disco. "Waiting in Vain" revealed a fragment of the dynamic between Bob and Cindy as Bob touchingly comments on the biochemical nature of jealousy. "Turn Your Lights down Low" is the tenderest ballad of Bob's career, while "Three Little Birds" is almost children's music, evocative of the carousel or a church fair. The album ends with a medley of the old Wailers' "One Love" with a revamped Curtis Mayfield chestnut, "People Get Ready." The use of the classic Rasta plea for unity and togetherness in "One Love" seemed to lift the curse laid on early in the record, promising a newer atmosphere of reconciliation that would become a reality for Bob Marley within a year's time.

Bob was restless during the recording sessions. The tracks took long, tedious hours to mix; when one was finished Chris Blackwell would send for "the Skip," who usually was found in a heated game of table football with other Wailers or members of Aswad. There was one special moment when Blackwell called Bob in to listen to the final mix of "Exodus." Bob leaned against the wall as the martial music unfolded around him. Then Bob erupted into a frenzied hop that galvanized the studio and sent all the cool steppers around him into motion. Bob liked the mix; it was an electric moment, the birth of "Exodus."

Bob's private life at the time was hectic. He was living alternately at Wailers headquarters in Chelsea and in a secluded town house in Colligham Gardens, Earls Court, where he could carry on in private. Around this time he was introduced to the Ethiopian royal family, which was living in exile in London. The family was headed by Haile Selassie's grandson, Crown Prince Asfa Wossan, the pretender to Selassie's abolished throne. It turned out that Asfa Wossan knew the Wailers' music, and he gave the awed Bob Marley a ring that he said had once belonged to Selassie. It was a gold band with a golden Lion of Judah rampant in a setting of black onyx. The ring immediately became Bob's most treasured possession, perhaps his only one, and he wore it every day for the rest of his life.

Early in April, the Wailers had finished recording and were beginning to rehearse for the upcoming 1977 tour to support *Exodus* in Europe and the States. One night Bob and Family Man were driving in Ladbroke Grove, a partially West Indian neighborhood in northwest London, when their car was stopped by police. When the constables searched them, they found a big spliff in Bob's pocket and another in Fams's cock. When the cops asked for Bob's residence so they could search for more pot, he gave them the Earls Court address to avoid a bust of the rest of the band back in Chelsea. They went back to Bob's house, found a pound of herb and arrested both Bob and Family Man Barrett for possession.

The two Wailers were tried at Marylebone Magistrates Court on April 6, found guilty and fined fifty pounds. The judge told Bob and Family Man: "Whatever the approach or attitude in your own country you must really appreciate that here it is still an offense. While you are here it would be very unwise to use or have possession of cannabis." The two Wailers nodded solemnly in agreement, relieved to be let off with a slap on the wrist. Outside, on the courthouse steps, Bob told reporters that he smoked pot because he didn't drink. The man from the *Daily Mail* asked Bob if he was planning to marry Miss World, and Bob laughed. "She's one of my girl friends," was his reply.

The Wailers' European tour began in Paris in May, a month after *Exodus* was released, and had jumped on the charts in Britain and Europe. The tour went well, but right at the beginning there was a bad accident. Bob was injured during a pickup football game between the Wailers' squad and a team of French journalists. "In Paris I was playing soccer and a man gave me a raas claat tackle in the rain," Bob recalled later. "The foot started paining me, and I wonder now why it kept burning for so long. Bwai, I score a goal and just hop off the field. When I took off my shoe, the toenail was completely out."

The same toe had been hurt years before in a hard-fought game in Trench Town in the early seventies. Now, a French doctor examined the foot, cut off a jagged piece of nail, bandaged the wound and told Bob to stay off his feet. But Bob Marley had a tour to do. *Exodus* was hot and Chris Blackwell thought that with the Wailers providing maximum tour support, the album could be Bob's first international number one. The pressure was on: Bob wore heavy socks and sandals over his bandaged right foot. He even juggled a football during the lulls between sound checks and the shows, hoping the toe would heal in time for the British dates of the tour. In the meantime he traveled around Europe in considerable pain.

The first show was in Paris, at a converted slaughterhouse called the Pavillion. That afternoon the Wailers played a two-hour sound check without vocals, leaning heavily on older material for the European part of the tour to make up for the previous year's shows when they played mostly from *Rastaman Vibration,* disappointing fans who came to hear familiar songs. As the band was dressing for the show later, Bob was mockingly reproachful when he spied Tyrone's multizippered New Wave jumpsuit. "I nuh want no punks in dis band," he said with a laugh. Twelve thousand Parisians showed up for the show (opened by veteran Jamaican trombonist Rico Rodriguez), an inspired performance with Bob acting out his lyrics, crying in exaggerated rage and anguish, strutting across the stage in exultation, his head in his hands, locks trembling like cobras. On his right, the I-Threes experimented with Judy's new choreography, running through complex mime movements like the pistol-shooting pantomime on "I Shot the Sheriff." At one point the audience gasped when a madman bolted through the security line and started to dance around Bob on stage. Memories of the shooting were fresh in everyone's mind, but the man only wanted to express himself, and eventually Bob put his arm around him and they sang a verse of "Lively Up Yourself" together before Don Taylor dragged the intruder offstage. The most sensational new presence in the band was Junior Marvin's; wearing tight pants, twitching his butt and throwing down histrionic rock riffs on his knees, Junior took some of the visual focus off Bob, leaving the Skip free to roam around the stage evolving his own exotic, pantomimic dances. Afterward, Island Records gave a post-concert party for the Wailers at a chic boîte called the Club Elysées Montignan. As Bob came in, Bianca Jagger ran up to him and kissed him on the cheek. Bob thanked her and said, "Who dat?" Still in the denims he wore on stage, he danced with a stunning African model for two hours before he disappeared into the Parisian spring night.

The next day Bob sat for interviews, receiving the press in his kitchen suite at the Paris Hilton, dressed in a blue warmup suit with a heavy coin-silver Coptic cross dangling from his neck. The gold Lion of Judah ring beamed talismanic from his left hand. To journalist Karl Dallas he gave his new improvised definition of the word reggae: "Reggae kind of come from a Spanish, Latin word, and it mean 'King Music.' Yeah, that what reggae means." Most of the writers wanted to know Bob's reactions to the shooting. Asked by Robin Denselow if he had been back to Jamaica since the incident, Bob said, "No man, not yet. Fear, I wouldn't say fear yunno, but I really wouldn't want to get people with me shot up again, yunno, get them involved . . . It nuh difficult for me a-go back, but I need some time out of Jamaica, in the quiet, because me cyaan t'ink vengeance. Cyaan do dat, just let it cool out, because yunno, man have feelings . . . I had feelings of vengeance, yes, but me just outgrow it yunno. Me realize this is madness, and I don't really want a vengeance." Asked if he knew who shot him, Bob laughed in his rolling, infectious bray. "Yeah . . . but dat top secret. Yunno? Really top secret."

Asked if *Exodus* sounded different because it was recorded in England, Bob said no. "We're all on it, seven of us, right? And it's roots music, so if one man get too giddy, the other all seh 'Hey, him gettin' giddy!' I mean, him get too psychedelic [referring to Junior Marvin] and the islands don't like that, not a giddy man. Dem love a *root* man, so everybody have to stay root . . . Like Aston Barrett and Carlton Barrett, yunno? Ya cyaan return to the roots, you must *be* the roots. Guy t'ink he can return to the roots when he was a leaf, he drop off and that how he return to the roots. We must *be* the roots."

From Paris, the self-contained Wailers entourage embarked for the next gig at Brussels by bus. Offstage Bob was a shy and withdrawn man who spent his coach time quietly. On this trip he perked up when Seeco's birthday was announced, a bottle of champagne was uncorked and everyone sang happy birthday to the Wailers' rhythm elder. Wine was the only alcohol Bob Marley would drink, and he loved good champagne. When the bus hit the Belgian border Bob yelled out to everyone to flush their herb, but the customs agents, perhaps appalled by a coachload of scowling dreads, let the Wailers through without a search. Bob played soccer between shows at The Hague, despite bad pain. The tour passed through Holland, Germany and Scandinavia, giving spectacular shows of Wailers greatest hits and depending on Gillie's cookpot and electric blender for sustenance. Concerning the tour's business affairs, Bob depended on no one and trusted no one. The books of the tour management, an English company called Alex Leslie Entertainments, were under the constant scrutiny of Bob's lawyer, Diane Jobson. It was painful for Bob to think of all the money that had been stolen from him over his long career, and he was determined never to let it happen again. Even Don Taylor, recovered from his wounds and dealing on Bob's behalf, was suspect. Later in the year, Bob and Diane would meet with Bob's old mentor Danny Sims to discuss Marley's suspicions of Taylor's handling of the Wailers.

On June 1, the Wailers began a week of concerts at London's Rainbow Theatre. (One of the shows was filmed by Island Records and shown in European theaters later in the year.) Bob was greeted as a messianic figure in blue denim against a lurid stage backdrop of Trench Town shanties and bonfires. The audiences in their urban guerrilla outfits of boots and berets were a sharp contrast to the sensual majesty of the I-Threes, swaying in African tie-dye dresses and green capes. Bob was dancing now as much with his arms as with his legs, stabbing the thick air during "Road Block," holding the bridge of his nose in deep thought as "Crazy Baldheads" cleverly faded into "Running Away," stretching into an eerie cruciform during the metallic clank of "War," while behind him Seeco banged a huge Niyabinghi bass drum and the Wailers pounded like a mechanized artillery column moving along bad road. "No Woman, No Cry" provided a breather, but then Bob was up and dancing madly with his guitar on a fast version of "Heathen." The show's finale was a transcendent "Exodus" that built chorus upon chorus in spiraling echoes and reverberation, *We the generation/Tried through great tribulation* over and over again until the boundary between musicians and audience vanished. Back in the dressing room, an exhausted and limping Bob Marley found his right boot filled with blood; the ugly wound on his toe had opened again.

When the British leg of the *Exodus* tour was complete in June, Bob traveled to Delaware to rest at his mother's house and prepare for the upcoming American shows, which were to begin at New York's Palladium in July. But the crushed big toe on his right foot had never healed, and the infection had become worse in Europe and was beginning to fester. Bob tried to relax in Delaware, where he took his youngest brother, Richard, to a school picnic at a public park where he was surrounded by a large group of teenagers amazed by his twenty-five-inch dreadlocks. But his foot was so painful that Bob could hardly walk, and the future of the lucrative American tour seemed in doubt. At Island Records there was consternation; no one could imagine a Wailers show without a leonine Marley prancing around, but *Exodus* had gone to number one in England and Germany after the Wailers had toured, and it seemed as if the album could do similar business in America if the Wailers provided proper support.

Bob then flew back to England to consult with a foot specialist on why the toe wasn't healing. The surgeon examined Bob and took some smears from the toe to study further. The next day, Bob was told that the doctor had detected cancer cells under the microscope. "Does that mean I have cancer?" an uncomprehending Bob asked. The doctor replied that it did. Bob asked what he could do, and the doctor suggested that Bob's toe and part of his foot be amputated immediately to prevent the further spread of the cancerous cells. Asked if there was an alternative, the doctor said if a small part of the toe was amputated and the area cleaned of infection, that the cancer might be localized and possibly contained with normal therapy. The doctor added that the alternative was a long shot, and recommended amputation as soon as possible.

Bob Marley was in a terrible quandry. If his toe were amputated, his foot would heal quickly and the American tour could take place with a subdued, but definitely *there,* Bob Marley. If the other course were taken, Bob would have to be off his feet for six months, the already-booked tour would have to be canceled and *Exodus* sales would suffer.

The situation bred serious tension between Bob and his business people, which Bob later described to interviewers Basil Wilson and Herman Hall: "Here is what happen now. They don't want to run this thing like how I want to run it. Them want to run me on a star trip, but I am not on a star trip. I want that any time I tour and I look at myself and realize that my structure [health] run down, I must rest. But they are not concerned with my structure. Dem run and plan a North American tour . . . I watch Muhammad Ali and Alan Cole and I see how these athletes take care of their structure. But the people who set up the tour do not work. Them just collect money and when night come you find them in bed with two girls while you bus' your raas claat and work hard all the time. When my toe was injured, they didn't even know . . . My toenail had just come out and the bwai-dem still set up a North American tour . . . Here what they had planned to do: they had planned to cut off my toe, just so I could make the tour. I say *the blood claat bwai-dem plan to cut off my toe to do the tour!* Y'understand what I say? I am in London and I consult a doctor. The record company phone the doctor and ask how long will the toe take to heal? The doctor tell them six months. Then they asked how long it would take if the toe was cut off. The doctor told them that should take about a month. So dem would cut off my toe just so I could work. I just go an' check a black doctor; 'I hear say me all have cancer and dem blood claat dey.' But I just took a little rest. *Exodus* was a-bubble, and if I mek the tour *Exodus* would sell over a million. His Majesty [Asfa Wossan] said to me in London, 'Is what sin you do to agree to cut off your toe?' So I just seh to dem, 'Fuck off and go away.' So I just decide, and take a rest."

Against the advice of his London doctors, Bob returned to the United States for a second opinion. Accompanied by his personal physician, Dr. Carl Frazier (known to the entourage as PeeWee), Bob went to Miami to consult with Dr. William Bacon, a surgeon who had saved Don Taylor's life after the shooting. That night he called his mother in Delaware and sounded very depressed. Bob told his mother that Dr. Bacon had said that part of his toe would have to be cut off, along with more flesh higher up on the foot, if the cancer had spread.

Cedella remembers the call. "He said to me, 'Why Jah let me have cancer, Momma? I never do anybody anything that is bad, I never dunno able to why. Why would Jah let me have cancer?' So I never couldn't find no answer for him. Jah love, dey teach us, tie it." Cedella did seek out a famous black herbalist in the ghetto of west Philadelphia for a remedy for Bob, but the herbalist said that because of who Bob was, he was afraid to take the case.

On July 20, Don Taylor's Miami office announced to the local promoters that the Wailers' American tour was being postponed until the autumn because of an injury Bob had suffered in a soccer match. All tickets were refunded, and the public relations stance was that Bob Marley would resume touring in a few months. Right after that, Bob's foot was operated on at Cedars of Lebanon Hospital in Miami. The surgeon cut away the rest of Bob's toenail and some adjacent flesh, cleansing the wound of as many of the deadly melanoma cells as possible.

Bob recouped quickly from the surgery. He bought a large suburban luxury home in south Miami, big enough for Cedella and her brood and the big extended family appropriate to a Jamaican clan chieftain. With a commodious screened patio and pool, it was a nice place to recover, and remodeling of the house to Bob's Rasta/Ethiopian taste began immediately.

The type of skin cancer that had been diagnosed in Bob's foot was extremely dangerous and often fatal but, when discovered and treated early enough, was curable in many patients. Bob was given medication and told by his doctors to change his meatless Rasta diet to get more protein. Lee Jaffe walked into the kitchen of the Miami house one day after the operation to discover the formerly strict Italist devouring a plate of spaghetti and meatballs. Bob said the doctor had told him to eat meat for the protein. He maintained a regimen of medication and regular checkups, and his doctors gave him a clean bill of health two months after surgery. Two months after that, Bob Marley was playing football again. There were some bad moments—Cedella remembers Bob stubbing his toe while he was playing with his brothers and weeping with pain—but everyone was optimistic and praying that Joseph's hands would be made strong by the hand of the Almighty.

Despite the canceled tour, *Exodus* was a big hit in the United States, which was a solace to Bob in a time of trial. He was pleased that the album was getting a lot of air play on black stations for the first time, that black Americans were beginning to get the message he was putting out. The Wailers had always been puzzled by reggae's lack of acceptance in black America. Tyrone Downie voiced most succinctly what Bob and the band might have been feeling at the time: "The blacks in America are into glitter; they're into platform shoes, fur coats and Cadillacs. They're tame, man, and they're not about to let their pretty Afros down. All that talk of revolution—it *vex* 'em, man, it vex 'em bad."

Bob Marley's own attitude was both deliberately vague and visionary, as he told a reporter for the New York *Times:* "In Africa, dey prepare for Zion. It is for dem me sing my song. Me only want to sing and spread the word. It slow to start yunno, but now it creep up and the time is right. The time is right to rise up against Babylon. It have to be, in America, all over the world. It is prophecy, and dat no man can change."

As Bob's toe continued to heal, he rested amid his family and entourage at the big manse on Vista Lane in Miami. The leftover tracks from the London sessions were being remixed and overdubbed at Criteria Studio in Miami under Bob's supervision, to be used on the next Wailers album. At the same time, early in 1978, Bob and Don Taylor were finalizing plans with their booking agent for a Wailers world tour that would begin in May of that year in the States, cover Europe in the summer and wind up in Asia by the end of the year. Even after the previous year's canceled tour, the Wailers had no trouble booking dates anywhere they wanted to go. They were the hottest band in Western pop music, in demand all over the world. Bob's absence seemed to make his fans' hearts grow fonder, especially after rumors of his illness began to multiply right after his surgery. (West Indians occupy many paramedical, service and custodial jobs in American hospitals. Within hours of his operation at Cedars of Lebanon in Miami, the word on the street was that Bob Marley had cancer.) In the press especially, Bob was accorded a reverence and even a moral authority that only grew as he recuperated; he was described variously as "reggae's shining prince," "revolutionary artist," "a superstar of contemporary music," "modern prophet," "first Third World superstar," "most important cultural figure of the seventies," "a righteous campaigner for truth and justice" and—perhaps best —"the psalmist of Jamaican reggae."

But not everybody loved Bob Marley. In Jamaica, where almost every Wailers lyric became a cultural watchword, the Wailers' records were rarely best-sellers after the shooting, as if Jamaicans preferred their own roots music to the Wailers' new international sound. Some Jamaicans, people who gave credence to the widespread rumors that the shooting had been a revenge hit for Bob's part in a racetrack scam, accused Marley of selling out his ideals for the thrill of gangland enterprise. Others said the racetrack story was planted by the Jamaica Labour Party to cover up the role of its gunmen in the shooting. And not all journalists were awestruck and groveling. One long interview with *Melody Maker* went badly, with the writer unable to make anything but Rasta jibberish from the torrent of Bob's slurred patois on his tapes. When Bob saw the article he was almost trembling with anger as he read the quotes someone had underlined in red: "some of what Bob said was little short of crazy" . . . "the absurdity of some of his thinking" . . . "his verbosity is one-dimensional, emerging out of his bottomless faith in Rastafari" . . . "his monomania is quite frightening" . . . "ideas which seem quite absurd" . . . "the madness of some of his statements" . . . "screwy" . . . "paranoic exaggeration" . . . "deluded" . . . "incomprehensible rant."

All this time, Bob continued to work on his music and write new songs. Island had released "Exodus" and "Waiting in Vain" as singles during the previous year, and was now releasing "Punky Reggae Party" in England. In Jamaica, the song was released on Bob's label, Tuff Gong, along with another Marley/Lee Perry collaboration, "Rastaman Live Up," a wordy and sublime Marley one-drop sermon with backing vocals by the Meditations. Another song of Bob's called "A Jah Jah," an extremely rootsy and hard-rocking reggae hymn, had been recorded by Rita Marley on Tuff Gong. Those two singles—"Rastaman Live Up" and "A Jah Jah"—were, along with the forthcoming Tuff Gong single "Blackman Redemption," Marley's hard answer to critics who said the Wailers had gone soft.

Two hundred miles from Bob's house in Miami, Kingston was on fire. Something had to be done about the city's wretched decline into violence and anarchy. And into a dangerous void of moral leadership stepped the Twelve Tribes of Israel. Their long-range plans would eventually provide the vehicle for the safe return of Bob Marley to Jamaica the following spring.

Two factors helped form the so-called Peace Movement, which sprang up under Twelve Tribes' sponsorship in January 1978. The first was crime, which everyone could see was destroying Jamaica. The island had never recovered from the influx of guns and the subsequent tribal warfare surrounding the 1976 elections. People were being murdered in petty robberies almost as an afterthought, and rape had literally become a national nightmare. So many children were raped in Jamaica that the island's doctors were emigrating in disgust, unable to treat any more half-dead raped children. Gunmen were breaking down doors with the butts of M-16s and raping women in front of their families. All over Jamaica, wives were urging their husbands to emigrate, find work and get their families out of Jamaica. Trying to stop the incredible crime wave, Michael Manley ordered the Jamaican army into the streets. Late in 1977, an army ambush slaughtered five leaders of the JLP-oriented South Side Gang, and began a policy aimed at the repression of gunmen and criminals, who were arrested on sight and jailed.

Two friends of Bob Marley's found themselves sharing the same cell. Their names were Bucky Marshall and Claudie ("Jack") Massop. Massop was one of the JLP's most powerful warlords, thought of as a vicious gangster and a master criminal by Manley and the PNP forces. Marshall was a minor PNP thug. Both men had grown up with Marley in the zinc-sided back alleys of Trench Town. On the streets Massop and Marshall, controlled by opposing political factions, were the bitterest of enemies. But in jail, their acquaintance with Bob gave them a common ground, and they talked of how the civil war in Kingston might be stopped. It was Massop who had the idea for the Peace Concert. The plan was simple: the two warring factions of the JLP and the PNP would agree to a truce and a cease-fire and would begin to negotiate peace in the ghettos. To seal the pact, Bob Marley would be brought back to Jamaica, his safety guaranteed by the people who shot him, in order to play at a Peace Concert dedicated to the new movement. Eventually, Massop thought, peace in the ghettos would end the army's repression of his gang. The hardest part of the plan was convincing Bob Marley to return. Claudie Massop wasn't in a position to approach Bob directly, because Massop was a JLP man and Bob assumed that the JLP was still out to kill him. So Massop and Marshall approached the leader of the Twelve Tribes of Israel, Vernon Carrington (known as Gad, or Prophet Gad), to sponsor the Peace Movement officially and act as intermediary between it and Bob Marley, a Twelve Tribes member known as Joseph.

Members of the Twelve Tribes visited Bob in Miami and told him of the plan, urging him to accept. Bob replied that he would not return to Jamaica until he received a personal guarantee from Claudie Massop that he and his family would be safe. The delegation offered to fly Massop to Miami, but Bob didn't want any more gunmen near his family, proposing instead that a meeting with Massop be held on neutral ground in London, early in February.

During these days, Bob received some of the new Twelve Tribes esoteric teachings from the Prophet Gad, ideas that became part of Bob's thinking and were repeated again and again, especially in interviews, for the rest of his life. It was a complex system of beliefs, difficult to summarize, that held that common astrology was a Babylonian science symbolized by the signs of the zodiac. Was not Aquarius the name of a Roman god? And was not Rome the headquarters of Babylon and thus the source of all evil in the world, with the Pope sitting as Antichrist? Black people, the Twelve Tribes taught, should renounce astrology and identify instead with the biblical twelve sons of Jacob: Judah, Reuben, Gad, Asher, Naphtali, Dan, Simeon, Levi, Issachar, Zebulon, Joseph and Benjamin. Thus black people would recognize themselves as the true lost tribes of Israel, struggling in Babylonian captivity, yearning for redemption and Zion. Bob Marley was no longer an Aquarius. He was now *Joseph,* and his safety was guaranteed by prophecy: "The archers have sorely grieved him, and shot at him, and hated him: but his bow abode in strength, and the arms of his hands were made strong by the hands of the mighty God of Jacob, the king of Israel." It was trying to explain this symbolic, mythopoeic doctrine of the Twelve Tribes that occasionally earned Bob Marley—not the most articulate of men when trying to explain himself—epithets of "screwy" and "deluded" from the music press.

Early in February, Bob Marley met with Claudie Massop in London to discuss the Peace Movement. Bob was still unsure of who had ambushed his house fourteen months earlier, and told Massop that the JLP could not guarantee his safety if it wasn't their men who attacked him. At that point, Bob said, Massop admitted to Bob that the shooting was political, that JLP elements had done it, but that all was forgotten and Bob should come home and help stop his beloved Jamaican ghetto youth from dying like flies in the burning city.

Back in Jamaica, there was consternation in PNP circles that Marley was meeting with Massop, and that PNP interests were being represented by Bucky Marshall, a henchman so small-time that not even PNP minister Anthony Spaulding, the party's top political enforcer, had heard of him. The PNP quickly sent another old friend of Bob's, a militant ghetto captain named Tony Welch, to London to join the talks. The three men lived together for a week and negotiated a pact that called for a truce in the Kingston ghettos, climaxed by a peace concert with Bob Marley and the Wailers. On February 23 the announcement was officially made in London; the concert was set for April 22. Later, Bob spoke of the meeting and of his hopes for the Peace Movement: "The unity is the best thing that ever happen in Jamaica. The youths have a chance to turn themselves around. The two badman like Jack [Massop] and Tony [Welch], I see to it that they come together and talk and shake hand. And then we go back together and live as brethren . . . because the youth realize that dem grow with me for so long. I am a man who grow up in

Darling Street, Back O' Wall, Trench Town, Ghost Town, Concrete Jungle, all those places they say is rebels' area . . . I neither go right nor left. I go straight ahead, seen? I can't unite the JLP or the PNP because these are two organizations set up to fight against each other. That is called politics and I'm not into those things. We are talking about *Rasta*. We black people have a root. We are uniting regardless of whether you are PNP or JLP, regardless of what you are defending. We are talking about our real heritage. We are talking about the real self."

In March, Bob Marley returned to Jamaica to a jubilant welcome from friends and family. Once again the lights burned late at 56 Hope Road, the sound system blared and rehearsals started for the upcoming world tour, for which the Peace Concert was to be the first show. Bob made a triumphant progress through the worst ghetto neighborhoods in Kingston—Rema, Concrete Jungle, Matthews Lane—as a demonstration of solidarity with the Peace Movement. At the same time, the Wailers were being reformed, joined by some old members who had returned to the ranks. Guitarist Al Anderson was rehired and paired with Junior Marvin for the two-guitar sound that Bob liked. And another lost Wailer, Earl "Wire" Lindo, was encouraged by his replacement, Tyrone Downie, to come to the band rehearsals at Hope Road. Tyrone says, "I really care for Wire; I respect him and I copied him a lot to get my chops down. He came back to Jamaica and wasn't doing anything and needed money and he was like—he wasn't crazy, but he was into his head. People didn't understand him. He was frustrated because he's a great writer and composer." As soon as Wire showed up at the rehearsal, Bob invited him back into the band.

The Wailers' new album, *Kaya,* was also released that month and provoked a storm of controversy and criticism. The ten tracks from the London sessions had been remixed into a mellow pastiche of love songs and easy-skanking dance tunes, with barely a hint of Bob Marley's familiar defiance and rebellion. Given a very "bright" mix like a rock record, *Kaya* was uncharted territory for most of the Wailers fans. The opening track,"Easy Skanking," set a theme of peace and harmony, with Bob crooning about "takin' it easy, takin' it slow." "Kaya," a Rasta word for marijuana, was an updated version of a song the old Wailers had cut for Lee Perry years before, a lovely doper's vision of rising above the clouds and the falling rain. "Is This Love" was a touching declaration inspired by Bob's ongoing romance with Cindy Breakspeare, as was "Satisfy My Soul," a highly charged song of passion and sex that also had been recorded for the Upsetter as "Don't Rock the Boat." The side was rounded off by a sinister version of the counting song "Sun Is Shining," another Upsetter oldie. *Kaya*'s second side had a slightly more provocative dynamic. "She's Gone" and "Misty Morning" (the latter one of the strangest songs Bob ever recorded) dealt with the cooling of the Breakspeare affair. "Crisis" described the brutal conditions that had led to the Peace Movement. The album's most important number was the trenchant "Running Away," a talking-reggae in which Bob, performing in a curious singsong voice, describes some of his guilt and self-doubt over the shooting: *You must have done something you don't want nobody to know about . . . Lord, something wrong, you must have done something wrong, why you can't find where you belong.* The album finished with a soothing Rasta akete hymn, "Time Will Tell."

Reaction to *Kaya* and its themes of love, doubt and dance were strong. Bob Marley was widely accused of going soft and selling out. Asked by interviewers what had happened to his protest lyrics, Bob tried to explain: "How long must I protest the same thing? I sing 'Get up, Stand Up' and up till now people don't get up. So I must still sing 'Get up, Stand Up'? I am not going to sing the same song again . . . I do not want to be a prisoner. I don't want to see people suffer and sing as if I'm glad to see people suffer and to make money off of that. I want people to live big and have enough."

In March, Bob traveled to New York and was installed in a suite at the Essex House Hotel on Central Park South in order to give interviews promoting *Kaya* and the Peace Movement. Journalist Don Rojas of the black newspaper *The Amsterdam News* asked Bob about his critics. "Dem cyaan get me out so easy," Bob replied. "Dem 'ave fe try harder than that. Dem seh me is a traitor to my people. No. No. No matter what propaganda dem spread about me, I remain true to the masses. No man can change that."

Then Bob was asked about racetrack racketeering in Jamaica. He answered, "Me nuh gamble yunno, Rasta! Man in Jamaica seh me a-win race horse. Me? I-man is a *saint.* My only vice is plenty woman. Other than that, I-man is a saint to all dem accusation." Bob launched into a discourse on the anti-astrology doctrine of the Twelve Tribes: "Plenty people read horoscope but all dem signs is nothin' but Roman gods. That mean, is *Rome* many people dealing with. But when you know you is one of the twelve sons of Jacob, then you know yourself as an African. Man is a whole universe in himself."

On the Peace Movement, Bob was enthusiastic and fervent. "I really respect the brethren that started it. It's a great achievement. And dis is it! *Dis is it!* Dis is black man redemption. *Dis is it!!*"

The Peace Concert held at Kingston's National Stadium on April 22, 1978, was the high point of Bob Marley's career, at least as far as Jamaica was concerned. Preparations for the event were feverish around Hope Road, with the Wailers rehearsing amid heavy security. During breaks Bob would come outside to juggle a soccer ball in the asphalt courtyard, a diminutive figure in T-shirt and tight warmup pants, gold chains around his neck and long locks pent up in a crocheted red and white tam. Claudie Massop was around the compound, a Jamaican "big man" in heavy gold jewelry, unintimidated by the squad of police guarding Tuff Gong in bulletproof vests and carrying loaded shotguns.

The concert was held on a Saturday, and all that day the streets of Kingston were swarming with people headed for the stadium. There was a persistent rumor about that the three original Wailers would reunite for the historic moment. But although Peter Tosh was prepared to play with his own group, Bunny Wailer was boycotting the concert, one of many Jamaicans cynical about the Peace Movement and its impossibly optimistic aims. For Bob Marley, the concert itself was enough. It had brought him back to his home.

By early evening the stadium was filled. Arranged in the front rows were Prime Minister Manley, opposition leader Seaga and the Jamaican political and judicial elite. Mick Jagger (who would sign Peter Tosh to a recording contract for his band's label) was in a conspicuous seat near the stage. Hundreds of armed police lurked around, watching for trouble.

The first half of the concert featured the cream of reggae's young singers, trios and deejays, all backed by Lloyd Parks and the We the People band. Dennis Brown, Culture, the Meditations, Dillinger, LeRoy Smart, Trinity, the Mighty Diamonds, Althea and Donna, Junior Tucker and Bongo Herman each played brief sets. After a long intermission, the night's big attractions came on. Jacob Miller and Inner Circle played fast and brash, followed by local hero/deejay Big Youth and an incongruous soul singer named Beresford Hammond, who was riding a string of hit singles in Jamaica.

Peter Tosh was up next, backed by Word Sound & Power, propelled by the rhythm battery of drummer Sly Dunbar and bassist Robbie Shakespeare. The audacious Tosh looked out at the crowd and realized he had a captive audience of the entire Jamaican political establishment. Pointing a long black finger at the nation's white and creole elite, Tosh harangued them for half an hour on Rasta political economy and the evils of the system, which Peter referred to as the shit-stem. Tosh then openly taunted the assembled police by firing up and smoking a huge ganja cigar. Tosh's monologue was as obscene as it was brave, and it deeply offended the politicians as Tosh described conditions for the poor:

"Me waan likkle oil fe cook all me food, me cyaan even get dem t'ing dere. I and I 'ave to set up dis cunchry here and eliminate all dose shit-stem, dat poor black people don't live in confusion, caa hungry people are angry people. I and I not a politishan, but I suffa de consequences. Yunnoseen?

"Right now, Mista Manley, me gwy taak to you personally, caa you and me is friends, so you say. Seen? . . . Well, right now, as a man of powa and a rula of dis likkle cunchry here—not you alone, Mista Seaga too. We would like de members of Parliament muss come togedda, if hoonoo dealin' wid de people and wid de suffering class, caa police still out deh a brutalize poor people for blood claat wha? *A likkle draw of blood claat herb! Seen?"* Down in front, the politicians and high police officials were squirming with rage at Tosh's arrogance. But high up in the sta-dium seats, the common people were on their feet, cheering Tosh on. (A month after the Peace Concert, Tosh was arrested outside a recording studio for smoking ganja and severely beaten in a police station.)

After Tosh's blistering performance with Word Sound & Power, the akete drumming ensemble Ras Michael and the Sons of Negus played while the Wailers set up. It was almost midnight when Bob Marley jumped on stage to a tremendous ovation from the crowd and the Wail-ers exploded into "Trench Town Rock." The whole stadium seemed to shake as Bob, dressed in jeans and a wheat-colored garment of soft bur-lap, locks writhing like pythons, directed the Wailers in a vulcanizing display of the power of fast reggae rock. The set was based on the *Exodus* songs, Bob tenderly singing "Natural Mystic" and assuming his magiste-rial, cruciform pose during "War." The climax of the show was "One Love," when Bob Marley asked Michael Manley and Edward Seaga to join him on stage and clasp hands to symbolize the government's support of the Peace Movement. Edward Seaga mounted the stage quickly, but Michael Manley held back at first. Manley felt that the Peace Movement had been cynically plotted by the JLP to get the pressure off their gang-sters and goon squads, and didn't want to be seen shaking Edward Sea-ga's hand in public. Manley knew that the Twelve Tribes truce wouldn't hold. But eventually he mounted the stage and stood next to an ecstatic, tranced-out Bob Marley, who grabbed the two leaders' right hands and held them over his head for all to see. It was an electric, historic moment for Jamaica, and a strange one as well. For while the little singer in the middle finished his song, Manley and Seaga seemed to freeze as they shook hands, looking uncomfortable and remote. (Later, Bob looked at a video of the moment and commented, "Guiltiness rest on their conscience." To another friend, he mused that he should have killed them both when he had the chance.) The concert ended on the Wailers plea for Rasta brotherhood and unity, "Jah Live."

But as soon as Bob got used to life at Hope Road, it was time to leave again, on the longest, most important, most grueling tour of the Wailers' career. Known as the "Kaya 78" tour, it would take the intrepid band of natty dreads as far from Trench Town as they could go. By the end of the year, the Wailers would become one of the top concert attractions on the planet, filling stadia and big indoor arenas all over the world.

The Kaya 78 tour was originally scheduled to begin in Florida on May 4 and pass through the South and Texas. But health problems forced Junior Marvin to miss the early dates, which were canceled because Junior's showmanship was crucial to a tour that depended on Bob Marley conserving his strength and protecting his still-tender right foot. The tour was rescheduled to begin in Ohio on May 19.

Bob used the extra time for a quick trip to London to make promotional videos for the two singles that Island had released from *Kaya*, "Is This Love" and "Satisfy My Soul." Tuff Gong in Jamaica had simultaneously released Bob's newest roots single, "Blackman Redemption," which celebrated the Peace Movement with Rasta slogans, a hard roots groove and the tough, impacted horn sound Bob loved. The video for "Is This Love" showed Bob at a children's party at the Keskidee Arts Center in London, with black and white kids playing together, ending with the laughing children dancing circles around a delighted Bob Marley out in the street. Back in Miami, Bob recorded two versions of a song called "Buffalo Soldier," written by the Jamaican producer King Sporty. Skating across a skewered historical time warp, the song compared Rastafarians to the black soldiers who fought with the U.S. cavalry during the Indian wars.

The 1978 edition of Bob Marley and the Wailers that began their world tour on May 19 at the Music Hall in Cleveland was the tightest, cleanest-sounding, most obsessively rehearsed band in the history of reggae. Bob, the Wailers and the I-Threes had reached a point of musical telepathy that allowed for extended jazzlike improvising in showpieces like "War" and "Exodus." It was a perfection that had been earned by Bob's relentless taste for band practice. Tyrone Downie remembers the regimen: "When on tour or just rehearsing, Bob was so obsessed. You wake up in the day and all you're supposed to think of is come up there and rehearse till you're too tired and it's too dark. It came from the days in Joe Higgs's yard, playing dominoes and singing; they were used to rehearsing all day." And if a Wailer made a mistake, especially during a show, Bob would mark it. "He just wanted it to be like we all know it's supposed to be. And whoever wasn't doing it right, he told them either to listen to the record, ask somebody who knows, try to do it or don't play. He wasn't rude, but very straightforward, a ghetto street person, aggressive, a little ignorant of manners. He just reacted naturally, from inside himself."

During the tour the Wailers rehearsed every day, and problems from the previous concert would be hammered out with Family Man at the next show's sound check. Rita Marley remembers Bob always reminding the band of things it already knew, irritating the musicians, who sometimes just wanted to be depended on to play it right. Bob was the Wailers' conductor, and he ran the Wailers the way an imperious Viennese maestro might run a symphony orchestra. "He wouldn't stop until he got a thing right," Judy Mowatt says. "I mean, if it takes six hundred times. Sometimes we got tired of repeating the same thing over and over, but he *never* got tired. And we did it just to please him, even though we feel a little disgusted inside doing the same thing over again."

The Wailers went on the road with the most modern sound in reggae. The sound system they carried had the latest, state-of-the-art hardware. The double guitar mix was very rockish, with Junior's jangly Stratocaster balanced by the rounder, more bluesy tone of Al Anderson's Gibson Les Paul. (Junior's Stratocaster had been a present from Eric Clapton, who had wanted to make a gesture when he visited the Wailers backstage at one of the shows. At Bob's suggestion, Clapton gave Junior the old Strat that Clapton had used to record the *Disraeli Gears* album when he was with Cream.) The two Wailers keyboardists could reproduce any sound Bob wanted, Wire on his "roots Rhodes" organ and B3 clavinet, Tyrone with his high-tech Oberheim synthesizers and every new keyboard toy on the market. The rhythm section—Family Man, Carlie, Seeco—provided the bedrock reggae against which the more rocky players like Junior and Tyrone had to contend if they wanted to push the beat. Occasionally Carlie Barrett (called "Field Marshal" within the group) would play too fast, and Bob would get on his case about sticking to the basic "one-drop" framework of Wailers music.

That May, the Wailers played Cleveland and Columbus, Madison, Chicago, Milwaukee and Minneapolis, selling out every show they played. With only a day's rest between gigs, in June the tour moved on to Pittsburgh, Rochester, Detroit, Philadelphia, Boston, Montreal, Toronto, Buffalo and Washington. In every city Bob worked hard at promotion, giving dozens of interviews and visiting every important radio station in every town. As for the rest of the Wailers, Al Anderson remembers that they were "on the rampage" most the time. At every stop there were beautiful young women available, attracted by Bob and the music, and there were always plenty left over for the band when Bob had made his choice. "It was like a party," Al says. "There were almost never any problems amidst the band. The trouble came from outside influences—too many sharks and only one piece of meat." In spite of other musicians offering Bob cocaine and girls showing up backstage with the finest Peruvian flake, Al maintains that he never saw Bob take cocaine. He recalls the late rock guitarist Tommy Bolin holding a loaded coke spoon up to Bob's nose, and Bob blowing the powder away. "Bob would say that Jah meant that one should anoint his head with herb oil, not powders and paste."

On June 15, during a five-day rest and promotion stop in New York between the Buffalo and Washington shows, Bob took part in a ceremony that was extremely moving for everyone present. At a press conference at the Waldorf-Astoria hotel, Bob was presented with the Third World Peace Medal by all the African delegations to the United Nations. Bob was deeply and visibly moved when Senegal's Mohammadu Johnny Seka spoke an extemporaneous tribute to Bob's efforts for equal rights and justice, and presented him the medal "on behalf of *five-hundred millions* of Africans." At the subsequent press conference, Bob was asked if his music was less revolutionary now than it had been. "No . . . Y'see . . . when you fight revolution, you use guns! A-true! If you fight a revolution, you use guns. Well, me no really want talk about revolution until me have guns, right? So me no want talk about revolution 'cause me nuh know if me *ever* get guns. Y'see, we don't mek guns, yunno. I want check ya now: even in Africa, we find seh the gun me buy kill my brother with, is *white* man we 'ave fe buy the gun from."

Reporter: "We're not speaking about guns, we're speaking about music."

Bob: "Well, yeah. The music is the *biggest* gun, because it *save*. It nuh kill, right? The other gun lick off ya head!"

On Saturday, June 17, the Wailers played a sold-out Madison Square Garden in New York. At last, reggae on Broadway. The long show began with "Trench Town Rock" and drew from every phase of the Wailers music. The final number, "Jamming," drew a tumultuous ovation and was followed by a long encore/medley of "Get Up, Stand Up," "War" and "Exodus." The building seemed to levitate with the high spirits the Wailers projected, caught by New York *Times* pop critic John Rockwell in his review of the show two days later: "Ultimately, the reason for both the unparochial impact of Marley's Rastafarianism and the success of the concert was his fusion of music with politics and mysticism. Mr. Marley's images of exodus, resistance and paradise on earth aren't just Jamaican or even confined to undeveloped parts of the world; they can speak to everyone through the power of his music as a modern day Utopian vision."

After a final U.S. show at Lenox, Massachusetts, the Wailers flew to London to begin a month of European dates. In London, Bob was heavily interviewed, denouncing Johnny Rotten of the Sex Pistols because Rotten, like many snobbish white reggae fans, had taken to downgrading the Wailers in favor of Jamaica's rootsier musicians. One reporter asked Bob about the National Front, a racist neo-Nazi group active in England. Did the National Front worry him? "Worry me? Blood claaat! Dem want fuck wit' me, dem blood claat, I and I give dem pure war. Fuck dem!!" Late in June the Wailers videotaped a soaring version of "Satisfy My Soul" for BBC television before embarking for sold-out shows in Paris, the island of Ibiza, Stockholm, Copenhagen, Oslo, Rotterdam, Amsterdam and Brussels and a final outdoor music festival in Staffordshire, England. Bob preferred playing in Europe. He felt the audiences were more sympathetic than in America, and he would let himself get further out in Europe than he would in the States. Rita Marley: "Bob worked on inspiration. In concert he gets very emotionally involved. He closes his eyes— that mean he lock off this world completely, on a different level of communicating. It is a natural, spiritual thing that happen to him each time he goes on stage. He gets involved spiritually. He gets *in spirit.* The I-Threes saw spiritual things happen to Bob onstage that no one else was conscious of. Languages, Bob talking in tongues in his songs."

From London, the Wailers flew to Vancouver in western Canada to begin a ten-day tour of the West Coast. After shows in Seattle and Portland, the band reached San Francisco on July 20 to play the Greek Theatre in nearby Berkeley. Guitarist Ron Wood of the Rolling Stones showed up backstage and introduced himself to Bob, who had never heard of him.

On the following day, July 21, the Wailers were backstage at the Starlite Amphitheater in Burbank, preparing for the show, when Peter Tosh showed up with Mick Jagger. After two excellent albums for CBS, Tosh was being recorded by the Stones, and backstage there was talk of Jagger joining the Wailers for a number. But Bob decisively vetoed the idea, saying that people paid to see the Wailers, not some English rock singer.

Tosh and Jagger watched the show from backstage, and at the show's emotional climax, the encore of "Get Up, Stand Up," Peter Tosh strode on stage and grabbed the mike from Bob to sing the battle cry the two of them had written. As Tosh sang the verses, Bob danced around him with a delirious smile, and the two reggae masters called the chorus home to an exhausted finale. Bob and Tosh walked off, and in the wings Bob stuck out his hand. When Peter slapped it Bob said, "Bwai, the pope feel *that* one." Two weeks later, Pope Paul VI died in Rome. Six weeks after that his successor, Pope John Paul I, died as well. The Wailers thought this was significant, a sign from Jah.

The final show of the West Coast tour was in Santa Barbara on July 23, Haile Selassie's birthday. With a vast red, green and gold backdrop bearing the emperor's image behind him, Marley performed a spine-tingling show which ended with twelve thousand fans, ninety percent of them white, chanting in unison the words "Rastafari! Rastafari! Rastafari!" It was another of those semimiraculous moments the Wailers were becoming famous for, and later a reporter asked Bob about the rare phenomenon in America of white people following a black man. "Is God who mek everybody," Bob answered, "and him mek a way for the black man that the white man have to follow, because out of the black man came the white man, all white men. It's Ham, Shem and Japeth, yunno, the sons of Noah. Ham the black, Shem the Asian and Japeth the white man, all come out of Noah. That mean the black man follow the white man in his direction for a time, then His Majesty come and stand up and say, 'Wait! Something wrong!' . . . What we black people cannot deal with in America is color prejudice. You musn't bow to the white man. You must be *superior* to him. That means you cannot be prejudice, because if you are superior, how can you be prejudice? Now we are not saying you have to mingle with them now. But you cannot walk with that half-and-half thing . . . We are superior people, but dem guys sort of took our thing and turned it back upon we. You have to show people who God is, man, *superior,* and deal with it."

The Wailers' last night in Los Angeles was spent at a party in their honor at an exclusive disco, the Daisy. Every black star in the city was there, and Bob danced for hours with Diana Ross's sister. It was sunrise when the Wailers got back to their motel.

From Los Angeles the Wailers made up the canceled southern U.S. dates before returning to Jamaica. In England, Chris Blackwell was working on a live double album culled from the London, Paris, Copenhagen and Amsterdam shows. It was a heavy rock guitar album at Bob's direction; he had urged Al and Junior to be dominant on the dates that were recorded, and Al confirms, "We were throwing *down.*" Later the two guitarists tried to keep that feeling—star guitar reggae—alive in the band, but Bob said no, not for the Wailers. It was only a commercial sound he wanted for the live album that would eventually be called *Babylon by Bus.* The title came from the headline of an article by a British writer who was being bused, along with other scribes, to the Wailers show in Staffordshire. The bus broke down on the road, and all the press missed the show. Neville Garrick found the clipping and titled the album while assembling the intricate die-cut album jacket in London that fall.

Back in Jamaica, plans were being made for the Wailers' upcoming Asian swing. Bob's foot had healed well, there was football all the time and great anticipation for the tour through Australia, New Zealand and Japan.

Bob was especially eager to record at the new Tuff Gong Studio that had been completed in the Hope Road house in his absence, supervised by Diane Jobson. But final construction and equipping of the studio wasn't quite finished, and the prolific Marley was fairly dripping with new material; the Wailers hadn't recorded any new songs since the *Exodus* sessions in London almost two years previous. While he waited for his studio to be finished, Bob got some new material off his chest by recording five demos on a four-track recorder under Lee Perry's supervision. The titles included "Jungle Fever," "Give Thanks and Praises," "I Know a Place (Where We Can Carry On)," "Who Colt the Game" [about an upset domino game] and the molten, dangerous-sounding "Burn Down Babylon": *Come we go bu'n down Babylon one more time/Come we go bu'n down Babylon one more time/Lord dem soft, Lord dem soft/So come we go bu'n down Babylon one more time.*

The Wailers' Asian tour was a triumph. The band had never played in that part of the world, and pandemonium attended the gigs. In New Zealand, Bob received a Maori tribal greeting from a dozen women before the Aukland show. They held him and rubbed his nose and cheeks with theirs. The dreadlocked poet, now a truly planetary figure, reddened with pleasure.

When the Kaya 78 tour finally wound down, Bob was exhausted. He planned to rest at his Miami house for a month, and then return to Jamaica. Dozens of new songs had accumulated in his head, and from them would come Bob Marley's masterpiece, the album called *Survival.*

9

Zimbabwe

We deal with creative power, yunno? And out of it you get rockers,
reggae, rock steady, every kind of music, a creative thing which is
roots . . .
Well, reggae music is a music created by Rasta people, and it carry
earth force, *people rhythm . . . it is a rhythm of working people,*
movement, a music of the masses, seen?

(1979)

Bob Marley had been trying to make his pilgrimage to Ethiopia since
1976, but the war between Ethiopia and Somalia over the contested
province of Eritrea had presented insurmountable visa problems. Bob
finally got a visa in late 1978, aided by Alan Cole, who had left Jamaica
after the Hope Road shooting and later turned up in Addis Ababa as
coach of the Ethiopian airline soccer team, which would eventually compete in the 1980 Olympics in Moscow. Flying from London to Nairobi,
Bob then made his way to Addis Ababa, where he visited sites associated
with Haile Selassie and Ethiopian history, lived on a religious communal
farm called Shashamani, went to nightclubs featuring the brazen and
passionate Ethiopian pop singing style and attended a giant rally staged
by Ethiopia's Marxist government in support of the liberation movement
in Rhodesia, which Ethiopians were already calling by its African name—
Zimbabwe. The mass rally broadened Bob's understanding of the issues
in Zimbabwe and his identity as an African. The Ethiopia visit changed
Bob Marley's life and his music.

He started to work on a song called "Zimbabwe" while he was still in
Ethiopia, which like most African states was preoccupied with the bitter
guerrilla war being fought by black nationalists against a minority white
regime. The struggle had originally begun in 1890, as the British settlers
led by Cecil Rhodes occupied the fertile tribal territory of Mashonaland.
Three years later the whites had crushed the Ndebele tribe in the south
and taken Matabeleland in the southwest. By 1896, under the leadership

of two spirit-mediums, Kaguvi and Nehanda, the Shona and Ndebele peoples rebelled in a bloody uprising called *Chimurenga,* which was suppressed by the British Army the following year. Rhodesia remained a rich British colony until 1965, when the right-wing Rhodesian Front led by Ian Smith declared Rhodesia independent. While the United Nations imposed economic sanctions and the British appealed for reason, Rhodesia continued as an apartheid state, insuring the continued oppression of the black majority. In 1971, the British proposed a settlement for Rhodesia in which African majority rule would have been postponed until the turn of the century. The plan was rejected by the African population, and later that year a new Chimurenga began with sporadic guerrilla attacks on white farms in northeast Rhodesia.

By the time Bob Marley arrived in Africa late in 1978, the Rhodesia war was reaching its climax. The Rhodesian Army was winning small battles against the Patriotic Front, but was losing the war just the same. Britain, the United States, all the African countries and even neighboring South Africa were demanding a political settlement between the Smith regime and rebel leaders Joshua Nkomo and Robert Mugabe. White Rhodesians were emigrating by the thousands, and the supplies were low due to UN sanctions. Ian Smith was attempting to bypass the guerrillas with an internal settlement with moderate Africans; he would install a black bishop, Abel Muzorewa, as a token prime minister. Out in the bush, Patriotic Front leaders Joshua Nkomo and Robert Mugabe swore to destroy the internal settlement. The second Chimurenga continued.

This was the backdrop of Bob Marley's most important song.

While Bob was still in Africa, Tuff Gong International was steaming along in Kingston under Diane Jobson, who was now running Tuff Gong as perhaps the only multimillion-dollar recording company in the Third World. With Bob due back in Jamaica by the end of the year, the various Rasta carpenters and artisans were rushing to complete the new studio at Hope Road in time for Bob to record the tunes for the new album that was expected to be called *Black Survival.* The first music to be recorded in the new studio was Judy Mowatt's *Black Woman* sessions, which included an obscure old song of Bob's called "Down in the Valley" and Mowatt's "Joseph," a song (written after the shooting) about the sense of paternity and respect the Wailers had for Bob Marley. *Black Woman* was completely remixed at Tuff Gong as an experiment to test levels and break in the studio for the upcoming *Black Survival* sessions.

When Bob returned to Jamaica ready to record, it was the beginning of a new era for the Wailers. Bob's new songs were the first body of work he had produced since the *Exodus* sessions almost two years before, and he was brimming with punch lines and catch phrases, many of them lifted from Psalms and Proverbs in the Old Testament. No recycled Wailers classics were among the *Black Survival* sessions. Bob's experiences in Africa had imbued his music with new hopes for black unity and an edgy but resolute new militance that was most obvious when the first of the songs, "Ambush," was released by Tuff Gong in Jamaica early in 1979: a graphic portrayal of his near-assassination, "Ambush" described a black nation in which factions fought for power, corrupted by imposed economics and "political strategy." The bumping, drama-heavy chorus tells what happens when a man resists the system: *Ambush in the night/All guns aiming at me/Ambush in the night/They opened fire on me/Ambush in the night/Planned by society/Ambush in the night/Protected by His Majesty.* "Planned by society" identifies the gunmen, "society" being a ghetto term for the Jamaican ruling class.

Bob immersed himself in his new studio. Small (some musicians said it was claustrophobic), well-run and equipped with the latest and best recording systems, Tuff Gong Studio got terrific keyboard, horn and vocal sounds. Patterned in many ways after Bob's favorite studio, Criteria in Miami, Tuff Gong also had what guitarists felt was the best guitar sound in reggae music. It was tiny, and when the Wailers were recording and eight musicians, drums, two or three keyboards and all the equipment were packed into the minuscule space, it was an extremely tight fit. But the music emerged as the tightest, clearest reggae yet to be recorded by the band. When the musicians listened to the playback of what they were doing—"Wake Up and Live," "Ride Natty Ride," "Africa Unite" and especially "Zimbabwe"—they knew that *Black Survival* was going to be pure *murder.*

The next track to appear in public after "Ambush" was "Babylon Feel This One," which was never actually released as a record but was given to Brigadier Jerry, the deejay of the Twelve Tribes sound system. "Babylon Feel This One" existed only as a "dub-plate," an acetate disk over which a deejay could toast with exclusive rights, and it was extremely hot at the dances. Other outtakes from the *Black Survival* period included "Jump Niyabinghi," "Mix Up Mix Up" and "Wounded Lion in the Jungle," a tortured ballad that reflected the intense period of sadness and depression that Bob Marley was passing through in this time.

Bob didn't complain, so only the people closest to him noticed how raw Bob's feelings were and how short his temper and attention span had become. Some thought that Bob's anticancer medication was making him ill, while others felt his melancholy was caused by other things. The

Peace Movement hadn't worked, the truce had broken and the violence in western Kingston was worse than ever as the two Jamaican parties struggled for the soul of the nation. Claudie Massop was shot by police at a roadblock in February 1979 amid rumors that he had stolen the money earned by the Peace Concert Bob had headlined the year before. The autopsy found forty-two bullets in his body. Bob's old recording mentor Lee Perry, one of the few men who Bob ever called a genius, suffered a mental breakdown and was in the asylum of Belleview Hospital in Kingston. Bob's black mood extended to his family and friends as well. Close friends say he roughed up Rita one night after he heard she was seeing another man. He had an old friend from the ghetto, one of the Hope Road regulars, stuffed into the trunk of a car and disappeared for a while for some major transgression. And there was the beating he gave his sister Pearl at his house in Miami after Pearl had been fresh to him. Cedella recalls: "He want to let her know that he put diaper on her and he didn't want her frownin' at him or anything, and he whipped her in her room properly. But everybody in the house cried, because it wasn't like him to do that, and even he was upset. Later I went to him and seh, 'What happen?' And he said, 'None a you nuh talk to me.' He vex with everybody then, and I didn't trouble him."

Back in Kingston, Bob worked to finish the new album in time for the U.S. tour projected for the fall of 1979. At Hope Road he was strumming his guitar for twelve hours a day, working on songs. Some of the crack Kingston session musicians who worked on the album—drummer "Santa" Davis, bassist Val Douglas, trumpeter "Chico" Chin—remember that Bob was abrupt and distracted during the sessions. One afternoon, after failing to get a guitar and keyboard overdub on the album version of "Ambush," Bob called in Jimmy Becker, a white musician who was the premier harmonica player on the reggae session scene. Halfway through Becker's take, Bob forgot what he was doing and wandered outside to join a football game in progress in the front yard.

Sometimes, though, Bob's shyness and reticence were mistaken for anger. His friend Neville Garrick says that Bob was so shy that "the word 'screwface' might have been invented for him. Bob built a shield with his face. He knew how to use his face so when someone want to approach him and Bob don't know him, they have to stand back and not bother him. That was his defense of the magnetism he had, or else the people would have squashed him. Sometimes I read the face and read the temperament and I say, *Cho,* yunno, well I can check and if he don't want to talk we can talk another time."

To combat his melancholy, Bob would play as hard as he worked. Despite his doctors' warnings not to constantly irritate his bruised foot with constant football, Bob continued to juggle a soccer ball and play in the swirl of football activity that was a feature of Hope Road life. The ganja chalice was always omnipresent, as were the constant streams of pretty girls attracted to Bob's scene by his own magnetism and the promise of life in the Rasta fast lane. Bob's tenth child was conceived at this time with Yvette Morris, a secretary at Tuff Gong who had been devoted to Bob for years. Several of the flashy Jamaican girls that Bob liked to party with in these days also later claimed to have mothered his children, but Bob kept close tabs on all the women with whom he had mated. He told Diane Jobson that he could always tell one of his children by its mouth; if the child seemed sometimes to speak from the side of its face, it was definitely his. Yvette Morris gave birth to a daughter, Bob's last child, who was named Makeba Janesta Marley.

One time at Hope Road, Diane Jobson made a remark to Bob about the girls with whom he was dallying, and Bob rebuked her for it. "I think it was actually a kind of warning," Diane says. "Like if I ever saw him with another woman, a sister who might be a glamour girl or a model type, in other words not a Rasta woman but a sporting child, a party girl, I wasn't to make any remark. It was like in the Bible where they were complaining that Jesus was eating with the publicans, and Jesus said, 'He that is well is not in need of a physician.' With regard to these women, Bob said that I was to have the attitude that there but for the grace of God go I. Because if it was not for the influence of him [Bob], who knows which way *I* might have gone. Bob used to say, 'Diane, if *she* seh she love me, and *you* seh you love me, then *you must love her too!*' "

The first half of 1979 was taken up with recording and mixing the *Black Survival* music. Added to Bob's sense of perfectionism was that of Alex Sadkin, the new producer brought in by Chris Blackwell to temper Marley's music for the international marketplace with a crispness and precise attention to detail that some complained was robbing the Wailers' reggae of some of its raw spontaneity and soul. As for Bob, he just wanted his records to sound as hot and as *black* as Stevie Wonder's sounded. And when the new album was released that summer as *Survival* (to appeal to Bob's old white audience as well as the new black one he was courting), Bob Marley got his wish. The music was so alive that it seemed to literally jump out of the speakers.

Reggae studios in Jamaica tend to take on the personalities of their owners. Whereas the scene at Harry J's was relaxed and casual, the atmosphere at Tuff Gong was true to its name, a tough yard full of smart new

BMWs and various cannibalized cars, populated by the heavies of the young Rasta community and various hoodlums and leeches from the slums looking for dope, women and a handout from Bob. If you hadn't been invited to Hope Road and weren't a regular, it wasn't a great place to hang out. So it was odd that one day in early June a white man in a coat and tie showed up at Tuff Gong asking for Bob Marley, saying he was from Boston and wanted Bob to come and play a benefit concert for African freedom-fighters in July, only a few weeks away. The man, whose name was Chester English, insisted on talking to Bob, but some of the motorbike boys and smart-ass Rasta youth with big chips on their shoulders started to hassle the white man, and were about to get physical and throw him out when Bob Marley emerged from the house to see what the commotion was all about. The man repeated his story to Bob; he represented a group called Amandla, which was raising money for humanitarian causes in southern Africa. Bob listened intently, and then told an aide to call Amandla's office in Boston to see if the story checked out. When word came back that the benefit would be held at Harvard Stadium in Boston and would include Dick Gregory and Babatunde Olatunji, the Nigerian drummer, Bob agreed to do the benefit for a fee of ten thousand dollars. He turned to Chester English and said to tell his people when and where they wanted him, and he would be there. Then he walked back into the house.

The Wailers' first gig that year was held at Reggae Sunsplash II, the Jamaican music festival held at Jarrett Park in Montego Bay early in July. The band went on at one-thirty in the morning on the small stage cluttered with equipment and people, and Bob moved in a tight circle wearing an Ethiopian striped sweater, brown leather pants and boots and a sensational mane of dreadlocks. It was the first Wailers concert in Jamaica since the Peace Concert, and the band opened with old favorites "Road Block" and "Them Belly Full" before dashing into newer songs. "Rastaman Live Up" was fast and fiery in contrast to a slow, beautiful, declamatory version of "No Woman, No Cry," delivered as a great folk poem being imparted to its native audience, picking up into reggae-rock at the chorus of "Everything's gonna be all right now." The 1979 edition of the Wailers kept crackling with "Hypocrite," an old song from the Ghost Town days which had just been reissued as a single on Tuff Gong with another classic, "Nice Time," on the flip side. It was probably the only live performance of "Hypocrite" ever given by the Wailers. It was followed by a taut rendition of "Lively up Yourself," as sharp as a dangling machete, with a similar latent menace and authority. "That's what it boils down to," a possessed Bob Marley shouted between verses; "I got *war* in my shoes!" The encore was "Get Up, Stand Up," reggae arson by Bob and the fast-dancing I-Threes (with Marcia heavy with child), all of them bathed in sweat, which faded into an incredible "Exodus" with Bob frozen into a position holding something out in front of him in his hand, an invisible object the size of a grapefruit or a grenade. Drenched in spotlight, Bob stood immobile as he sang, eyes closed, small mouth open, sharp features, bushy eyebrows and scraggly Rasta beard shiny with perspiration. The rockers' anthem put everyone there into trance, and Bob was joined on stage by his sons Ziggy and Stevie, who danced around him with boyish movements. A minute later another boy went on stage and began to dance, a tall Rasta child with a head of long locks who was said to be one of Bob's sons out of wedlock. The concert ended with Bob melted back into the band while the boys carried on upstage. Bob was revealed as a master musician of the new age, his sons out in front as dancing boys in a timeless ritual of tribal musical tradition. Tuff Gong Night at Reggae Sunsplash II (Tuff Gong Records artistes Junior Tucker and Light of Love had opened) was a smashing success.

While rehearsing the band for the upcoming benefit show in Boston and supervising the final mixes for the new album, Bob took time out to talk with journalist Vivien Goldman of *Melody Maker.* Responding to a question on the lack of the usual Wailers militance on *Kaya* he said, "Me *too* militant. That's why me did *Kaya,* to cool off the pace . . . I don't have an army behind me. If I did I wouldn't care, I'd just get more militant. Because I'd know, well, I have fifty thousand armed youth and when I talk I talk from strength . . . Maybe if I try to make a heavier tune than 'Kaya' they would have tried to assassinate me because I come too hard. I have to know how to run my life, 'cause that's what I have, any nobody can tell me to put it on the line, you dig? Because no one understands these things. These things are heavier than anyone can understand. People that aren't involved don't know it. It's my work and I know it outside in."

Because 56 Hope Road had been transformed from a decrepit old house to a modern twenty-four-track studio and an up-to-date Rasta office complex with IBM typewriters and sophisticated communications gear, Bob was asked if he found it difficult to stay in touch with his ghetto roots. Bob was incredulous: "Find it difficult? Watch now: you look into my yard—it's a ghetto. This is a ghetto you're looking at. Look out there —I've just brought the ghetto uptown."

After expressing some reservation about Chris Blackwell's stewardship of his music and telling Goldman that he was getting tired of saying the

213

same things in interviews (by then Bob Marley had been talking to reporters almost nonstop for six years), he was asked which bit of his career had meant the most to him. His answer took twenty years within its scope: "I love the development of our music, that's what I really dig about the whole thing. How we've tried to develop, really trying to understand what we're trying to do, yunno? It just grows. That's why every day people come forward with new songs. Music goes on forever."

On July 19, the twenty-five-member Wailers touring party—musicians, technicians, family and cook—gathered at Hope Road, where a bus took them to the Kingston airport for the flight to Boston and the Amandla benefit and the "Festival of Unity." Bob was excited about the show, since it was in support of his favorite cause, African liberation, and it offered a chance to try out some of the new Wailers songs before Boston's avid reggae audience. Also on the bill were Patti LaBelle, salsa star Eddie Palmieri, master drummer Babatunde Olatunji and Dick Gregory, the black social activist who would act as master of ceremonies. Although Bob had originally said the Wailers would play for ten thousand dollars to cover their travel expenses, Don Taylor had later hiked the fee to twenty thousand dollars, with a stipulation in the contract that Dick Gregory personally introduce the band. At a press conference before the show on July 21, a reporter asked Bob how he could demand twenty thousand dollars when the show was a benefit for Africans fighting for their freedom in the bush. Bob was angry and nonplussed, and was about to answer when Dick Gregory stepped in and deflected the question. Later it was said that Bob hadn't known about the change in fee and was furious with Don Taylor.

The Amandla concert (so-called for the phrase *Amandla Ngawetu,* "Power to the People" in the Shona language of Zimbabwe) was another of those epiphanic Wailers shows where twenty-five thousand people filling Harvard University's football stadium were treated to a delicate, craftsmanlike set that reprised the band's hits and introduced the group's hard new music. The police had asked that the Wailers perform in the afternoon to minimize the difficulties of a late concert in racially unstable Boston (the organizers had received bomb threats), so Bob came out at 3 P.M. in a khaki shirt and jeans as Dick Gregory was finishing a moving introduction. After blaming the United States for "what goes on over there in South Africa," Gregory introduced Marley as "a young man who understands racism, who understands poverty, who understands *all* the hurts, and *he didn't let it defeat him.* He set out to share his joy, his love, his great respect, his religion, his *spiritual power* with the whole

214

world. And we say to you, Brother Bob, we thank you, we thank you, we thank you!" As the crowd roared when Bob Marley walked on stage, Dick Gregory took Bob's hand and pulled it to his mouth and kissed it.

With the I-Threes throwing their bare shoulders and dancing hard and frisky, Bob launched into a long show whose highlight was "Exodus," with Olatunji sitting in on bongo drums. When the audience refused to stop cheering even after a long encore, the Wailers came back to offer the first public performances of "Zimbabwe" and "Wake Up and Live." During the first, Bob brought the I-Threes to center stage and sang with his arms around his three reggae priestesses, the four of them swaying as Family Man led the band with his thunderous bass. It was always the most touching part of any Wailers show, and one that sometimes had a practical side according to Judy Mowatt, who said that Bob occasionally joined his three singers to coax them back on key when they had strayed from the harmony Bob wanted to sing over.

Then, as "Zimbabwe" melded into the war cry of "Wake Up and Live," Bob Marley did something he rarely, if ever, did. He made a speech, a dub screed for unity and brotherhood within the context of the song and its rhythm. It was a free-form meditation and exhortation, as fierce and direct as Bob Marley ever got on a stage: ". . . Third World struggling, yunno, and we must come together for Zimbabwe . . . *Yeah!!* . . . Women and children shall fight this revolution . . . We can be free, we must be *Free,* yunno. Four hundred years plus, this captivity, so we want go home to we yard . . . Rastafari know that . . . *Yes!!* . . . Don't let propaganda lead you astray, false rumors and false propaganda. Haile Selassie I the *Almighty!!* . . . Zimbabwe must be free by 1983, Jah seh, *Africa must be free!!* . . . So everyone have a right to decide his own destiny, *yeah!!* . . . See me, looka dat, *wake up and live y'all/wake up and live/Life is one big road with lots of signs* . . . Put your feet in the dust . . . A people without knowledge of their past is no better than a tree without roots . . . We smoke herb so we get one meditation, and they don't wan' fe see us in unity, *C'mon children!! Yeah!!!* . . . I couldn't mek a speech, I could mek a speech, but I'm gonna tell ya that I'm gonna fight for my rights. I'm a Rasta man and we are Rasta people. Consciousness cover the earth . . . *Hey sisters!!* Awake from your sleepless slumber, emancipate yourself from mental slavery, none but ourselves can free our mind, yunno what I'm saying? Babylon *burning!!* It's vibration mek the whole world stop. *Burning!!* No more force . . . *A free the people!!* . . . Yunno something? We're gonna do it . . . with a nuclear bomb! Wake up and live! Rastafari, the Almighty God!! *With no apology!!* . . . Yunno, it's time for us to be *freee!!!*" Bob furiously rubbed the front of his head as he sang, as if he were trying to imbue the spirit right into his skull. His khaki shirt and the I-Threes' red, green and gold skirts were soaked in the heat of the July afternoon. It was the most inspired show many people had ever seen from Bob Marley, and by the end of the day the Amandla organization had raised almost a quarter million dollars for African liberation. Twenty-thousand people left the stadium after the Wailers' part of the show.

Survival, Bob Marley and the Wailers' ninth album for Island Records, was released that summer, not long after the Amandla concert. Longtime Wailers fans were relieved at the band's return to militance, although the new Wailers militance had greater meaning in a different setting. Marley's concerns now had broadened from the perspective of a Jamaican ghetto sufferer to that of a pan-African freedom-fighter, a man who had the world as a captive audience for his message of black survival and unity. The change was symbolized by Neville Garrick's cover art, the myriad particolored flags of every African nation (Zimbabwe being represented by the battle pennants of the two contending factions of the Patriotic Front, Robert Mugabe's ZANU and Joshua Nkomo's ZAPU) on a black background, divided by a diagram of Africans packed like sardines inside the hold of a slave ship bound for the West Indies.

"Wake Up and Live," cowritten with Anthony Davis, opened the LP on a tight and biting note of rejuvenation, and featured a blistering saxophone battle between session players Dean "Youth Sax" Frazier and "Deadly" Hedley Bennett. Like many of Marley's later lyrics, some of the verses were lifted directly from the Bible. "We're more than sand on the seashore/We're more than numbers" is a direct paraphrase of Hebrews 11:12. Verses of "Africa Unite" were taken from Psalm 2. "One Drop" referred to the primal reggae drumming style, and how this rhythm was a psychic spur that prodded people to higher consciousness and "fighting against ism and schism"; in other words, toward human unity and dignity.

"So Much Trouble in the World" paved the way for the themes that dominated the second side of *Survival*—conflict, competition, black nationalism and survival. Conflict was represented by "Zimbabwe," which would later be credited with helping build the climate that led to a political solution of the "internal power struggle" being waged in that country. "Zimbabwe" expressed the solidarity with Africa felt by black people in the West. "Top Rankin' " described in apostolic terms a political system of competition and murder that was the most "Jamaican" thing about an otherwise internationalist album. But it seemed only a setup for what followed, one of Bob Marley's most prophetic, most disturbing and, ironically, most beautiful songs. "Babylon System," an akete drumming chant descended directly from the mystic burru tradition, was a quiet indictment of a capitalist industrial world that used people for profit, grinding them in its inhuman machinery. *Babylon system is the vampire/ Sucking the children day by day/Sucking the blood of the sufferers.* And in his most remarkable and touching eight lines, Bob Marley the poet issues his own declaration of black heritage and pride: *We refuse to be/What you wanted us to be/We are what we are/And that's the way it's going to be/You can't educate I/For no equal opportunity/Talking about my freedom/People freedom and liberty.*

The album ended with a brilliant, wordy rumination on the theme of survival. In the past year Bob had been jousting with the issues of nuclear power and atomic war. He thought both were manifestations of Babylon's final era, in that Marxism and capitalism would cancel each other out in a nuclear war, leaving a Third World force—Rastafari—to inherit the earth. Africa will be free, he kept saying, by 1983. His favorite book that year was the apocalyptic *The Late Great Planet Earth.* But on a more personal level, he was concerned that nuclear power and its attendant low-level radiation had given him the cancer that had robbed him of his greatest pleasure, unlimited, all-out quick-striking football. And there was a subtext to Marley's message here as well. Early in 1979 the Anglo-Jamaican dub poet Linton Kwesi Johnson recorded a song called "Reality Poem," widely interpreted in the reggae world as an attack on the appeal Rastafari had for black youth in the West: *This is the age of reality/And some a we a-deal with mythology/This is the age of science and technology/But some a we a-check fe antiquity/When we cyaan face reality/Me leggo me clarity . . . Some get vision/And start preach religion/But dem cyaan mek decision when it come to a fight . . . This is the age of decision/Mek we leggo religion.*

Bob Marley's answer to this, and to a "world that forces lifelong insecurity," was "Survival," which proclaimed: *We're the survivors . . . in this age of technological inhumanity . . . scientific atrocity . . . atomic mis-philosophy/We're the survivors."* And never one to let go of religion, Bob Marley concluded: *We've got to survive/But to live as one equal in the eyes of the Almighty.*

Soon after *Survival* was released in 1979, the song "Zimbabwe" struck Africa like a smart bomb. Within two months, African musicians in the West African recording centers—Lomé, Abidjan, Lagos—had recorded cover versions of "Zimbabwe" which sold well all over the continent, alongside the Island album and bootleg Wailers cassettes. Years before, Bob Marley had been adopted by the guerrilla fighters of Zimbabwe's

Patriotic Front; now, still in the bush, the ZANLA and ZIPRA battle groups had a new anthem with which to fight. For them, the song helped win the war. And in Africa, as in much of the world, Bob Marley was becoming a household word.

As winter descended on North America in October 1979, Bob Marley and the Wailers began a tour in support of *Survival* at the Apollo Theater in Harlem, an appropriate address since in Bob's mind the purpose of the tour was to cultivate what for him had been his most elusive audience—black America. The year before he had seen a 1933 quote from the writings of W. E. B. Du Bois, the American black nationalist, that had stirred him: ". . . if the young Black American is going to survive and live a life, he must face the fact that however much he is an American, there are interests which draw him nearer to the dark people outside America than to his fellow white citizens." To this end, Bob was touring to establish a Rasta presence in black America that would eventually evolve into Bob's ideal third alternative to the rigors of socialism and the psychic damage of capitalism. In addition to playing four nights at the Apollo beginning October 26, Bob hired a black publicist to coordinate interviews with black newspapers and magazines and visits to important soul stations in New York. "Hi," Bob said on one New York promo spot, "this is Bob Marley and *Survival* on WLIB, the best of both worlds."

It was a heady time for the Wailers. Just before, at the Philadelphia convention of the Black Music Association, a trade organization of black music professionals, Stevie Wonder joined the Wailers for the encore of "Get Up, Stand Up" and "Exodus." Sparks seemed to fly between the American superstar and his Jamaican counterpart.

Bob's health deteriorated as soon as he hit the chilly streets of New York in his quilted jacket and work boots. He caught a bad cold, but continued to walk between his usual hotel, the Essex House on Central Park South, and the midtown rehearsal studio ten blocks away, dragging an improbable retinue of dreads (including reggae singer Jacob Miller) strung along behind him for several blocks. Despite a worsening sore throat and fatigue, he conducted daily seven-hour rehearsals with the three horn players that had been brought along from Kingston for the tour.

The Apollo shows, seven concerts on four nights, were of historic proportions for the Wailers. Marcus Garvey had preached in the famous black vaudeville theater on Harlem's 125th Street, and its boxlike walls had rung to the music of the great heroes of black music—Bessie Smith,

Duke Ellington, Billie Holliday, Sam Cooke, James Brown. Despite what Bob called "a crack in my throat," the Wailers deployed the band's superbly organized new shows, which began with the incantatory "Natural Mystic" and ended with the show-within-a-show encore of "Get Up, Stand Up," "War" and "Exodus." The songs now melted into each other like the shimmering hues on Joseph's coat of many colors, as the Wailers burned away behind Bob, a slight, denim-clad, dreadlocked, hollow-cheeked and haunted-looking man who seemed to explode with pent-up energy as the almost inhuman roar of his loyal audience poured over him.

As the Wailers embarked on an exhausting, seven-week tour of the United States (forty-seven shows scheduled in forty-nine days), Bob's cold failed to improve. All his extra energy was used to promote Island's "Survival"/"Wake Up and Live" single at black stations around America. By the time the journalists came around for interviews at the end of the day, Bob was usually too tired to do them. He would ask his articulate keyboard player Tyrone Downie to sit in, and most of the interviews from this tour quoted Tyrone's ardent analysis of the Rasta life more than they did Bob, who was happy to sit there and supervise the talk, adding an occasional aside if he felt well enough. One subject that irritated Bob enough for him never to refuse comment was disco music, which was then dominating pop culture all over the world, keeping the more aware and socially evolved reggae movement in second place, much to the fury of the reggae musicians. A month earlier Peter Tosh had been quoted saying, "Death to disco, mon. I am here to make reggae the international music, because disco doesn't have the spiritual potential of reggae. The devil created disco, telling black people to get down get down all the time. But I-mon seh to black people, 'Get up stand up for your rights.'" Not to be outdone, Bob had his own analysis of disco: "America is pure deviltry, dem t'ings dat go on there. Dem just work with force and brutality. Dem lock out the punk thing because they see something is happening. So the oppressors bring another man to blind the youth to the truth, and dem call him—John Tra-vol-ta."

In mid-November the Wailers began another progress down the west coast of North America with a show at Vancouver. Backstage after the concert, Bob was visited by an Indian chief and members of his tribe who told Bob Marley they regarded him as a prophet and wanted to see his spirituality for themselves. Bob had long been interested in Indians and was pleased by their calling on him. But his health was bad on the way to San Francisco, where guitarist Don Kinsey picked up the tour for a few dates. "Bob was beginning to feel he was sick again by then," Kinsey says. On the bus to the concert at the university town of Santa Cruz, Bob told Kinsey that he was "getting tired of this business," and Don said Bob's energy level was definitely slipping. There was a big press conference after the Santa Cruz show, attended by dozens of reporters firing questions at Bob, but Bob was flustered and confused, and couldn't think through or finish his answers. Tyrone, sitting next to Bob at the table, took over until the press had gotten what they wanted.

Yet Bob continued to work and compose. He had already written many of the songs for the Wailers' next album and was strumming the chords and experimenting with the lyrics of a new autobiographical tune he was crafting called "Redemption Songs."

On a late Tuesday afternoon in November, in the nearly empty Roxy nightclub on Sunset Strip, the Wailers held a three-hour rehearsal for that night's show to benefit the Sugar Ray Robinson Foundation. It was to be the only nightclub-sized date of a stadium-weight tour. The Wailers wore mostly expensive leather and cheap army surplus, their locks pent up in bright, swollen knitted tams. In the club's lobby Al Anderson was quietly working out a new guitar riff on his unplugged Strat, while onstage Family was adjusting the tone settings on his amplifier, feeling for that penetrating bass vibration that anchored the Wailers' sound. As the horn players walked in the door and the band began to slide into their groove, Bob Marley stepped up and plugged in his Les Paul, wearing an intricate tam of red, green, gold and silver. A laconic "Lively Up Yourself" slid into a perfect dub of "Is This Love," Bob singing only a word or two from each verse, always on the off-beat: *"Is this . . . Is this . . . ,"* a gentle guitar break, and *". . . love that I'm feeling?"*

As the evening grew later the band changed instruments among themselves and friends wandered in to jam. The band played all of *Survival,* and Bob dubbing "Zimbabwe" right and tight. As the session wound down, the Wailers played a twenty-minute version of the new "Redemption Songs." If Bob was thinking of playing the new song's debut at the show that night, he changed his mind later. "Redemption Songs" would remain a secret for another few months.

Bob's illness improved while the Wailers spent time in southern California. Bob liked Los Angeles despite the hot, mood-swinging Santa Ana winds that blew the city dry during that time of year. The Wailers were living in a motel in West Hollywood, while Bob and his immediate retinue were installed in a rented house on Alta Vista, right off the Sunset Strip. One late night after a concert, a large group gathered at the house to screen the videotape made the night of the "Smile Jamaica" concert in

Kingston three years earlier. That afternoon Bob had signed albums at Tower Records in Hollywood, and that evening the house was full of glamourous black models and starlets, drawn to the smoky scene by the powerful Rastaman from Jamaica. As the video started, Bob had wandered off and someone was sent to look for him, since Bob had been keen on seeing it. He was found—blundered upon—in an unlocked bedroom where he was enjoying the ardent embrace of one of his new girl friends.

By now, Bob Marley's generosity had become something of a legend. Never comfortable as a multimillionaire, Bob gave money away to friends and favorite causes by the hundreds of thousands. His family estimates that in these times he once gave away almost two hundred thousand dollars in one month. So perhaps it wasn't so odd that Bob, at the urging of his old road manager Tony Garnett, financed a Tuff Gong record shop for Tony G., located in the heart of L.A.'s black Crenshaw section. Just before the Wailers left California for the tour's last stop, Bob gave Tony Garnett a check for the new branch of Tuff Gong Records, telling Tony that eventually he planned to manufacture and distribute Wailers records in America independently of the big music monopolies. Bob told Tony that he would return the following year to inspect the new shop.

Trying to regain his strength, Bob cut down press interviews now. When the occasional reporter wanted to talk about Rasta, Bob reflexively referred him to Tyrone or another reggae star in the Wailers' entourage, deejay Michael "Mikey Dread" Campbell. Fortunately for Bob Marley, he had survived seven years as a pop star with an ever-growing popular following among the press. As London's *New Musical Express* had put it that winter: "Few major rock stars at the age of thirty-four can boast the same on and offstage vitality, commitment and creative genius that Marley continues to exhibit and which shows scant signs of disappearing. That the future holds new developments seems extremely likely, with Africa looming as the next target for musical conquest." The Wailers then flew to Trinidad for a concert, and police fired tear gas to keep thousands of ticketless fans away from the show.

The last date on the *Survival* tour was in Nassau, the Bahamas. It was a benefit for the United Nations' International Year of the Child. In addition to the concert, Bob donated the royalties from the song he had written for his own kids four years before, and which his company, Tuff Gong, had just released. The record by the Melody Makers (Sharon, Ziggy, Cedella and Stephen Marley) was called "Children Playing in the Streets."

As the year turned into the beginning of a new decade, Bob Marley and his management team—Don Taylor, Diane Jobson and Chris Black, well—had important plans in store for the year 1980. After a short band visit to Africa, the Wailers would record a new album, to be called *Uprising,* followed by the biggest Wailers tour ever to support the new record and so Bob would be conspicuously absent from the Jamaican general elections to be held that year. The tour would cover every European nation, every major North American market (sometimes on the same bill with Stevie Wonder) and then swing through Latin America before attempting the first major reggae tour of Africa the following year. The name of Bob's company was changed from Tuff Gong Limited to Tuff Gong International, more appropriate to Bob's planetary following.

On January 1 the Wailers left Kingston for London on their way to Gabon in West Africa, where the band had been engaged to play for the birthday party of President Omar Bongo. It was supposed to be the Wailers' proudest moment, the band's first concert on African soil. Instead, Gabon was a disaster. As Diane Jobson put it, "Gabon is where we found out Don Taylor was a thief."

Months before, Taylor had been approached by the Gabonais president's two daughters, the Bongo sisters, who wanted the Wailers to play at their father's birthday party. When Bob was told, he was so happy to have been invited to Africa that he said he'd do the show for nothing. But Taylor told Bob that a forty-thousand-dollar fee would cover their expenses and be just a drop in the bucket to the oil-wealthy Bongo family. Bob told Taylor to negotiate the deal.

The Wailers arrived in Gabon on January 4 and stayed two weeks. Gabon is one of the richest countries in black Africa, and Bob was glad to be in a place where, he said, "black people have it together." The group had been expecting to play some shows for the people of Gabon, and so were disappointed when the two concerts were held at a small tennis arena for about two thousand of the young Gabonais elite. But the band was given a beautiful beachfront hotel to live in, which was invaded at all hours by young Gabonais who knocked at Bob's door to check him out. Some of them wanted to know what a Jamaican thought he could tell Africans about Ras Tafari, and Bob held long discussions and "reasonings" with them on the beach and in his suite until dawn.

The trouble started when it was time for the Wailers to be paid and leave Gabon. According to Diane Jobson, there was some minor dispute over the fee for Bob and soul singer Betty Wright, a client of Don Taylor's who had opened the shows for the Wailers. It was clear that some chicanery was under way, which Taylor blamed on a black American employee of the Bongos named Bobbitt. But before the Wailers left Gabon, Bobbitt heard he was being blamed for an internal dispute among the Wailers and went directly to Bob, asking if there was some problem with the sixty-thousand-dollar fee that had been paid to Don Taylor. At that point, Taylor was accused of defrauding Bob. Having negotiated with the Bongos for sixty thousand dollars, Taylor had told Bob the fee was only forty thousand dollars, thus allegedly netting a quick twenty thousand dollars for himself on the side. Bobbitt went to President Bongo with the story, and the Wailers' departure from Gabon was delayed when Bongo called everybody on the carpet to clear the air. Bob was extremely upset, according to Tyrone, that he, a Rastaman, had been disgraced in front of an African ruler. That night, back at the Wailers' hotel, there was a brutal three-hour confrontation between Bob and Don, witnessed by the whole touring party (and even tape-recorded by Neville Garrick), in which Taylor was beaten and forced to confess his sins. It was a sad story: for years, according to Diane Jobson, Taylor had been getting fifteen thousand dollars for concert advances and giving Bob only five thousand. Bob would give Taylor fifty thousand dollars to send to Family Man in Jamaica, and Taylor would allegedly change the money on the black market at triple the rate and give Family Man only the legal rate. Bob had never even made any money on tour until 1978, when he first took Diane Jobson along to learn the business and keep an eye on Don. Bob told Don he wanted all the stolen money back, and Taylor sobbed that every penny had gone to pay his huge gambling debts. Bob was so enraged that he reacted like a Trench Town gangster. "At that point," one witness said, "Bob almost beat Don Taylor to death." Tyrone recalls a livid Bob kicking Don Taylor in the head and the testicles. More diplomatic, Diane Jobson said Don Taylor "got a kick in the ass. He should've gotten two."

Don Taylor was fired as Bob Marley's manager on January 14 in Gabon. The next day, the Wailers flew back to London to begin recording *Uprising* and try to pick up the pieces. Later, Bob commented to a reporter: "Don too tricky, yunno? Juggling people, him too tricky . . . Is better that somebody ask you for something, and get it more, then try trick me fe take it. I'm no fool."

The *Uprising* sessions produced almost twenty songs, only half of which would appear on the album when it was released the following May, and a change in the Wailers sound. The horns and rock mannerisms had been discarded in favor of Africanisms like Junior's Nigerian "high-life" guitar on "Could You Be Loved." Junior Marvin and Tyrone Downie were singing male harmonies behind Bob on "Coming in from the Cold" and "We and Dem." The lyrics drew more heavily than ever from Scripture, with "Forever Loving Jah" taken in part from Psalm 1 and the starkly autobiographic "Redemption Songs" adapting the lines from the story of Joseph in Genesis. "Redemption Songs" was a total departure, a deeply personal verse sung to the bright-sounding acoustic strumming of Bob's Ovation Adamis guitar. Although a band version was recorded and later released, the album version had just Bob and his guitar, the most intimate and plaintive moment of communication that Bob ever allowed himself in a commercial recording. And after the pan-Africanism of the *Survival* era, *Uprising* seemed almost totally personal. "Bad Card" was in part about Don Taylor. "Pimper's Paradise" was Bob's analysis of the girls who flocked to his scene. "Work" was a classic Wailers counting song that advised black people to work in the sense of Marcus Garvey's proposed independent black economy. "Real Situation" spoke of a Jamaica again riddled by the violence of an election in which a now-failed socialist program was obviously succumbing to an aggressive push by Edward Seaga's free-market forces. "We and Dem" was Bob's most bereft song, courageous in its seeming frankness about the inner life of Bob Marley as a cancer patient trying to survive a disease for which there is no cure.

The Wailers were by then so *hot*, so telepathically *on*, that even the outtakes of these sessions produced wonderful songs like "Stiff Necked Fools" and "Give Me Trench Town," as well as the first experiments with a new song about Jamaican politics called "Slogans."

By early February, Bob was ready for a break from recording. He went to his house in Miami for a rest, conferring with Danny Sims on his management situation. Bob's contract with Island was over with *Uprising*, and Sims told Bob he could get the Wailers a better deal with Polygram, the international recording conglomerate. Sims recalls that Bob was surrounded by a swarm of amateur music experts trying to run his career, but doing much more harm than good. Bob then went to Kingston, where he gave himself a birthday party on February 6 to which he invited all the children of the Hope Road tribe. Sitting close to his father, little Stevie Marley held Bob's hand while Bob cut the big white-iced carrot cake with thirty-five candles burning bright.

Kingston was turbulent, and Bob felt it was no place for him to be, especially since the scene at Hope Road was in the center of a storm of complaint. It was the era of the "rub-a-dub" style of deejaying, when sound system oracles like Papa Michigan and General Smiley savaged the

Kingston dances with a steady new throb they were calling rub-a-dub. Since Michigan and Smiley's big rub-a-dub single "One Love Jamdown" had been released on 56 Hope Road Records, a Tuff Gong subsidiary, the Tuff Gong sound system dubbed out the song over its huge loud-speakers day and night. That was more than the neighborhood could stand. More than ever, the house and studio were the big hangout for Bob's ghetto friends and the Twelve Tribes Rasta element. Articles appeared in the conservative *Daily Gleaner* denouncing Tuff Gong for being dirty and noisy and creating a "ghetto environment" in Kingston's showplace. Hense the lines in "Bad Card": *I want to disturb my neighbor/Cause I'm feeling so right/I want to turn up my disco/Blow dem to full watts tonight/In a-rub-a-dub style, in a-rub-a-dub style.*

In March, Bob, Junior Marvin and singer Jacob Miller flew to Brazil in a private jet to plan a series of concerts featuring the Wailers and Jacob Miller's Inner Circle band, set to take place after the North American segment of the planned "Tuff Gong Uprising" tour that year. The South American shows were postponed, but not canceled, after Jacob Miller's tragic death in a Kingston car wreck the following month.

But Bob tried to keep his personal profile as low as possible in a tense Jamaica that was beginning to undergo the violent rigors of another national election. The flashy silver BMW Bavaria was gone, replaced by a Jeep. "An *old* Jeep," he emphasized, "so nobody will say I'm driving a BMW anymore." Part of the parade around the Tuff Gong complex included the inevitable foreign reporters looking to pry quotes from Bob on the international reggae movement he was spearheading. But now he had less tolerance for the press, especially a nasty middle-aged interviewer from Australian television who asked Bob if he was rich.

"When you say rich, wha' you mean?" Bob asked haughtily.

The reporter asked if Bob had many possessions.

"Possessions mek you rich?" Bob sniffed with contempt. "I nuh 'ave dat type of riches. My riches is *life.*"

The reporter then asked what he would have to do to become a Rasta like Bob. The answer came hard and fast.

"Well, the first thing you have to do is . . . born again!"

The reporter asked if he would have to be reborn black.

"Do you have a choice? If you have a choice, you better be born black if you have a choice, and if you don't have a choice, come as what God send you."

When Bob returned to Miami he received two pieces of news. The first was that Bucky Marshall, who had worked on the Peace Concert, had been shot to death at a dance in Brooklyn. Bob's fatalistic sadness was offset by a formal invitation to attend the independence ceremonies of the new nation of Zimbabwe on April 17. For Bob Marley, it was a singular honor and a stunning fulfillment of the prophecy in the song "Zimbabwe." When the Smith/Muzorewa government realized their position was hopeless, they submitted to talks with the Patriotic Front forces in London. New elections were called, with the guerrilla factions allowed to take part. The result had been a landslide for Robert Mugabe's Marxist-oriented ZANU party. When the ceremonies marking the independence of Zimbabwe were announced for that April, Bob Marley, whose music had played such a vital role in the struggle, was among the dignitaries invited at the personal request of Edgar Tekere, the General Secretary of ZANU and one of the fiercest warriors for freedom and dignity in Zimbabwe.

Until early April, two weeks before the event, it was assumed that Bob alone was going to Zimbabwe. Then a pair of African businessmen from Zimbabwe arrived in Miami with another invitation, asking Bob Marley and the Wailers to appear at the independence ceremony as part of the official program. Everyone was stunned. Nobody had really dreamed that "Zimbabwe" would go this far. Nobody except Bob, who offered to perform just for the honor and to pay the Wailers' expenses. It was a week before the ceremony.

Three days later, the Wailers arrived at Salisbury airport on a flight from London. Their plane was met by ZAPU leader Joshua Nkomo, minister of home affairs in Robert Mugabe's new government, and the rest of the cabinet. Mugabe himself had driven into Salisbury with Britain's Prince Charles, who had arrived an hour earlier to lower the Union Jack for the last time in Africa. Not long after that a chartered Boeing 707 freighter also arrived from London, carrying twenty-one tons of Wailers equipment, including the stage, a full thirty-five-thousand-watt public address system and a twelve-man road crew. The trip to Zimbabwe cost a quarter of a million dollars, which Bob paid out of his own pocket.

While the stage was being built at Rufaro Stadium, ten miles outside Salisbury, the Wailers spent the night at a motel on the outskirts of the city. They talked to many of the former guerrillas who were also billeted there, and accompanied them the next night to Joby's, a nightclub in the heart of Salisbury. Edgar Tekere, sporting twin nine-millimeter pistols on each hip, drove Bob and a few others out to one of the guerrilla camps to visit the troops. Bob remembered the visit with pleasure: "One night we go to a soldier place and a guerrilla call out to me, and give me a touch of something. *Tell ya, bwai* . . . Good herb dem smoke, man! Dem tell me they smoke that herb and feel brave. Dem tell me it mek dem . . . *invisible!"*

It was Tekere who made the deepest impression on Bob. The tough combat veteran of the wars for African liberation told Bob sternly not to return to Jamaica. When Bob answered that he still had work to do back in Jamaica, Tekere told him that was foolishness. Tekere told Marley that he was *home* now, an African man who should stay in Africa and become part of the destiny of the continent. "That was the best invitation you could get," Bob said later. "Man who fight for the land tell you to stay, it's your home. Him risk him life, him was fighting. Plenty people shoot after him and him still alive, come tell me stay in Zimbabwe. It's the best."

On the night of the ceremony, the Wailers left for the stadium at eight-thirty, and slowly made their way behind the stage they had brought with them. Thousands of uniformed schoolchildren were performing gymnastic displays on the field as the Wailers tuned up. Musical accompaniment was provided by a Scottish pipe band and a choir made up of guerrillas. Prince Charles and Bob Marley were introduced and talked quietly in a corner for a few moments. (Bob wouldn't say what they talked about.) Then the ceremony of independence began, and the Wailers watched in total awe as the ritual unfolded. Rhodesia had been the last colony in Africa (apart from Namibia, not a colony in the literal sense). Now Zimbabwe became the fiftieth independent state in black Africa. The independence process, the fruit of a great tree with Marcus Garvey at the roots, which had begun in Ghana in 1957, was now at an end. As the British flag was lowered, the assembled troops took two steps backward. As the red, gold, green and black flag of Zimbabwe was raised, the troops took two steps forward. Twenty-one guns boomed out a salute as the crowd cheered and jet fighters roared overhead. And then, at ten o'clock, a voice announced Bob Marley and the Wailers! As the stage lights went on, Junior began shouting "Viva Zimbabwe" and the audience roared for Bob Marley. The band lit into "Zimbabwe," but stopped ten minutes into the show when the crude Rhodesian riot police set off tear gas outside the stadium to rout a large band of ZANLA guerrillas trying to crash the gate to hear the Wailers. As the tear gas drifted in, the audience started to panic and the I-Threes were rushed off the stage and back to the hotel. After a few moments of chaos and brandished AK-47s, the Wailers resumed playing "War" as the guerrillas marched into the stadium with clenched fists. At ten-thirty Bob called it quits after annoying officials and thrilling the audience by playing twenty minutes longer than planned. The Wailers would play their full show at another concert the following night. As Bob was coming off stage, he was met by the I-Threes, who had returned to the stadium when they heard the danger had passed. "Now," Bob joked when he saw them, quoting himself, "we'll find out who are the *real* revolutionaries."

The next night at the stadium, under a banner that read "Welcome to Salisbury, Sun Capital of Africa," the Wailers played an inspired show for forty thousand Zimbabweans that started with "Natural Mystic" and built into an ecstatic moment for the Wailers. Dressed in leather, thick locks cascading down his back, Bob slapped and scratched his face as he sang, improvising kinky bongo dance routines and high-stepping in half-time during the instrumental sections. It was perhaps the single greatest moment of Bob Marley's life. He felt that he had influenced history with his music, and now was a part of the solution.

Yet, even with this triumph, some of the Wailers sensed something wrong with Bob. He looked ill on the plane back from Africa. In London the eight male Wailers crowded into an elevator for a group shot by photographer Adrian Boot. The camera caught Bob in his gray tweed jacket and bloated tam, his face gaunt and haggard, a faraway, distracted gaze veiling his normally piercing eyes.

Uprising, the Wailers' tenth and last album for Island Records, was released in May 1980 to an initially mixed reception. Critics liked the upbeat tracks like "Work" and "Could You Be Loved," and were impressed by the dark, folkish power of "Redemption Songs." Others, like *Rolling Stone*'s critic, found the album "pessimistic and broody." But whereas *Survival* had sold only moderately, *Uprising* was commercially successful as soon as it was released, helped by the Afro-beat dance groove of "Could You Be Loved," which Island had released as a single.

Later that month, the Wailers began their epic "Tuff Gong Uprising" tour in Zürich, Switzerland, the most arduous series of concerts the Wailers ever gave. Playing to more than one million fans in twelve different European countries in only six weeks, the Wailers had to perform every night for six nights a week, a different venue in a different city every night, often playing without sleep. The forty-strong Wailers entourage, traveling by jet and by bus, included a Swiss film crew for part of the trip and Alan "Skill" Cole, back on the road with Bob as a sort of bodyguard and field commander. Skill's return also meant that the Wailers' five-a-side indoor soccer squad (Bob, Skill, Seeco, Gillie the cook and Rasta roadie Naphtali in goal) remained undefeated for the duration of the tour.

For two months the Wailers crisscrossed Europe like tribal jet nomads in their flashy new red, gold and green satin battle jackets, each musician's name stitched on the breast. The pace was sheer madness. On one afternoon in July they played outdoors for one hundred thousand English at the Crystal Palace Garden Party. That night they flew to Munich and were trapped all night at the airport when no bus arrived to pick them up. That afternoon, playing with no sleep, the Wailers opened an outdoor show for Fleetwood Mac and blew the place away. After the Wailers set, twenty thousand people left the stadium before Fleetwood Mac's show.

For a long swing through Scandinavia and Germany, the band traveled by bus. A fierce Jamaican-style domino game raged out of control in the back of the bus, while up front the video hummed with interesting tapes. One favorite was a black-and-white duet on "Redemption Songs" by Bob and Wire Lindo on acoustic guitars, taped for JBC television earlier in the year. And there was the black-and-white, monaural tape of a Wailers rehearsal, taped at Tuff Gong Studio just before the tour. Looking thin and tired, but singing hard and clear in his dub-wise rehearsal style, Bob is serious, spontaneous and passionate, the dangerous young rebel of 1973 turned into the thoughtful young father of 1980. The tape had a long version of "Pimper's Paradise" with a shining and reflective solo by Junior Marvin. Family Man is pictured crammed into the furthest corner of the little studio in an attempt to isolate the resonating boom of his bass. Bob's favorite tape was a Tina Turner spectacular with Sister Turner at her most carnal.

In many ways the German concerts were the strongest of the tour. Bob had a special feeling for Germany, and the Wailers consistently played two-and-a-half-hour sets, reprising all their greatest hits and showcasing the new songs from *Uprising*. In Dortmund, and on many other shows that tour, the I-Threes served as opening act, backed by the Wailers. Looking regal and utterly elegant in almost formal gowns, the I-Threes gave devastating performances. Marcia Griffiths, who had toured in Germany before she joined the Wailers, would address the audience in German after the women had sung Marcia's "Precious World." "Good evening and welcome to the Tuff Gong experience," Marcia would say. "This is where we bring you the message so that your souls will be uplifted." Then they would sing Judy's "Slave Queen," Rita's "That's the Way Jah Planned It" and Marcia's militant, utterly stirring "Stepping Out of Bablon," with Carlie Barrett beating his drums as if for his life and Tyrone throwing down bolts of orchestral synthesizer illumination.

Then Family Man would commence a suspenseful bass dub pattern while Junior began to chant: "Mar-ley . . . Mar-ley . . . Mar-ley." Finally, when the cheering had built like a thousand sirens and the tension was humid in the air, Bob would apotheosize on stage and speak: *"Hail, Rastafari! I-tinually ever faithful, ever pure, Jah live, children . . .* And there's a natural mystic flowing in the air . . . YEEEEAAAAAAAHH-HHHHHHHHH!" Almost three hours later, after the second encore, the shows would end with Bob playing "Redemption Songs" alone on stage, a bantamweight lone locksman strumming a big red Adamis guitar: *Old pirates yes they rob I/Sold I to the merchant ships/Minutes after they took I from the bottomless pit/But my hand was made strong/By the hand of the almighty/We forward in this generation, triumphantly.* As he sang, first Seeco took up his hand drums, then the rest of the band gradually dropped in and turned "Redemption Songs" into a joyous song of Bob Marley's identity and self-worth, and of the sadness that came with living inside his own vision.

After playing for one hundred eighty thousand Italians in Milan and one hundred thousand in a park in Dublin, Ireland, the Wailers returned to England for some shows and settled into a flat in the West End. At a gym called Eternity Hall in Fulham, the Wailers five-a-side football squad beat a team from *Record Mirror* 50 to 36. Bob played with his hair down and scored an even dozen goals. It was Skill Cole, the onetime striker for Santos Brazil, who sent the score flying. A few weeks earlier at Nantes, France, a larger Wailers squad had performed well against the French national team.

In London, Bob was preoccupied with a new song titled "Slogans." Strumming his guitar, reaching into his experience for new lyrics, he was singing all the time. A tape made in the London flat with Anglo-reggae singer Delroy Washington and a bunch of girls is the only known recording of one of Bob Marley's final songs about the horror then taking place on the streets of Kingston: *Wipe off the paint and the slogans/All over the street/Confusing the people/While asphalt burns our tired feet/I see demonstration, segregation and riot/False prophets, dictators and traitors/I see boundaries and barriers . . . Can't take your slogans no more/Can't take your slogans no more . . . No more false talk from the hypocrites/No more sweet talk from the pulpit . . . Can't take your slogans no more/Can't take your slogans no more.*

When the European segment of the "Tuff Gong Uprising" tour had wound down, the Wailers returned to Jamaica, all except Bob and his inner circle, who flew to Miami. With no professional manager at the helm, Bob Marley's business affairs were in turmoil. Don Taylor was suing Bob for a million dollars, and Bob was countersuing.

Even more ominous was a warning Danny Sims had received. Sims had been called to Miami to consult with Bob over management and the potential multimillion-dollar offer from Polygram upon expiration of Bob's Island contract. When Bob told Sims that he wanted to return to Jamaica to see his children and take care of business, Sims gave him some bad news. The civil war raging in Kingston was so hot that an associate of Sims's with links to the Central Intelligence Agency had passed on the warning to Sims that if Bob Marley returned to Jamaica and it even looked like he might support Michael Manley against Edward Seaga's CIA-supported challenge, then what had happened to Bob Marley and his family in 1976 would, according to Sims, "look like a fuckin' skirmish." Bob Marley never returned to Jamaica in his lifetime.

Exile, even self-imposed, was a bitter pill for Bob Marley. Despite years of Rasta rhetoric about Ethiopian repatriation, he still loved Jamaica and was distraught with the killings in western Kingston. After his old cronies Take-Life and Frowzer, among many others, had been murdered in the streets during the long campaign, Bob summed up his feelings to a reporter in London: "Yeah, mon. Survival. I think what is going on down there, it is a dreadful t'ing, like some mass execution without control or anyt'ing. And Jamaica is a likkle place. Jamaica is sufferin' people who have nothin' else. All dem do is fight. Fe what? Dem nuh fight fe Jah or nothin'. Just WAR! *Foolish t'ing.*"

10

Berhane Selassie

Well I know that, way I figure seh, maybe things get worse for the better. Yunnerstand? They just get . . . worse for the better!

(1980)

Bob Marley's appearance began to change drastically that summer. At first it wasn't easy for the other Wailers to notice because they were with him every day. But then, Judy Mowatt says, "we sense the changes in him even though he wouldn't tell anyone that something is wrong. He had lost weight, he wasn't eating much and he wasn't talking much either. Bob was always a jovial person and we realize now that he was very quiet for him, and the bones of his cheek projected a lot. But he's a person like, yunno, something will be wrong with him and he will not say it. He was like a father to us, a man who would never burden anyone with his problems."

By August, a month before the "Tuff Gong Uprising" American tour was to begin, Bob's health had deteriorated. The Wailers were in Miami. Al Anderson recalls, "We saw him getting thin and not eating as much. We thought he was just tired from too much touring, burnt out like the rest of us." Most of the Wailers assumed that Bob's cancer had faded and been held in check by the regular checkups Bob was supposed to have. In Miami the band was given the tour schedule, beginning in Boston on September 14, then moving to New York to share the bill with the Commodores for two nights at Madison Square Garden. It was a prestige gig in black music, promoted by Frankie Crocker, the powerful program director for WBLS, New York's premier black radio station. The tour would later intersect with Stevie Wonder, who had just released his first reggae single, "Master Blaster Jamming," which Bob first heard in Miami with a combination of pleasure and mild shock: *From the park I hear rhythms/Marley's hot on the box/Tonight there'll be a party/On the corner at the end of the block. . . . Peace has come to Zimbabwe/Third World's right on the one/Now's the time for celebration/'Cause we've only just begun.* For the first time it really seemed that Bob, the Master Blaster according to Stevie Wonder, had a chance to make his mark on America.

Al Anderson first noticed that Bob was in trouble in Miami, when Chris Blackwell showed up to videotape an acoustic version of "Redemption Songs." As he was about to play, "Bob was coughing a lot, and his breath rattled. I asked him what's the matter and he said, 'Nothing, man, me alright, everything cool.' After the video session, Bob lay down and looked tired and really sick. I said, 'Listen, man, what the fuck, I *know* something's wrong with you.' He said, 'Al, I got a pain in my throat and my head, and it's killing me. It's like somebody's trying to kill me. I feel like I've been poisoned. And something wrong with me voice. I've never felt like this before in my life.' "

Despite Bob's frail health, plans continued for the upcoming tour. Since *Uprising* had already been out for several months and sales had fallen off, Chris Blackwell gave Danny Sims eighty thousand dollars and a two-point override to promote the U.S. single, "Could You Be Loved." Sims went to work in late August and within two weeks the single was being played on every important black station in America, building an audience for the tour. To some of the Wailers the big puzzle was Bob's health. He had had a supposedly complete checkup from his personal doctor, Carl "PeeWee" Frazier, just prior to the tour. The musicians were told that Bob was OK, just tired. Rumors began to circulate that Bob was maintaining the pace by "freebasing" cocaine, smoking pure cocaine base freed of waste alkaloids by a simple chemical process. A lot of accusation and denial flew back and forth about Bob's use of cocaine. The only thing for sure was that Bob wasn't talking about it.

On September 1, Bob Marley served as grand marshal of the annual West Indian Carnival Parade held on Labor Day in Brooklyn. Two weeks later the Wailers flew to Boston, where the American tour began on September 16. The I-Threes were supposed to open the show in Boston, just as they had during the European shows, but at the last minute Bob changed his mind and played the "old" show, starting with "Natural Mystic" and running through the Wailers' songbook before hitting the new songs from *Uprising* near the end of the performance, which seemed abnormally subdued for the Wailers. On the following day the Wailers bused south to Providence, where a tired-sounding, husky-voiced Bob Marley made the rounds of radio stations before a long sound check at the Providence Civic Center, where another subdued set was played. On Thursday, September 18, the Wailers arrived in New York, where Bob was planning to do two days of interviews and visit radio stations prior to the two-night stand at the Garden.

From the moment the Wailers arrived in New York, the band knew something was wrong. The Wailers had been traveling together for years, sharing the same quarters. The I-Threes' room had always been on the same floor as Bob's so that they could rehearse new routines as they came to Bob and so Rita Marley could iron Bob's clothes before the show. But in New York, Bob was deliberately isolated from the rest of the band for the first time. While the Wailers were assigned rooms at the Gramercy Park Hotel on East 21st Street, Bob and the inner circle checked into the Essex House on Central Park South, almost forty blocks and a five-dollar cab ride away from the rest of the band. When the musicians protested (Bob was using Island Records' six-door stretch limo), they were told that Skill wanted Bob away from the rest of the tour so he could concentrate on publicity and then get some rest.

But Bob's suite at the Essex House was a circus, day and night, crowded with friends, musicians, dope dealers, reporters, photographers, freeloaders and hangers-on talking loud, guzzling drinks and ordering room service. Bob was tired and spent a lot of time lying on the big bed, observing the flickering skyscrapers of New York through the floor-to-ceiling windows of the suite. It seemed like every reggae-bizz hustler in New York wanted something from Bob. One trooped in with lights and a video camera, asking Bob to do a couple of tunes for the reggae program the young Jamaican had on a local cable channel. Bob was exhausted, lying on his back, but he asked for his guitar and sang "Redemption Songs" in a weak voice flat on his back while the tape rolled.

The confusion and chaos that were building around Bob Marley increased the next day, Friday, September 19, the Wailers' opening night at Madison Square Garden. That afternoon, after fortifying himself with ginseng tea and lots of herb, Bob visited radio stations and put in an appearance at the Jamaican Progressive League before leaving for the sound check at the big arena on 34th Street. When the Wailers arrived the road crew was still building the gaudy Commodores' stage set on which the Wailers would play that night. (Although the two groups were equally billed, the Wailers were opening both shows, swallowing a little pride to capture a new audience for the band's message.) So the sound check was delayed, then postponed, then canceled. That night when Bob Marley and the Wailers took the stage, lively red, green and gold characters on a gaudy red and white stage that looked like the interior of a Cadillac, the sound was abysmal and the first few numbers were ruined until engineer Errol Brown could mix the levels the way Bob wanted them. Dressed in his usual denim jacket, jeans and construction boots, Bob gave a bravura show, throwing his hair until it seemed a whirlpool around his face. Twenty thousand New Yorkers cheered the amazing magical presence of the man, as Marley once again cast his own darkling spell: *There's a natural mystic blowing through the air/If you listen carefully now you will hear/This could be the first trumpet/Might as well be the last/ Many more will have to suffer/Many more will have to die* . . .

The following day, Saturday, Bob was totally beat. He stayed at the Essex House with his courtiers. Lying on his bed, he talked with journalists and friends; when an aide brought in a huge bundle of cash, the receipts from the previous night's show, Bob waved the package off as if it contained something unworthy of consideration. Part of the intrigue swirling around Bob in New York had to do with his lack of a manager and even a record label. Bob had become dissatisfied with Island, which he considered a white rock label unable to channel the Wailers' music toward the black audience at which Bob was aiming. That night at Madison Square Garden the president of Polygram Records was present backstage offering, according to Danny Sims, a ten-million-dollar label deal with Tuff Gong International. The deal was to have involved an immediate three-million-dollar advance to Bob, with the rest to be paid out over the course of five albums, as well as the rights to other Jamaican artists in the Tuff Gong stable like the I-Threes, the Melody Makers, Freddie Mac-Gregor, Burning Spear, Junior Tucker, Nadine Sutherland and others.

Early on Sunday morning, Rita Marley called her husband to see if he wanted to go to the Ethiopian Orthodox Church with her. Bob told Rita he didn't feel well because he had gotten to bed late after the final New York concert.

Later that morning, Bob put on a warmup suit and went out to run in Central Park with Skill and a few others, including Dr. Frazier. The group had almost reached the reservoir track when Bob shouted out in panic, "Alan! Alan!" Skill Cole turned and Bob Marley collapsed into his arms. Bob remained conscious, terrified. His body felt "frozen," and his neck was immobile. He could hardly move at all. His friends carried Bob back to the hotel, and after a couple of hours the seizure seemed to pass, and Bob could walk again.

Hours later, someone called Rita Marley at the Wailers' hotel and told her what had happened. Rita immediately went to Bob's suite at the Essex House, where she found a crowd of people smoking herbs in the living room while Bob tried to rest in the bedroom. Bob told Rita that he was feeling better and would see her later that night at a new reggae club in Greenwich Village called Negril. But when the I-Threes arrived at the club that night, they were told that Bob had gotten sick at the club and had just left with Skill Cole in the limo, bound for the hotel.

The next morning, on Monday, the Wailers were scheduled to fly to Pittsburgh to continue the tour. Again Rita called Bob to pick him up for the ride to the airport, but Bob told her he wasn't making the flight. He was vague with her, saying he had some business, an interview to do. So the band flew on to Pittsburgh; everyone now knew about Bob's collapse. As Al Anderson says, "The band knew there was a big, big problem."

Bob Marley didn't make the flight to Pittsburgh because Dr. Frazier had taken him to a neurologist, whose diagnosis came fast and came very bad. Bob had a large cancerous brain tumor that was killing him. The collapse in Central Park had been a stroke. The neurologist ventured that Bob had only between two and three weeks left to live. Bob was stunned, speechless. Carl Frazier asked if there was a chance of another diagnosis, and was again shown the irrefutable results of the X rays and brain scans.

An immediate decision had to be made on the tour. Marley's doctors demanded the rest of the dates be canceled at once. But Bob wanted to go on to Pittsburgh. Bob muttered something about knowing what was going on and wanting to get another opinion from another doctor.

That afternoon, Rita called Bob's suite from Pittsburgh, where the Wailers were waiting for him. One of Bob's publicists answered the phone and told Rita that Bob had suffered a stroke. Rita assumed that the tour was canceled but was told no, that Bob was insisting on coming to Pittsburgh. Hearing this, Rita Marley burst into a rage. "If anything happens to Bob," she shouted, "somebody's gonna *feel* it." Later, Rita lay down to rest and had a vision of Bob wearing hospital clothes, with no hair, talking to her from the other side of a fence.

Bob and the rest of his group arrived in Pittsburgh that night, and Rita went to see him as soon as he checked into the hotel. Bob looked dazed and hardly seemed to recognize anybody. He looked so different that Rita blew up and tried to stop the tour right there. She called Cedella in Miami and told her Bob was too sick to play but was being pushed by his friends to play that night. But Bob was adamant, and the Wailers played their last concert ever the next night at the Stanley Theater in Pittsburgh on the feeling that if Bob was going to die anyway, he might as well die on tour the way he wanted. Such was the sense of desperation felt by all the Wailers.

The afternoon of that final show, there was a sound check at the theater late in the afternoon. Bob brought the whole band on stage and without saying a word started to sing "Keep On Moving," the classic old Wailers ska. Bob sang it over and over and over for forty-five minutes until the I-Threes were in tears and the rest of the band got upset and wanted to leave the stage. But everyone understood. It was, Judy Mowatt said later, Bob's way of saying good-bye to the Wailers when he had them all together one more time.

That night's show was magnificent, burning with the furious insight of a dying man's eyes. Bob came out without an introduction and shouted into his microphone: "YEEEEAAAAHHHHH!! *Greetings* in the name of His Imperial Majesty, *Emperor Haile Selassie I, Jah,* Rastafari, who liveth and reigneth with I and I I-tinually, ever faithful, ever sure. They say that experience teaches wisdom, but there's a natural mystic blowing through the air . . ." And the Wailers launched into a fast ninety-minute version of their show, the Barrett brothers rushing the beat so Bob wouldn't get too tired. Although Bob's voice sounded a little raspy on "Natural Mystic," it improved as the band charged into "Positive Vibration," "Burnin' and Lootin'," "Them Belly Full," "Heathen" and a medley of "Running Away" and "Crazy Baldhead." Bob's dance was a little less spry than usual, but other than that the Wailers played like any other night where the band wanted to really throw it down on stage. Still moving fast, Bob sang hard on "War"/"No More Trouble," "Zim-babwe," "Zion Train," "No Woman, No Cry" and the long finale of "Jamming" and "Exodus."

After a few minutes of pandemonium, the Wailers came back for the encores. Bob performed "Redemption Songs" alone with his guitar, and offstage many of the touring party cried in the wings at the poignancy of the moment. They finished the set with "Coming In from the Cold" and "Could You Be Loved" and left the stage again. But Bob wanted to play more, so they came back and did "Is This Love" and "Work." As Bob sang the backward numerical verses—*Five days to go working for the next day/Four days to go . . .* —the rest of the band realized the show was over at last. Bob was literally counting the Wailers down to the end. "Work" was the last song he ever performed.

After the show, Rita Marley called Danny Sims and threatened to "make war" if the tour were not stopped. Sims asked her what she wanted to do, and Rita said she would take Bob home to his mother in Miami and find the best doctors for him. So the tour was stopped. Skill Cole called all the Wailers to Family Man's room. Choked by his own words, Skill gravely cleared his voice out spoke out of his bushy black beard. "Well, I-ya . . . it's like this . . . It's a thing where Bob . . . isn't physically capable . . . of continuing working." Nobody was able to speak any further. The Tuff Gong Uprising tour was canceled on September 23, 1980. The Wailers' "official" position was that Bob was suffering from exhaustion.

Bob Marley was flown to Miami the next day in a state of devastation. A year's worth of planning, touring and recording commitments had gone for nothing. Bob couldn't believe he was really a dying man, but he knew his career was over. It was a terrible moment for him. He underwent tests at Cedars of Lebanon Hospital, where his foot had been operated on, but the doctors decided to send him to New York for further tests at the Memorial Sloan-Kettering Cancer Center. Bob flew to New York supported by Cindy Breakspeare, Skill and Dr. Frazier, who checked Bob into Sloan-Kettering as soon as they landed. Bob had hoped his stay at the famous cancer hospital could be kept secret, but Jamaica's traditional ties to nursing and hospital work undid him. When Bob's test results came in on October 7, he was found to have cancer in his lungs and stomach as well as a malignant brain tumor. The Sloan-Kettering doctors told Bob Marley that at best he had perhaps four to five weeks to live, and started radiation therapy in an attempt to reduce the growth of the tumor on his brain. On October 8, the day after the results of the tests came in, the New York black-oriented radio station WLIB broadcast the news that Bob Marley was a cancer patient at Sloan-Kettering. That same afternoon, Bob left the hospital and checked into the Wellington Hotel on 56th Street so he could maintain his privacy while continuing the radiotherapy at the hospital as an outpatient. Initially Bob began to respond to the radiation. He felt strong enough to watch his friend Muhammad Ali's last fight against heavyweight champion Larry Holmes. Friends took him to a concert by the British rock group Queen, and one Sunday afternoon he went out to play soccer with Skill Cole in Queens. But Bob was unable to run and tackle with his usual fervor, and soon limped off to the sidelines to watch.

Lee Jaffe found Bob a few days later, at Danny Sims's house at Fifth Avenue and 103rd Street. Even with lung cancer, Bob was smoking a spliff with his hangers-on while around him controversy raged. Until the cancer story broke in the press, some unscrupulous elements in Bob's entourage wanted Sims to keep Bob's illness a secret from Polygram Records so Bob could take the huge advance and run. Sims refused, but the point became moot when Bob's cancer became public and the offer was withdrawn. There was also arguing back and forth over Bob's treatment. Some wanted him to stay at Sloan-Kettering, while others like Danny Sims and Lee Jaffe wanted Bob to be put on the controversial nontoxic and dietary treatments that were generally disdained by the orthodox cancer establishment. Sims wanted Bob to go to the Mexican clinic where actor Steve McQueen was then being treated, but didn't want to be the one to take the responsibility of sending him. Later, Lee Jaffe was appalled to find Bob living in a squalid two-room suite at the Wellington with no light and hardly any air, the atmosphere filled with smoke from his cronies' spliffs and cigarettes. Bob looked tired and very sick. One weekend, Lee took Bob up to his country place in Putnam County so Bob could get some fresh air. Bob was quiet but still optimistic, playing new songs; but Lee noticed that it was getting harder for Bob to hold his guitar.

Back in New York, Bob suffered a setback. Another small stroke left him barely able to stand, and the Sloan-Kettering doctors began chemotherapy. Within a week Bob had lost twenty-five pounds and his hair had begun to fall out. One afternoon at the hotel, Bob's scalp was burning so much from the chemotherapy that he began to literally pull his locks out of his head. A few minutes later Bob asked for a scissors so he could cut the rest off himself. When Lee walked in and saw Bob he made a remark about Bob looking like a rude boy again. "You're not easy," Bob replied with a small laugh. As Bob lost more weight and began to look deathly ill, his family pressured him to be baptized in the Ethiopian Orthodox Church. Actually, Bob's mother (who herself had been baptized in St. Ann with Bob *in utero*) had been trying to get Bob baptized in the E.O.C. for years but he had always said to her in putting it off, "I baptized by *fire.*" There had also been the problem of the Twelve Tribes, which looked upon the E.O.C. as a rival organization. But now, fearing for his life, Bob agreed to baptism as a favor to his mother, thinking he had only another week or two to live. So on November 4, Bob was baptized at the Wellington Hotel, as a tearful Rita Marley and their children watched, by Abouna Yesuhaq, Archbishop of the Ethiopian Orthodox Church in the Western Hemisphere. Bob was christened Berhane Selassie, "Light of the Holy Trinity." After the ceremony, Bob took his wife and children in his arms and wept.

Right after that, Bob Marley began to die. The chemotherapy was having little effect other than making Bob nauseous every moment. The brain tumor had paralyzed him from the waist down so that he was unable to walk. Bob was passive and confused, not knowing what to do, and his friends were frightened because he looked so bad. Bob was obviously slipping out of their hands.

A couple of weeks earlier, PeeWee Frazier found out that Dr. Josef Issels, a German specialist in nontoxic cancer treatment, would be addressing a cancer seminar in New York. Issels's name had been frequently mentioned to those around Bob as the one man who might be able to save Bob Marley. Although blacklisted by the American Cancer

Society as a quack and persona non grata to Bob's New York doctors, the seventy-three-year-old Issels had a solid reputation within the "holistic" medical community. Said by some to be thirty years ahead of his time, Issels specialized in terminal cancer patients who had been given up by their physicians. His therapy included altered diet, hyperthermia (heat treatment), injections of drugs some considered experimental and a holistic philosophy that called for an almost psychological transference, or identification, of patient with doctor. Although there were shadows in Dr. Issels's past (he was an officer in the Nazi S.S. during the Second World War, had served a jail term for manslaughter and had lost a famous patient, the British Olympian Lillian Board, in 1970 while she was under his care), Issels's Sunshine House clinic in Bad Wiessee, West Germany, treated roughly fifty cancer outpatients per day for about two thousand dollars per month.

Bob Marley was in such agony that something had to be done. PeeWee and Skill tried to speak to Issels at the cancer seminar, but failed because it was closed to the public and security was tight. Later they managed to penetrate the question-and-answer session by almost beating down the door. Frazier asked Issels whether he had ever treated melanoma, and Issels replied that he had, but that it was usually too difficult to treat. Before they were able to speak with him about Bob, the session was over and Issels had slipped out. Later they tracked him down at another lecture he was giving, and persuaded an aide to give them Issels's personal phone number in West Germany.

Now, at the Hotel Wellington, Bob was going downhill. It seemed to those taking care of Bob that chemotherapy itself was killing him. He was partially paralyzed and having difficulty eating and breathing. Dr. Frazier called Josef Issels in West Germany, and arrangements were made to receive Bob as a patient at Sunshine House. Bob's clothes were hastily packed and a four-car caravan organized to take Bob to Kennedy Airport. Bob, accompanied by Skill, PeeWee and a friend called Bird who was cooking for Bob, rode in singer Roberta Flack's limousine and flew to London aboard the Concorde because it was faster. The friends Bob left behind in New York wondered if they would ever see him again.

Bob arrived at Issels's clinic in the Bavarian Alps on November 9, 1980, unable to walk without support and expecting to die within days. But within hours, the charismatic, white-haired, iron-willed Issels had captured Bob's complete faith and trust and had stabilized some of his symptoms. After an initial diagnosis confirmed the brain tumor as well as cancer in the lungs and stomach, Bob was put on a regimen that included blood transfusions, hyperthermia and injections of an anticancer agent called THX, the use of which was illegal in the United States. Slowly, Bob began to regain a bit of his strength, as well as a bit of hope.

To the outside world, Bob had all but disappeared. The Wailers and Tuff Gong refused to publicly admit that Bob was suffering from cancer. Before Bob had left New York, Chris Blackwell had taped a statement by Bob that was later issued to radio stations: "Hail Rasta! Ya t'ink anyt'ing can raas kill me? I understand that writers and people in the press are very interested and concerned about my health. I want to say thank you for your interest and that I'll be alright and I'll be back in the road again in 1981—really, performing for the fans we love. Beautiful yunno, it's Bob talkin' to ya, have no doubt, seen? Good." In New York, Bob's publicist continued to insist that Bob was being treated for "severe fatigue," while in a London radio interview Rita Marley denied Bob was ill and said that he had gone to the Shashamani farm in Ethiopia to rest. But on November 25 the London papers broke the story that Bob was at the Issels clinic, and the ruse was dropped. Nothing was heard from the clinic at Bad Wiessee for another three months.

11

Nine Miles

Why do you look so sad and forsaken?
When one door is closed
Don't you know another is open?
   "Coming In from the Cold"

A month after Bob Marley arrived in Germany, instead of dying as predicted, he began to fall into a routine. He lived in a ground-floor flat in a two-hundred-year-old *Gasthaus* with his mother and whatever friends were visiting. Strictly forbidden to smoke or drink even a little wine, he would walk with support down the hill to Issels's clinic for twice-a-day hyperthermia treatments that were called "heat sessions": intense 180-degree beams of ultraviolet heat were aimed at Bob's tumors (five in all had been diagnosed) in order to weaken the malignant cells in hopes they would respond to the drugs Dr. Issels had prescribed. The heat sessions were an ordeal for Bob, one which he bore with a silent, stoic courage. Rita Marley says, "He handed himself over, innocently. From that time on, Bob was led."

Early in February 1981, the Wailers family gathered at Bad Wiessee to celebrate Bob's thirty-sixth birthday. All the Wailers were there except for Family Man and Carlie Barrett. Bob was in good spirits and in better shape than anyone expected. He was taking transcontinental phone calls and conducting Tuff Gong business with Diane Jobson's help. He was able to kick a ball around in the clinic's gym and was allowed to take walks of up to an hour along the mountain roads and paths. Cedella Booker and Diane Jobson had gone to Germany for the purpose of bringing Bob back to Miami if his condition was stable, but the idea was overruled by Drs. Issels and Frazier. Bob was in no condition to travel and was continuing to lose weight. But his hair had started to grow back —"He looked just like he did when he was a little boy," Cedella says— and his face was bright and handsome again. Still, Diane was frightened by Bob's thinness and blank mood. His diet had been restricted to organically grown food, and since it was winter in West Germany no vegetables or fruits were in season. Bob sorely missed his roasted yam and other Jamaican specialties: the boxes of food Diane had sent from Jamaica and Florida had been intercepted by the clinic staff. Bob's weight had dropped below one hundred pounds, and Diane was insisting the Issels treatment was "breaking down Bob's physical structure." She pleaded again with Bob's doctors to let her take him to the Mexican hospital where Steve McQueen was in treatment. Again, Diane was refused. Throughout the ordeal, Bob maintained his faith in Issels.

In March, a writer and photographer from London's *Daily Mail* showed up at the clinic to do a story on Bob. Diane Jobson was angry that Issels, who had invited them, was seeking publicity by using Bob's fame. Bob was photographed wearing a woolen cap and his Wailers jacket, his face childlike but for his mustache and light beard. With the reporter, Bob was frank as ever. He was quoted as saying, "Like so many other patients who have come here, I was given up by the doctors to die. Now I *know* I can live. I have proved it."

Asked if his experience had changed him, Bob said, "Yes, of course. I've gone inside myself more. I have had time to explore my beliefs, and I am the stronger because of it."

As for Issels, Bob was quoted: ". . . I believe he is the best doctor a man could have. I have faith in him. He is of wide understanding. He gives me the strength to live."

The published report in the *Daily Mail* received wide attention, and revived hope that Bob might regain his health. Several music magazines published reports that Bob would be back in Jamaica, working on new music, by June.

But Bob was confined to the slow and lonely walks between treatments. One day Bob and Diane were walking home slowly from the clinic, when a little girl stepped out from behind a house gate and offered Bob a bouquet of spring flowers. As Diane's eyes moistened in spite of herself, Bob murmured that he felt surrounded by love.

One night Dr. Issels came to the flat to socialize with Bob, Cedella, Diane and Neville Garrick. A bottle of wine was opened for the occasion, although Bob couldn't drink. Issels told them a story about a German acquaintance who had advised Issels not to treat Bob, saying that Bob Marley was the most dangerous black man in the world. Under the conversation Bob's cassette player boomed out *Uprising*. Suddenly, for the first time in months, Bob began to sing along with the music: *Weeeeeee can make it work.* Bob looked straight at Issels as he sang. When the song ended, Issels nodded in agreement. "We will," he said. "We will."

Back in Jamaica, there was great speculation over Bob's health. A rumor spread through Kingston music circles that Chris Blackwell had said, "If Bob dies, reggae *mosh.*" Meaning that reggae music might be unable to survive any longer as an international force after Bob. There were many rumors that Bob had died, fueled by the closing of the Tuff Gong Studio for several weeks that spring and the firing of Tuff Gong's marketing director, Tommy Cowan. Some Rastas proclaimed esoteric reasons for Bob's sickness, complicated scenarios involving the story of Samson and Delilah and the Book of Judges. Through his press agent, Peter Tosh released a statement that he hoped Jah would help Bob to overcome the pollution of the planet. Later, just before the end, the new Jamaican government of prime minister Edward Seaga (elected the year before after seven hundred and fifty Jamaicans had been killed during the campaign) awarded Bob Marley the Jamaican Order of Merit. The award was accepted by Bob's oldest son, Ziggy. It allowed his father the title of the Honorable Robert Nesta Marley, O.M.

Cedella Booker noticed her son begin to get weaker by the end of March. Day after day Bob lay in bed, saying he was too weak to walk to the clinic. When he refused to eat or drink water she complained, and Bob replied, "Momma, it's not you feelin' the pain, yunno, it's me. I know how I feel, and I can't eat." As much as possible, Bob would keep silent. In the evening he read the Bible with Cedella or just meditated, while Cedella sang to him: *I know Jah Jah will find a way . . .* By the middle of the month, Bob was too weak to read, and friends had to read the Bible to him. He felt the injections he was given were poison, and in bad moments thought they were trying to kill him. Early in April, Dr. Issels went on vacation, leaving Bob to be cared for by his staff. Again Diane Jobson protested. How could Issels go on vacation? Bob was down to seventy pounds and could no longer even hold his guitar. Al Anderson had to walk him around. To make matters worse, other Wailers were calling Bob from Jamaica, trying to collect money owed them. There were rumors among the band that Bob was on his deathbed and was refusing to make a will. The multimillion-dollar Tuff Gong empire was at stake, with Rita as sole heir if Bob died without a will. At one point, Bob sent word to Don Taylor that he wanted to see him, but Taylor didn't come.

Late in April, an intestinal operation was performed on Bob to allevi-ate intense pain that had developed in his bowel. Two weeks later, on

May 3, Dr. Issels examined Bob Marley and gave up. Issels told Diane and Cedella that Bob had two weeks to live at most, and if they wanted to get him home he would have to leave within a week or he wouldn't even be able to survive the flight. Diane went in to see Bob to break the news gently. "Bob," she said, "Dr. Issels says you can go home now. He says you can continue the treatment from home."

Bob had been gazing out the window. Now he turned to face Diane and kissed his teeth bitterly. "Dr. Issels is a madman," he said softly.

Diane Jobson chartered a plane to fly Bob back to Miami. They arrived at midday on Saturday, May 9, and immediately checked Bob into Cedars of Lebanon. The hospital staff examined Bob and said they could do nothing for him but keep him comfortable.

On Monday morning, May 11, Bob's doctors told Rita Marley, who was sitting with Bob, that Bob's vital signs were slipping and that it would only be a matter of hours. Rita shook Bob awake, crying for him not to leave her. She started to sing a hymn—*God will take care of you*—but stopped when Bob seemed not to be listening. But then Bob said to her, "Keep singing, man, keep singing." Again, Rita begged Bob not to leave her, and he said he wasn't really going anywhere, that he was just going to prepare a place for himself in the hills. Then his breathing became very shallow, and Rita shook him a little more and blew on his face. Then she called Cedella, who was at home, and told her she better come to the hospital.

By the time Cedella got to the hospital, Bob had revived a little. He said he felt positive and stronger. His wife and mother began to pray aloud, and Bob told them to pray for everyone else, but not for him. Then he spoke to his two sons, Ziggy and Stephen, saying good-bye and telling them what he wanted them to do.

At eleven-thirty, Cedella Booker was praying in tears at Bob's bedside. Suddenly Bob said, "Don't cry for me, Momma. I'm gonna be alright." Cedella answered that she wasn't crying for him, but was crying to God. Bob said, "Oh." A few minutes later he asked Cedella for some water, which he drank to the last drop. Some nurses arrived to take an X ray and Cedella helped them move Bob onto his side. He complained that he had spent the last six months with needles sticking out of his body. Then he lay back and said he wanted to sleep. He stretched out his hand to Cedella and beckoned, saying, "Come closer, come nearer." Then his eyes rolled back and he lost consciousness and began to snore until a nurse put an oxygen mask over his face to help him breathe. A few minutes later, the doctor came out into the hall and told them Bob was gone. Cedella and Diane went into his room. Bob looked quiet and peaceful for the first time in months. Then a nurse turned to Cedella and said, "I'm sorry, ma'am."

A few days later, Bob appeared to his daughter Cedella in a dream, asking her to tell her uncle, Anthony Booker, to stop telling people that he was dead. "Every time dem call 'pon the phone," the little girl dreamed her father said, "him tell people, seh me dead, and me nuh dead!"

At eleven forty-five on Monday morning, May 11, Neville Garrick was working in his studio off Hope Road, listening to reggae songs on his cassette player, when the sky became dark and he and his wife heard three loud thunderclaps and saw a bolt of lightning. Garrick's wife said, "Umm, I don't like that." At Judy Mowatt's house two miles away, the phone rang and when Judy answered it a friend in Miami told her that Bob was dead. Judy hadn't even known that Bob was in Miami. "And at the same time there was a great thunder, just as Marcy [Marcia Griffiths] drive up. It was broad daylight, and rain didn't start to fall, but there was this great huge thunder in the heavens and a flash of lightning that came through the house. It came through the window and lodged for a second right on Bob's picture . . . like the heavens were really responding to a great force being taken away from the physical plane of the earth." Half an hour later, the JBC announced that Bob Marley had died in Miami, and the entire nation of Jamaica went into deep mourning.

The Barrett brothers, Family Man and Carlie, were working at the Tuff Gong Studio on Hope Road when the bulletin of Bob's death came over the radio. Knowing that Bob had died without a will and that technically all of Bob's possessions would go to Rita and the children, the Barretts were fearful that a delegation from the Twelve Tribes of Israel would now try to physically assert a claim on the property, which some members maintained Bob had verbally willed to the organization. The Barrett brothers immediately locked down the studio and the whole compound until a decision was made as to who were Bob's legal heirs. A long struggle for control of the Tuff Gong empire had begun.

As the news of Bob's passing filtered around the world, many people were caught by surprise. In their obituaries, the wire services and newspapers emphasized Bob's music and his mixed racial heritage, calling him "one of the world's most popular performers." Reuters quoted a London spokesman for Island Records who estimated that the Wailers worldwide sale of albums exceeded one hundred and ninety million dollars. In its long obituary the *Times* of London stated: "Whether on stage or on record Marley conveyed a vivid intensity heightened by his use of the fiery Biblical texts appropriated by the Jamaican cult of Rastafarianism, of which he was a prominent disciple. He was a deeply expressive singer whose range extended from the melodic lament of 'No Woman, No Cry' to inspiring and politically loaded dance tunes like 'Exodus' and 'Zimbabwe.' He came to be seen as the embodiment of reggae, but possessed an originality that would have ensured his prominence in any type of popular music. Reggae will survive the loss of his unique vision, but it may never have another spokesman of such eloquence and broad appeal." In Africa, the popular magazine *Spear* editorialized: "Bob Marley's music will be sung wherever men and women come together to demand justice and freedom. Bob Marley has left a legacy of hard work, a spirit of love and freedom for black people which will prove an inspiration to many as the crisis of the Babylonian system deepens."

On the following Thursday, a memorial service was held for Bob Marley at his house on Vista Lane in south Miami. Outside the big yellow house a large Ethiopian banner flew from the roof, while in the backyard a line of hand drummers kept up a steady akete tattoo, passing a burning chalice among themselves. Inside the house floral arrangements bedecked every flat surface, and Cedella and Rita stood in the doorway receiving a daylong procession of guests—many of the Wailers, Chris Blackwell, Don Taylor, Danny Sims and dozens of other old friends, employees and strangers who said they were just fans. In the main hall of the house Bob's body was laid out in a bronze casket, open from the waist up for the viewing. Bob's long locks, which had been saved, were restored to his head under a knitted Ethiopian crown. Bob's face was composed and waxen; his body had shrunk from weight loss and the folds of his skin hung over his crossed hands. The fingers of his right hand rested on a Bible opened to the Twenty-third Psalm, while his left hand rested on his old guitar, which Diane had placed in the coffin. The body was dressed in Bob's favorite denim jacket.

Around the coffin, Bob's family and friends held a traditional Jamaican wake. Some people stood facing Bob, speaking loudly to the body. Others offered religious testimony or anecdotes about how contact with Bob Marley had changed their lives. Before the short religious service, Cedella Booker, her face swollen from anguish, sang "Redemption Songs" while someone played the organ. Outside, the drummers continued their stark, tribal vigil.

Bob Marley finally returned to the Jamaica whose violent politics had made him an exile on Tuesday, May 19, two days before the state funeral planned, with Rita Marley's consent, by the office of the prime minister. As the coffin was being unloaded from the plane which had flown it home, a *Gleaner* photographer was pushed around by Rita Marley and others after he tried to take some pictures of the arrival. The following day, Bob's body lay in state at the National Arena, where thousands of Jamaicans had queued up to view Bob Marley one last time. There was a carnival atmosphere outside the arena; vendors were selling food and every manner of Bob Marley bauble, and when the surging crowds broke through their own lines, the police set off waves of tear gas to try to beat them back. Before the day was over, forty thousand Jamaicans had filed inside and past the coffin covered by a Jamaican flag and guarded by uniformed police and members of the Twelve Tribes. When the viewing ceased, the coffin was taken to a funeral home for the night.

The first funeral observances were held for Bob Marley early the next morning, when the coffin was driven to the Jamaican headquarters of the Ethiopian Orthodox Church on Maxfield Avenue, in the heart of the old Kingston slums. As a dozen foreign film crews set up their cameras and lights directly in front of the altar, blocking the mourners' view, Ethiopian Orthodox priests in ornate red, gold and silver vestments chanted prayers in Amharic and Geez, waving frankincense burning in golden censers. After the church service, the motorcade containing the coffin headed for the National Arena, detouring so the hearse could pass 56 Hope Road one final time in a gesture of farewell.

By the time the motorcade reached the National Arena, the crowd in the building far exceeded its twelve thousand seating capacity. The coffin was placed on the stage and again covered with the Jamaican flag. The back of the stage was draped in Ethiopian colors with a banner reading "The Hon. Robert Nesta Marley O.M." hung over the top. A bright neon sign flashed the word "Joseph," Bob's adopted Twelve Tribes name. There were portraits of Bob, Marcus Garvey and Haile Selassie, and from the balconies hung black banners proclaiming "The wicked is driven away in his wickedness, but the righteous hath hope in his death" and "Death is swallowed up in victory. O death where is thy sting? O grave, where is thy victory?"

At ten o'clock, there was a musical "presentation" by the Wailers (minus Tyrone Downie, who was too overcome with grief to go to the arena; instead he stayed in his hotel and—weeping—watched the funeral on television). First Cedella Booker, her daughter Pearl Livingston and a friend named Ora sang a song Cedella had written called "Hail." Then the I-Threes came on stage in long gowns and headwraps, faces puffy from weeping. Backed by the Wailers, they sang "Rastaman Chant" and "Natural Mystic," while Bob's sons Ziggy and Stevie danced on stage with some of their father's patented moves.

The funeral service itself began at eleven o'clock, presided over by Archbishop Yesuhaq, who had baptized Bob in New York the previous year, and a chanting line of Ethiopian Orthodox priests wearing ornate Coptic crosses. Rita Marley, Cedella Booker and Bob's children watched from seats in the second row. After Governor-General Florizel Glasspole and opposition leader Michael Manley each read their lessons, there was a snag in the service. Skill Cole, dressed in pure white and a red, green and gold tam, stepped to the lectern and deviated from the scriptural passage chosen for him by the Ethiopian Orthodox priests. As Skill boldly called out greetings to the Twelve Tribes of Israel, whose members felt left out of the ceremonies in favor of the E.O.C., he was greeted by loud applause and shouts of *Jah Rastafari*. A priest stepped up to correct Skill, but the tall footballer shouldered him aside as the rest of the priests clucked in disapproval. Skill read a passage from Isaiah: ". . . the righteous is taken away from the evil to come," and told the congregation his lesson had been different from the verses in Psalms that had been assigned to him. The archbishop followed Skill with Matthew 5: "Blessed are the peacemakers, for they shall be called the children of God."

After the mourners stood for the Lord's Prayer, the prime minister gave his "remembrance," an eloquent tribute from a man who was professionally and politically Bob Marley's opposite. In his eulogy, Seaga said of Bob: "His voice was an omnipresent cry in our electronic world, his sharp features, majestic locks, and prancing style a vivid etching on the landscape of our minds . . . Most people do not command recollection. Bob Marley was never seen. He was an experience which left an indelible, mystical imprint with each encounter. Such a man cannot be erased from the mind. He is part of the collective consciousness of the nation."

After the service, Bob Marley was carried out of the arena on the shoulders of Twelve Tribes members, as Archbishop Yesuhaq reassured the huge crowd: "He is not dead, but only resting." The cortege making the fifty-five-mile trip to Bob's burial site at Nine Miles was joined by dozens of rented buses and cars containing journalists, Twelve Tribes members and friends. It drove past streets and sights familiar to Bob Marley, down Tom Redcam Avenue and South Camp Road to Marcus Garvey Drive, skirting Trench Town. The crowds were thick as the cortege drove through Six Miles and Spanish Town, and as the long line of cars snaked into the deep country the roadsides were filled with black people gathered together in solid walls and perched in houses and trees, waving flags and banners, pictures and paintings of Bob, palm fronds, tree branches and umbrellas. From the whole Jamaican interior, the people had come to line the roads to say good-bye. The hearse carrying the coffin began to have engine trouble in Bog Walk and, at a place called Cotton Tree along the Ewarton Road, it broke down. The cortege was delayed for fifteen minutes until the coffin was transferred to a pickup van and the funeral motorcade to St. Ann continued. The cars wound slowly through Mt. Rosser, Moneague, Claremont, Bamboo, Brown's Town, Alexandria, Alva, Calderwood, Stepney and on into Nine Miles. After five hours of weaving through the hot green hills of the parishes, Bob Marley's body was carried up the hill on which he was born, now choked by thousands of Jamaicans milling about, and placed in a small plain white cement mausoleum that had been built next to the tiny house that Omeriah had built for his daughter and new grandson thirty-six years earlier. Over the mausoleum grew a large pear tree, laden with fruit. Edward Seaga was already there, surrounded by security. Archbishop Yesuhaq was there too, trying to administer the last rites of the church as pure Jamaican chaos swirled about him in a bewildering array of color and emotion. Over a loudspeaker, a voice announced: "Bob Marley, the king of reggae, has chosen to come here to rest." Rita and Cedella sang "Angels of mercy, angels of light, singing to welcome the pilgrim of the night" as the sun danced in and out of clouds and then behind the mountain on which Bob's ledge was perched, pitching the bishop's sermon into a cooling shade. As the words echoed out over the hills, the vault was sealed three times. (There had been talk in heavy Rasta circles of an attempt to steal the golden ring of Haile Selassie, which was being interred with Bob, so that a living Rasta might be anointed with the ring's power.) The first seal was a red metal plate with a gold Star of David. The second was a steel grill that was bolted on and covered with cement, the third seal of Bob Marley's tomb. The formal interment over, thousands of people trooped down the hillside, mingling with those thousands heading uphill for a look.

Much later, as darkness was falling, the crowd had thinned out and the smell of cook fires took over Nine Miles. All the priests, politicians, police and film crews had left for Kingston, and only a relatively small group of Rastas and friends of Bob were sitting up on the hill, watching over the tomb. At seven o'clock, drummer Babatunde Olatunji walked around the tomb striking a Yoruba ceremonial bell from his native Nigeria, called an *agogo*. Chiming out an African scale of bell syllables, Olatunji stopped at Bob Marley's head and sounded a loud, clarion peal that seemed to linger forever in the still air of the mountainous St. Ann night.

12
Aftermath

Me wake up Monday morning on the 11th of May
Me hear a news flash me seh around mid-day
And this was what the announcer say
That the great Bob Marley pass away
Said the great Bob Marley pass away
Seh Bob Marley was the king fe reggae
Me heard that him die inna Miami
And at his bedside was his family
His children and his wife Rita Marley
Me seh the whole world is in sympathy
Me seh me love Bob Marley
Jah mek me tell ya that we love Bob Marley . . .

> Lui Lepke
> "Tribute to Bob Marley"

Whatta weepin' and a wailin' and a gnashin' of teeth
Cos me feel it in me heart and soul
Cos we must find a cure fe cancer
Cos it kill off me reggae fadda
And left me with me one madda Rita—GO DEH!

> Ranking Joe
> "Bob Marley Special"

Him sing a lotta LP for you and me
Him sing a lotta LP and a lotta 45
Me seh him nuh tek no bribe and him nuh build no strife
Oh Lord my God I wish him was alive . . .

> Errol Scorcher
> "Sounds of Honorable Bob Marley"

In the aftermath of Bob Marley's death, his friends and those who loved the Wailers' music tried to take stock of what was left behind. While the Jamaican deejays recorded their own rhyming tributes, in New York Miles Davis was playing "My Man's Gone" in concert as a memorial to Bob. In Jamaica, Tuff Gong released an old song of Bob's called "I Know," which had originally been recorded in 1975 for the *Rastaman Vibration* sessions. Remixed by Family Man for release as Bob had requested as he lay dying, "I Know" sounded as spooky and sepulchral as if it had come from beyond the grave. Yet, for Marley devotees, the message of acceptance and redemption was reassuring. At the same time in New York, Danny Sims released an album called *Chances Are,* containing rerecorded and remixed version of songs that Bob had cut for Sims between 1968 and 1972. Because the LP had a recent picture of Bob on its sleeve, it was denounced widely as an exploitive fraud, anathema to the spirit of Bob's music. "I got worse reviews than Hitler," Sims said later. And later in the summer of 1981, the fourth Reggae Sunsplash festival was held at Montego Bay as a tribute to Bob. At the show's climax Stevie Wonder came onstage to jam with Rita Marley and the Wailers. Later, the open-air park would be rededicated in memory of Bob.

Later in the year, as part of a film biography of Bob that Chris Blackwell had commissioned, Cedella Booker and Tyrone Downie joined Blackwell at the bottom of the Grand Canyon in Arizona where members of the Havasupai Indian tribe venerated Bob, playing his records all the time. Bob Marley, who was interested in the Indians, would have loved it. Cedella and Tyrone sang for the Havasupai, who then in turn sang Bob's songs back to them.

Not long before Bob left Germany, he spent thirty thousand dollars on a golden, custom-made Mercedes 500 SL sedan. Six months later, in January 1982, the car arrived at the port of Kingston on a freighter. It took Rita Marley three days of haggling and a one-hundred-percent import duty to get the car off the docks. Back at Hope Road, fourteen-year-old Ziggy Marley started to drive the car around his father's old compound.

Bob Marley left behind a huge number of unissued songs, enough for five more albums according to some estimates. And then there were the hundreds of songs that evanesced into the night air. Diane Jobson remembers: "One time it was raining at Hope Road, and we were sitting down on the front step. And Bob siddung with his guitar and made a beautiful song. And then we never heard anything more about it. That particular one, I remember him making a remark, he said, 'Alright now, you see me a-sing, you should be writing down the words what I'm doing.' I said, 'True, Bob.' I picked up the phone directory and turned to the back page and wrote the words of the song on it. He just did a verse and stopped. Two years later, I picked up the phone book and was marveling at the lyric. It was so beautiful."

After his death, many of Bob's friends began to think of him as a Christ figure.

Tyrone Downie: "Bob was a little like Christ for me. Christ wasn't perfect. Christ fucked women. He swore. He did what we all did. He was studying the laws of nature, the laws of the universe. He wasn't trying to teach us to be good, 'cause life is not about being good. Life is about being yourself, being free. How could he know so much about society if he wasn't part of it. Look at Mary Magdalene. So Bob . . . when he was alive I wasn't sure. Since he died, my perspective is that he is really *the* prophet. Because I was right there with him, I never considered him as Bob the prophet. I considered him as Bob my friend."

Diane Jobson: "Bob must be seen as a Christ figure, and his songs as a new book of psalms. There will be no more prophets, so his message *had* to reach the ends of the earth. Even Japan, even Italy, where Rome is. 'This could be the first trumpet, might as well be the last.' "

Danny Sims: "I think Bob was a very mythical character. He was like Jesus Christ. Not to say that he *was,* but he was a saintly kind of figure."

Cedella Booker: "There was something about Bob's eyes; the magnet in them was so strong that sometimes you couldn't look full at him when he was staring at you . . . He always maintained that he was just a farmer. If you took away his money, he wouldn't starve."

Since Bob Marley died intestate, without a will, all of his money and property went to Rita, causing some resentment within the Wailers organization and Bob's extended family, including the various girl friends who bore his children. Gradually, Rita moved to consolidate the Tuff Gong enterprises, but she had to do without the help of the person who knew Tuff Gong the best. When Bob had died, Diane Jobson resigned, telling Rita that her services as lawyer and adviser had been personal to Bob only. (Eventually, Diane would rejoin the organization.)

Later Danny Sims reflected on his end: "We had the two point override, I had the publishing. So the only thing I didn't get part of was the tour money, and they didn't make any money on tour. The Wailers sold out everywhere, but Bob got robbed a lot. I'm not calling any names, but Bob Marley got robbed more, because he was bigger, than any act in the history of the business."

But it was the music that was really important, and it meant all things to all people. For the religious, the appeal was obvious. Marxists heard in the music a call to arms and rebellion. Black people could identify with everything Bob ever wrote, while his young white fans heard a message of universal love and brotherhood. Rita Marley: "Bob was born rich, that was his quality. His richness was on the spiritual level, the gift of God. The inspiration that he had to give was his glory."

The invitation bore two embossed Lions of Judah. It read:

PSALM 2

How good and how pleasant it is for brethrens
And sistrens to dwell together in one inity
Give praises unto the Almighty JAH Rastafari

Mrs. Rita Marley and Family request your presence at their
Birthdate Anniversary of the Hon. Robert Nesta Marley O.M.,
our beloved brother and friend.
To be held at Nine Miles, Rhoden Hall, St. Ann, Jamaica W.I.
on the 6th February, 1982, at 5 p.m.

The morning of the sixth dawned bright and clear. At 9 A.M. the JBC began broadcasting a long birthday tribute to Bob that had been produced by an FM station in San Francisco, California. The road out of Kingston was free of trucks on that Saturday morning, which made the climb over the Blue Mountains faster and much less exhausting. Outside Spanish Town my rented Toyota was pulled over by the police at a speed trap; a Jamaican justice of the peace was holding roadside court, and gave me a pink summons for a court appearance in Kingston the following week. Back on the road, I wondered what Bob Marley would have done with this Babylonian ticket. His spirit told me to throw it out the window, which I did.

Further on, a stop at the famous roadside shanties near Moneague, where one can buy thirst-quenching water coconut, buttered roast yam and salt fish, giant pineapples and papayas, exotic naseberries, blushy red Ethiopian apples and long strings of oranges and tangerines—the great bounty of the St. Ann hills. Turning off the main road, I drove toward Browns Town, deep in the heart of the garden parish. Cruising the tops and sides of inland ridges and vales, one can see the impossible deep azure of the ocean on the other side of the hills. The roads are rural, narrow and infrequently traveled except by flocks of goats and the intervillage vans that hurl passengers along these country lanes with breakneck abandon. Along the flat open spaces, steel poles have been erected at intervals along the roads to try to cut down on illicit ganja missions flown by Florida-based Cessnas and Beechcraft. Deep in St. Ann, the land is heavenly and green. The ghostly great houses of the late sugar empire watch over the landscape from their promontories. A few people walk along the road. A man carrying water gently sways as he ambles slowly onward.

Through the teeming market town of Browns Town on a busy Saturday, a riot of dark stalls and bright fabric in primary colors, a sea of faces that recall Togo and Benin as much as the West Indies. A stop at a roadside shop for an ice-cold bottle of Ting, Jamaica's grapefruit soda, the best soft drink in the world. Standing in the shop, I watched reggae star Dennis Brown roar by with locks flying, at the wheel of his fancy new VW van, headed toward the party at Nine Miles.

Suddenly the road turns to gravel and a winding, rutted country track. Jamaicans of all ages were heading up to Marley's hamlet on foot, carrying food and radios. Some shouted for rides as we passed, but we were running full from Kingston.

Nine Miles, Rhoden Hall, Stepney District, Parish of St. Ann. We parked, walked up a little hill past vendors of curried goat, roots tea and sensemilla, and found seats next to the sound board in front of a stage erected across the lane from Bob Marley's birthplace and tomb.

The landscape consists of rolling green hills, whose granite outcroppings were covered with people waiting for the show to begin. The afternoon was alternately brightly radiant and then gray and cool, as oceanic cumuli rolled in from the sea. The sun set behind the big hill in the back of the stage late in the afternoon, and from then on the proceedings were illumined by a single powerful bulb suspended over the stage. The crowd was mostly Jamaican, but with a lot of youngish tourists who found their way inland from the north coast. People were building spliffs and waiting out the afternoon in good humor and expectation. In front of the stage was a sign that read: NO FILMING BY ORDER OF MANAGEMENT. The management here was strictly Rita Marley, heiress to the entire Tuff Gong empire. Back on Hope Road in Kingston, Rita was

257

having a huge concrete wall built around the Tuff Gong Studio compound, turning the onetime tropical mansion into a fortress.

Bob Marley's simple cement tomb has been covered by a little chapel, gray-roofed and sided (perhaps temporarily) with sheetrock. Light pours in through stained-glass windows and flickers from the dozens of long candles and tapers that burn silently for the late reggae avatar. Outside, police stood guard with riot shotguns slung casually over their shoulders. On the roof of the tomb, a solitary white dove was perched.

The audience was full of dreads basking in the deep blue twilight, calling to new arrivals: "Sky is clear!" "Pardon me, sir, would you give me a likkle sensemilla thing?" Just as half a dozen dreads fired up their meticulously crafted spliffs, a uniformed colonel of the Jamaica Defence Force stalked through the crowd brandishing his swagger stick, making ostentatious sniffing noises, turning up his nose at the sweet aroma of St. Ann's finest draw. "Haarruummph!" The Rastas mocked the colonel without mercy and dissolved into peals of derisive laughter as they puffed happily away.

The view into the little hills from my seat was *long,* surrounded by Jamaican mountain jungle. Giant turkey buzzards swooped low over the crowd, perhaps drawn by the spicy scent of stewing goat and Ital food. Vendors were selling oranges. "See the orange man! Get your blood claat orange right here!"

The large painting of Bob holding his guitar that was displayed at his funeral was propped up against the stage, along with blown-up sepia portraits of Marcus Garvey and His Imperial Majesty Haile Selassie I. Red, green and gold bunting draped the stage.

At four-thirty the sound system was switched on. Lui Lepke sings "Tribute to Bob Marley" on tape. An hour later, after various members of the new Wailers set up their instruments on stage, Rita Marley, dressed in red and sporting tennis sneaks and a Tuff Gong eyeshade, appeared on stage. She welcomed the throng, announced the program and asked for good behavior with all the prim propriety of the lady schoolteacher on the skank of "One Draw." Then she introduced her priest, a handsome Ethiopian from the Ethiopian Orthodox Church who walked onstage in a black burnoose and prayed, in heavily accented English, for the soul of Bob Marley. Then the priest held his small black cross aloft in the St. Ann twilight and simply said, "Our Father . . ."

It was like a dub version of the Lord's Prayer.

As night fell, a white-smocked Ethiopian reggae band took the stage, but not before an intense Rastafarian woman announced that tape recorder and cameras are *dangerous diseases* and would be confiscated if discovered. Around this time, small groups of hard youths in mirror sunglasses and berets filtered through the guests, threatening the various professional photographers trying to cover the event.

Dallol was basically an Ethiopian copy band, and they covered Wailers songs like "Who the Cap Fit" with little grace. They were followed by a Rasta dub poet who delivered a shining poetic rap/invocation that set a sharp tone of spirit for the evening. As his staccato poetry jabbed into the audience he was greeted with appreciative cries of *"Murder"* and *"Bim!"*

Then the Wailers came on. I should say, the *new* Wailers came on. Seeco was absent, reportedly exiled for some transgression. Tyrone Downie, the band's avant-garde keyboard man and Bob Marley's musical alter ego, was touring with Grace Jones. Al Anderson was in New York. Carlie and Family Man Barrett remained as one of reggae's greatest rhythm sections, and Earl "Wire" Lindo was on keyboards. Lead guitar Junior Marvin took Bob's lead vocals, sometimes singing in partial phrases, so the Wailers now sounded like Wailers-in-dub. Artman Neville Garrick was on percussion, and the band was filled out with veteran guitarist Gitzroy and Steven Stewart on keyboards. From their sound that night, it seemed that the Wailers were still trying to regain their automatic transmission while mourning their leader. Certainly, to almost everyone present, the old Wailers drive was absent that night.

But the musicians, obviously experimenting, still managed to mount a soulful and very satisfying show in tribute to Bob Marley, martyred by the epidemic scourge of our unhappy century. Cute Tuff Gong chanteuse Nadine Sutherland, not yet fourteen years old, came out first and did quick versions of her single "Starvation" and the last major Marley anthem, "Redemption Songs."

Then, a dramatic moment. The I-Threes walked on.

Rita Marley. Judy Mowatt. Marcia Griffiths. The three reggae goddesses. Judy and Marcia wore scarves around their heads, long dresses and red, gold and green silk Wailers tour jackets. Onstage, the I-Threes don't smile much. They just look . . . awesome.

"It feels like a *party,*" Rita exclaimed. But it didn't. It felt like something else. Rita tried to get the crowd to sing happy birthday to Bob, but the people seemed stunned, reminded again that Bob rests in that tomb over there with the candles and the incense. Rita tried again for a rousing happy birthday, but it wasn't working. It felt like a wake.

But that's all right, too, and the I-Threes, arguably the best harmony singers in Jamaica, delivered a short set that began with a subdued but beautiful rendition of "Nice Time," continued with an even more beautiful a capella harmony orgy on "That's How Strong My Love Is" and

259

finished with a long scatting skank with the Wailers on the theme: "Some like it hot/Some like it cold/Some like it in the pot/Nine days old." It looks silly on the page but that night in Nine Miles, it *burned.*

The I-Threes stepped off to great cheering and "Mother Booker," Cedella Booker, Bob Marley's mother, came on to sing. Mother Booker is a queen-motherly woman, robed in salmon-colored silk and golden Coptic crosses. Backed by hand-drummers, she improvised a chant based on Bob's last words to her in the Miami hospital from which he passed on: "Mama, don't cry. I'll be alright."

The night's entertainment was finished by her grandchildren, the Melody Makers, Bob's four children with Rita—Sharon, Cedella, Ziggy and Stevie. The kids did juvenile versions of their father's stately songs, and I decided to leave, feeling overcome with sentiment. Of all people, *of all people,* why did Bob Marley have to go? He was so important to so many, one of the few truly international people.

It was hard to keep my eyes on the undulating red dirt road, trying to find the way to Claremont and the main highway to Kingston. I kept thinking of how Bob Marley had emerged from these limestone hills and his grandfather's clan to become not only the key figure in reggae, but the most important and charismatic world champion of human freedom and dignity in the 1970s. The old road looped about itself as it threaded east through the hill country, and my eyes were wet from the red dust and all the emotion of the day.

At darkened Claremont we stopped at a roadside bar for a cold Red Stripe and a taste of the jukebox. Bob Marley was singing, "Could You Be Loved?" The night air smelled of ginger lily and sweet St. Ann dew. A mile on down the road, we turned south for Kingston and home.

13

Postscript

Kyaan Get Me Out of the Race

It has now been twelve years since Bob Marley left us. Yet Bob lives on, discarnate. Recently the *New York Times* ran a big picture of him in its Sunday arts section with a caption that noted that his music still has worldwide impact. Ziggy Marley and the Melody Makers have grown into an arena-filling act with record sales that have reached the millions their father could only dream of in his own lifetime. But in death Bob Marley has become a Third World saint and godling. When Amnesty International sponsored a planet-circling benefit tour in 1988 that featured some of the most important rock stars of the day (Sting, Bruce Springsteen, U2), the massive outdoor shows always opened and closed with the musicians assembled onstage singing "Get Up, Stand Up." As the 1990s progress, careening toward the millenium, Bob Marley's life and music continue to inspire, instruct, and touch his listeners in many ways.

Within a few months of Bob Marley's passing, recording began to resume at Tuff Gong Studio in Kingston. Late in 1981 Ziggy Marley and the Melody Makers released their first record, "What A Plot"/"Children Playing in the Street." Rita Marley's 1982 single, "One Draw," was also a worldwide smash. But not until 1983, when Island Records released *Confrontation*, did any significant posthumous Bob Marley music surface in the marketplace.

Confrontation was a mixed bag of old singles, demos, and rehearsal tracks rerecorded with new backing by the Wailers, the last time (to date) that any "official" BMW material has been issued. It included two 1970s singles resurrected from the Tuff Gong vaults ("Rastaman Live Up!" and "Blackman Redemption") and two posthumous 12-inch singles, "I Know" and "Trench Town." The molten dub plate "Burn Down Babylon" was included after it was transformed into the less threatening "Chant Down Babylon." "Jump Nyabinghi," "Mix Up, Mix Up," "Give Thanks and Praises," and "Stiff Necked Fools," all less-than-magic Bob Marley compositions, were used to fill out the package.

The "hit" song of *Confrontation* proved to be a remixed version of "Buffalo Soldier," the unfinished song that Bob had cut in 1978 (in at least two versions) with Jamaican producer King Sporty in Miami. (Sporty, according to rumor, sold the tracks to Chris Blackwell for $80,000, which Blackwell paid to keep Sporty's brilliant version out of the market.) Although "Buffalo Soldier" was never officially recorded by Bob Marley for release, and although Bob Marley and the Wailers never played it in any concert, the song has become heavily identified with Bob by the generation that was too young to have seen the Wailers in the misty Seventies.

Legend, subtitled "The Best of Bob Marley and the Wailers," was released by Island Records in 1984. It was an immense success, despite sloppy annotation and packaging. Two separate versions were released. The English edition merely reissued 14 tracks that spanned the era from "Stir It Up" to "Redemption Song." However, the American *Legend*, although packaged in the same jacket, contained quite different material. The 1975 concert "No Woman No Cry" on the English album became an overly slick remix for America. "Buffalo Soldier" was completely remixed—by the dreaded Eric Thorngren—to sound more like the riotous King Sporty original. "Waiting In Vain," "Exodus," and "Jamming" also were remixed in ways Bob Marley never heard, yet "Jamming" sounds just like the original album track. Island also released at least five remixed 12-inch Bob Marley singles of varying degrees of interest during this same time. These included "Waiting In Vain" backed by a four-song mix-up medley; "One Love"/"People Get Ready," whose B-side contains a special epistolary version of "Keep On Moving" recorded by Bob in London in 1977 (with members of Aswad and Third World) as a post-assassination message to Ziggy that he was safe; a 12-inch dub version of "One Love"; "Could You Be Loved"; and "Three Little Birds." Ironically, the British 45-rpm single of "Three Little Birds" released by Island contained a special bonus track—a white-label, seven-inch version of the original King Sporty "Buffalo Soldier," the best and hopefully final edition of this strange, anthemic glide through hyper-history.

To promote *Legend*, the I-Threes and the Wailers undertook a tour in 1984. It was a somewhat bizarre affair. Junior Marvin and Tyrone Downey traded Bob Marley's lead vocals while the ladies warbled, and slides of the Wailers' old albums were projected in the background. It was the final hurrah of the whole BMW era, the last time the old troupe gathered onstage to play this epochal music. Significantly, Ziggy

Marley took some time off from high school in Kingston to join the *Legend* tour in Los Angeles, where he took the stage and fronted his father's band with much elan and confidence.

Everyone who saw those shows knew that a new era was at hand.

●

This new era began in 1985, when Ziggy Marley and the Melody Makers released their first album on EMI Records. *Play the Game Right* was an impressive debut; its songs, including "Naah Leggo" and "Natty Dread Rampage," were written mostly by Ziggy himself, with the help of his mother's production team, Grub Cooper and Ricky Walters. (The previous year Ziggy had recorded under the guidance of English producer Steve Levine. Most of these tracks were scrapped, except for "Lying' In Bed," a visionary song in which Ziggy describes a visitation by his late father, which was released as a single.) Since Ziggy and his brother and sisters Sharon, Cedella, and Stephen were still in school when *Play the Game Right* was released, a tour by the Melody Makers had to wait until 1986 with the release of their second album, *Hey World.*

The *Hey World* tour was a fascinating hodgepodge, with all the telltale signs of a travelling Tuff Gong road show. Reggae chanteuse Nadine Sutherland opened, followed by the regal I-Threes, who had just released *Beginning,* an appallingly bad album whose one saving grace was Marcia Griffith's "He's a Legend," a touching memorial to Bob that was written for the *Legend* tour. After the I-Threes, Ziggy and the Melody Makers took the stage, backed by the all-star 809 Band led by Tyrone Downey. Ziggy and his sibs ripped through the best songs on *Hey World* ("Reggae Revolution," "Say People," and "Lord We A Come" with Bob Marley-soundalike Stephen Marley on lead vocal). They also played some of their father's greatest hits, especially a hot rendition of "Rat Race." It was a good show, but there was nary a dreadlock nor a spliff to be seen anywhere near the production.

Ziggy Marley and the Melody Makers had to wait until 1988 and the triumph of *Conscious Party* to claim their place as a world class reggae act. The album was produced by Tina Weymouth and Chris Frantz (of the band Talking Heads) for Virgin Records. *Conscious Party* coupled with the Melody Makers' nonstop touring propelled Ziggy into the same arenas his father had finally conquered after years of slaving and suffering. Songs like "We Propose" and "Lee and Molly" (with Keith Richards playing guitar) provided Ziggy with the kind of material he needed to establish himself as an artist aspirant to the spiritual goods and unassuming moral authority of his father.

Yet no one should confuse this "success" with Bob Marley's real triumph. Ziggy Marley and the Melody Makers are an act, heavily coached and stage-managed by mother Rita. Unlike Bob Marley, Peter Tosh, and Bunny Livingstone, who were outlaw victims of the Jamaican political economy, Ziggy Marley and the Melody Makers were raised as Jamaican cultural royalty, isolated from the ghetto of their parents' childhoods, and, in Ziggy's case, educated by Jesuits. Whereas the old Wailers' shows inspired trance states and felt like a visit to another planet, Melody Makers' shows are more like a voyage to the senior prom of some nicely integrated secondary school. Yes, the music sounds great. The band, led by Earl "Chinna" Smith and staffed by the Ethiopian members of Dallol, is crisp and clean. Cedella Marley and Sharon Marley Pendergrast (her married name) contribute nice backing vocals with the help of Erica Newell. And Stephen Marley plays the bongos and does some toasting. Yet anyone who populated the murky basement clubs where Bob Marley's show once lurked cannot fail to notice that where the father's music was his life and his means of survival, the son's music is a show, an act, a pageant of reggae-rock and Rasta sentiment.

But one must also acknowledge that somewhere in his soul Ziggy might have a dash of his father's fire. The same year that *Conscious Party* was such a huge hit on American campuses, Ziggy's little-noticed Jamaican single "Ghetto Youth," which urged Jamaicans to give ghetto kids a chance in life, was a hit at home as well.

It is clear that Ziggy Marley and the Melody Makers can thrive for years by just doing their own music and the occasional Bob Marley song, which in the past they have tended to downplay. A Melody Makers show at the Apollo Theater in Harlem in February 1989 included "Survival" and "Stir It Up." The encore was "Buffalo Soldier," which the whole audience sang along with, like it was an old friend.

The torch has been passed. Not long ago I heard two seventh graders talking. "Did you know," one asked the other, "that Ziggy Marley's father was in a reggae band too?" Soon after that, I heard about two kids dancing in a club when a video of Bob Marley came on. "Who's that?" the girl asked. "Ziggy Marley's father," the boy answered.

●

Jamaica has always been a land of spiritual revelation, a land where the dead traditionally materialize and speak to the living. Today Bob

Marley is seen all over the island, dispensing wisdom and soul-info as he makes his spectral rounds. Consider the following document, distributed by the classic reggae singer Stranger Cole:

REGGAE NEWS FLASH

BOB MARLEY SPEAKS TO STRANGER COLE IN A VISION

It was May 28, 1988 that I vision Bob Marley and I sitting on a tomb stone in Alms House Burying Ground in Jamaica. We both was singing one of my original compositions, when Marley said to me, "The time has come for Rasta to cover the I brain and tek up the fight against Babylon. Tell Joe Higgs fe cover him brain too, cause Jah already give uno both you Strange Jah Cole and Rasta Joe Higgs the words fe the music that will free the people and free up the land seen."

The last thing he said to me before he walked away was that, "I man a go cross the bush go look fe Rita and the pickney dem." I meeting Marley in this vision brings me back to the days at 2nd Street when we used to sing in the kitchen with such greats as Joe Higgs, Delroy Wilson, Alton Ellis, Ken Boothe, and many, many more.

Even as Peter was given a vision by the Almighty, even so I, Strange Jah Cole, was given a vision with Bob Marley.

●

The battle for control of Bob Marley's multimillion dollar estate began almost immediately after his death. Early information indicated that Bob died without a will, so the entire estate was inherited by his legitimate wife, Rita Marley. Later, Rita produced what she claimed was a valid will leaving everything to her.

Rita ran Tuff Gong with an iron fist. With the aid of Bob's American retainers, lawyer David Steinberg of Philadelphia and New York accountant Marvin Zolt, Rita reorganized herself into what came to be known in Jamaica as "The Rita Marley Group of Companies." Under her reign, Tuff Gong studios and production offices were moved from 56 Hope Road to a site on Marcus Garvey Drive. The old house on Hope Road was transformed into the Bob Marley Museum, an attractive (if rather spare) destination for the earnest Euro tourists who came to Kingston and Nine Miles to pay homage to old Bob.

By 1986, Rita had run afoul of most members of the old tribe. The Wailers musicians faced starvation when their royalties were cut off. They were forced to sign ironclad contracts buying out their interests in return for immediate though inadequate cash payments. Most of the old Tuff Gong employees, all of them fanatically loyal to Bob in his day, were dismissed or left in disgust. Meanwhile the legacy of Bob Marley languished in a gnarled knot of litigation and ill will.

All this came to a dramatic end in 1987. BIG RACKET UNCOVERED IN MARLEY ESTATE screamed the headline in the *Daily Gleaner.* COURT SACKS RITA AS ADMINISTRATOR. The newspaper revealed that after Bob's death, lawyer Steinberg and accountant Zolt had allegedly schemed with Rita to withhold some of Bob's offshore assets from the Jamaican estate. Allegations of fraud and forgery (with regard to Bob's will) abounded. The Jamaican Supreme Court removed Rita as manager of her late husband's estate, which then reverted to a shady Jamaican bank, the other court-appointed estate administrator. The bank-run "Estate" seized Tuff Gong Studio, 56 Hope Road, Rita's country house in St. Mary, and Cedella Booker's house in Miami. The bank even tried to evict Bob Marley's mother from the house Bob had bought for her!

One can only wonder what Robert Nesta Marley would have thought of all this. Old friends know he'd be madder than hell.

Meanwhile, other tragedies also marked the year 1987 as a bad one for the Wailers family. In April, Carlton Barrett was shot to death at the gate of his home in Kingston, murdered by an unknown killer. A few days later, Carlie's wife and her boyfriend were arrested and charged with his death, but were eventually acquitted for lack of evidence.

Five months later, Peter Tosh was also murdered in Kingston, during a robbery at his house. Tosh had spent much of the 1980s cruising on his laurels. He enjoyed a hit single with his reggae version of "Johnnie B. Goode" in 1985, and his backing band, Word Sound and Power, continued as one of the hottest in the world, playing stadia from Brazil to Asia. Although Peter was squabbling with his label, Polygram, he was preparing to deliver another album in 1987 and then go back on the road. Around that time, Dennis Lobban was released from prison in Jamaica. According to rumors, back in 1973 when the Wailers were poised on the brink of international fame, Peter Tosh had caused some malefactor to be stuffed in the trunk of a car that then disappeared. When the police took notice, Dennis Lobban was persuaded to take the fall for Tosh, with the promise of just rewards somewhere down the road. Indeed, when Lobban got out of jail, he moved into Tosh's house, but soon fell out with Tosh's American wife. Thrown out of Tosh's Kingston residence, Lobban came back with a gun and some cronies to rob the place. They found Tosh, his wife, his drummer Santa Davis, and the prominent Kingston disk jockey Free I winding up a little party. Tosh and his friends were ordered onto the floor, the victims of a friendly robbery, when Tosh's wife began to scream. Dennis Lobban shot everyone in the head. Tosh and Free I were killed. Santa Davis and Tosh's wife survived. Dennis Lobban was sentenced to hang.

A pall fell over the tight-knit world of reggae musicians. Along with Bob Marley, Tosh had been reggae's architect and avatar. Now only Bunny Wailer was left alive, but there were persistent reports he had gone into hiding and was living under armed guard.

●

Anyone interested in the life, death, and works of the late Bob Marley cannot fail to be fascinated by the results of a lawsuit filed against Bob's estate by Danny Sims. The suit, which was heard in the Supreme Court of the State of New York in November, 1987, was officially titled "Cayman Music Inc. vs. Rita Marley as Administratrix of the Estate of Robert Nesta Marley, Tuff Gong Music, Bob Marley Music Ltd., Almo Music Corp., Rondor Music Corp., Island Records Inc., Atlantic Recording Corp., etc. et al." In this legal action, Danny Sims claimed that between 1973 and 1976 Bob Marley avoided contractual obligations to Cayman Music by publishing songs under pseudonyms (the names of Trench Town cronies, and under the name R. Marley, namely Rita). During this period, the suit contended, Bob Marley and the other defendants conspired to defraud Danny Sims and Cayman. Sims claimed in his affidavit that he had first learned of this fraud when he read this book when it was first published in England in 1983. Sims sued for damages and for the rights to all the songs Bob Marley issued during this period, including such classics as "No Woman No Cry," "War," "Exodus," and many other crucial works in the BMW canon. Since publishing is where the real money lies in the music business, these "properties" were potentially worth millions.

By the time the suit came to trial, Rita had resigned from the estate, and charges against her, Steinberg, and Zolt were still pending. The Jamaican bank that ran the estate chose to fight, and indeed filed a countersuit against Danny Sims. The judge threw part of Sims' suit out of court, explaining that some of his charges were covered by statutes of limitation that had already expired. While the fraud charges also came under expired statutes of limitations, Sims' lawyer argued that it would have been impossible for Sims to have discovered this fraud in Jamaica while Bob Marley was still alive. According to Sims, Bob Marley directed campaigns of violence and intimidation against anyone who stood in his way. To prove this point Danny Sims brought Bob's former managers Don Taylor and Alan "Skill" Cole to New York to testify that the climate around Bob Marley's Jamaican business affairs was one of threats, beatings, and fear.

Don Taylor testified first. He confirmed that he had been beaten by Bob in Africa in 1980, as described earlier in this text. Taylor also testified that he went to Bob's house in Miami in August 1980 and Bob beat him again while Skill Cole held a Uzi submachine gun to Taylor's head. He said Bob wanted Taylor to sign a paper relinquishing all his rights. Don Taylor said in open court: "He [Bob Marley] beat me up. Alan had the submachine gun. Every time he hit me, Alan had that gun. I couldn't believe Alan holding the gun on me. Finally Bob's kids, Ziggy and all of them, come through the door, and that's how it stopped. He [Ziggy] said, 'Don is so good to you. He take six gunshots for you' ..."

Skill Cole confirmed Taylor's story when he testified but Skill claimed the gun was a shotgun rather than an Uzi. He went on to describe his own role as Bob Marley's enforcer and song-plugger.

Skill Cole: "Well, in those days [1971-1974] it was very difficult for Rastafarians to get airplay unless we were aligned with the big recording companies. When I started working at that time as manager [of Tuff Gong], we went independent. So we had a lot of problems getting our songs on the radio. It was my duty to see that we got proper airplays, that our music was on the charts ... We had to put a lot of strength, what you call muscle, to get things played from various disk jockeys. ...Well, sometimes we had to go there and beat disc jockeys and deal with program directors, things like that. We had to beat them, send guys to smash their cars, things like that. Threaten them ... 'If you don't play our records, you have to leave the station.' [We forced] disc jockeys and program directors to leave their jobs. Some went out and left the country."

Skill also described how he and Bob ordered three men to beat up Danny Sims' Jamaican sublicensee, Ted Powder. Sims then flew to Jamaica and paid Bob some money he owed him. Cole testified that some gangster cronies of Bob's threatened Sims with a gun in Bob's suite at the Essex House in New York during the Wailers' last tour in September 1980. All this testimony was designed to show that people were so scared of Bob Marley that the truth about Bob's song-publishing machinations could not be revealed while he was alive.

Other interesting bits of Marley history also came to light at this trial.

One of the lawyers asked Taylor who had attempted the assassination of Bob Marley. Taylor testified: "There were two guys. It was a mixture of political, [and] a thing that [Alan] Cole had run a racketeering horse race and they thought that Bob was behind it because Alan was driving Bob's car. Alan, he fix horses at the track. He had fixed this big race and took off with the money. And they must have felt that Bob must have financed it, because Alan didn't have no way to get that kind of money away from Bob." Taylor also described "this mixed up idea that he [Bob] believed in the Peoples National Party, and so did I. And we had a lawsuit against Clement [Coxsone] Dodd, who was Bob's first recording company, that I had started for not paying Bob, and tried to get back some of the copyrights—all those factors together caused the assassination."

Taylor was asked what had happened to the frightened youths who had tried to kill Bob Marley. "They were hanged," he testified. "I saw one hung. I was thirty feet away when they tried them and hung them, the people in the neighborhood, in the gully. They tried them in the gully. They had me fly down. They had me say that's the one who shot me. Then they hung them. None of the assassins are alive." Asked who had carried out this execution, Taylor replied: "Because of the love of Bob Marley by the people, the people took it upon themselves."

Eventually, the jury retired to deliberate. The main issue had boiled down to whether Danny Sims knew of the alleged fraud before October 1982, when the statute of limitation expired. The estate had subpoenaed an interview with Danny Sims that I had recorded in March 1982. On this tape, Sims can be heard discussing Bob's songwriting subterfuges and his plans for taking legal action. Considering this, the jury found for the estate. Cayman Music had lost its three-year legal battle, but even today the case is still pending while awaiting review at the appellate level.

Several months after the verdict was announced, the Jamaican government put Bob Marley's estate up for sale. The asking price for Bob's recordings, song catalogues, all future composer's royalties and real estate was just over eight million dollars. The only major bidder was Island Logic Inc., the New York holding company directed by Chris Blackwell. The Marley family, led by Bob's mother, tried to fight the sale in court, arguing that the price (for an estate potentially worth hundreds of millions over time) was absurdly low. When one of the estate's lawyers complained that the estate might lose value if the sale was postponed because of the family's objections, one of the more tuned-in Jamaican judges remarked that with the [poor] quality of reggae music in Jamaica now, Bob Marley's music could never lose its value. But in March 1989, the Appeals Court in Kingston ordered that the estate be sold to Blackwell for $8.6 million. This decision is currently under appeal. In another development, Chris Blackwell in turn sold Island Records to the German recording conglomerate Polygram during the summer of 1989.

But even the richest of men cannot own a spirit, and Bob's wild spirit still exists. You can hear it in every new Bunny Wailer album, especially the 1989 masterpiece *Liberation*, and earlier records like *Marketplace* and *Rule Dance Hall*. You can hear it when Andrew Tosh, Peter's son, tours with Tosh's old band. You can hear it in the hard fast reggae of the young African Bob Marleys: Majek Fashek from Nigeria, and the brilliant Alpha Blondy from the Ivory Coast. You can hear it in the precious collector's cassettes that surface among Marley disciples. These Wailers rehearsals, demos, broadcasts, soundchecks and concert boardchecks are filled with wonderful and poignant material that will never be released legitimately. You can hear Bob's spirit when his band, the Wailers, come to town to play his music. Tyrone is gone now, and Carlie is dead, but Family Man still runs the show from behind his impassive, bubbling basslines, and Junior Marvin sings both Bob's and the I-Three's parts with authority.

And if one is patient, one can expect to hear more Bob Marley music someday. There's "Rainbow Country" and a long Lee Perry version of "Natural Mystic" that came out on English 12-inch singles. Island put out "Roots," a rare B-side, on the 1986 *Soul Rebel* anthology. Trojan released the extremely rare *Soul Revolution* dub album in 1988, which was almost immediately suppressed by Danny Sims. Other old Marley tracks — "Adam and Eve," "Mr. Chatterbox," and "Redder Than Red" — have appeared on various Trojan collections. And there are dozens of unreleased songs in various forms, among them "Jungle Fever," "Wounded Lion in the Jungle," "Who Colt the Game" and many others.

Bob Marley lives. He's a *god*.

"History proves."

A Bob Marley
Bibliography

Amandla (concert program) Cambridge, Mass. July 21, 1979.

Anon. *Marly, or, the life of a planter in Jamaica.* Glasgow: Griffin, 1831.

Anon. "Sister Judy Had a Vision," Kingston *Star,* December 7, 1976.

Anon. "Miss Universe, Cindy Breakspeare," *People,* December 1976.

Anon. "Marley's Battle," *Record Mirror,* April 1981.

Anon. "Reggae Star Marley Dies," New York *Post,* May 12, 1981.

Ashford, Nicholas. "Zimbabwe flag raised for first time at midnight ceremony," London *Times,* April 18, 1980.

Barrett, Leonard. *The Rastafarians.* Boston: Beacon, 1977.

Bell, Rob. *The "King" Kong Compilation* (liner notes). Mango Records MLPS 9632, 1981.

Bilby, Kenneth M. *Bongo, Backra and Coolie/Jamaican Roots,* vol. 2 (liner notes). Ethnic Folkways Records FE 4232, 1975.

Black, Clinton V. *History of Jamaica.* Kingston: Collins Sangster, 1979.

Boot, Adrian, and Michael Thomas. *Babylon on a Thin Wire.* New York: Schocken, 1977.

Boot, Adrian, and Vivien Goldman. *Bob Marley—Soul Rebel, Natural Mystic.* London: Eel Pie/Hutchinson, 1981.

Bradshaw, Jon. "Blackwell's Island," *Rolling Stone,* May 27, 1982.

Bradshaw, Jon. "The Reggae Way to Salvation," New York *Times,* August 14, 1977.

Brazier, Chris. "Punks not Rasta but them fight down the Babylon system an' love black people," *Melody Maker,* February 11, 1978.

Bourton, Keith. "Marley," *Black Echoes* (undated photocopy).

Campbell, Thorace. "Bob Marley Lives," *Spear* (Nigeria), August 1981.

Cioe, Crispin, and J. Sutton-Smith. "Bob Marley and the Roots of Reggae," *Musician,* April 1980.

Clarke, Colin G. *Kingston, Jamaica.* Berkeley: California Press, 1975.

Clarke, Sebastian. *Jah Music.* London: Heinemann, 1980.

Cohen, Scott. "Bob Marley Is Reggae, Man!", *Oui,* February 1976.

Coleman, Ray. "Marley Speaks," *Black Music,* June 1976.

Coleman, Ray. "Root Strong in Funky Kingston," *Melody Maker,* June 12, 1976.

Coleman, Ray. "Marley: still a life and death struggle," *Melody Maker,* May 21, 1977.

Cooper, Carol. "Tuff Gong: Bob Marley's Unsung Story," *Village Voice,* September 10, 1980.

Cooper, Carol. "Confronting Marley's Legasy," *Record,* September 1983.

Cromelin, Richard. "An Herbal Meditation with Bob Marley," *Rolling Stone,* September 11, 1975.

Daily Gleaner. Kingston, May 20–24, 1981.

Dalton, David, and Lenny Kaye. *Rock 100.* New York: Grosset & Dunlap, 1977.

Davis, Stephen, and Peter Simon. *Reggae Bloodlines.* New York: Doubleday, 1977.

Davis, Stephen, and Peter Simon. *Reggae International.* New York: Knopf/R&B, 1983.

Davis, Stephen. "A Conversation with Peter Tosh," *Oui,* November 1979.

Davis, Stephen. "The Last Interview," *Black Music,* July 1981.

Davis, Thulani. "Bob Marley: No Exile," *Village Voice,* August 20, 1980.

DeVoss, David. "Singing Them a Message," *Time,* March 22, 1976.

Dwyer, Ed. "This Man Is Seeing God," *High Times,* September 1976.

Fairweather, Jean. "Wailers," *Xaymaca,* August 11, 1974.

Faristzaddi, Millard. *Rastafari.* New York: Grove/R&B, 1982.

Farrell, Barry. "Bob Marley, the Visionary as Sex Symbol," *Chic,* November 1976.

Fergusson, Isaac. "So Much Things to Say," *Village Voice,* May 18, 1982.

Fitzsimons, Ross. "The Magic of Marley" (undated photocopy).

Futrell, Jon. "The Continuing Story of Marley's Ghost," *Black Echoes,* November 29, 1980.

Gayle, Carl. "Dread in-a Babylon," *Black Music,* September 1975.

Gayle, Carl. "Getting My Share of Humiliation, Just Like the Blackheart Man," *Black Music,* October 1976.

Gayle, Carl. "Positive Vibrations," *Black Music,* November 1976.

Gayle, Carl. "One Love Equal Rights Integration Peace Concert," *Jahugliman,* October 1978.

Goldman, Vivien. "Munchies in Munchen: Wheeling Across Europe with the BMWs," *Sounds,* May 28, 1977.

Goldman, Vivien. "So Much Things to Say," *Sounds,* June 1977.

Goldman, Vivien. "Uptown Ghetto Living," *Melody Maker,* August 11, 1979.

Goldman, Vivien. "Knocking off the Opposition," *Melody Maker,* March 29, 1980.

Goldman, Vivien. "The 3 Wise Is," *New Musical Express,* August 9, 1980.

Goodwin, Michael. "Marley, the Maytals and the Reggae Armageddon," *Rolling Stone,* September 11, 1975.

Grass, Randall. "Sir Coxsone." In Davis, Stephen, ed., *Reggae International.*

Harris, T. Boots. "Bunny Wailer, the Man with the Richest Dreadlocks Voice," *Jamaica Daily News,* August 12, 1976.

Holloway, Danny. "Remembrances of Brother Bob," *Reggae Beat,* May 1983.

Irwin, Colin, with Roz Reines and Paulo Hewitt. "From Jamaica's Slums to Reggae Master Blaster," *Melody Maker,* May 16, 1981.

Isaacs, James. "Chicka-Boom and the Wailers," *Real Paper,* July 18, 1973.

Issa Paul. "The Real Bunny Wailers," *Daily Gleaner,* August 8, 1976.

Johnson, Linton Kwesi. "Bob Marley and the Reggae International," *Race Today,* June 1977.

Johnson, Linton Kwesi. "Some Thoughts on Reggae," *Race Today,* December 1980.

Kaye, Lenny. "Bob Marley: I & Unity," *Hit Parader,* December 1979.

Lake, Steve. "Burnin' with Marley," *Melody Maker,* November 24, 1973.

Lee, Hélène. "La Maison dans L'Ile," *Rock et Folk,* July 1980.

Livingston, Pearl, ed. *Unity of the Strong Heart,* Bob Marley Fan Club newsletter, May 1978.

Manley, Michael. *Jamaica: Struggle in the Periphery.* London: Writers and Readers, 1982.

May, Chris. "On the Road with the Wailers," *Black Music,* September 1977.

May, Chris. "Starting from Scratch," *Black Music,* October 1977.

McCormack, Ed. "Bob Marley with a Bullet," *Rolling Stone,* August 12, 1976.

Meeks, Brian. "Duppy Conquerors," *Embryo* (Trinidad), October 1971.

Miller, Jim. *The Rolling Stone Illustrated History of Rock & Roll.* New York: Random House, 1980.

Narine, D. J. "The Bob Marley Odyssey," *Class,* September 1981.

Needs, Kris. "Marley Uprising," *ZigZag,* August 1980.

Nelson, Barbara. "Marley Laid to Rest," Jamaica *Daily News,* May 22, 1981.

Noel, Peter. "Marley: Mama Don't Cry for Me," *Amsterdam News*, May 16, 1981.

O'Brien, Glenn. "Bob Marley, So Much Things to Say," *Interview*, May 1978.

Ojenke, Raspoeter. "Bob Marley: Revelations from a Warrior," *Soul*, September 18, 1978.

Partridge, Rob. "Natty Dread It Ina Zimbabwe," in *The Rock Yearbook, 1981*. New York: Delilah/Grove, 1980.

Pickering, Clinton. "Marley-Splash," Jamaica *Sunday Sun*, July 8, 1979.

Ramsden, Dave. "Junior Wailer," *Melody Maker*, October 15, 1977.

Reel, Penny. "The Words and Works of Bob Marley and the Wailers," *New Musical Express*, June 6/June 13, 1981.

Reines, Roz. "Babylon In-a Europe," *New Music News*, May 1980.

Reines, Roz. "Bob Marley's Fight to Live," *The Face*, January 1981.

Rockwell, John. "Reggae: Bob Marley in Jamaica Program," New York *Times*, June 19, 1978.

Rodney, Walter. *The Groundings with My Brothers*. London: Bogle-L'Ouverture Publications, 1969.

Rohlehr, F. G. "Sounds and Pressure: Jamaica Blues," *Moko* (Trinidad), June 1971.

Rudis, Al. "Rasta in the Material World," Chicago *Sun-Times* (undated).

Santelli, Robert. "Pressure and the Pursuit of the Promised Land," *The Aquarian*, September 17, 1980.

Seaga, Edward. "Eulogy on the occasion of the official funeral for the Hon. Robert Nesta Marley, O.M." Press release of the New York Consulate-General of Jamaica, May 22, 1981.

Smiley, Xan. "Misunderstanding Africa," *Atlantic*, September 1982.

Spencer, Neal. "Me Just Wanna Live, Y'unnerstand?", *New Musical Express*, July 19, 1975.

Spencer, Neal. "Jamaica Lion inna Concrete Jungle," *New Musical Express*, November 10, 1979.

Spencer, Neal. "Bob: 'I'll Be OK,' " *New Musical Express*, November 22, 1980.

Stevenson, John. " 'I Know I Can Live,' Says Rebel Superstar Marley," *The Daily Mail* (undated photocopy).

Stokes, Niall. "An Interview with Bob Marley," *The Hot Press* (Ireland), May 13, 1983.

Survival, Tuff Gong newspaper, Kingston, July 1979.

Thomas, Michael. "The Wild Side of Paradise," *Rolling Stone*, July 19, 1973.

Thomson, Doogie. "BMW—The Last Five Years," *Ital Rockers,* March 1978.

Tribute to a King. Memorial edition of the Jamaica *Daily News,* May 21, 1981.

Verena. "Bob Lets It All Hang Out," Jamaica *Daily News,* September 5, 1975.

Waters, Anita. "Bob Marley: One Final Major Interview," *Everybody's Magazine,* Fall 1981.

West, Bob. "Bunny Wailer: It Won't Be Long Before You See Me in Action," Jamaica *Sunday Sun,* November 29, 1981.

White, Tim. "Bob Marley's Jamaica," *Crawdaddy,* January 1976.

Wilson, Basil, and Diane Ellis. "No prescriptions, but a resonant, visionary message of protest," *Weekly Gleaner,* June 20, 1976.

Wilson, Basil, and Herman Hall. "Marley in His Own Words," *Everybody's Magazine,* July 1981.

In addition, the Reggae Beat Archives in Los Angeles, which specializes in Bob Marley documents, made available the following recorded and transcribed interviews and tapes:

Bob Marley: interviewed by Neville Willoughby, Jamaica 1973.
interviewed by R. A. Allen, London 1975.
interviewer unknown, Paris 1976.
interviewed by Karl Dallas, London 1977.
interviewed by Robin Denselow, Paris 1977.
interviewed by Neville Willoughby, 1978.
United Nations press conference, 1978.
interviewed by Brian Anderson, England 1980.

Rita Marley: interviewed by Roger Steffens, Los Angeles, undated.
interviewed by Joe Menell, Jamaica 1981.
interviewer unknown, London 1980.

Joe Higgs: interviewed by Roger Steffens, Los Angeles 1981.
Chris Blackwell: interviewed by Roger Steffens, Los Angeles 1982.
Judy Mowatt: interviewed by Roger Steffens, Los Angeles 1981.
"The Bob Marley Memorial," broadcast KCRW-FM, Santa Monica, California, May 1981.
"The Bob Marley Birthday Special," broadcast, KCRW-FM, February 1982.

Index

INDEX

INDEX

INDEX

Tuff Gong, new name acquired, 48–49, 83
Wailers reduced to basic trio, 53
in Wilmington with his mother, 61–62, 64–65
year's absence from Jamaica, 179, 180, 181–93
youthful associations, 26–29
Zimbabwe visit and conference, self-financed, 226–28
Marley, Captain Norval, 8, 9–15, 17, 19, 21–22, 106
Marley, Cedella, 69, 221, 247, 260
Marley, Constance, 19
Marley, Damian, 180
Marley, David "Ziggy," 72, 166, 213, 221, 245, 246, 250, 260
Marley, Edith, 9, 11–12
Marley, Justin, 131
Marley, Karen, 107
Marley, Kimane, 141
Marley, Makeba Janesta, 211
Marley, Marguerite, 19
Marley, Peter, 19
Marley, Rita. See Anderson, Rita
Marley, Robbie, 106, 153
Marley, Robert, 9, 12, 19
Marley, Rohan, 106
Marley, Sharon, 221, 260
Marley, Stephen, 106, 213, 221, 224, 246, 250, 260
Maroons, 2, 3, 5
Marshall, Bucky, 194, 195, 225
Martyn, John, 132
Marvin, Julian "Junior," 182, 184, 185, 187, 188, 196, 200, 201, 204–5, 223–24, 225, 227, 229, 259
Massop, Claudie "Jack," 194, 195, 198, 210
Mayfield, Curtis, 32, 45, 74, 87, 185
Maytals (Vikings), 41, 68, 77, 101, 111
See also Toots and the Maytals
Meditations, 182, 183, 193, 198
Melodians, 68, 78, 111
Melody Maker, 122, 125, 156, 157, 160, 161, 193, 213
Melody Makers, 221, 236, 260
Mighty Diamonds, 198
Miller, Jacob, 198, 218, 225
Mittoo, Jackie, 42, 43, 81
Moore, Johnny "Dizzy," 42, 45
Morgan, Derrick, 51
Morris, Yvette, 211
Mowatt, Judy, 104, 127, 128, 137, 143, 167, 172, 173, 174–75, 177, 178, 187, 201, 208, 215, 229, 233, 238, 247, 259
Mugabe, Robert, 208, 216, 226
Murvin, Junior, 183
Music in Jamaica
burru drumming, 38

early, 4
government recognition of, 46–47
mento, 18, 29, 33
quadrille, 8–9, 29
recording industry, 33–34, 40–41
reggae, 77–78, 79, 81, 82, 96, 103, 108, 109–10, 248
rockers, 184
rock steady, 67–68, 70, 74
rub-a-dub, 224–25
Rude Boy, 46, 50–52
Sir Coxsone's Downbeat, 38, 39–40
ska, the new sound, 29, 47, 51, 52, 74
sound system men, 38, 39–41
Muzorewa, Abel, 208, 226

Naphtali, 228
Nash, Johnny, 73, 74–75, 89, 91, 92, 96–98, 102, 104–5, 125, 126
Negro World, The, 5
New Musical Express, 114, 146, 149, 161, 169, 221
New York Times Magazine, 156
Nibbs, Lloyd, 42
Nkomo, Joshua, 208, 216, 226
Nkrumah, Kwame, 7
Now Generation, 110
Nyerere, Julius, 7

Olatunji, Babatunde, 212, 214, 215, 251–52
Oui magazine, 161

Palmieri, Eddie, 214
Papa Michigan, 224–25
Paragons, 68
Parks, Arkland "Drumbago," 43
Parks, Lloyd, 198
Patterson, Alvin "Seeco" (Franseeco Pep), 32, 37–38, 39, 41, 42, 104, 140, 188, 189, 201, 228, 230, 259
Paul VI, Pope, 204
Peace Concert (April 1978), 194, 196, 198–200, 210
Peace Movement (1978), 193–94, 195–96, 197, 198, 199, 200, 209
People magazine, 172
People's National Party (PNP), 24, 95, 96, 108–9, 118, 171, 176, 177, 180, 194, 195, 196
Perkins, Lascelles, 31, 41
Perkins, Wayne, 104
Perry, Lee ("Upsetter"; "Little"; "Scratch"), 40, 80–87, 89, 92, 93, 94, 111, 113, 143, 152, 153, 171, 172, 183, 184, 193, 196, 205, 210
Peter Tosh. See McIntosh, Winston Hubert
"Peter Touch," 89
Pioneers, 77

284

INDEX

285

INDEX